RUMI'S SUN

The Teachings of Shams of Tabriz

RUMI'S SUN

The Teachings of Shams of Tabriz

Translated by Refik Algan
and Camille Adams Helminski

THRESHOLD
BOOKS

Revised edition published by Threshold Books, 2017

First published by Morning Light Press, 2008

Library of Congress Cataloging-in-Publication Data

Names: Shams-i Tabrīzī, -1247, author. | Algan, Refik, 1952- translator. | Helminski, Camille Adams, 1951- translator.
Title: Rumi's sun : the teachings of Shams of Tabriz / translated by Refik Algan and Camille Adams Helminski.
Other titles: Maqālāt. English
Description: Louisville, Kentucky : Threshold Books, 2017. | Includes index.
Identifiers: LCCN 2017028314 | ISBN 9780939660193 (pbk.)
Subjects: LCSH: Sufism--Early works to 1800.
Classification: LCC BP188.9 .S519513 2017 | DDC 297.4092--dc23
LC record available at https://lccn.loc.gov/2017028314

THRESHOLD BOOKS
1288 Cherokee Road
Louisville, Kentucky 40204

This opening, this translation, is dedicated to

My mother, Azize Algan,
who was always a true teacher to me all through her life.
Without her help this work could never have been done!
—*R.A.*

To the Truth that is Sought,
and all those who seek It.
—*C.A.H.*

Introduction

Living with Shams

In the Name of our Infinitely Compassionate
and Infinitely Merciful Source

It has been a long journey—living with Shams. For many years now Refik Algan and this poor one have been consulting and reflecting within the universe of Shams. It was many years ago now that Refik recognized the treasures within the *Maqalat*, the teaching conversations of Shams that were transcribed in his presence almost eight hundred years ago, and began to share them with us, translating little by little, moment by moment, word by word.

We are grateful that this work is at last coming to fruition in the form of a book, *Rumi's Sun, The Teachings of Shams of Tabriz*, published by Morning Light Press. It feels so appropriate for Shams, the "Sun," to be able to radiate further in this way. Alhamdulillah, all praise belongs to God, and may God and Shams forgive us for our mistakes.

As we write this introduction, we have embarked upon the "Year of Rumi," the year 2007 being recognized by UNESCO as the year of remembrance and awareness of the gifts of Mevlana Jalaluddin Rumi, during this year that is the 800th anniversary of his birth. The message of Love and Unity he conveyed is certainly sorely needed in this world of ours which still in the midst of its many difficulties can continue to be illumined by the light of "the Sun." Shamsuddin-i Tabrizi, the "Sun of the Religion from Tabriz," may God make his abundance eternal, arrived in Konya on the twenty-sixth day of the month of Jamadhi-al Akhir, 642 A.H., or by the western calendar, the 29th of November 1244 C.E.

Shams' heart was the perfect mirror for the heart of Mevlana who had such a deep spirit from birth and had been so beautifully educated by his mystic father and mother. Shams awakened Mevlana to his second "birth"—into complete oneness with his Creator. Many accounts exist of the history of their meeting and friendship so we will not go into detail here. We will leave Shams' words (and Mevlana's) to reflect the meaning and expanse of their friendship. Suffice it to say that with the opening of that friendship, a new paradigm appeared and through that shift of matrix, Love flowed out into this world in such abundance that even after almost 800 years the ripples are still widening to encompass the whole of this world within the field of their nurturance.

As publishers for many years of Rumi's works, we at Threshold Books would receive requests for permission to quote his words from such varied directions as home-builders, poets, social workers, makers of tea, doctors, and glass-blowers . . . "Fall towards the Glassblower's breath!"

One can still hear the sound of the companionship of Shams and Mevlana through the voice of the *ney*, the reed flute that is prepared to be an instrument of music by being burned clear through its core. As Shams said, "I do not have the power to cry out—that is the sound of the ney." For Shams, Mevlana was that ney—as Mevlana says in the beginning of his masterwork of 25,700 verses, the *Mathnawi*, "Listen to the *ney*, and the tale it tells. . . . " That "ney" expresses the longing of return—return to its Source. Shams and Mevlana provided that possibility for each other—diving into the Presence of God—moment by moment.

The *Maqalat* is the record of Shams' teaching conversations and we offer it here in its traditional order. In the original Persian, it flows like a stream of consciousness with no indication of paragraph breaks, changes in hour, or day, or who exactly is present in any moment. For the ease of the reader we have divided our text into paragraphs and sections with titles to orient.

The pronouns are also often elusive. In Persian, as in Turkish, a single pronoun indicates he, she, and it. To broaden the reader's awareness of that and the fact that within the Qur'anic universe, which was Shams' universe, God is far beyond gender or any formulation by which we might try to describe Him/Her and every soul has its own connection with his/her Lord, closer than one's jugular vein, we sometimes use He/She in reference to the Divine, as well as he/she for the individual soul.

Passages from the Qur'an included in this text are italicized, followed by citation of *surah* (chapter) number and verse. Quranic translations included here are either adapted from *The Message of the Qur'an* by Muhammad Asad or excerpted from *The Light of Dawn, Daily Readings from the Holy Qur'an*.

The text upon which this translation of the *Maqalat* is based was calligraphed in the original Persian script by Ayashli Shakir, an annotated copy of manuscripts #2144 and #2145 of the Mevlana Museum in Konya, which were moved in recent years to Ankara for safe-keeping. We have referenced the Turkish translation of this manuscript by Dr. Mehmet Nuri Gencosman, as well as the original manuscript from Konya, and the text that was published recently by Muhammad-Ali Movahhed in Iran. The original manuscript is referenced every five pages of original text by page number in the footnotes. Names and terms are also challenging to render into English because of the differing usages in Turkish, Persian, and Arabic. We have simplified and regularized transliteration based on most common usage in English and chosen not to use diacritical marks in the text. We have omitted the more obscure passages and some that were repetitive, hoping that what is provided here will be most helpful. We would like to thank all the friends who have helped support this work, especially Amer Latif, Saeid Rahmanpanah, Ahmad Rezwani, Uzeyir Ozyurt, and Mahmoud Mostafa for their help with locating manuscripts and the verifying of translations along the way, and all the wonderful folks of Morning Light Press, especially Dennis Pence, Steve Jadick and Darcy Sinclair. May God bless all their efforts.

God willing the words of Shams will be able to be heard. As Shams says in his *Maqalat*,

Even if the whole world would hang me by my beard, still if something needs to be said, I will say it. But without a doubt, even after a thousand years, these words will be heard by those whom I want to hear.

A few people became the Prophet's scribes for the revelation—those who wrote down the divine commands—and a few people became the place where the revelation descends, that is, the place of its effect. Work hard so that you may be both! In other words, be both the object of the revelation and the scribe of the revelation that comes to the heart.

The universe of the Truth is an infinitely wide expanse. Shams throws open the shutters, reveals the vista, and brings us out into that infinite expanse of clear air, and strong life, into the Presence of the Beloved.

Within footnotes to passages we have occasionally noted references to similar passsages in Mevlana's writings, so that one might witness some of the flow of inspiration between Shams and Mevlana. When one spends time with the words of Shams and also with Mevlana's it becomes clear how Shams' words were the powerful seeds that opened through Mevlana's words into a beautiful garden in which many could walk and catch the fragrance of the Beloved.

If one enters the tomb of Mevlana in Konya and turns around to look over the door, one will see the calligraphy of the double "*Hu*," the pronoun of Divine Presence: *Hu/Hu*. Shams and Mevlana were that for each other and each for the Divine. . . . The Prophet Muhammad said, "The faithful are mirrors for the faithful." Shams reminds us that this might also be understood as "The faithful are mirrors for the Faithful," for God. The human being has the possibility of being the field of display of the Divine attributes.

Shams and Mevlana met in the realm of Love of God. Both were bound with a great love to the Prophet Muhammad and the way that opened with the revelation of the Qur'an. They breathed the air of the Qur'an and all their words are woven with its meanings. As Shams says, "We have such a tether that nobody has the power and courage to pull it. Only Muhammad, the representative of God, pulls it."

From a place far beyond dogma, where the mysteries unfold, they called, "Come!" Shams reminds us that the saying of the Prophet Muhammad, "I have such a moment with God . . . ," is an invitation.

As Mevlana says,

Love is the astrolabe of God's mysteries.
A lover may be drawn to this love or that love,
But finally he is drawn to the Sultan of love.
However much we describe and explain love,
When we fall in love we are ashamed of our words.
Explanation by the tongue makes most things clear,
But love unexplained is clearer.
When the pen came to the subject of love, it broke.
When the discourse reached the topic of love,
The pen split and the paper tore.
If it tries to explain it, intellect sticks fast, an ass in mud;
Only Love itself can explain love and lovers!
None but the sun can display the sun,
If you wish to see it, don't turn away from it.
Shadows may be a sign of the sun's presence,
But only the sun offers life-giving light.
Shadows bring on slumber, like evening talk,
But when the sun rises the *moon is split apart* [54:1].
In the world there is nothing so wondrous as the sun,
But the Sun of the soul never sets, it is eternal.

Though the external sun is unique and single,
one can imagine other suns like it.
But the Sun of the soul, beyond the heavens,
Has no similar, neither manifest nor imagined.
Where is there room in conception for His essence,
So that the like of Him might be conceivable?
The sun (Shams) of Tabriz is a perfect light,
A sun, yes, one of the beams of God!
When praise was heard of the "Sun of Tabriz,"
The sun of the fourth heaven bowed its head.
Now that I have mentioned his name, it is but right
To offer some signs of his beneficence.
That precious soul caught my skirt,
smelling the fragrance of the garment of Joseph;
and said, "For the sake of our ancient friendship,
speak a hint of those sweet states of ecstasy,
that earth and heaven might rejoice,
that intellect and spirit, and eye might increase a hundredfold."

[*Mathnawi* I: 110-127]

Welcome to the universe of Shams.

Al-fakira al-Mevlevi,
Camille Adams Helminski

Ya Hazrati Mevlana, Ya Hazrati Shams, Ya Allah Hu

The Shining Sun

I begin in the name of God, the Infinitely Compassionate and Infinitely Merciful, and I ask His help. This book was gathered from the words of the beloved Mevlana Shamsuddin Tabrizi, the sultan of those who have attained. May God not deprive us of his abundant blessings.[1]

The Palace of the Ancient One

If you pass beyond the body and reach the soul, then you will have reached "createdness." The Truth is the Ancient, Eternal Being. Where can the one who is created find the One who is Eternal? What connects the earthly creature and the Lord of lords?

In your opinion, that by means of which you move and attain liberation is the soul; then what use is it to put the soul in your hand, ready to give it away?

---

1 This prayer was written by the person who was beginning the transcription of Shams' words. The tradition of transcribing was such that a few people might be designated to transcribe in order: one to write the first sentence spoken, the second to write the next sentence spoken, the third to write the third sentence spoken and the first to write the fourth sentence spoken, and so forth, so that the whole might be recorded. In this case, the names of those who transcribed follow at the end of the manuscript. No notation was made as to changes of time however, so the manuscript comes to us somewhat as a stream of consciousness. We break it into titled sections here in order that the reader might more easily receive it.

> Even if Your lovers bring You their own heads,
> the gift of their life,
> they will have only brought cumin seeds to Kerman.[2]

What is it worth to bring cumin to Kerman? What renown will it bring? What price will it fetch? There is a palace where *He is without need*,[3] so take your need there! Because the One without need loves need, and you, due to that need may suddenly leap out of these created affairs. Something from the Eternal One, is connected to you; it is love. The ambush of love comes and embraces you, just as it says in the Qur'an: *They love God* is the effect of *God loves them* [5:54]. Then you will see the Ancient Eternal One through the Ancient Eternal One because *He perceives all vision* [6:103].[4]

This is the entirety of the words that do not end and will not end until the day of resurrection.

---

2 The region of Kerman is the source of all cumin.

3 *Truly, God does not stand in need of anything in all the worlds* [*Surah al-Imran* 3:97]. See also such verses as *Surah al-Anam* 6:12-14:

> *Say: "Unto whom belongs all that is in the heavens and on earth?" Say: "Unto God, who has willed upon Himself the law of grace and mercy." He will assuredly gather you all together on the Day of Resurrection, [the coming of] which is beyond all doubt: yet those who have squandered their own selves—it is they who refuse to believe [in Him], although His is all that dwells in the night and the day, and He alone is All-hearing, All-knowing.*
> *Say: "Am I to take for my master anyone but God, the Originator of the heavens and the earth, when it is He who gives nourishment and Himself needs none?" Say: "I am bidden to be foremost among those who surrender themselves unto God, and not to be among those who ascribe divinity to any beside Him."*

4 *No vision can grasp Him/Her, but His/Her grasp is over all vision: He/She is subtle beyond comprehension, and All-Aware* (*Huwal Latiful Khabir*) [*Surah al-Anam*, 6:103]. This verse from the Qur'an also brings to mind the *hadith* (saying of the Prophet Muhammad): God says, "When my faithful servant draws near to Me through his or her voluntary devotions, then I love him/her and I become the ear with which he hears, the eye with which he sees, the tongue with which he speaks, the hand with which he grasps, the foot with which he walks.

The Friend of the Friend

They say that I am a saint; suppose I am, what honor and pride could I take from such words? Rather, it would cause me intense shame if I were to be proud of this. Instead, I am proud that I am a friend of Mevlana who, if one looks at the attributes indicated by the Qur'an and the sayings of the Prophet, is a saint. So, I am the protector[5] of the saint and the friend of the friend; from this point of view, I am stronger.

The Mirror

Even if you prostrate yourself a hundred times in front of a mirror, it won't flatter you. If any ugliness begins to appear on the mirror, know that it's your own; don't blame the mirror. If you say to it, "Hide that defect on his face from him, because he is my friend," it says, "Impossible."

He said, "Now, friend, you say, 'Put the mirror into my hand so that I may look!' I can't find a reason not to; I can't deny your request."

Yet in his heart he is thinking, "Let me find some excuse not to give you the mirror, because if it says that there is something wrong with your face, perhaps you won't be able to bear it, and if you then say it's the mirror that's defective, it will only be worse for you."

But again love doesn't allow me to find any excuse. I say, "Okay, let me give you the mirror, but if you see some fault on its face, don't blame the mirror. Find the fault with that which is reflected on the mirror, know that it has appeared there from your own image; find the fault within yourself! The only condition by which I agree to offer the mirror is that you don't find fault with the mirror. And if you are unable to find the fault within yourself, then put the burden on me, as I am the owner of the mirror. Don't say the mirror is defective."

---

5 Here Shams is playing with the word *wali/veli* which means both "saint," "friend," and "protector."

"I accept the condition. I promise. Give me the mirror, I can't wait any longer!" he said.

Again, the heart of the mirror-owner hesitates: "Let me find some pretext to avoid this situation. The work of the mirror is subtle." But still, Love didn't allow us any excuse. "Okay, let's remember the condition once again," the mirror-owner said, and gave the following advice: "The condition and the agreement is that no matter what defect you see, you will not throw the mirror on the ground; you won't destroy its jewel-essence, even though its jewel-essence is unbreakable."

"God forbid," the person said, "I would never intend or even think of such a thing. Now let me have the mirror so that I can prove to you my good manners, and you can witness my fidelity."

"But if you break it, its essence is this great . . . , and its cost is this much . . . ," and he brought witnesses and evidence for its value.

Then, after all these words, when the person was given the mirror, the mirror-owner ran away. Then, that person said to himself, "If this mirror were so valuable, why did he leave it and run away? Has it begun to break?"

When he held it in front of his face, what he saw was ugliness. He wanted to throw the mirror to the ground, crying, "Such agony because of this!"[6] But he recalled his agreement, the bill of sale, the witnesses, and the money he would have to pay for the crime of destroying the mirror. He said, "I wish there had been no conditions, no witnesses, no money involved, so that I could cool my heart and do what needs to be done."

While he was saying this, the mirror was rebuking him with the tongue of its state: "You see? What did I do to you, and what are you doing to me? You love yourself and are finding fault with the mirror, because the one who loves himself respects only his *nafs*; while the one who loves the mirror, renounces both."

This mirror is Reality, Itself; he thinks the mirror is something other than himself. Even so, just as he is inclined toward the mirror,

6 Literally, "My lungs have filled with blood," indicating the intensity of advanced tuberculosis with which someone is on the verge of death.

the mirror is inclined toward him. Because he is inclined towards the mirror, the mirror is inclined towards him. If he had broken the mirror, he would have broken me, too. Wasn't it said, "I am with those who have been broken."[7]

In short, it's impossible for the mirror to incline towards itself. It is like a touchstone or a balance-scale; it always inclines towards the Truth. If you try to tell it, "O scale, weigh this less as more!" still, it will only show the Truth, even if you were to coddle it or prostrate yourself in front of it for two hundred years.[8]

Be Honest

Mevlana (Jalaluddin Rumi) expressed such gratitude to you. Just listening to him and receiving his generosity and kindness, when we went there together, pleased us so much that we didn't want to leave.

Remember that people are easily pleased when even hypocritically you flatter them; and when you pay attention to them, even just by listening to what they have to say, it pleases them. Otherwise, they quickly get bored with the conversation.

But even if people don't get along well with us, we have to be honest. Always to behave with honesty is right for the human being. As God said to His prophet, "*Be honest, as you have been commanded to be!*"[9] You are honest; stay honest. Demonstrate honesty!

> No matter how much I call something crooked
> "straight," it won't change it.

---

7 It is repeated that God said to one of His Prophets, "I am with those whose hearts are broken for Me."

8 Shams echoes the *hadith* "The faithful are mirrors for the faithful." The saint is the clearest of mirrors, and the purest of saints, the reflector of Reality Itself.

See Mevlana Jalaluddin Rumi's *Mathnawi* I:3153-3227 for the story of the Prophet Joseph and the mirror which is another reflection of this story. "The beautiful face is in love with the mirror: it is a polisher of the soul and a kindler of *the fear of God in hearts. . . .* "

9 See *Surah Hud*, 11:112 and *Surah Shura*, 42:15.

Dervish Words

"The One" is one of the pure attributes of the Glorious and Powerful God, one of His happy names. Who are you and what is your word?[10] These are the words spoken by the Truth, full of wisdom. Others are indications of the great ones. Yes, they are, but come, which one—which "word"—is yours?

I speak from my own state. I don't hold on to those words. If you also have something to say, tell me. If sometimes words become subtle, then for the sake of bringing witnesses as Mevlana has said, "One has to seal the words with the Qur'an or the *hadith* of Muhammad so that their meaning might be explained." This is what is appropriate.

Someone said, "He has both beautiful (*jamal*) and stringent (*jalal*) attributes. Among his beautiful attributes is his modesty, and among his stringent aspects is his unrelentingness, but his stringency outweighs his beauty."

But one thing about you is that you are not resentful. The fact that you don't bear a grudge is better than a thousand other attributes. Why were you left in fear and panic because I didn't speak with you for a few days? This is an extremely good sign.[11]

When I ask you to speak, my intention is to show you that meaning is like a tiger that we don't control. I only have some power over words; call it the power of the meaning or call it Divine assistance. Sometimes, I just throw words forth and there are no other words like them. We trick some of the meanings to come out, but others don't. When you speak, as if you are speaking my words, how full of

---

10 Each human being is a "word" spoken by God, each with a different quality: *Be, and it is* [*Surah Ya Sin*, 36:83].

11 *Taqwa*, "vigilant awareness" sometimes translated as "fear of God," is an important aspect of the path. Rather than feeling hurt and bearing a grudge because he was ignored, instead he was fearful of what he might have done to rupture a connection. *Taqwa* is our vigilant awareness of God and sensitivity to the continual vibrancy of the connection wth the Divine.

meaning and beautiful it is.[12] Just as you were speaking to that dervish the other day, how many meanings showed themselves! Doors open, and wide views are revealed.

Compounding the Good

Now, due to your words and the benefit you caused, double benefit occurs: one benefit for you and one for the doer of the good. According to a *hadith*, "The one who is the means of a good is as good as the one who actually accomplishes it." Part of the benefit is for the doer and part of the benefit is for the one who was the cause behind it.

Subtle Conversations

Don't be hurt if I speak honestly with my friends. I gave my word not to be hypocritical.

Because you couldn't wait for the word I wanted to say, it was lost. No other words come to mind. If you have something to say, wait until I have finished speaking. These dervish conversations are subtle. If something is lost now, it will be lost; the words that will come later will be different.

Sema

In the people of God, these Divine Self-disclosures and visions of God occur more often during the *sema*,[13] when they have emerged

---

12 Here it seems that Shams is referring to Mevlana. One can witness how the *Mathnawi* of Mevlana Jalaluddin Rumi is an unfolding garden from the seeds of Shams' conversation and verses of the Qur'an and *hadith.*

13 *Sema* (*sama*): a gathering for the sharing of music and chanting, "listening" inwardly to the Divine. During the time of Mevlana and Shams, poetry would be spontaneously recited and spontaneous whirling would take place during the *sema* gatherings. Later, a formalized ceremony of whirling developed that was based on the mystical principles shared by Shams-i Tabriz with Mevlana's son, sultan Weled. The movement of whirling is also referred to as *sema*. During

from the universe of their own existence. *Sema* carries them out of other universes and joins them with the Truth. It is true that there is a *sema* that is forbidden; but it is blasphemy to say that the *sema* performed by the people of God is a sin. The hand that is lifted without that state will burn in hell for sure, and the hands that are lifted with that state will reach paradise—without a doubt.

There is a *sema* that is permissible but not obligatory. This is the *sema* of the pure ones who live practicing ascetic disciplines. To them it brings tears and softness of heart. Of course they will reach Paradise.

And there is also a *sema* that is obligatory. This is the *sema* of the attained ones who have reached a holy state; for them *sema* is obligatory just as the daily prayers and the fast of Ramadan, and just as food and water are obligatory in the time of hunger and thirst. This *sema* is obligatory for the spiritually mature, because it supports their life. If one of the mature ones makes *sema* in the East, another one begins moving in the West. They are aware of each other's states.

Attributes of Beauty and Wrath

Someone said, "Mevlana is all kindness, while in Mevlana Shamsuddin, there are both the attributes of kindness and wrath."

Someone else said, "It is like this with everyone."

When my words are repeated, he comes, interprets, and then apologizes! "My objection was to his words, not to your qualities."

Fool! Once I have spoken why do you interpret my words? What excuse do you have? He was defining me by the attributes of God, who has both wrath and kindness. But those were not his words; it is my word not *Qur'an* nor *hadith*. These were my words that have come forth from his tongue.

---

this whirling movement of the Mevlevis (those who follow the teachings and example of Rumi, i.e. Mevlana), the dervishes raise their arms—the right hand extends upwards to receive Divine blessing, and the left hand is turned towards the earth to bestow the blessing received. Thus the one whirling becomes a conduit for bringing Divine Presence and blessing more directly into this existence.

What made you say that everyone has these attributes? How can the wrath and kindness that is attributed to me be in everyone?

Now, with such manners and words, these people need to catch up with Bayazid, Junayd, or Shibli and drink from the same cup as they did. If they were to be told of the attributes and manners of those shaikhs, just from hearing about it, they would lose their minds. Even so, those shaikhs were all humble in the presence of God.

Even with all this, he died veiled from God. A dervish passed by that person's grave and said, "There was only one veil left between this man and God." This was the generosity and beneficence of that dervish. Ask another dervish about it.

Mevlana has a lot of beauty, and I have beauty and ugliness. Mevlana has seen our beautiful side, but he has not seen our ugly side. This time I will not be hypocritical and will show my ugliness, so that he may see all of me—my beauty and my ugliness.

Focusing

The sign of someone who has found his way to our company is that he chills towards the conversations of others. He doesn't just lose interest in their conversations, he won't even be able to speak with them.

No Dope!

Some of our friends have become fond of hashish—it is the devil's fantasy. Here, there is no place even for the fantasy of the angels, much less for the fantasy of the devil! We don't even accept the illusions of the angels, so how could we accept those of the devil?

Why don't our friends taste of this pure and endless universe of ours? This universe embraces them and intoxicates them without their even being aware of it. Everyone is in unanimous agreement that it is not a forbidden substance, but wine is forbidden.

Someone who was dubious said, "It's written in the Qur'an that wine is forbidden, but it doesn't say anything about hashish being forbidden."[14]

I replied, "There is a reason for every verse in the Qur'an. It has descended upon humanity for a reason. In the time of the Prophet Muhammad, people didn't smoke hashish. If the Prophet's companions had smoked it, he would have ordered their punishment. Every verse has come down according to a need. When his companions used to disturb him by reciting the Qur'an too loudly, this verse was revealed: *O you who have faith, don't raise your voices louder than the Prophet's* [49:2].

Prophets Recognize Each Other

All the prophets confirm each other. Jesus says: "O Jews, you don't know Moses well; come and be with me so that you may also know Moses." Muhammad (may God's peace be upon him) used to say: "O Christians and Jews, you don't know Moses and Jesus very well. Come and be with me so that you may also know them better. All prophets accept and confirm each other. And their words are always words that explain and complete each other."

After this the companions said: "O Messenger of God, since every prophet has acknowledged the one who came before him, who is going to confirm you, since you are the last of the prophets?"

He answered: "The one who knows his own soul, knows his Lord."

And so the one who knows my soul, knows my Lord as well.

One Step to the Goal

The more learned a person is, the more distant he is from the goal. No matter how advanced such a person's thought becomes, still he remains far from the goal.

> This is the work of the heart,
> not the work of the head.

---

14 M. 5.

It's like the story of the man who had found a treasure map. The map said, "Go out such and such a door; you will find a dome. Turn your back to that dome, and turn your face towards the *qiblah*[15]; release an arrow, and the treasure is hidden where the arrow falls."[16]

The man did so, and shot the arrow, but he couldn't find the treasure. News of this reached the king who then commanded his archers who could shoot great distances to let fly their arrows from that spot, but still nothing was found.

Then the man sought help in the Divine Presence and received an inspiration, "We didn't say to draw the bow!" He returned to the spot, put the arrow in the bow, but did not draw it. Upon release, the arrow fell right in front of him. When Divine help arrived, it was only a step to reach the goal. *"Two strides and he arrived. . . .* "[17]

Now what does this story imply in relation to actions? And what in relation to spiritual exercises? Those who shoot the arrow far away remain more deprived, because only a step is necessary to reach the treasure. But what is that step? Who has that step? "He who knows his/her self, undoubtedly knows his/her Lord (*hadith*)."

And the one who is called the commanding self[18] reaches satisfaction and peace.[19]

---

15 The *qiblah* is the direction of prayer for the Muslim, toward Mecca and the Kaaba.

16 See the story of the fakir and the treasure in the *Mathnawi*, VI: 1908-2043; 2257-2375. I.e.: That [Divine] King said, "[*those who*] *have striven in Us*"; He did not say, "[*those who*] *have striven away from Us*," O restless one . . . [*Mathnawi* VI: 2358].

17 This is a reference to the moment when during his *mi'raj*, Muhammad's journey through the heavens into the presence of God, with God's help he approached within two bow lengths or nearer [53:9]. *And thus did [God] reveal unto His servant whatever He deemed right to reveal* [*Surah an-Najm*, The Star 53:10].

18 The commanding self (*nafs ammarah*) is the aspect of self that is full of desire, compulsion, and self-interest.

19 As the self becomes purified, it moves through being repentant (*nafs al-lawwamah*), to being inspired with the Divine (*nafs al-mulhimah*) to being content with God's commands (*nafs al-mutmainnah*) and through the states in which it is both then pleased with God's commands (*nafs-i radiyah*) and also pleasing to its Lord (*nafs-i*

❁

Love and Intellect

A preacher preaches for the sake of informing people about the signs of the Beloved; he shows the way to the wayfarer. The imperfect shaikh and the poet recite verses in order to explain and indicate signs, but these people appear ridiculous in the presence of one who really knows.

It's like the case of the person who was talking about fish, and someone said, "Be quiet; you don't know what you're talking about! How can you explain what you don't know?"

The man said, "You think I don't know anything about fish?"

"OK, if you do know, tell us about the signs of a fish."

"A fish has two horns just like a camel."

The other man began to laugh and said, "I thought you didn't know anything about fish, but now I realize that you don't even know the difference between a camel and an ox!"

> If the red tulip hadn't laughed foolishly,
> who would have seen the darkness within her?
> She's all dressed up in her own blood;
> That's the punishment for those who
>   are black-hearted.

Yes, all these words come to this: "Speak with people according to the measure of their understanding (*hadith*)." And so, the limitation of their understanding is their downfall.

> Intellect ties people in knots,
> but love dissolves those tangles.

---

mardiyah) until at last fully purified (*nafs-i kamilah*) it is able to enter the Garden, the Abode of Peace.

And God invites to the abode of Peace. [*Surah Yunus*, Jonah 10:24-26]

But to the righteous soul will be said:
"O soul in complete rest and satisfaction!
Return to your Sustainer well-pleased and well-pleasing!
Enter then among my devoted ones! Yes, enter my Garden!" [*Surah al-Fajr*, The Daybreak 89:27-30]

Intellect says, "Too much ecstasy!"
Love says, "Nevermind."

❖

The Sea Bird[20]

During my childhood years I experienced a strange state. Nobody could understand this state of mine.[21] Even my father didn't know what was happening. He used to say, "You aren't crazy, but I don't understand the way your life is—you haven't had the training of spiritual exercises, or fasting, or anything like that."

I said to my father, "Listen, the situation you and I are in—it's as if someone had placed a duck's egg underneath a hen. When the egg is hatched, the little duck heads for the water. Of course the mother hen panics with a flutter of wings around him, but she is made for the farmyard; it's impossible for her to enter the water. This is how we are, father. I see a sea where I can swim; it is my home. And my state is like the state of the seabirds. If you are of me or if I am of you, come into this sea! Otherwise, go and mingle with the birds of the farmyard. Let these words be a touchstone for you."

If this is how you act with friends,
how will you behave towards an enemy?

---

20 See *Mathnawi* II:3766-3787.

21 See *Menaqib al-Arifin* #537 (translated by Susan Blaylock, may peace and blessings be with her, in a manuscript pending publication):

Sultan Weled said:

Shamsuddin told my father this: "When I was a child, I saw God and angels and contemplated the mysteries of this and the world beyond. I thought that everyone could see these things, but later realized that they could not. Shaikh Abu Bakr forbid me to speak about it."

Sultan Weled continued: "My father told me this: 'This is our Master Shamsuddin's gift granted to him from Eternity, not from his devotions or his asceticism.'"

On whom We had bestowed grace from Ourselves and unto whom We had imparted knowledge issuing from Ourselves [*Surah al-Kahf*, The Cave 18:65].

The Spirit of Intimacy

Yes, one group is left in suspicion and doubt, while another group experiences intimacy with God. Mansur al-Hallaj departed in doubt, and another group stopped between doubt and intimacy: "The spirits of the martyrs are within the craw of the green bird. The spirits of the faithful are within the white bird's craw. And the spirits of the unbelievers are within the craw of the black bird (*hadith*)."

Sema is permitted for the pure servants of God, because their hearts are clean. They love for the sake of God, and their anger is for God's sake;[22] their hearts are clear and sound.[23]

If my swearing and shouting reaches the ears of someone who has been an unbeliever for a hundred years, he becomes a believer. If it lightly touches the ears of a believer, he becomes a saint and enters paradise. I told you before in my dream I had told you, When my heart joins with his heart, this becomes his station.[24] He had seen lots of visions before this one, too. In the end, he will leave as one surrendered (*muslim*), free.

Muhammad

If the prayer of Muhammad, peace and blessings upon him, "O God, guide my people for they do not know," did not exist, how could Abu Jahl[25] have thrown a sheep's stomach on the Prophet without his hands shriveling?

In the end, the Prophet is a lone horseman on their path. Anyone who intends discourtesy towards him is overcome with an affliction. The Prophet is the kind of person before whom human beings and

---

22 See the story of Ali and the infidel Knight: *Mathnawi* I: 3721-3843; 3975-4003.

23 See *Surah ash-Shu'ara*, The Poets 26:89: *Bring to God a sound heart.*

24 Shams reminds us how the spiritual station is transferred through the melding of hearts.

25 Abu Jahl was one of the strongest opponents of Islam among the Meccans during the time of the Prophet Muhammad.

angels put their ladders down in recognition of his greatness and in awe of his words. Tight-rope walkers, trapeze artists, and acrobats are amazed at the height and strength of his rope and his fearlessness and courage. How could those who have seen him riding and cropping a black lion as if it were a lazy donkey ever forget him?!

Forgetfulness

Forgetfulness is of two kinds. The first is from this world: those who are caught by this world forget to remember the next world. The second cause of forgetfulness is to be busy with the work of the next world which causes one to forget even oneself. This world in the hands of such a person is like a mouse in the paws of a cat. Through companionship with a real servant of God, a person attains a state that no shaikh reaches even after thirty years on a prayer carpet.

A third reason for forgetfulness is love of God. The one who falls into that love forgets both this world and the next. This is the rank of Mevlana. The meaning of, "This world is unlawful to the folk of the next world, and the next world is unlawful to the folk of this world, and both this world and the next world are unlawful to the folk of God," is this: they forget both worlds. Mevlana has drunkenness in love but doesn't have awareness in love, but I have drunkenness in love as well as awareness.

For me, there can be no forgetfulness in drunkenness. What value does this world have that it should either veil me or veil itself from me?

The Carnelian

A shaikh told the friends, "The Caliph has forbidden the *sema.*" This prohibition became a knot within the heart of a certain dervish. He fell ill and they took him to a specialist. The specialist examined his pulse and looked for the cause of illness; it was unlike anything he had ever seen. The dervish died. Afterwards, the doctor performed an autopsy and found the knot within his chest. It had become a carnelian.

When the doctor came upon hard times, he sold the jewel. It passed from hand to hand, until at last it reached the caliph, who had the gem set into a ring. One day, that same caliph was attending a *sema*, which he had once again permitted. He glanced down and saw that his clothes had become splattered with blood. He checked himself but could find no wound. Then as he felt for his ring, he discovered that the stone had dissolved. He summoned the person who had sold him the gem. He traced the gem back to its first owner, and that doctor told him the whole story of its origin.

> If you see drops of blood spilling here and there,
> know them to have fallen from my eyes.

☼

Sema of the Sensual

What does a sensual man have to do with *sema*? His *sema* is eating! His eating is in his soul; all of him has become eating! *They eat and take their enjoyment like the eating of cattle* [47:12].[26] As if he were created and given existence so he could eat! Can someone who has found the meaning within his soul eat like this?

☼

Do Your Own Work

You are saying, "Mevlana has light and greatness, and power." But if someone believes in a person who is unproven and misguided, and he follows and obeys that person, then how can there be power and light in him? Again you say, "Fifty saints should walk behind Mevlana." How could he be following someone who is blind? You say that the saints have signs: who are you to know about the sign of a saint?

When a person is left helpless, from that helplessness either light or darkness emerges. The devil deepened in darkness because of his helplessness, but the angels became brighter because of theirs. Miracles are like this, too. This is also how words of truth

---

26 *Truly, God will admit those who have faith and do rightful deeds to Gardens beneath which rivers flow; while those who turn away from God will take their enjoyment and eat as cattle eat: and the fire will be their abode* [*Surah Muhammad*, 47:12].

become manifest. When people are left helpless, they prostrate in front of God.

The one who says, "With just one glance I can know a person," is greatly mistaken.[27] What he and those like him have found to trust in, what pleases them and makes them drunk is a fiery glance. Watch yourself so that you might keep progressing through your own inner universe, and try to pass beyond it because it is empty, only air.

I have nothing to do with ignorant people in this world. I didn't come here for them. I put my seal upon these people who show the path to the Truth.

True Yearning

If a person wants to listen to my words in order to debate or to compare them with the words of shaikhs or Qur'an or *hadith*, neither will he hear those words nor will he benefit from me. But if he comes and listens out of need and yearning for benefit, for need is the real capital, he will benefit. Otherwise, not one day or ten days, but even if he speaks for a hundred years, we will put our hand under our chin and just keep listening.

The Beauty of the Spirit

It is not surprising if a jewel put into a coarse container, wrapped in a black handkerchief, and hidden under ten coverings or in a sleeve or a sheepskin cannot be seen. It is like the situation of Sayyid through whose self (*nafs*) the spirit and the happiness of the spirit reached him, even though still he had not yet seen his own spirit.[28] The rank of reaching the happiness of the spirit is far from that of seeing one's

27 Shams reminds us of Iblis (Satan), the fiery one who would not bow to Adam at God's command because he thought Adam who was "only made of clay" was beneath him. See *Surah Sad*, 38:71-76. Likewise, this is also perhaps a reference to those who cursorily reject Shams.

28 Here Shams refers to those who awaken on the Path of God. In particular, Sayyid Burhanuddin—though the fragrance of the beauty of spirit had come

spirit. And after having seen the spirit, one must still then walk on the Way of God until with a discerning eye one can see God in this life; I'm not saying "in this very world."

Although that jewel is hidden within those veils, still its light shines through to the outside. One who has mature sight is aware of that which hasn't yet emerged.

It's not astonishing that someone isn't aware of what hasn't yet emerged, but what is astonishing is that when it is brought out and is placed on an open palm in front of them, still no one sees. If that were not the case, who could utter the words of Socrates, Hippocrates, the Brethren of Purity,[29] and the Greek philosophers in the presence of the Prophet Muhammad, or his descendents—the children of Muhammad's soul and heart, not the children of earth and water! And when God is present, too!

One day, Umar was reading from the Torah, Muhammad (may the prayers of God be upon him) took the pages from Umar's hand, and spoke to him, "If the person upon whom the Torah descended were alive now, he would be following me."

☸

Ibrahim Adham

Before he gave up the kingdom of Balkh, Ibrahim Adham was continually giving away his possessions and tiring his body through ascetic practices and vigils.[30] "What must I do?" he would ask, "so that I might find an openness of heart within myself?"

One night he was asleep on the throne; though his eyes were asleep, within he was awake. The night guards were beating the drums with mallets and sticks, playing reed flutes (*neys*), and making a

---

to him, he hadn't yet fully beheld the beauty of his own spirit. See *Surah al-Muddhaththir*, The Enfolded One 74:1-4: *O you who are enfolded, arise and warn.*

29 The Brotherhood of Purity (*Ikhwan as-Safa*) was a society of spiritual friends begun around 951 C.E. in Basra. They compiled one of the first encyclopedias, the *Rasa'il ikhwan as-safa* which included philosophical, metaphysical, and scientific knowledge.

30 M. 10.

racket. Ibrahim Adham said to himself, "Which enemy are you trying to keep away? The enemy is asleep here with me. Such a poor one as we are is in need of the compassionate glance of God; what security can come from you? There is no safe haven other than in the refuge of His kindness." With these thoughts his heart was troubled; he kept raising his head from the pillow, and then lowering it again.

> How strange! How can a lover sleep!
> Sleep isn't allowed for one who loves!

Suddenly, he heard strong footsteps and noises from the roof of the pavilion as if a large crowd of people were marching on the roof. The footsteps echoed in every corner of the pavilion. The sultan said to himself, "What has happened to the guards? Where have they all gone? Don't they hear this crowd running on the roof?" Then due to this noise of footsteps a strange perplexity and terror came over him; it was as if he had forgotten both himself and the palace; he was unable to shout, or to call the guards to come with their weapons.

Just then, someone leaned his head downwards from the roof of the pavilion and asked, "You who sit on the throne, who are you?"

Ibrahim answered, "I am the king! Who are you, walking on the roof?"

"Well, we lost a few strings of camels, and we're looking for them on the roof of this pavilion," the man replied.

"Are you crazy?" Ibrahim asked.

"Ibrahim Adham, you are the crazy one!" the man responded.

"Did you lose the camels on the roof of the pavilion? Who would ever search for camels here on a roof?!" Ibrahim Adham asked.The man answered, "Would one ever really look for God on the throne of a kingdom? Are you really looking for God here?"

Nobody saw Ibrahim Adham again.[31]

---

31 Mevlana echoes this story, intertwining it with that of the Prophet Solomon and Bilqis in Book IV of his *Mathnawi*, IV:717-1112. To be with Shams, to immerse in the Divine Presence, Mevlana himself gave up the "throne" of his respected position.

The Meaning of Sainthood

What is the meaning of sainthood?[32] Does it mean having soldiers, a crown, and a throne? Perhaps the one who has sainthood in his *nafs* is a saint. Sainthood is to have sovereignty over one's self, one's states, one's attributes, one's speech, and one's silence. The one whose wrath or grace is appropriate while he is speaking or silent, is a saint. The people of wisdom (*arif*) don't say, "We are incapable, and He is the Powerful One." You have to become powerful and strong in every attribute, that you might be silent at the time when silence is called for, respond at the moment for response, and show wrath when it is the moment for wrath, and kindness when kindness is appropriate. Otherwise such a person's attributes become a calamity for him or her, and they cause pain because they are not ruled by him, rather they rule over him. A person becomes a ruler, if he is not a slave.

Die before You Die

A philosopher was explaining about the agony after death.[33] He was saying: "The soul comes to this earth to mature itself; it tries to gather the capital of maturity from the world[34] so that when it emerges from this world, it might not have any regrets." We must come out of form into meaning now.

After having merged with the body, the soul becomes occupied with images. If the soul merges too closely with the flesh, then it falls into difficulty; the soul loses its expansive and joyful aspect. On the one hand it begins to pay attention to possessions and becomes

32 *Veli*-hood (*Wali*). Shams is again making a play on words here, referring to the various meanings of sainthood/sovereignty/guardianship.

33 It is believed that after death, after the body is buried, a person suffers for a time as purification for sins he or she has committed.

34 Capital of maturity: Shams refers to the idea that we come to this world to become acquainted with many attributes, to ripen. This development of maturity, the experiencing of the qualities and what we learn from that experiencing, is our real capital.

attached to the high opinion of others; the soul gathers relationship with a spouse and with friends who are close to his or her heart. He or she becomes involved with many kinds of pleasures. And so, from the point of view of the aspect of the soul tied to the body, to speak about a single "death" is faulty; really a thousand deaths are experienced.[35]

If the soul were in expectation of the fulfillment of its wishes from the other universe [of Non-existence], he or she would struggle to go there. Then death would not be death; rather it would be life. Mustafa,[36] peace and blessings upon him, said, "The faithful do not die, really they immigrate from one universe to another." According to the individual situation, immigration is one thing; death is another.

A person cannot walk around freely in a cramped and dark house; one cannot feel comfortable and joyful in such a place; one cannot even stretch one's legs out and sit comfortably. But, if one immigrates from that very tight house to a large house that has gardens all around it and flowing waters, then that immigration is not referred to as "death."

These words are like a bright mirror. If you have joy and an inner light, then you fall in love with death. May God make this a blessing for you; and don't forget to pray for us, too! If you don't have such a light or sense of taste, then work for it! The Qur'an informs us that if you are looking for such a state you will find it. God says, "If you are of the truly faithful, seek death." *You should seek death—if you are sincere!*[37]

One should not forget that just as there are among the real men of God, among men of faith, those who seek "death"; women who seek "death" are also not absent among the women of faith. This is a bright mirror in which you can see the clear reflection of your state. If you are continually holding awareness of death and longing for that passage, in every state in which you find yourself and in the

---

35 This is due to the number of attachments that are severed at death.

36 Mustafa is another name for the Prophet Muhammad.

37 See *Surah al-Baqarah* 2:94 or *Surah al-Jumu'ah* 62:6.

midst of everything that you do, then whatever endeavor you are involved in will be beneficial. So when you find yourself hesitating between two things, wondering which to choose, look into this mirror. Of those two things, choose the one closest to death.[38] You must be ready for death and wait for it like a pure light.

The Pearl

Sultan Mahmoud of Ghazna showed a pearl to the door-keeper.[39] The door-keeper had heard the king praising his vizier profusely [when he had praised this pearl]. The sultan asked the door-keeper, pointing to the pearl, "Is this a good pearl?"

"To say it is 'good' is to say nothing at all. It would be contrary to good manners to even speak about its worth—it is so precious. A hundred thousand times over it is a good pearl! Calling it 'good' is like referring to our sultan as 'good' when his majesty is so great that to say such a thing would be ill-mannered."

Then the sultan ordered him: "If that is true, then break it!"

"How can I break it! The vizier says that this pearl is four times more valuable than the rest of the sultan's whole treasury. The most appropriate thing is for it to remain in the treasury."

"All right. Then let it continue to keep good company with the other treasure, let it be so," the sultan said, and bestowed upon the door-keeper robes of honor and increased his pay.

---

38 Shams indicates that it is incumbent upon us to choose death for the ego, and reach for the purity of the soul, for the essential Self. We are called upon to turn away from the demands of the compulsive ego, and rather to open to faith, journeying with awareness of our Sustainer, so that we might be ever ready for the moment of return to our Lord.

39 The door-keeper was the representative of the vizier. In the palace doorways had curtains, and there were doormen who stood at the place of entry. When someone would come to the room of a sultan, the "curtain-man" or "door-keeper" would be the one to pull the curtain aside and allow the person to enter. The door-keeper was the general secretary of the vizier who was the king's right hand man or prime minister.

This test was made in such a way that no one could witness how the others in the palace who were tested were responding. At last the challenge came to Ayaz.[40] The sultan was thinking to himself: "I hope that Ayaz, who is dear to me, doesn't respond in the same way." He kept thinking: "If he responds the same way as the others, what shall I do? But he is the apple of our eye! Let him say whatever he wishes."

The turn of examination of the pearl came to Ayaz. The room where the pearl had been placed was enclosed by a curtain so that nobody could approach. When the king pointed towards the pearl for Ayaz to take it, he was afraid and trembling; he was still thinking to himself, "What if Ayaz says the same thing as the others!"

Ayaz, looking at the king, examined him as though asking, "Why are you trembling?" meaning, "trembling before the grandeur of the sultan is appropriate for Ayaz; such trembling isn't appropriate for the king." He had matured in the sultan's palace, he had learned good manners, and in reality, his heart was filled with love of the sultan.

The sultan turned to Ayaz and said in an uncustomary way, "O sultan, take the pearl." He didn't say, "O slave, take the pearl." But, to Ayaz, a thousand times more sincere a compliment was hidden in the word "slave" than in "sultan." Being called "slave" pleased him a thousand times more. When referred to as "sultan," he suffered.

Ayaz took the pearl. The king asked, "Well, how is it; is it beautiful?"

Without adding a word, "Beautiful," Ayaz replied.

And when the sultan asked, "Is it very fine?" again not adding any words, "It is very fine," he answered.

---

40 Ayaz is the name of the loyal slave of sultan Mahmoud of Ghazna. He was famous for his literary genius, intelligence, and strong fidelity to the king, and these qualities of his had won the heart of the sultan. Ayaz, who had won the trust of the sultan, had a very pleasing character, a beautiful face, and a beautiful temperament. The story of Mahmoud and Ayaz has become a theme for many legends and poems.

See the story of Ayaz and the pearl in the *Mathnawi*, V: 4035-4238.

"If so, then break it!" said the sultan. Ayaz had prepared two stones and had hidden them in his sleeve. He had had a dream about this happening. As soon as he hit the pearl with the stones, it shattered into many pieces. From every direction sighs and screams arose.

"Is this a place for sighs and screaming?" Ayaz asked.

"But you broke such a precious pearl into pieces!" the other courtiers who had been nearby exclaimed.

Ayaz answered, "The command of the sultan is more precious than this pearl."

Upon hearing this answer, all those who had gathered bowed their heads, glancing at the floor. And this time, they were moaning to themselves again and again: "Alas! What did we do?!" as they realized their own insolence.

The sultan ordered his sergeants: "Call the executioners and have them take these men away; let them sweep away these fools who have surrounded us! Let them be hanged.

Ayaz threw himself forward, "O, gentle-tempered sultan!" He said, "The best thing to do is to *forgive*."[41]

---

41 See *Surah an-Nur*, 24:21-22:

O you who have attained to faith! Don't follow Satan's footsteps: for the one who follows Satan's footsteps, witness, encourages corruption and all that is contrary to reason. And were it not for God's blessing with you and His compassion, not one of you would ever have remained pure, for it is God Who causes whomever He wills to increase in purity: for God is All-hearing, All-knowing.

And so, do not let those of you who have been graced with God's favor and ease of circumstance ever be neglectful of helping their near of kin, and the needy, and those who have turned from the domain of evil for God's sake, but let them forgive and endure. Do you not desire that God should forgive you your sins, seeing that God is Ever Ready to Forgive, and is Most Merciful?

Shams reminds us here of our tendency to honor idols—money, possessions, wealth, position and our own self—rather than the command of God. Ayaz represents one who is willing to offer up even the pearl of the soul to his Beloved Lord, knowing that alignment with the command of God is more valuable than all else.

It is the Creator who has the power to restore. As Rumi often reminds us, in order to find the treasure buried beneath it, the house must be demolished, but then once the treasure is found, the house (the self) is able to be rebuilt better than before. Empty of self, the soul is then filled with the Divine.

All of You

One day your image came to me:
I became intoxicated from such pleasure,
from the wine of union.

All night long we lay embracing each other;
when the face of morning shone, we parted.

My whole being has been sacrificed for all of You;
all of me is occupied with all of You.

Looking for God

So, you set out to look for God . . . He is such a God that He has created this sky which is so vast that intellects and imagination become lost in it. It's not possible to understand even a single star. Whatever philosophers, astronomers, or physicists say, it isn't as they say. Now, such a star[42] has come into existence from a universe from which all these beings have also come. What kind of a universe is it?

Even a worm that crawls in manure wants to see and know God! On this way, God has granted new life to those who have sacrificed themselves until their livers were torn to shreds. Some people's stomachs have filled with blood; when God kills them in this universe, they give up all their possessions, properties, and all attachments to self or others, and just like Ibrahim Adham they reach another life.

Mevlana was looking for the path of Truth. After all, someone who falls in love with a woman or a man turns away from his or her shop or business. And if someone were to say, "They're going to hang you," to such a person, "So what, hang me," he or she would answer. The lover has no fear for his life; possessions and properties no longer have value for him either. He or she would willingly die for such an ephemeral darling—they will both be buried beneath the earth. Instead, be the lover of the Pure One who has no beginning

42 Star: not only the heavenly body in the celestial universe, but also a sign of an illuminated human being.

nor end, and who is pure of any kind of incompleteness—love Him because it is He who is Everliving.[43]

Ibrahim Adham gave away a lot of money and possessions. He would give them as gifts to the dervishes that he encountered, so that he might reach the Eternal Beloved. He would wear rough woolen rags under his clothes, and during the day he would secretly fast and retreat in solitude. Sometimes his heart would become contracted, and he would feel sad when there was no opening.

> What harm comes to the dervish
> from the sourness of others?
> If the whole world were swallowed by the sea,
> what would it matter to a duck?

❊

Pre-destiny and Free-will: Be Willing to Serve

Sometimes a person may have a single shameful aspect, and yet it veils all of the person's thousand positive qualities; what one needs is a single positive quality capable of veiling a thousand disgraceful aspects.[44] There is a kind of person who has no defects except that he is resentful; this state veils all of his positive qualitites. In the end his portion is like Iblis: *Let there be a curse upon you* [15:35].

---

43 See *Surah al-Furqan*, Discernment 25:58: *And so, place your trust in the Living One who dies not, and extol His limitless glory and praise.*

Also, witness the unfolding of this in the *Mathnawi* in lines such as:
"Only Love and the lover can resurrect beyond time.
Give your heart to this; the rest is second-hand.
How long will you embrace a lifeless beloved?
Embrace that entity to which nothing can cling.
What sprouts up every spring will wither by autumn,
but the rose garden of Love is always green."

(*The Rumi Collection*, selected and edited by Kabir Helminski, Shambhala Publications, p.40.)

44 A person may have many positive qualities, but his one, single shameful quality may mask his good qualities. Shams is recommending the development of one good quality so strong that it can mask all of one's mistakes before God.

The eye of the good man doesn't see that which is offensive. When a shaikh was passing by a carcass he saw that people nearby were holding their noses, turning their faces away, and passing by hastily. The shaikh neither held his nose nor turned his face aside, nor did he quicken his pace. And when they asked him, "What are you looking at?" he began to praise it, saying, "How white, how beautiful its teeth are!" The carcass spoke to him with the tongue of its state.[45]

Your book of deeds[46] is of many colors.[47] And this many-coloredness comes from looking from the point of view of "predestination," thinking your destiny was written that way.[48] Pay attention that you don't write in different colors in your book.[49] There are some people who know a lot about predestination—if you look only with the eye of predestination, you may miss a lot. You can't sit back and say, "We'll just go to sleep and wait to see what God will command."

A good man doesn't complain about anybody; he doesn't keep watch for faults or mistakes. Most of the time, one who complains is really himself at fault. When someone catches him by the throat, then he reveals that the fault really is his own. Each person thinks in his own way and sees things from his own perspective in order to justify what he does. When a person considers his own situation, he joins those who believe in free will [considering that he is free

---

45 The tongue of its state: i.e., "with the tongue of its reality." Telepathic communication passes from the state of one being to another, whether human or animal or even stone. The Prophet Muhammad used to hear rocks speak.

46 Book of deeds: the book in which angels record one's good and bad deeds. It is said that each person has an angel over each shoulder. The one to the right records his or her good deeds and the one to the left records his or her wrongs in that soul's book of life.

47 Many-colored (*talween*) as opposed to unicolored (*tamkin*) . . . that is, one is scattered, not unified in one's actions.

48 Some believe that what we live was written in a book before we were born—God's handwriting of our destiny.

49 Our intentions and our actions are colored with different qualities depending on the level of the soul from which they are initiated. One strives to be consistently pure.

to do as he pleases], but when he looks at his friend's situation, he joins those who believe in predestination [and thinks that his friend is under a predetermined obligation].[50]

The Sufis know about the inner meaning of the belief of predestination. What do others really understand about it? Among those who speak of predestination, there are those who really understand it, and there are those who only imitate understanding. Why do you look at the imitation?[51] Why don't you look at the Truth? Increase your service for us, so that we may increase our prayers for you.[52] Be like *Those whose good deeds weighed heavier on the scales* [7:8] and who then attained liberation.

❁

A Real Lover

> Ever since I was separated from you my eyes darkened;
> The clouds of my eyes pour rain.

There is an awesomeness and majesty in the words of lovers. They cause one to reflect, "Has my ego (*nafs*) developed to such an extent that it can blame itself? He swore *By the blaming self*[53] [75:2]. He doesn't give the self at peace (*nafs al-mutmainnah*) to be auctioned off. Has this

---

50 Predetermination or predestination: according to this view, what a person does is based upon a blueprint previously made; it is his destiny and cannot be changed. Free-will: according to this view the creature of God is the creator of his own deeds, he has the power to choose and is free to determine his own destiny.

51 One may consider the three stages of imitation, investigation or experimentation, and verification.

52 Shams is indicating that there is a certain amount of predestination, but that service is in our power. Use your free-will for service. That service will draw prayers and goodness to you, will help to purify you, and, with God's help, enable you to attain liberation. Focus on the Truth.

53 According to the Sufi path there are seven stages of the soul: *nafs al ammarah*—the commanding self (commanding to follow its desires), *nafs al-lawammah*—the repentant self (the self that repents of its waywardness), *nafs al mulhimah*—the inspired self (the stage of the self when one recognizes more fully one's connection with the Divine Reality), *nafs al-mutmainnah*—the contented or tranquil self (the one who begins to be content with God's Presence); *nafs ar-radiyah*—the

contented self in you begun to manifest? I am speaking about a love that is real and a seeking that is real. Your remembrance and seeking are not yet real, they are still only wishful thinking. You're still saying, "I wish. . . . " Where does that leave you?

Shadow Players

I wouldn't trade the dust of the old shoes of a real lover for the heads of today's lovers and shaikhs. Shadow players who display images behind a curtain are better, because at least they openly admit that what they are doing is illusion; they admit that it is false. "We do it in order to earn our bread," they say. Because of this, they are better.

I said something to a person in such a way that, if I had spoken in this way to others, they would have been hurt. But he desires that desire and sensuality might embrace him from every direction. He is full of desires; from above and below, and from every direction, desire has gripped him. Well, just then when he was speaking, the brightness and the beauty in his words was really coming from desire. Every tiny wave of desire that emanates from him also returns to him. When his words are conveyed to him he feels pleased. When desire ebbs, he diminishes. He becomes enamored of the words and goes about his business; that itself becomes a proof against him.

He should have a *madrasah* position come to him so that he might fulfill his desires. Then he'll start being buddies with everyone; he'll get all dressed-up in new clothes, and start thinking ill of some of those who are respected and also some people he doesn't even know. Then, he neglects the dignity of the dervish, and he won't look after their needs. He begins to say, "Who is more intelligent than I am? I've learned wisdom from Sirajuddin; who can advise me? When it comes to the burden of carrying on one's head the labor of looking

---

pleased self (the one who is pleased with all that God gives); *nafs al mardiyah*—the self that has become pleasing (to God); *nafs as-safiyyah*—the purified self.

for God, who is a higher authority than I am?" he says, and soon he is really deluded.

From the first shaikhs until now, those who have come and gone are divided into certain classes. One has to start at the beginning. We were talking about desire (*hawa*). Let's continue. We can't have different criteria: we can't say, "For Sanai it's one way; and for Sayyid it's another, or for someone else, other rules apply." Even someone who is crazy wouldn't say that.

In short, give up this habit of yours for a year; while you yearn and pray, wear a coarse cloak; otherwise, they will sell you like a young Armenian slave. Stop trying to make an effortless living for yourself with your false words.[54] You weren't created for your desires. Keep this advice within your soul. Be careful not to speak falsely with people, and be careful not to hurt them.

> A lover who has won her beloved
> may play the coquette,
> but putting on coquettish airs (*naz*)
> before gaining the beloved would be foolish.

The vizier we spoke of asked, "How can I break this pearl?

The king replied, "Yes; how can you break it?!" And kissed him on his eye.

By kissing the vizier's eye he indicated that he had found an ignorant man, but in the test he was making he really was looking for someone wise.

❊

Two Kinds of Action

In a gathering, someone was sarcastically complimenting someone who could not sit still: "On your own impulse, you are continually receiving and then giving. All the time you are doing this and that, speaking according to your impulse—is this the result of your state?"

---

54 Shams is talking about a false shaikh who has no real knowledge and yet tries to make a living from his teaching about the Way.

I explained, "There are two kinds of action. One is like the desperate struggle of a man being tortured, writhing beneath blows of the stick. The other kind is like joyful frolicking amid sweet herbs and wild roses in the tulip gardens. Don't run after just any kind of action!"

> The moth that flew to the candle was lost:
> it went after the light and fell into the fire.

Now, since he is fiery, and his movement is from fire, he thinks the same of the servants of God.

> He looks at everyone with dark looks,
> seeing from the circle of his own self-existence.

He doesn't know that the work of this one is just the opposite—he went after fire and fell into light. Don't look at him[55] with that eye [of your own existence] or you will lose him!

Keeping Close to the Beloved

> I won't let you become just a thought in this heart.
> I don't want you to be brought low by these eyes.
> I'm keeping you within my soul,
> not in my eye or my heart,
> so that with my last breath you might still be my beloved!

If stringency[56] looks at beneficence[57] with its own eyes, it sees everything as wrathfulness and pain. I, this servant of God, said to a *kafir*,[58] "You are also of God, and I am, too. But you were created from His stringent attribute, and I was created from His

55 Don't look at "this person," i.e., Shams. Shams is cautioning the listener that if one looks with one's critical eye, from the perspective of the endarkened self, one may not be able to see the light of the Sun of Shams and so would lose him and any benefit he might lend. The bat is blind to daylight.

56 *Qahr* is the attribute of God which is overwhelming power, stringency.

57 *Lutf* is the opposite quality (*latif*) which is God's subtle mercy and grace.

58 The word *kafir*, often translated as "unbeliever," is actually "one who is covered," or veiled from the Truth. This is the term used for those who deny Reality and

beneficence. Gentle mercy actually overwhelms wrathfulness.[59] Let go of the attribute of stringency and connect yourself to gentle mercy; its taste is more pleasing."

The Prophet left something to his community, something that did not exist before. Actually, perhaps it existed, but it was veiled. People have tried many ways to remove that veil—casting spells and talking and talking. The summary of all the advice of the prophets is this: Find a mirror!

An Appropriate Response

Now, if you are going to respond, say something appropriate. That is, just as when both wings of a double door are well-placed, neither is larger or smaller than the other, you also need to give an answer that fits the question.

A king said, "I don't want someone who comes to me to start speaking unless I speak. And when I ask a question, let him give an appropriate answer; let him never speak more than enough."

The king asked a visitor, "Do you have a wife?" "I have a wife and three children," the visitor answered. This answer did not find favor with the king; instead the king said, "Send him away."

Before leaving the visitor wrote something on a piece of paper for the king: God asked the Prophet Moses, "*What is it that you have in your hand* [20:17] ?" and Moses did not speak more than enough when he said, "*This is my staff, I lean upon it; with it I beat down leaves for my sheep . . .* [20:18]." The king wrote an answer at the bottom, "There was a different wisdom in the lengthening of Moses' words; the wise person is the one who responds appropriately."

---

would be better translated as "the unfaithful one," or "the denier," not referring to any particular religion, but to one who denies the Truth of Ultimate Reality.

59 See *My mercy overwhelms my wrath* [7:156].

❁

The Joy One Receives from the Words of God

Those great and perfected ones for whose sake He gave existence to the cosmos also have a veil so that they aren't totally annihilated. Sometimes they speak about secrets with God. Sometimes the veil thins or disappears. Now I'm telling secrets; I'm not just speaking words.

One wonders how it is that these great ones even give a place to words and don't just keep silent. Though he may seem to be among them, Bayazid[60] is not, but the Prophets and the Messengers who bring Holy Books are of this group. They became intoxicated from that Divine speech and could hear nothing else. A hundred thousand barrels full of wine can't do what the words of God do.

Those who know the Qur'an are in a tight place, but the one who first becomes a knower of God's speech finds spaciousness. Then he can explain the Qur'an's meaning.

> I said to the night, descend,
> Now that the moon is asleep.

The night is a veil between the two [lovers] and others, or it may be a veil between the lover and his beloved.

---

60 Bayazid Bastami, a Sufi mystic who lived from 804-874, emphasized the importance of ecstacy, but some felt that his drunkenness limited him. When Shams first met Mevlana, he asked him, "Who is greater, Muhammad or Bayazid Bastami?"

Mevlana replied, "What kind of question is that; Muhammad of course is greater."

Shams replied, "But Bayazid said, 'Glory be to me, there are eighteen thousand universes within my armspan.' Whereas Muhammad said, 'My Lord, I have not known you as you ought to be known.'"

"Yes," replied Mevlana, "but that is because Bayazid's cup was filled with one sip, whereas Muhammad's thirst was never quenched."

Veils

Someone said, "O Messenger of God! How can I speak to that dark-faced, cold, and hypocritical Arab about the attributes of yours that belong to prophethood?"

The Holy Prophet replied: "It's important that not even all of the Arabs together should become a veil for you. Has this one Arab become a veil for you?"[61]

"But, O Messenger of God! He is a denier of the path and an enemy," the man replied.

Then the Holy Prophet answered: "What good does your speaking ill of him do? Only through the words of the Truth can you raise his head and plant the seed of longing in him; perhaps then, he might benefit."

Those students who blindly serve their masters[62]—that half-complete work of theirs is their veil, their night. Despite the jealousies among you, we[63] are sending our wishes of forgiveness (*'astaughfirullah*) to God. Praise be to God: we are winging prayers, and they fly.

To the best of your ability, look at your enemy with consideration and love! If you go to someone's door with caring love, it pleases him or her—even if he or she is an enemy—because when he or she is expecting hostility and harshness from you, but instead sees your love, he or she will be pleased.

---

61 See *Surah al-Ma'ida*, The Feast 5:8: *O you who have attained to faith! Be ever steadfast in your devotion to God, bearing witness to the truth in all equity; and never let hatred of anyone lead you into the sin of deviating from justice. Be just: this is closest to being God-conscious. And remain conscious of God: truly, God is aware of all that you do.*

62 Historically, a poor theology student would serve the teacher in return for board and tuition. A dervish might serve his teacher/shaikh, but less than whole-heartedly, without real commitment, and without real perception of the Light of that spiritual luminary.

63 Shams sometimes uses the "royal we" to refer to himself.

Purifying the Heart

The Lord of the dominion spread a feast for everyone,[64] so that it might be a compassion for all the universes, but the finest foods He keeps for the finest guests.

O faithful soul who has triumphed! Return to your Lord [89:27]: you are not one of those from whom it is appropriate to hide this morsel of Divine blessing.[65]

Shaikh Muhammad[66] said, "The field of words is very long and wide; everybody speaks as they wish."

And I said, "The field of words is actually quite narrow, but the field of meaning is wide. Go further, beyond the words, that you might witness the vastness and might watch this field! Take a look and see to what extent you are among those who are "far away," or those who are "near" yet still distant.[67]

"You know these things so well," he said.

"Words are not our concern," I said. "You are what you are, but look beyond the forms; 'community is a mercy (*hadith*).' If they [ordinary people] don't come to speak with you, don't be upset. Because they [beings of the spiritual world] speak from beyond forms, the secrets of the path aren't spoken to me when there are

---

64 See *Surah al-Ma'ida*, The Feast, 5:114-115: *Said Jesus, the son of Mary: "O God, our Sustainer! Send down upon us a repast from heaven: it shall be an ever-recurring feast for us—for the first and the last of us—and a sign from You. And provide us our sustenance, for You are the best of providers!"*

God answered: "Truly, I [always] do send it down unto you.

65 In other words, you can appreciate this taste (*dhawq*), whereas others may not have that discernment.

66 It seems that Shams is referring here to Ibn al-Arabi.

67 When we fail to turn our attention toward the Divine Reality, we remain distant from that Reality, even though It always is near—God is closer than our jugular vein (See *Surah Qaf* 50:16). However, as human beings no matter how closely we may approach the Divine Reality, we are still under the limitation of our existence and still distant from God until the self is finally purified and returned to its Sustainer.

strangers either on the outside or on the inside; they come when I am alone."

Even though you are of good character, and you don't bear grudges, or house treachery or thievery within you, yet still within this human body there are hidden potential treacheries. It is like in the time of the Prophet David when the chain of justice vanished into the heavens—it was because of a hidden treachery. When everybody saw that the chain of justice had vanished, they realized there must be a reason.[68]

If the chain of justice of illumined heart, purity, and savor pulls back from the seeker, there must be a reason. *Allah never changes the grace He has bestowed on any people unless they first change that which is in their hearts, and Allah is the One Who Hears, the One Who Knows* [8:53]. If you are vigilant with your own purity and goodness; if you work to purify your inner self from those hidden potential treacheries, the purity and goodness within you increases.

---

68 M. 15.

During the time of King David, a chain hung from heaven near his seat of judgement. One who was innocent would be able to reach it, but one who was guilty or untruthful would not be able to reach it—the chain would recede into the sky. A man to whom a hundred dinars had been given said he had returned them to the owner who claimed he had not received them. The man who took the dinars had melted them down and placed them in his cane. While making his statement he gave it to the other man to hold, so that for that moment it might be true that he had given the money back to him. Because of this deceit which was still not evident to the people, the chain of justice receded into the heavens and did not reappear.

King David himself was covetous of his neighbor's wife and contrived to have her husband die in battle so that he might marry her. Later while judging against a man who coveted his kinsman's sheep though he himself had sheep in abundance, he suddenly recognized his own sin and sought repentance: whereupon "he asked his Sustainer to forgive him his sin . . . and *turned unto Him in repentance* [38:24]," opening a purified heart to his Lord, and enabled once again to receive His grace.

❊

Completing Work

O truthful seeker, keep your heart happy! For the One who makes hearts happy is busy working to complete your work, for *Everyday He is about some new endeavor* [55:29]. He is occupied with the task of either the seeker or with the one who is sought.

Whoever says anything other than this, is a fool, even though such a person doesn't see his own foolishness. Only those who possess Divine discernment, who see with the light of God, understand and know that what most people consider to be skillfulness and subtle discernment is stupidity and fogginess from the point of view of one who has remained (*baqa*) after annihilation (*fana*).

Now, O truthful one! God is busy with the completion of your work, both outwardly (*zahir*) and inwardly (*batin*), He is completely occupied with you. He will never abandon you. He tells us: *You cannot will unless God wills* [81:29], that is, unless He wills, you cannot will anything; *Allah is the One who Knows and the One who is Wise* [76:30]. That is, "O Muhammad (may the peace of God be upon him), whatever you will, that is Our will!" It is not egoism; it is not desire.

Some people say that here, the words "*you cannot will*" have been spoken to the companions, and the community. That is, *You cannot will* what is proper for you, you don't even know how to look for the right path, but as the Messenger of God, I can will it.

> In order to unlock the treasury of mystery,
> There is no other key but the hand and
> heart of Muhammad.

I swear by God that the mature ones of Truth who have withdrawn into seclusion (*halvet/khalwah*) become dizzy even from the mere form of these words. Imagine what the meaning of these words does to them!

❊

Beyond Words

So maybe I don't have a poem or written work in which to rejoice. Even so, I feel pleasure and exhilaration from my words. There's never been such a little-known poet. So who am I? God created me all alone, thrust me forth, and then left me alone on the top of a mountain. Because my mother and father died, wolves and birds fed and raised me.

In short, the field of words is wide, but in that wide field, meaning is becoming narrower and narrower. If there is no other meaning beyond this narrowing field of meaning, then the width of the field of writing and words won't survive either. The voice of writing that can't be conveyed by a pen becomes quieter and quieter. And then, keeping silent is not necessarily due to the insufficiency of meaning, but rather to its brightness.

❊

Read the Letter of the Friend

As soon as he was born, the Prophet Jesus spoke; Blessed Muhammad began speaking after forty years. This isn't due to his incompleteness, but perhaps to his perfection. Because Muhammad was the beloved of God. They ask a servant, "Who are you?" He or she answers, "*Witness, I am the servant of God* [19:30]." No one ever asks the sultan, "Who are you?"

The ignorant one with faulty thinking is continually reading his own letter. He doesn't read the letter of his Friend. If he had read even one line from it, he would never have said the things he does, but he just keeps reading his own letter, and that's it. However, in that page of his, all the letters are bent and crooked, dark and unreal; they are only his own strange delusions, his imaginings. He becomes the slave of the idol that he makes with his own hands, and he becomes its servant and stands guard at its door. Like those idols, these religious holy days[69] say, "O people who are unaware of your own selves! You are looking for blessing from us, but we want you to look at us in such a way that there might remain no dayness in day, no hourness in hours, and that the lifelessness of the lifeless might end."

The Veil of Being

An "*alif*"[70] leapt forth from the universe of meaning. Whoever understands that *alif*, understands everything, and those who cannot understand it, cannot understand anything. Seekers tremble like a willow trying to understand that *alif*.

Long explanations have been made to them about the various veils, and how there are seven hundred veils of light and seven hundred veils of darkness between people and the Truth, but these explanations haven't been able to guide them to the Truth; instead they have waylaid people and caused them to despair, "How will we pass through all of these veils?"

All of the veils are really a single veil; and there is no other veil than this one, and that veil is this existence (*wujud*).

---

69 Shams refers here to the holy days of Ramadan and the like when intensified practice is invited. People lose sight of the real value and intention behind the holy days, and observe them only externally, making an idol of the obligations. Instead, real blessing would come from diving fully into the practice that could lead one into a deeper sense of Essential self, beyond time and space in ever-deepening connection with the Ever-Living One.

70 An "*alif*" is the first letter of the alphabet in Arabic. It's form is a single straight line. It is often referred to as the witness of the Unity of Being. In the sema ceremony, when the dervishes pause between cycles of turning they stand straight, with arms crossed and hands upon the shoulders, in what is known as the "alif" position, witnessing to the Oneness of God, the Oneness of Reality.

✲

Looking with the Eye of Love

I can speak to myself; with everyone in whom I see myself, I can speak. He was your enemy; he suffered because he was not you. But how could I hurt you? Even if I were to kiss your foot, I would be afraid that my eyelashes might prick your foot and wound you.

They have said, "Mevlana Jalaluddin is free of the world, but Mevlana Shamsuddin-i Tabrizi isn't." And Mevlana answered them: "You don't love Mevlana Shamsuddin; if you loved him he wouldn't seem so disagreeable and ugly to you."

> Tolerance blinds the eye to mistakes,
> But angry looks reveal even the smallest fault.

"Your love for something makes you blind and deaf"—that is, concerning the faults of the beloved. When love diminishes, right away you begin to see defects. Don't you see—because the mother loves her baby so much, she tolerates even its dirtying its bed. She doesn't feel disgusted, but tells it, "Bon Appetit!" These words show her devotion to her child.

Now Mevlana Shamsuddin says, "Mevlana previously gave this answer. Now, listen to it from me:

Someone takes a lame donkey into a stable, and both day and night he gives it fodder. The donkey keeps defecating on its master. That is one situation. Another person rides an Arabian stallion, and the stallion saves him from all kinds of dangers, troubles, and the evils of highwaymen.

Well, this example shows the power of that secret. In the end, the truth (*haqq*) of the steed upon which a person is riding becomes obvious.[71]

✲

Seeking the Blessing of the Poor Ones

Desire won't take us anywhere. Only the need of the poor ones, their entreaties must be our companions. Truly, *Alms are for the poor* [9:60]. What we need is that need.[72] The real form together with its meaning . . . these are such prayers that they aren't possible near a frowning and sour-faced shaikh.

I said, "O sour-faced master! You've reproached us, saying that we were fighting with you."

"No," he said.

One shows a sour face to a person by whom one has been hurt; with others one laughs and gets along fine. When he sees a certain person, he frowns; but he sees another and smiles, and when that person causes him no problems, he continues to like him. If he encounters suffering or loss, it is a struggle related to his own *nafs*.

He turns his face towards himself and frowns; but when he turns his face in the direction of the friend, he starts to smile. To know this is a kind of maturity. To know it and yet appear not to know it is the maturity of maturity.

I would like to learn about a person's main goal in life in order to know his meaning, and I want to know a person's meaning in order to know his main pursuit.

---

71 The *nafs* eventually reveals itself to be either an unmannerly or a noble steed.

72 The Prophet Muhammad said, "Poverty is my pride." Dervishes were referred to, or referred to themselves as "the poor ones," rather than saying "I." In poverty, in humility, the soul approaches closer to its Creator who is the Satisfier of all Needs. Truly, God is always with us, *closer to us than our jugular vein* [50:16], yet as we increase our yearning for nearness with God the reality of His Presence can become our meaning.

Transforming the Ego

These heedless people who go into the presence of the great ones aren't aware of the reality of their state, because they go without aptitude.

A man walking on the path comes to a river. If he tries to go through this fast-flowing water, it's deep and he will drown; if he tries to jump over it, it's wide and he will probably fall into it. To solve this difficulty, *Kill your nafs* [2:54] just as Abraham killed those four birds,[73] and immediately all four of them came back to life. But in this case, they resurrect in a different sense. The inner qualities of the friends of God (*awliya*) are like those four birds. Those four birds died, but these have become alive again in another way. How different they are! Those who live with their *nafs* are of one sort, and those who live with their hearts are of another. Those who live with their hearts are again different from those who live with their Lord.

There is no other remedy, because this is the Way.

Serving God

Lend God a goodly loan [73:20].[74] What need could God possibly have?

Once God said to Moses, "O Moses! I am hungry. Are you not going to feed me? If I come to your door, how will you welcome Me?"[75]

Moses said, "O my Lord! You are beyond such things."

---

73 See *Surah al-Baqarah*, The Cow 2:260.

74 *Recite, then, [only] as much of [the Qur'an] as you may do with ease, and be constant in prayer, and spend in charity, and [thus] lend unto God a goodly loan: for whatever good deed you may offer up in your own behalf, you shall truly find it with God—yea, better, and richer in reward. And [always] seek God's forgiveness: behold, God is much-forgiving, a dispenser of grace!*

See also *Surah at-Tawbah*, Repentance 9:111: *See how God has purchased of the faithful their lives and their possessions; in return, theirs is the garden, and so they struggle in God's way. . . .*

75 See *Surah al-Waqi'ah*, That Which Must Come To Pass 56:73.

God repeated, "O Moses! What if I come to your door?"

No matter how many times Moses said, "How could this be?" God kept on saying, "What will you do if I come?"

Finally, He said, "I've become very hungry. Stop arguing. Go and prepare some food, and I will come tomorrow."

Moses prepared food. Early the next day, he looked and saw that all was ready, except that there was no water.

Just then a dervish appeared and said, "For the sake of God, give me some bread."

Moses said, "It's good you have come," gave him two jugs, and said, "Bring some water."

The dervish said, "I am at your command." He brought the water, and Moses placed some bread in the dervish's hand. The dervish then thanked him and left.

Now, how is it possible that Moses should fall into such difficulties on God's path? Moses knew alchemy quite well because he had been ordered, "Write the Torah with gold!" Yet the hour grew late, and Moses distributed the food he had prepared among his neighbors. He was considering, "What is the secret of this? Perhaps it was to help these people or to serve them from the heart, for I did what God commanded."

Then the moment of expansion arrived, and Moses questioned God, "You promised to visit me, but you did not come!"

God answered, "O Moses! I came. But how was it that you did not give us bread without first making us carry two jugs of water?"

❊

Futile Discussions

Two scholars were proudly debating about the secrets of gnosis, the gatherings of the people of wisdom and their conversations. One of them said, "The person who is riding on that donkey and coming towards me is God."

The other said, "No, in my opinion, his donkey is God." In short, one can see from these words that they had fallen into the abyss of predestination.

One understands a different meaning from the words of Bayazid and other wise ones like him. To be occupied with such discussions as these scholars is a veil. The journey is a different kind of journey.

They said "Why would this be different?"

I answered, "Let's say that while you were listening to our conversation a coldness came to your heart, well it's that kind of a veil. They are on a path which is close to the path of incarnationism (*khulul*—as if God as a spirit enters your body). But the words of the attained ones who belong to the universe of the Spirit penetrate into one's soul; one who is full of desires and ambitions, how can such a person understand this."

❊

Love Annihilates Sensuality

The words of the mature ones who belong to the universe of Holy Spirit penetrate hearts; how can you who are full of desire and lust understand this? I don't want to talk about desire; I've explained this issue of desire before. I've said that Love annihilates desire and lust and ambition. Love and affection are such things that when they become active, even if someone were to bring a hundred *houris*, a hundred beautiful maidens of paradise, in front of you, they would seem as lifeless as mud bricks to you. Whenever you hear a word of wisdom or begin contemplation, that love and affection start to move.

Love is the light of the veils of holy light (*nur*) indicated by "God has seventy veils of light (*hadith*)." Now that you are drowned in desire, how can you discuss the radiance of light? And if you do talk about it, it all turns into desire. That Sufi Imad gets drunk and swings his head; that movement, too, becomes desire. But where is desire, and where is the radiance of the Holy Light of God?

❊

Look Deeper

From time to time, ask us, "How are you?"

I am your servant.

If they serve the servants of God with their possessions, then an affection awakens. Their work opens by means of that affection.

A single coin given by a true friend is more valuable than a hundred thousand given by someone else. Whoever accepts this help of a friend, becomes bound to him; that which is given by the friend opens a closed door.

Never be satisfied with the beautiful outer appearance and words and deeds of a shaikh! Because something is hidden behind them; ask for that.

Longing for True Words

He (Mevlana) has two kinds of words: one is hypocritical, diplomatic and beautiful, and the other is straightforward and true. The souls of the saints and their spirits are longing for those hypocritical words, but Mevlana wants to find Shamsuddin-i Tabrizi and sit and talk with him. The spirits of the Prophets long for his true and sincere words: "We wish we were in his time, and might be able to attend his gatherings and could hear his words!"

Now, don't miss this opportunity! Don't look with this eye; look with the eye with which the souls of the prophets are looking—with heartache and longing.

Layla and Majnun

Harun ar-Rashid (the famous Abbasid Emperor) said one day, "Bring Layla to me that I might see her just once. Majnun has fallen into total difficulty because of his love for her; from East to West, lovers have made the story of their love their mirror." After spending lots of money, and with many sly ruses they managed to bring Layla. They placed her into a secluded room in the palace of the Caliph Harun ar-Rashid. In the evening the Caliph came to the secluded room. Candles had been lit; he looked at her carefully for some time, and then for some time he sat with his head bowed. Finally, he said to himself, "Let me make her speak; perhaps the beauty of her face becomes more apparent when she speaks." Harun turned his face to Layla and asked, "Are you Layla?"

"Yes, I am Layla. But you are not Majnun. The eye that is in Majnun's head is not in yours."

> How can you see Layla
> with an eye with which you look at others?
> Unless you wash it clear with your tears!

Look at me with the eye of Majnun! One should look at the beloved with a loving eye because *He loves them* [5:54]. But the problem is that they don't look at God with the eye of Love. They look at God with the eye of knowledge, or from the viewpoint of gnosis or philosophy, but to look with the eye of love is another work all together.

Do You want to Know a Secret?

Someone full of himself came and said, "Tell me a secret."

I said, "I can't tell you a secret. I can only tell a secret to a person in whom I don't see him in himself—I must see myself in him. Then I'll have told my secret to myself. But I don't see myself in you; I see someone else in you.

"When someone comes to someone it is due to one of three possibilities: either he is a disciple (*murid*), or he has come out of friendship, or he wants to display his own greatness. Which one of these three are you? Don't you sit in front of so and so?"

"Is it clear to you what kind I am?" he asked.

"Yes, it is clear: I see him in you. Since he is in you, I am not in you, for he is not me."

Real Bravery

The really brave person is one whose outside appears exactly like his inside. My inside and outside are all of one color. If this matter were revealed and my sovereign power (*wilayat*)[76] were to rule, the whole universe would become one color: no sword, no grief or oppression would remain. But that the universe should be that way is not the law of God.

☼

Crossing the River

In order to leap further forward, some people first go backwards so that they might better jump across to the other side of the river.[77] If their backward movement is in order to jump further forward, it's good, but if they go backwards for any other reason, then the outcome is desolation. There is no doubt that this river's water will be crossed; everyone will cross it, the blasphemer, the Muslim, and the Jew. If you stay behind, robbers will weaken you and leave you helpless. On the other side of the water, bandits can't attack you. There, you receive help and things will be made easy for you. Now, in order to jump to the other side of the water, if you go very far backwards, you will soon become exhausted; yet you must make such a leap that both your feet must land firmly on the other side. If one of your feet slips into the water, then your other foot will also slip, for the water is flowing strongly and you will be pulled in.

☼

Making Space in the Heart

Someone was saying: "If you had become a scholar of Muslim religious law, what subtle points you could find!" And the other, a Christian, said: "If you had been a Christian, you would be the light of the religion; you would bring a brightness to Christianity." And a Jew said something even better than this: "If all Muslims

---

76 Again Shams brings into resonance the multiple meanings of *veli/wali*: friend, protector, saint. If his friendship were really to be known, grief and difficulty would vanish.

77 The river of the *barzakh* is the boundary between the two worlds. Jump strongly into Non-Existence!

were like this, what a happy religion the religion of Muhammad would be."

Knowledge can be an understanding of the inside or of the outside. If it belongs to the inner universe, people call it "wisdom" or "philosophy." But consider just once: where will it fit? The house is full—there isn't even space for a needle.

He was saying, "If you are patient, you won't complain about difficulties." But where will that thought fit? How can it find a place in the house of the heart, when this house is so full that there isn't even room for a needle?

True Manners

In the city of Nishapur, when people want to accustom a child to righteousness and teach him about good manners, they ask him, "What do you say about such and such a child?[78] He seems nice to us; is he good-natured?" If the child says, "Yes, he is good-natured; he isn't bad," then he, himself, is also like that. If he says, "He's far from such good qualities," then they ask, "If that's so, then what are you right now?"

How Do You Soften?

There are some people who become muslim[79] within while they are listening to a sermon, but when they leave that gathering, they solidify like tin having left the fire. And there are some who do not even soften during a sermon and must be softened by other things, by difficult illnesses. And some soften through still other things, just as in the physical world everything is softened by means of some tool.

---

78 M. 20.

79 To be *muslim* is to be surrendered to God. "Islam" might be translated as the "peace that comes with surrender."

Relinguishing Robes

In my view, if a person throws off his *khirqa* (robe) during the *sema* he shouldn't pick it up again even if it is worth a thousand precious gems. If he picks it back up, then he has been deluded in that *sema* and in that state.

It would be like saying, "I thought that that taste was worth this *khirqa*, so I gave it away. But now if I look at it again, I see that I was deceived. It wasn't."

When Bitter Words Become Sweet

To some people, these words seem bitter, but, if they endure that bitterness, a sweetness comes to them. One who smiles during the time of bitterness smiles because his eyes are seeing the sweetness that will come in the end. And so according to this point of view, patience means to witness the end result of an action and impatience means to be so short-sighted as to not be able to see the outcome. The foremost rank always goes to those who know very well what the outcome of deeds will be.

Choosing a Far-Sighted Companion

A mule asked a camel, "Why is it that most of the time I am stumbling at the front of the caravan, and you are walking at the back?"

The camel said, "When I come to the beginning of a slope, with one look I can see ahead, all the way to the end. Because my head is high, the spiritual resolve (*himmet*) that comes to me is from an exalted station. Also my eyes are bright and clear, so with a single glance I can see the top of the slope as well as what's in front of my foot."

Here, the camel symbolizes "the shaikh," because he has complete vision. Everybody who clings to him acquires his qualities.[80]

80 See *Mathnawi* IV:3370-3422 for a version of the mule and camel story offered by Mevlana:

There is no doubt that you take on the nature of the one with whom you are closely in contact, the one with whom you sit.

If you spend time looking at straw, dryness constricts you; if you look at greenery and roses, freshness opens within you. Your companion pulls you to his own universe.

This is why reading the Qur'an purifies the heart. You remember the prophets' words and their states. Their forms unite with your spirit; they become your comrades and sit with you. By means of that great, immortal, and infinite jewel I gained such a warm, high knowledge that I merged with it and became filled with its fire.

May the Fire Be Cool

The companionship of the people of this world is like fire, you need to be an Abraham so that that fire might not burn you. Nimrod set a fire burning on the outside, and Abraham also set a fire burning.

"You'll see whom the fire will burn," he said. "O Nimrod! You have been born from overwhelming power (*qahr*), and I was created from mercy (*rahmat*): let's see who will get burned in the end."

Didn't God say, "*My mercy overwhelms my wrath*?"[81]

Abraham said, "The overwhelming is known, what need is there for the test?"

He said, "No, the work is necessary."

Abraham said, "In the name of God (*Bismillah*)." He said, "The foot of mercy overwhelms overwhelming power (*qahr*); even so, mercy annihilates suffering and wrath. The foot of mercy is like this."

Yes, one has to test the friends. Yes, Abraham is a friend. Just as they say, "If you behave like this with a friend, what will you do to the

---

"... you have gained *Enter in among My servants* [*Surah al-Fajr*, The Daybreak 89:29]; you have brought near *Enter into My Paradise* [*Surah al-Fajr* 89:30]. . . "*Guide us*," you said, "*in the straight path*" [*Surah al-Fatiha*, The Opening 1:5]: He took your hand and led you to the abode of bliss."

81 This is a *hadith qudsi*, a saying of God conveyed through the Prophet Muhammad, outside the revelation of the Qur'an. See also *Surah al-A'raf*, The Faculty of Discernment 7:156.

enemy?" He threw the friend into the fire and tested him to see what he would do. Only the One who threw him knows about his state.

☼

The Great Wings of Need

I remembered that person because of his need. He used to show his need in such a way—you should also show your need like that.

Someone rejected this, saying to himself, "What's this?! Boasting that so and so served this way, by showing need!"

I am not exaggerating—I am showing the way, because need is the way. Need is the foremost wing feather on the way.[82]

☼

The Moaning Pillar

Now we'll speak about the speech of lifeless beings and their actions. Philosophers deny such things, but how shall I tell you what I see with these eyes? Remember the tradition of the moaning pillar.[83]

---

82 Mevlana echoes this in verses like *Mathnawi* III: 3204; 3208-3213, (*Jewels of Remembrance*, p.31):

It was Mary's painful need that made the infant Jesus
begin to speak from the cradle.
Whatever grew has grown for the sake of those in need,
so that a seeker might find the thing he sought.
If God most High has created the heavens,
He has created them for the purpose of satisfying needs.
Wherever a pain is, that's where the cure goes;
wherever poverty is, that's where provision goes.
Wherever a difficult question is,
That's where the answer goes;
wherever a ship is, water goes to it.
Don't seek the water; increase your thirst,
so water may gush forth from above and below.
Until the tender-throated babe is born,
how should the milk for it
flow from the mother's breast?

83 The moaning pillar: When the first mosque in Medina was being built, between its two walls a niche was built where the trunk of a date palm was used as a column or support. When Muhammad gave his Friday sermons, he

"There is a secret hidden within the folds of one's tongue." Blessed Ali said, "When a man speaks, I come to understand what kind of person he is at that very moment, and if he does not speak I come to know what he's like within three days." . . . It was also Ali who said, "Even if the veil were lifted, my certainty would not be greater."[84]

A Talent Is Needed

What prevents people from coming into the presence of the great ones, into their gatherings, is a lack of aptitude. Capacity is needed, receptivity is needed, and freedom from busyness with the world is necessary in order for such a visit to bear fruit. Those who visit with real need, even if they are deficient, still, their visits won't be wasted. But one has to make an effort to improve oneself. In some

---

would lean against this pillar. But then someone provided a pulpit for him. When he no longer leaned upon the pillar, just then the wood gave out such a sound that it seemed it would nearly break into two. The Blessed Prophet went near it, and a sound like the longing cry of a newborn baby was heard.

Even so, the pillar was filled with love for the prophet, and so when it spoke, one heard and recognized the longing within it. Otherwise one might not have recognized it as more than a simple trunk of a date palm. Unless the heart is open, we usually do not recognize the ways of worship of the inanimate beings. See *Surah al-Isra'*, The Night Journey 17:44: *Limitless is He in His glory, and sublimely, immeasurably exalted above anything people may say. The seven heavens acclaim His limitless glory, and the earth, and all that they contain; and there is nothing that does not celebrate His immeasurable glory—but you fail to grasp the manner of their glorifying Him! Truly, He is forbearing, always ready to forgive!*

The saints and prophets had such sensitivity. A favorite song attributed to Yunus Emre reflects this: "The rivers all in Paradise flow with the word Allah, Allah, and every longing nightingale—he sings and sings Allah, Allah."

See *Mathnawi* I: 2113-2153 and III: 1496-1500.

84 Ali, the cousin of the Prophet Muhammad, the fourth caliph of the Islamic community was known for his eloquence. He and his wife Fatima, the daughter of the Prophet, are recognized as the first mystics of Islam. Many of the sufi lineages trace back through Ali to the Prophet Muhammad. For such as he, this world is already the Resurrection, his sight and hearing are already clear.

See also *Mathnawi* II: 843-1046.

I don't see the hope of improvement—that they might wake up before they regret the opportunity that they have lost.

Don't Cling to Anything but Him

One has to make amends for one's faithlessness. We have spoken of making amends and we have taught the Way, and that Way is to offer up the world. *Those saved from the covetousness of their own souls, they are the ones who achieve prosperity* [59:9]. Make such an effort that it might be useful enough to protect you when the Day of Separation comes—if you keep Him in front of your eye, nothing else remains.

Finding the Pearl

There was a jewel merchant who had fifty agents who traveled around the world wandering across land and sea trading for him. This man was looking for a pearl. He heard the fame of a certain diver. He passed by that diver, but then the diver came looking for him. The kind of pearl he was seeking and where it was to be sought was a secret between the merchant and the diver. The merchant had seen the pearl in his dream. He had faith in that dream and he trusted in it, just like the Prophet Joseph, who (peace be with him) had confidence in his dream of the moon, the sun, and the stars all prostrating themselves in front of him. The Prophet Joseph had known the interpretation of that dream and passed his nights pleasantly even when he was thrown into the well and while he was imprisoned.

Now, the diver is Mevlana [Jalaluddin Rumi], I am the jewel merchant, and the pearl is between us. They say: "The way that leads to the pearl is between you. Can we find a way to it?" I said, "Yes, this is the Way: I am not telling you to give anything, I am telling you to come in the form of need." Ask, "Is this the way to God?" with the tongue of that state. This is the Way of God.

❊

Crossing the Bridge

Certainly, when one is going to Aksaray,[85] you have to cross the bridge. *They struggled by means of their possessions and their own selves* [9:21] is the bridge on the way of Truth. First one must give away one's possessions; after that there are many things one must do. First Aksaray must be passed. There is no other way except the path through Aksaray, unless you go through the desolate plains. But when wolves and demons see that you've left the path, like an arrow shot from a bow, they will catch you from behind, overpower you, and swallow you in one bite.

What do you want to do now? What will you give for the Way of God? What is in your heart? Tell me what you think. If there is an obstacle for you, tell me about it so that I might teach you a way around that obstacle, so that it might be easy for you. I know the Way better than you do. I was telling the story of the pearl, but you are not buying it even for a copper coin. Shall I speak in a veiled way now, or shall I speak openly?

❊

Seeing

This Mevlana is the Moon; eyes cannot reach the Sun of my Being. They can only reach the Moon. Due to the intense brightness of its light, and its brilliant luminosity, eyes cannot look at the Sun. That Moon can't reach the Sun, but the Sun can reach the Moon. *Eyesight cannot perceive Him, but He perceives all vision* [6:103].

❊

Happy Is the One Whom This Arrow Strikes

Which arrow is this? From whose bow has it sprung? Who knows the Truth with real maturity and understands God's power? This arrow is without limit. *Say: though the sea became ink for the words of my*

---

85 Aksaray is one of the cities adjacent to Konya. Here Shams uses it as a metaphor for one of the first stages of the journey.

Lord, truly the sea would be used up before the words of my Lord were exhausted, even though we brought the like thereof to help [18:109]. Happy is the one whom this arrow strikes. This arrow is for those who recognize the Truth. There are many other arrows in my quiver, but I can't shoot them. The arrows I have shot keep returning. Those that are left in the quiver have other things to do.

At least, wherever you are, don't turn your face away from us. Don't talk about leaving us and going away. Whatever state you are in, give of what you have. If you have nothing, strive to work and earn, so that you may gather other friends around you. Pay a little attention to us, too—a coin or two because of the debt you owe us. A person is responsible for the word he/she gives.

Learning Unity

What is the promise with God like?[86] Likewise, don't neglect to keep a portion from everything towards our debt, even if the portion is just a coin or two, until the moment comes when suddenly an opening is gained. Then you will be free of these things. In the same way, don't turn away from us even for a moment, and don't forget your promise.

Let's say reason orders something; desire demands just the opposite. It is as though the master says, "Bring me pickles." But the servant says, "No, bring some sweets; sweets are better." This isn't appropriate. The servant must first say, "Bring what the master ordered." In reality what the master orders is sweet.

The master says, "I am going to such and such a place." The servant says, "May God be with you, I'm not coming."

"Why aren't you coming?"

He answers, "I'll come later; now, I have an excuse."

86 This refers to our covenant with God in pre-eternity (the Day of *Alast*) when the souls were gathered and God asked of us, "Am I not your Sustainer," and we responded, "Yes." We are reminded, *you will be called to account for your promise* [*Surah al-Isra'*, The Night Journey 17:34].

This isn't appropriate. This is the opposite of what one needs to learn. On this path, one must learn unity not opposition. But no, you teach me opposition, and I teach you unity; that is, you are teaching me about self-absorption, and I am teaching you about crying out with need.

Who Are We Listening to?

If you are sad or full of grief, you need to be re-energized; if one is old, one has to become young. You have to engage with your head, ears, and reason so that you might receive your portion, so that you might both hear meaning and eat. In other words, so that you might both listen to subtle meanings and do something. Now you are saying, "At the moment, I already am doing something."

How can anyone do two things at the same time? One must. God has given me the ability to carry seven or eight works all at the same time. God is dominant over everything. Because some saints appear very active and quick they seem dominant to you, but they aren't really. And some saints seem to be soft and gentle, but actually they are extremely active and dominant; what they want to happen comes to be. They don't proclaim miracles.

People like Sharaf Lahawari who blur our words with their words are drowning in muddy water. He saw in his dream that he was drowning in muddy water and that he was waving his fingers asking for help, calling, "O Shamsuddin-i Tabrizi, take my hand." This dream didn't turn out to be enough advice for him though, because again, in my presence he started talking about the difference between the miracles of the prophets and the wonders of the saints. "Whenever they want to, the prophets display miracles," he was saying.

But where are the words of the saints, and where are you?

Whose Business Is It, Anyway?

Whoever curses me, I pray for him saying, "O God! Give him something better and more pleasant to do than this cursing so that instead of this, he might recite glorifications, remembering You, and busy himself with the world of the Real."[87] How did they fall into discussions about whether, "he is a saint" or "he is not a saint"? What is it to you if I am a saint or not?!

It's like when they said to Juhi,[88] "Look over there for a moment; they're carrying trays!"[89] Juhi responded: "Is it any of our business?" And when they answered, "But, they are taking them to your house," Juhi said, "Then, is it any of your business?"

Now, I will also say, "Is it any of your business?" Well, it's because of this that I keep away from people.

❊

Sugar Samples

Within myself I love many great ones. I have an affection for them, but I don't show it. Once or twice I have revealed it, and I still have a memory from the time when I began my work.

There is a kind of affection that never cools, but nobody knows the value of this friendship or appreciates it. The love I have shown to Mevlana has only increased and never decreases.

I can't speak the full Truth for when I first began speaking the truth, I was sent away; if I had completely spoken the truth, instantly they would have exiled me from every city.

But a little reveals a lot: that is, words may be few but meaning great. Let's say they have placed a big sack of sugar over there, and they have brought a little sample from it; well, that small sample is the evidence for the rest. It is enough to tell us about it. A little righteousness shown by a person reveals a lot, and likewise a little crookedness and hypocrisy also reveals a lot.

---

87 M. 25.

88 Juhi is the Mullah Nasruddin (the wise jokester) of the Arabs.

89 Such trays usually hold sweets or borek.

✲

Ahmad-i Zindik

The details about Ahmad-i Zindik[90] were entrusted to Junayd as follows:

Ahmad-i Zindik lives in such and such a city and the knot of the difficulties you have encountered cannot be untied without him. Even if you were to undergo a hundred forty-day retreats (*cille*), still you couldn't solve your difficulties without him!

So Junayd left Baghdad and set out for that city. He said to himself, "If I ask where the house of Ahmad-i Zindik is, it wouldn't be courteous." So he interpreted the name and inquired for him as Ahmad-i Siddiq.[91]

In his dream he had received a pure word, but he listened to it in an altered way. For this reason, for sixty days he wandered around idly, and of those whom he encountered, he would ask, "Where is the house of Ahmad-i Siddiq?" Due to the misfortune of interpreting the name that had been correctly conveyed to him, he was unable to find him.

Suddenly, a remedy came to his mind: "Let me pass through the door of that ruined mosque." He was just about to pass through and to walk inside when a recitation of the Holy Qur'an came to his ear. Immediately his heart began to race. A young man was just leaving the ruined mosque. "Now let me ask about the man by his real name," he thought and he inquired.

The young man said, "O, do you hear the voice of the person reciting Qur'an?" Junayd gave out a loud cry, fainted, and fell to the ground. The young man fell down at his feet. Junayd had attained the reward of speaking the truth and had reached his aim. When he came back to himself, he entered the ruined mosque and sat down to the side.

---

90 *Zindiq* means heretic. I.e., Ahmad the Heretic.

91 *Siddiq* means the true/loyal/faithful one; the adjective is used for the faithful companion of the Prophet, Abu Bakr-i Siddiq—i.e., "Ahmad the Faithful."

Neither did Junayd make any gesture of greeting nor did Ahmad-i Zindik open any opportunity or space for it. After remaining like this for a long time, Ahmad-i Zindik's heart softened and he looked at him and began to speak: "Welcome Junayd!" he said.

Within himself, Junayd was thinking, "How did you know that I am Junayd?"

Ahmad smiled and said, "How could I not know? From the first day you began looking for me, I was watching you suffering in difficulties and trying to untie the knot of this puzzle, and I was wondering, 'What should I speak about with him when he comes?' In this moment there is nothing for me to tell you. If there is a topic you want to talk about, you indicate it and let's speak about it. Recite something and let us listen."

Junayd began speaking, and Ahmad-i Zindik stood up and whirled[92] a few times. Holy souls from the invisible universe gathered around him and said, "If you turn like this a few more times you're going to break the rope of the cycling heavens." Ahmad, contrite, sat down.

Playing for God

This is the way it is: "If you speak a truthful word, and you comment on and interpret it, people cheer up a little; they are affected, and become pleased. But if you speak it plainly without interpretation, people neither are touched by it, nor are they pleased, unless these words are spoken to those chosen by God to receive the Truth. At this station, questions are not needed and mustn't be asked, for how can a question reach the speaker when he is in a state of bewilderment?

"What am I saying; with whom am I speaking?" he says to himself in bewilderment. "Why don't these people understand?" he wonders.

Someone was playing a musical instrument beside a house. Somebody called to him, "There is nobody in this house, whom are

---

92 The expression here is "to strike the wheel." "To turn the wheel" is also a term used for the Mevlevi whirling practice *(sema)*.

you playing this instrument for?" The man responded: "Be quiet! Everyone is having tekkes and caravanserais built for God; I am playing this instrument for God. I am playing it for God's sake, so why are you questioning me?"[93]

❁

Walk Straight On

You need to walk straight forward on the path. You don't need to discuss things while you are walking; just move ahead on the path, you ass! You are neither one of those asses that can pass over the bridge,[94] nor one of those Egyptian asses that can go one station[95] ahead and come back in a single day! After thousands of boasts and much haste, you can't even go half of the way to the next station in a day."

Witness: God does not change people's condition unless they change their inner selves [13:11]. Complain about and weep for your own self *(nafs)*.

God said to His Prophet: *Truly, you cannot guide aright everyone whom you love: but it is God who guides him that wills to be guided* [28:56].[96]

"I know," he responded. "The reality of this struck me very strongly."

---

93 For a version of this story by Mevlana see *Mathnawi* VI:845-887.

94 The bridge between this world and the next.

95 Station: halting place—a place where people stopped, watered their horses, and rested. This is also a term used to denote a level of spiritual attainment.

96 . . . *He is fully aware of all who would let themselves be guided* [28:56]. According to several extremely well-authenticated Traditions, the above verse relates to the Prophet's inability to induce his dying uncle Abu Talib, whom he loved dearly and who had loved and protected him throughout his life, to renounce the pagan beliefs of his ancestors and to profess faith in God's oneness. However, the Qur'anic statement *you cannot guide aright everyone whom you love* has undoubtedly a timeless import as well: it stresses the inadequacy of all human endeavours to "convert" any other person, however loving and loved, to one's own beliefs, or to prevent him from falling into what one regards as error, unless that person *wills* to be so guided. ~ Muhammad Asad, *The Message of the Qur'an*, commentary on [*Surah al-Qasas*, The Story 28:56].

Only the Heart of a Faithful Servant of Mine Can Contain Me

When someone is in the special guesthouse of the king—the king himself puts the morsel in his mouth. Now, where is such a person compared to those who have only crumbs of bread and pieces of bone thrown into the street for dogs?

I said, "Tell us about the *hadith qudsi*[97]: 'The earth and the heavens could not encompass Me, only the heart of a faithful servant of Mine can contain Me.'"

He said, "This subtle saying has the same meaning as the verse, *Truly We offered the trust to the heavens and the earth, and the mountains; but they refused to bear it because they were afraid of it. Only man took it up, yet truly, he is very foolish and ignorant* [33:72]."

That is, this is the knowing (*marifat*) of God, and it has degrees. The meaning of the *hadith qudsi* is also related to this verse.

"In your opinion, is there anything else to be said about the meaning of this tradition?" he asked.

"Truly, one's power isn't enough for this," they said and couldn't stop talking.

"This is a subject to speak about," they said; but they are running away from it. If this aspect were really spoken about, it would be very useful. This world is bad, but only for the one who does not know what this world is. When he knows what this world is, it no longer remains "this world" for him.

He is asking, "What is the world?"

The other says, "Other than the afterworld."

He asks, "Then what is the afterworld?"

He says, "Tomorrow."

He asks, "OK, what is tomorrow?"

Expression is extremely narrow; language is narrow. All of these religious wars (*mujaahida*) are because people could not be liberated

---

97 A *hadith qudsi* is an expression of God conveyed through Muhammad, but outside the revelation of the Qur'an.

from the constricting bondage of language—it is so narrow. They go to the world of Attributes. I wonder at what they say about the high pure attributes of God.

Theologians (*mutakallimun*) discuss: "Are the Attributes identical with the Self of God (*Dhat*) or are they other than the Self?" Do they ever agree about this? No, they don't, because the world has many varied colors; a word isn't pronounced with only one intonation.[98]

❋

The Path of the Broken Heart

Someone asked a dervish who had been visiting Hakim Sanai: "What has that many-colored one told you?"

The dervish bowed his head, "He said that the people of the world are constantly shifting colors,[99] but one who has liberated himself from this continual variation is slowly, gradually going home [to God]. He doesn't go too far away from the path, because the world is extremely multi-colored. That one is a Jew, a Christian, a fire-worshipper."

The Mu'tazilites[100] say, "If the Word were eternal then this world would have to be also." This path is not the path of the Mu'tazilite. This path is the path of the broken heart, of sorrow, and helplessness; it is the path of giving up jealousy and enmity.

When a secret is revealed to you, you must be thankful for it. Now would you like me to tell you about the meaning of this gratitude in a veiled way or straightforwardly?

---

98 People have difficulty being freed from their particular way of expression and this causes misunderstandings . . . "the field of words is narrow."

99 Again Shams refers to the idea that one should become unified, of one color, reliable in oneness.

100 The word "Mu'tazilite" means, "one who has separated from the alliance." The Mu'tazilites were considered heretical from the point of view of the Sunnis (especially the Ash'arites) because they turned away from the perspectives of Hasan of Basra, insisting on the importance of rational debate, and the primary importance of the intellect.

Thanks be to God. Don't despair. Your face has turned towards peace and pure light. You are facing Spirit, health, and ease. Painful and blurry days have passed.

❊

The Best of Human Beings Is the One Who Most Benefits Others

"The best of human beings is the one who most benefits others (*hadith*)." How can one who doesn't know what good is do something good? How can those who don't know what a "year" is, and who haven't understood what "life" is, wish each other long lives? A single small silver coin given into the hand of a man of God is better than a thousand silver coins that come into the hand of a man who is fond of his *nafs*. I can't explain this to you, because your "nafs" is too lively and rebellious; if I tell you this, you'll only answer me back with a thousand words of opposition, and then you'll be cut off from us.

❊

Who Is Seeking Who

In addition to these shaikhs of the outside who are famous among people and who are talked about on pulpits and in gatherings, there are hidden servants more perfected than the famous ones. And there is one who is sought among them whom some do find. Mevlana thinks I am that, but I don't think so. If I am not the sought one, I am the seeker. In the end, the seeker raises his head also amid the sought. God is seeking me now, but the story of that sought one has not become famous in any book; nor is it spoken about among the orders. . . . These words are all to tell you about the path, and no one else speaks about it like this.[101]

---

101 As Shams says elsewhere in his *Maqalat*, "One of His Holy Names is *the Seeker.* And I am the sought, because every seeker has something he is seeking."

True Assistance

Maybe a blasphemer is carrying water on a path, and there is someone who needs water. When the water comes to that person, he doesn't turn around to question where it came from, but right away his insides relax owing to that water. On the Day of Reckoning, that blasphemer will hold the hand of a hundred thousand Muslims. The work of God is beyond reason. One man may spend two hundred silver coins for the dervishes and it has no effect, while five silver coins given by someone else prove more useful.

If it were possible to understand these meanings by study and discussions, then the best thing to do would be to put dust on one's head, and on Bayazid's and Junayd's and apprentice to Fakhr-i Razi for a hundred years.[102] They say that in writing his commentaries on the Qur'an he used a thousand rolls of paper. Others say that he wrote five hundred reams, but one hundred thousand Fakhr-i Razis can't approach even the dust of the path of Bayazid. Fahkr-i Razi is like the knocker on the door—not on the inner door of the house, but rather the knocker on the outside door. The special part of the house where the sultan is secluded with his favorites is something else.

Risking the Journey

Your difficulties and discussions indicate that you want to learn by means of information, but one has to walk and struggle on this path. Let's say, for a hundred years you have talked about the way to Aleppo and Damascus, but you can never bring the goods of Aleppo here unless you endure the difficulty and dangers of the journey. You must undergo the concern and fear of having your property plundered by robbers; only then can you arrive.

102 Both Bayazid or Abu Yazid Bastami and Junayd al-Baghdadi were Sufis of great renown. Bayazid was known for his ecstatic approach to God and Junayd for his sober approach within everyday life. In knowledge of the Qur'an and its interpretation, Fakhr-i Rahzi was renowned, yet his real knowledge was limited.

Someone asked, "Should the student prefer the way of discussion first, so that later walking on that path might be easier?"

He answered, "I have already told you the story of the way to Aksaray and given you information about the journey. You didn't go and now you are asking what it is like there, and I am telling you, 'Go there; I am with you. And from now on, you yourself pay attention to see which way is safer—which way is most free of thieves, wolves, and other dangers.'"

And then, what about the path to Malatya or the path to Ilbistan?

A Qiblah of Coins

Money is the *qiblah* (the direction of worship) of the majority of people, though the wayfarers have sacrificed it. One coin is dearer to worshippers of this world than their sweet souls. You could even say they have no soul, for if they really had a soul, money would not be dearer. By God! A single coin is the *qiblah* for the one who worships this world.

Becoming Trustworthy

The angels and the spirit rise up to Him in a day whose measure is fifty thousand years [70:4]. You don't understand the hidden allusions (*ramz*) of the Qur'an. If you die only with this outer meaning, then it will take fifty thousand years until you smell the fragrance of paradise. If you keep imagining, "Where is the universe of the prophets, where is the universe of the saints (*awliya*)?" you'll get dizzy, lose your balance, and fall down. Just start walking.

"He who comes to me by an armspan . . . "[103]: but between armspan and armspan, between one knee and another knee there are differences. "Two strides and he arrived," but you don't have the stride of Muhammad. A pharaoh raised his head inside you; Moses

103 *Hadith qudsi*: "When someone comes toward Me by a span I come to him by a cubit; . . . when someone comes to Me walking, I come running to him."

came and drove him out. Again pharaoh came; Moses left. These are indications of the shifting of colors. How long is this going to go on? Hold onto Moses himself in such a way that another pharaoh is unable to come. This shifting fickleness of colors is not the Way.

✲

Resurrection

Those who say, "Our lord is God," and then stand steadfast . . . [41:30].[104] They spoke this in this very world. On the other hand, the ignorant ones say, "No! We have no God." And yet the faithful stand in that faith without any change. On the Day of Resurrection, when the faithful are gathered from their graves, they will see a hundred thousand divine lights. Where is the angel of death? Instead it is the angel of life there for them. Where is the grave? For them there is liberation, liberation from the grave and the prison.[105]

"This world is the prison of the faithful (*al-mumin*)." (*hadith*). If someone is told, "As soon as you come out of this prison, you will become the companion of the sultan—you will go to Him and sit with Him on the throne forever," then he will say, "Seize me by my throat and press quickly so that I may find freedom." *Seek death, if you are truthful, sincere* [2:94].

When they are gathered in the field of resurrection, see what a resurrection it will be! That day is the day when secrets are unveiled. Their hidden secret is the Truth (*al-Haqq*) and Truth will be revealed,

---

104 *Surah Fussilat*, Clearly Spelled-Out 41:30: *[But,] behold, as for those who say, "Our Sustainer is God," and then steadfastly pursue the right way—upon them do angels often descend, [saying:] "Fear not and grieve not, but receive the glad tiding of that paradise which has been promised to you! We are close unto you in the life of this world and [will be so] in the life to come; and in that [life to come] you shall have all that your souls may desire, and in it you shall have all that you ever prayed for, as a ready welcome from Him who is much-forgiving, a dispenser of grace."*

105 M. 30. *Surah as-Sajdah*, Prostration, 32:11: *Say: "[One day,] the angel of death who has been given charge of you will gather you, and then unto your Sustainer you will be brought back."*

but if the Truth is made manifest, how can resurrection remain?[106] They will be bound in chains of divine light so that they might not come into the field of resurrection. They [the angels] do whatever they do by means of these [chains of divine light] that that which needs to be done might be done: they bring the paradise-dweller to paradise and the hell-dweller to hell. They break off their chains so that they might come into the field of resurrection, but they will be tied with more chains of divine light, and until the last moment their chains are not undone.[107]

Tears that Wash the Soul

Now, words are for the work[108]; the work is not for words. It is so that you may come to know that ease is with the dervishes.

Ablution upon ablution is "light upon light." The kernel that matures is freed from the shell. Some people consider them to be perfect and some don't. And another group says, "Ablution upon ablution is light upon light." These aren't suitable for the role of leadership, but they are the shelter and security of the people of the universe.

There is no doubt that one has to clean the filth that is inside. Even a single particle of dirt within our inner universe is a hundred thousand times more foul than dirt on the outside. Which water cleans that filth inside? Only a few teardrops, but not just any teardrops, the teardrops from which truthfulness grows—perhaps innocent and clear tears from a real eye that can see. From then on, the fragrance of security and liberation reach that person and he or she wakes up from sleep. In such a person, sleep changes, and slumber also

---

106 There would not then be any resurrection, for resurrection would dissolve in the presence of the Truth (*al-Haqq*), the Divine Reality.

107 Everyone passes through the fire. When the faithful pass through the fire, the fire says, "Pass on, O faithful one, your light will extinguish my fire (*hadith*)." Their presence in the field of resurrection would convert the field of resurrection into the Truth. So that the process of everyone can take place they are bound by the light.

108 Words are to enable the deepening of spiritual practices and prayer.

becomes something different.[109] But tears without yearning for God, *salaat* without yearning, does not go further than the edge of the grave. They return with those who come back from the funeral. But prayers made with yearning and supplication enter into the grave with the person, and they are together with that person on the Day of Standing before God, too. Like this, they go even to Paradise, and precede that person up to the exalted station of the Truth (*al-Haqq*).

❊

Awakening

If such a heart has awakened, he or she cannot sleep. And even if he does sleep, if he sleeps even on the bank of a torrent, still it is easy: if you just tap him, he wakes up. When you point out the flood coming from far away, he shivers from fear; he forgets about the pain, prostrates at your feet, and gives thanks.

But there are also those who are in a deep sleep, and even if the enemy comes and cuts half their throat, still they can't open their eyes. And when at last such a person does open his eyes, the rest of his throat gets cut.

I am joking. Mevlana is a man of Truth. What suits him is that one should speak beautiful words in his gatherings. Don't you see that we have been speaking words of love this whole time, even now? In front of people of the world, one has to also speak frightening words, so that they might wake up at least a little.

---

109 Note references to *ayat al-kursi: God—there is no deity but Hu, the Ever-living, the Self-Subsisting Source of All Being. No slumber can seize Him/Her nor sleep. All things in heaven and on earth belong to Him/Her. Who could intercede in His/Her Presence without His/Her permission? He/She knows all that lies open before human beings and all that is hidden from them, nor can they encompass any knowledge of Him/Her except what He/She wills. His/Her throne extends over the heavens and the earth, and He/She feels no fatigue in guarding and preserving them, for He/She is the Highest and Most Exalted.* [The Throne Verse, *Surah Baqarah*, The Cow, 2:255]

✲

There is Hope

Now, someone has fallen asleep on a dangerous path. One of the people of God comes and wakes him up. But that sleeping person is still asleep according to God's servant. If I were ever to tell about the states of this sleeping person, you would lose hope about yourself. At least, let me not talk about it, so that you might not fall into despair about your own self (*nafs*). Do not be hopeless, because there are many hopes.[110]

When one gets old, one becomes like a child. But these words of mine don't refer to everyone; the Prophets and saints are not like that. Also our great Mevlana (*sultan ul-Ulema*) was not like this either: Muhammad Bahaeddin Weled,[111] the sultan of the Learned, although he lived more than eighty years, used to seem more mature and knowledgeable every day. His awareness and intelligence never diminished.

I don't disagree with this word; perhaps I would like to explain it—"I wonder how can a lover sleep?" [112]

---

110 See *Mathnawi* I:723-724:

> Plant the love of the holy ones within your spirit,
> don't give your heart to anything
> but the love of those whose hearts are glad.
> Don't go to the neighborhood of despair: there is hope.
> Don't go in the direction of darkness: suns exist.

111 Muhammad Bahaeddin Weled was the father of Mevlana Jalaluddin Rumi.

112 Witness this reflection from Mevlana, *Mathnawi* VI, 578-581:

> This Beloved, like the sun, neither sleeps nor eats:
> He makes souls sleepless and hungry,
> saying, "Come, be Me, or one with Me in nature,
> so when I unveil Myself, you may behold My Face.
> And if you had not beheld it,
> how would you have become so distraught?
> You were earth, and now
> you long to be quickened with spiritual life."
> Already the Beloved has bestowed gifts
> from that world of spacelessness,
> otherwise why would your spiritual eye keep gazing there?

The Gem of Love

Know that the universe is a veil in front of the eye of the *fakir*,[113] and the *fakir* is the precious jewel of love. The precious jewel of love exists from the eternal beginning. The universe (Adam) is just yesterday's existence.

Everyone speaks about his own Pir.[114] In a dream, the blessed Prophet gave a cloak (*khirka*) to me. But this is not one of those cloaks that would become old after only two days and fall to pieces, to be thrown into the furnace or to be used for dishcloths. Rather it is a cloak of companionship and conversation. Not a companionship with any limits, but a companionship that has no yesterday, today, or tomorrow. What does love have to do with "yesterday" and with "today" and with "tomorrow"?

Be Silent

Now, one doesn't ask questions in the gathering of that Pir. It is like shaking a tree to make its fruit fall down. A time comes when less fruit comes from that shaking—all of it is not like that such that it would come down. The only thing to be done then is silence and surrendering. It is not this way with every tree, but here, there is no other way. Here one should only be silent and surrender. It was said, "*When the Qur'an is recited, listen to it and keep silent* [7: 203]."[115]

---

113 *Fakir*: a humble dervish. Mevlana speaks about *fakr* (poverty) as the ore. Everything besides *fakr* (*faqr*) is an attribute, non-essential. *Fakr* is the remedy. The whole universe is nothing but headache and illusion, and *fakr* is the secret and goal that is sought by all the universe.

114 A Pir is the head of a spiritual lineage. I.e., each person speaks about his own teacher. Shams speaks about Muhammad as his beloved Pir.

115 *Say: "I only follow whatever is revealed to me by my Sustainer: this revelation is a means of insight from your Sustainer, and a guidance and grace to those who will have faith. And so when the Qur'an is voiced, pay attention to it, and listen in silence, so that you might be graced with God's mercy."*

And remember your Sustainer humbly within yourself and with awe, and without raising your voice, in the morning and in the evening; and don't allow yourself to be unaware.

See how those who are near to your Sustainer are never too proud to worship Him; and

❊

Maturity

Let's say someone has begun to speak and wants to make a subtle point. You can't reject his idea until after he finishes; after you understand the words, from the beginning to the end, then you can discuss it. If you have a doubt in your heart you can reveal it then. But people have the habit of discussing that point after only half understanding—that's inappropriate. Such behavior isn't right.

He says, "This is what maturity is: maturity is when even if he speaks thousands of words, still you grasp it perfectly." Now let's look at maturity in a different way. It is maturity when one recognizes one's own deficiency. You admit, "I couldn't understand it completely, I couldn't grasp the meaning."

In this matter, it is useful to ask questions, too, but then, you will have lost the fruitfulness of the first word—like the blessing of the first word that is indicated when the fakir was asked, "Why has the abundance of the gathering disappeared?"[116]

---

they praise His limitless glory, and prostrate themselves before Him alone. [*Surah al-A'raf,* The Faculty of Discernment 7:203-6]

See also Mevlana Jalaluddin Rumi, *Mathnawi* V, 3244-3250 (*Jewels of Remembrance*, p.123):

The Companion of the Prophet said,
"Whenever the Prophet recited verses of the Qur'an to us,
at the moment of abundance that chosen Messenger
would ask attentiveness and reverence."
It's as when a bird perches on your head,
and your soul trembles for fear of its flitting,
so you don't dare to stir lest that beautiful bird take to the air;
You dare not breathe, you suppress a cough,
lest that *huma* should fly away;
and if anyone speak sweet or sour words to you,
you lay a finger to your lips, meaning, "Hush!"
Bewilderment is like that bird: it makes you silent:
it puts the lid on the kettle and fills you with the boiling of love.

116 Rather than asking questions too readily, be silent and let the words cook you so as not to lose the fruitfulnesss of the words that may not come again.

My heart has become kabob from the fire of Love.
My face is flushed with the liver's blood.
The moisture of the Beloved's lips is my wine.
Don't blame me now—what good is giving me advice?

❊

Take One Morsel at a Time

There is an advantage in being able to eat one single morsel. You can benefit from that morsel to the extent that you are patient; and then you eat another morsel. This is wisdom.

But there is a kind of person who is in such trouble and pain that he wants to eat quickly; that is a different matter. He knows [about it], but he doesn't test our food.

If a wise man of God had begun to learn these outer (*zahir*) sciences, he would not begin another course without finishing the first one. For example, if such a person had studied this subject several times as Mevlana had suggested, he wouldn't be facing difficulties, and he wouldn't be speaking too much.

Because, unless he is kneaded within these ideas, all the benefits and the difficulties could become habitual. If he is kneaded within these ideas, then he could benefit from all the benefits and overcome the difficulties. This would then become his habit.

Rather than begin a new lesson each day, repeat the same lesson. If a person immerses deeply in a matter, then it is his right to reach a good result. A thousand other things emerge from that.

Some ideas give an openness of heart when they come; some give an openness of heart when they go. Pay attention to whether this openness of heart in you appears when these ideas come or when they go.

Careful! Union with her can't be achieved
　　by just anyone.
They don't serve milk to drunkards
　　from the goblet of the Law (*shariat*).
There, the attained ones who've passed beyond
　　worldly passions drink the moment;

And they don't give a sip to those
who worship themselves.

Words of Grandeur

When I recite a poem in the middle of my other words, I am opening wide the subject and speaking about the secret within its meaning, and then you fall into silence when I stop speaking. Today, there are some people here who are being overcome by the meaning—their tongues have become paralyzed.

Mevlana is not in such a state. Why would this state be in him? And especially not in me. Being overcome by the meaning and sometimes the lack of meaning! I have neither of these.

These people are right in not being able to become accustomed to my words. All my words are coming from Majesty. Everybody acknowledges that the Qur'an and the words of Muhammad are all through yearning, through need. Truly, the longing is seen; it appears in every meaning. These people listen to words, but without real longing. These words are from such a height that, if you were to look up at them, your hat would fall off your head. But this being proud of oneself is not something to be ashamed of from God's perspective. When they say, *God is the Most Great* (*Muttakabir*), they speak the truth; why would anyone be surprised at that?

Countering Hypocrisy

Let me tell you something: these people like to speak insincerely, they like hypocrisy; they find truthful words dreary.

If I tell someone: "You are the greatest, most honorable person of the age, you are unique," without a doubt, he will like it, and grasp my hands, complimenting me: "I've missed you so much; I've made a big mistake [not to have called or visited you for such a long time]." But last year I spoke honestly with him, and he became my enemy. This isn't surprising—if one wants to have a pleasant time with these people, one has to act hypocritically in order to get along well with them. But if you have chosen the path of sincerity, then you have to run away to the mountains or the countryside.

* * *

If you accept these words, that day, a state of mercy will come to you; great good fortune and happiness will reveal their faces to you. If you show respect and listen with yearning and remembrance, there is no doubt that he will be pleased.

Then to the eye of the dervish, this gathering will appear beautiful. He will keep remembering it. His heart will incline towards it, and he won't want to run away—his heart will find ease.

Presence of Heart

Your intention in asking questions and speaking is so that hearts might accept you, and that you might be seen as lovely by hearts. But when the opposite thing happened and when a disturbance came to the hearts instead, and when the pain of this sadness comes back to you, then your heart is troubled by it.

Muhammad, peace be with him, said, "There is no *salaat* without recitation of the Qur'an"[117]; and also, "There is no *salaat* without presence of heart (*huzur*)."

A group of people think that those who reach presence of heart, don't need to do *salaat* any more. They say: "After the aim is attained, to continue to look for a means to reach it is irrelevant." For a moment, let's assume that what they think is true. Let's say the Truth has completely shown its face to them, and sainthood, and presence of heart have appeared in them. Despite all that, abandoning the form of *salaat* would be an imperfection for them.

---

117 The Muslim ritual prayer is not valid without inclusion of recitation of the *Fatiha*, the first chapter of the Qur'an, *The Opening*, which is similar in form and content to The Lord's Prayer in Christianity. Without the offering of the *Fatiha* and the request within it for guidance from the Infinitely Compassionate One, the Sustainer of All Worlds, the prayer loses its meaning; without the presence of heart of real supplication, the prayer would become just an empty form.

Didn't this state of perfection and maturity that has come to you, also come to the Messenger of God, blessed Muhammad, too? . . . So why don't you follow the noble Prophet? Why don't you follow the footsteps of that enormously benevolent, unique Prophet who is so generous and both a giver of good news and a warner; why don't you follow the traces of that bright light of the Truth?"[118]

The Place of the Poor One

I was in a corner of a caravanserai when someone asked me, "Aren't you coming to the *khanaqah*?"[119]

"I don't see myself as appropriate for the *khanaqah*," I said. "It seems they have built the *khanaqah* for those who have no concern about cooking and striving to do things. Their time is precious, but they can't catch the moment. I am not one of them."

"Okay, so why don't you come to the *madrasah*?"[120] they asked.

"I am also not one of those who engage in discussions; even though I understand them, debates and discussions don't suit me. Because, if I speak in my own way, they laugh at me saying, 'He is a heretic.' They brand me with blasphemy.

I am a poor stranger, and the place of the poor stranger is the caravanserai."[121]

---

118 *[And as for thee,] O Prophet—behold, We have sent thee as a witness [to the truth], and as a herald of glad tidings and a warner, and as one who summons [all men] to God by His leave, and as a light-giving beacon. And [so,] convey to the faithful the glad tiding that a great bounty from God awaits them; and defer not to [the likes and dislikes of] the deniers of the truth and the hypocrites, and disregard their hurtful talk, and place thy trust in God: for none is as worthy of trust as God.* [*Surah al-Azhab*, The Confederates 33:45-48]

Muhammad not only continued *salaat*, but increased it, often standing in prayer late into the night.

119 A *khanaqah* (or *tekke*, Tr.) is a Sufi center where dervishes gather for training.

120 A *madrasah* (or *medrese*, Tr.) is an Islamic school attached to a mosque.

121 Shams was critical of both the sincerity of the dervishes of his time, as well as the knowledge of the more strictly religious. He preferred a caravanserai, a way station for those on a journey.

❊

Opening Doors

You want a key to open the door. Does one give the key to a thief? Do you think that friendship with thieves is pleasant? The one who trusts leaves the house to thieves, but he is brave and wakeful; he watches over the house.

Friendship with heretics is pleasant, because at least they know that they are heretics.

❊

Know the Good News

Good news and words of liberation don't seem to mean anything to people; words about the people of Hell are more appealing. They don't like hearing about the good news of liberation; liberation is in righteousness. So they [the imams] talk about Hell in such a way as to make their listeners die of fright.

Fatima, may God be pleased with her, was not a theologian; she was an ascetic (*zahid*, one of abstinence and worship), so she would often ask the Prophet to tell her about Hell; she wanted to hear about it from him.[122]

❊

Searching and Being Sought

The value of one who travels the path of need is beyond price.

---

122 As Shams says later in the *Maqalat*:

> When the Prophet came from the *mir'aj* (ascension), each person asked him whatever question came to his mind. One wanted him to tell him about seeing God, and another about the attributes of Paradise. Fatima (May God be pleased with her) said, "I am fearful—tell us about Hell." The intention of our Mother Fatima was to show herself as faulty. She had learned about courtesy (*adab*) from Solomon (May the greeting and peace of God be upon him). "*I can't see the Hoopoe, what's happened?*" [*Surah an-Naml*, The Ants 27:20] Rather than finding fault with the animals, he found fault with his own self. In the same way, "*Whatever harm comes to you is due to your own self*" [*Surah an-Nisa'*, Women 4:79]. Fatima's faith was also like this.

There are two attributes in the human being. The first is need—one is hopeful about this attribute! Be patient so that the face you are yearning for might appear to you.

And the second attribute is being without need. What can you expect from lack of need?

What is the end result of need? Finding the One who has no need. What is the end of the seeker? To find what he seeks.

What is the end of the one who was sought? To discover the seeker.

A Real Man Is One Who Pleases Others

Someone said, "I am an unbeliever." You are a muslim! The unbeliever also has a muslim within him.

But where in the universe is there really an unbeliever? Let me prostrate myself in front of him. Say, "I am an unbeliever," so that I may kiss you. They do not recognize me, so who are they worshipping in this universe?

"Show me a proof!" you say. They ask for proof from me; they seek Truth from the proof, but they don't want proof from the Truth.

How are you? Are you pleased with these words? If you are saying, "I am well-pleased," remain pleased all the time![123]

A real man is one who pleases others. And there is also the kind of person who pleases his own self (*nafs*). Yes, the servant of God can always please himself, but to please others is God's work.

Be More of A Muslim—Increase Your Surrender

They say: "Openness of heart doesn't come to us from Mevlana Shamsuddin." Someone who expects openness of heart from us is just a fire-worshipper—he finds me and expects an opening from

---

123 See *Surah al-Fajr* (The Daybreak) 89:27-30: *[But unto the righteous, God will say,] "O thou human being that hast attained to inner peace! Return thou unto thy Sustainer, well-pleased [and] pleasing [Him]: enter, then, together with My [other true] servants—yea, enter thou My paradise!"*

me! You are not such a fire-worshipper. You are a muslim, a faithful one (*mumin*).

A muslim doesn't hurt another human being; he covers the other's faults. For example, if a monk kills a muslim, and he takes shelter in your house, and if he says that he is running away from those who are looking for him, and if he says, "I have found only you as a place of refuge. Protect me," you shouldn't tell him, "Even if a Muslim kills a Muslim, he isn't shown mercy."[124] You just protect him. It may be possible that he might incline toward Islam. It's true that you are a muslim, but don't be content with just this, be even more muslim![125]

Every muslim needs to have an unbeliever within, and every unbeliever needs to have a muslim within. What savor is there in being a muslim? The savor is in lack of belief. Sometimes you cannot find any sign or way of muslimhood in a muslim, but you may find the ways of muslimhood in an unbeliever. "The final state of the sought, is to find the one who seeks," they say, but one needs to say something better than that. However, they aren't used to our way of talking. They get dizzy.

❊

Chant through the Darkness to the Light

In addition to everything we've said, the disciple who is a traveler of the way of Truth can't be liberated from following his desires unless he matures. It's not suitable for him to be away from the eye of the shaikh, because then instantly a cold breath cools him and becomes a fatal poison, like the breath of a dragon. It darkens whatever it touches. But, once the disciple has matured, his being away from his shaikh doesn't harm him.

Chant the name of God through the long nights [76:26]. In other words, when a veil comes between the disciple and the guide—that is the

---

124 M. 35.

125 To be a *muslim* means to be surrendered to God. Let it not be just an outward behavior. Increase the reality of your surrender.

"night." When the darkness begins, you need to remember him seriously, and you need to work so that that veil might be removed. Whenever the darkness increases and the guide seems ugly to you, then work even harder to get closer to him. Don't grieve, don't worry, and don't fall into despair! After the lengthening of darkness, after long nights, the bright, luminous days begin.

❊

Breathing the Fragrance of Paradise Dispells Thorns

They say, "If a man strengthens his religion, his troubles also increase. And the trouble of the man who weakens his religion, gets lighter." Just as Amir Kabus said, "Exalted ranks are attained only to the extent of the difficulties faced."

At times when there is no obstacle or veil, that pleasure and light start to move spontaneously; then whatever he finds, he finds by means of the light of the subtlety of God, Most Great: *I breathed into him of My Spirit* [15:29].

However, when he becomes veiled and alienated, such a state comes to him that he becomes unaware of his state and sets out to lead his own *nafs*.[126] He is unable to connect with love and the universe of light, even though he wants to show his *nafs* a different way.

Yes, consider yourself a fool, because it was said, "Most of the people of Paradise are fools."[127] Most of the people of Hell are philosophers and scholars like these, because their intelligence has become a veil for them. From each imagining of those people of knowledge ten more imaginings are born. Like the people of Gog and Magog,[128] they either say that there is no path, or they say that the path is very long. Yes, the way is long, but once one sets out to walk, with great exuberance and joy, the distance of the way disap-

---

126 He begins to live according to his own *nafs*, rather than Divine inspiration.

127 They are ignorant in the worldly sense, recognize the foolishness of their *nafs*, and depend upon God alone. This is reminiscent of the words of Jesus in the Gospel: "Unless you become as little children, you shall not enter the Kingdom of Heaven."

128 See *Surah al-Kahf*, The Cave 18:94: *Behold, Gog and Magog are spoiling this land.*

pears. Just as it was said, "Paradise is surrounded by things we dislike. (*hadith*)." All around the garden of Paradise are thorns. But when the fragrance of Paradise reaches our nose, bringing news of the beloved to the lover, then that place of thorns becomes very pleasant. The thorns that surround Hell always seem to be roses and basil, but the unpleasant odor of fire comes to us from them.

If I were to try to explain about the beauty of this path, it wouldn't be appropriate.

❁

Avoiding Snakes

The seeker of Truth can say, "These imams aren't explaining the outer meaning of the Qur'an correctly," because the outer meaning of the Qur'an is known by the light of faith and can be seen by it and not by the fire of desires. If these imams had the light of faith, how could they spend thousands to buy judgeships and official government positions?[129]

A man buys a snake from a snake seller, paying him a skirtful of gold; but it wasn't such a non-poisonous snake; it was perhaps a mountain snake that spits poison.

A person who runs away from the position of being a judge (*cadi*) or a state official, for God's sake, escapes from them because of the light of his faith, not any other reason. Someone who can recognize a snake can recognize the snake's friend, too.

> The Blessed Qur'an is a shy bride who opens her veil
> only if she sees that the land of faith is safe from war.

❁

Grapes Under the Snow

One has to protect grapes that haven't ripened yet from the sun, so that they don't get burnt. But when they have ripened, no harm comes to them from the sun. Until they sweeten the caretaker of the

---

129 Shams is indicating that people in the thirteenth century bought these positions through bribes, etc.

vineyard protects them from the winter, but when they have ripened well, they can survive even under the snow.

The person who has attained this station of maturity has immersed in the Light of God and become intoxicated with the taste of the Truth. Being a guide is not appropriate for him, because he is drunk—how can he bring others to sobriety?

There is a sobriety beyond this drunkenness, as we have explained before. The beneficence of those who have attained this sobriety has overcome their wrathfulness.[130] But the beneficence of those who get drunk and can't attain that sobriety is still mixed together with wrath. When his self becomes completely filled with beneficence (*lutf*), then his mercy becomes dominant.

☼

Intimacy with God

Revelations used to come to the Prophet through Gabriel, and also through the heart. It comes to saints only through the latter. Just as the blessed Prophet said, there is a moment when, "Neither a Prophet with a book nor one of the recording angels can come between us."[131]

☼

Let Yourself be Carried by the Sea

If a person who falls into the sea doesn't know how to swim, if he flails his hands and feet, even if he is a lion, the sea will break his strength and kill him. The nature of the sea is to drown someone who is alive; but when he sinks into the sea and gives up life, then the sea lifts him up and carries him. So, in its first killing him and then lifting him up to the surface of the water, you have an indication:

---

130 *My Mercy overwhelms My wrath.* [*Surah al-A'raf,* The Faculty of Discernment 7:156].

131 The complete tradition (*hadith*) of Muhammad is: "I have a time with my Sustainer when neither a Prophet with a book (a Prophet who has brought a holy scripture) nor an angel (one of the two angels that sit upon our right shoulder and our left, recording our deeds) can come between us."

"If someone wants to see a dead man walking on earth, let him look at Abu Bakr as-Siddiq (*hadith*)."[132]

He has emerged from the earth and has been nourished with a beautiful water[133] that adds soul to soul. That sea is one of God's servants.

Even if these are not ordinary things for you now, one day they may become ordinary for you. Even if it doesn't happen today, at this hour, it will happen in some future moment.

My being works such an alchemy that there is no need to pour it on the copper; even if the copper is just sitting in front of me, it turns completely into gold. And the perfection of alchemy should be like this.

Light upon Light

God has servants who, when they see that someone has covered himself with the cloak of honor, conclude that that person will be honorable, but when they see a robe on a person's back and a conical hat on his head, they conclude that that person has gone astray. There is another group of people who see with the light of God's stringency. They have left behind the battle and the world of color and scent: "If you take off that person's cloak, you'll find him suitable for Hell. And the person who has hidden himself under a coarse, woolen robe, if you take off his robe, you'll find a perfect man suitable for Paradise."

If a person is praying in the sanctuary,[134] but his mind is occupied with worldly things, then what he does is no different than the deed of a man who commits adultery in a tavern. People quickly

132 Abu Bakr as-Siddiq, one of the closest Companions of the Prophet Muhammad, was especially known for his sincerity and true faithfulness and devotion. He became the leader of the Muslim community, the first caliph, after the Prophet's death.

133 This water is a metaphor for divine knowledge that helps him to emerge from the earth of the body.

134 Shams is speaking about someone making *salaat*, the ritual prayer, in front of the prayer niche, the *mihrab*, which also means "sanctuary."

thrash those who commit adultery. If they repent, *God exchanges their bad deeds with good deeds* [25:70]. But when things are as they are, if someone gossips, even if he fasts, becomes subtle, and flies in the air, he can't be saved. If a person has both the garment of goodness and spiritual maturity, then it is *light upon light* [24:35].

Prayers

I cannot see myself in your heart as I used to in the past. May God make us appear lovely in your heart—let's pray for that. Let's recommend to the friends, too, that they pray. From now on, this will be our work. When it becomes impossible to give advice, let's raise our hands in prayer.

Wasn't it said, "*Peace be upon you! I will ask for forgiveness from God for you* [19:47]."[135]

Doing What the Doctor Orders

Whoever becomes our friend will worship more than he used to; I'm not saying this just for the sake of conversation. "The best way to

---

135 Shams is reminding us of how Abraham turned to God in prayer when his advice was not heeded by his father. See *Surah Maryam* 19:41-48:

And call to mind, through this divine writ, Abraham. Behold, he was a man of truth, [already] a prophet when he spoke to his father: "O my father! Why do you worship something that neither hears nor sees and can be of no avail whatever to you?

"O my father! Behold, there has indeed come to me [a ray] of knowledge such as has never yet come unto you: follow me, then; I shall guide you onto a perfect way. O my father! Do not worship Satan—for, truly, Satan is a rebel against the Most Gracious! O my father! I dread lest a chastisement from the Most Gracious befall you, and then you will become [aware of having been] close to Satan!"

He answered: "Do you dislike my gods, O Abraham? Indeed, if you desist not, I shall most certainly cause you to be stoned to death! Now begone from me for good!"

[Abraham] replied: "Peace be upon you! I shall ask my Sustainer to forgive you: for, behold, He has always been kind to me. But I shall withdraw from you all and from whatever you invoke instead of God, and shall invoke my Sustainer [alone]: it may well be that my prayer [for you] will not remain unanswered by my Sustainer."

give alms is when nobody sees it *(hadith)*."[136] And the least of alms is that which is given in a way that others witness, because the one who gives it becomes proud of it immediately.

What the shaikh does is measured, just like counted walnuts.[137] Certainly what they measure is useful, and they don't miss the mark. And some people do what is recommended, but can't find any benefit in it, and then they attribute the fault to the shaikh.[138] They do something the way they want to, thinking they will accomplish what they were given to do more quickly. Instead they have made success a hundred miles more distant.[139] Procrastination and inattention, neglect at the beginning of that work, causes the loss of a hundred possibilities. If the child had known he was behaving childishly, he would never have acted like this.

> Most people think a lot of their own *nafs*;
> I wish I knew the ignorant one.
> Perhaps at last you are liberated from doubt,
> but that idol of doubt you worship still remains.

. . . "I gave an order, why didn't you do it?" I asked you.

He told me, "I've given you my excuse."

"I didn't accept that excuse," I said. I acted hypocritically. A voice within me was saying, "If you had done the things that I told you, you would have been saved from pain."

Well, if we had saved you from grief in this universe, you would be pleased; but how can we help you go joyfully to the other universe? There everybody is left alone with his own pain at the door.

---

136 Shams is indicating the increase of one's efforts and worship in private, unseen by others—he and Mevlana often withdrew into seclusion.

137 I.e., one can count walnuts one by one; it is clearly measurable. One can give 10 or 15 to someone. What the shaikh does or recommends can be exactly as precise.

138 Some people practice these things and can't benefit from them, and then think it is the shaikh's fault, even though they have not really followed instructions properly.

139 They've made the process more difficult by following the interpretation or inclination of their own *nafs*.

Do Your Best to Cure What Can Be Cured

While the shaikh was preaching, someone was complaining: "What kind of advice is this? From the pulpit of the mosque he tells some stories, he plays a few tunes, but he doesn't give any advice to his own *nafs*. Why doesn't he tell these things to his own children? If he had, they wouldn't be like this. God forbid, why can't he say something to his wife?"

To be a shaikh is self-sacrifice. When his preaching shows signs of the intercession of the people of Truth, then the shaikh's sermon will stir even a stone.

For instance, they say to the doctor: "You are treating that patient, but why didn't you treat your father and son who died?" They said to Muhammad (may the peace of God be upon Him): "Why couldn't you free your uncle, Abu Lahab, from that prison of misbelief and bring him into the Light?"

He replied: "There are diseases that are impossible to cure. For a doctor to occupy himself in vain with such a patient is ignorance. There are also diseases that have a remedy and that can be cured, and to neglect those is to be lacking in mercy."

Planting Crops

A farmer was planting something in the earth.

"Why aren't you planting the land next to your house?" they asked.

"It's barren soil; it's not worth planting there," he said.

Likewise, those words of mine aren't harmful; instead, perhaps they are useful. But how are they useful? In a universe where there are people who might benefit from them. If in a moment the water of the Nile appears to be blood to a Copt, is it any fault of the water of the Nile? If the sweet voice of the Prophet David doesn't please someone who doesn't understand it, and if it seems ugly to him, does this diminish at all the value of that voice?

> The light of the Sun isn't harmed
> by the blindness of the eye of the denier.

❁

Be Respectful so that You Might Be Respected

Today if these words of mine don't please you, be wary. Respect my words so that you might be respected by me, and so that you might strengthen the aspects of faith and conviction that you claim to have, and bear witness to your own and your father's vision. The service and respect you showed before were all out of blindness. You were misleading others, and degrading me. Actually, you have been degrading yourself, because you were bearing witness to your own blindness and laziness, because you yourself had fallen down, when you said, "Why are they showing him such reverence?"

I'm afraid that at the moment, ignorant of the pain of separation, you are sleeping comfortably in the shadow of affection, but the way you are acting may cause that affection to come to an end. Then you may see this state in your dreams, but you won't see the shaikh, because it's not possible to see the shaikh unless he chooses—you won't see him either in a dream or while awake.

❁

The Teeth of the Lion

When you see the teeth of the lion opened wide,
Don't ever think that it's smiling at you; it is the terrible lion.
Be fearful of kings when they honor you.

❁

The Reality of Affection

I was speaking in a dream. The shaikh was telling me about them, one by one. Still, they don't consider the shaikh truthful. They don't want to believe either in his words or in his deeds. The reason is clear—it's because of the loss of affection.

I wonder why he doesn't confirm the shaikh's truthfulness! Let him put that on the palm of one hand and what he might expect from the shaikh on the other. Then let him weigh them—which is worth more?

The shaikh has a universe full of pleasing tastes; he's always occupied—doesn't he occupy himself with the final state of his disciple? In this life, what more can one do than this—to harmonize oneself with this affection?

Unity

This is just like the story of the ten Sufis, one of whom fell in love with a Zoroastrian. The lover used to spend his whole day following his beloved around; he followed her to the temple and everywhere. One day, the fire-worshipping girl asked him, "Why are you following me?" The lover spoke of his state. She said: "We view people other than our own as dragons; we always avoid them. How could you hope that I would be suitable for you?" The lover was left helpless.

Quickly, he went to his friends—he would say farewell to them.

"What's going on?" they asked. "God willing, it's something good!"

The dervish told the story. "Well, now I am taking my leave," he said. "Let me buy a sash [worn by non-Muslims] and tie it around my waist."

The friends all said, "OK, we'll do that, too. Let's buy ten sashes—let's all tie them around our waists. For in the end, are we not one single spirit, just in separate bodies?"

When the Zoroastrian girl saw them, she asked what was the reason of their coming all together. They told their story and said, "There is oneness among us."

A fire fell into the heart of the Zoroastrian, she tore off her own sash and threw it away, and told them: "I am the servant of that community among whom there is such fidelity! In no other community have I ever seen such unity."

The girl's father and relatives all came to her and began to reproach her. "How can you be charmed by these Sufis; how can you destroy your own religion?" they asked.

The girl answered, "If you had only seen what I've seen in them! Wouldn't hundreds of great ones be lovers of such as these!"

Love the Polishing

If someone is happy in his own essence, then advice polishes and enlightens him. But for one who is discontented, words of advice only darken him, and increase the rust on his mirror.

> O soul! Appear to me once, before my last breath comes
> to an end.
> Finish my work quickly; let me not speak another word.
>
> A lover is needed so that we might learn about this
> secret together.

Brothers

The story of the man whose brother was immoral is strange. Every day they used to catch this man in some bad deed, and they would lead him all around the city—they would take off the load on his brother's donkey, and make him ride on that donkey facing backwards. At last, one day his brother could stand it no longer. He told him, "Brother since you keep insisting on this bad behavior, I'm going to have to buy you your own donkey."

Companionship of the Way

Now there is a difference between us and the great ones. Our outside is the same as our inside. God has given me patience and endurance to get along well with strangers. But it is even better to spend time with friends.[140] If a person benefits from doing things in a certain way, he clings strongly to that way. If someone is bewildered, he should take a hint. Immediately he should follow the well-tried way and try to be a true companion. Such a person doesn't see his companions as ignorant and foolish; he doesn't have such opinions about them.

---

140 M. 40.

✲

Pay Attention to What's Important

Someone who runs from difficulty is like the blind grammarian. One day, the blind grammarian fell down into a hole full of filth. Someone came near to him and called, "Your hand. Give me."

Because this way of speaking was not grammatical, the scholar became angry and yelled, "Pass on! You're not one of us."

Someone else came and called, "Your hand. Reach out." With the same words, the grammarian sent him away, too.

And so, the one who saw the grammar mistake with such careful attention couldn't see the filthy state of the hole he had fallen into. All night long, he waited amid the filth in that terrible place and didn't take anyone's hand.

When day broke, someone came near to him and called, "O Uncle Omar! You have fallen into filth!"

"Then grasp my hand, you are one of us," the grammarian said.

But this man wasn't strong enough. When he took his hand, they both fell back into the hole. . . . [141]

Similarly, another grammarian was listening to the song of a singer and he started tearing his clothes and shouting. People gathered around him. Together with the other people there, a judge was

---

141 Mevlana recounts a similar tale in his *Mathnawi* and also in the *Menaqib al-arifin* by Aflaki there is an account of his reflections on the grammarian's preoccupation:

> "In the same way," continued Mevlana, "Until you remove from your personality the *hamza* [a letter in Arabic that indicates an aspiration of breath] of doubt and preoccupation with your own existence, you will never be delivered from that darkness which is the well of the *nafs* and of passion. You will never enjoy the delightful fragrances in the vast plain described in the Qur'an: *And remember, wide is God's earth* [39: 10].
>
> We caught the grammarian in his own net,
> and in this way taught you the grammar of detachment.
> Know that self-effacement, not grammar, is the way to knowledge.
> If you have died to yourself, you can dive safely into the sea of becoming.
> Jurisprudence, syntax, and morphology will only drown you, dear friend."

also astonished by the situation. "This man doesn't usually behave like this," they said.

The poor singer, thinking that his voice was pleasing the man, repeated his song. Again, the grammarian shrieked, and gestured to them. "Listen, O Muslims!" he said.

The people thought, "Voices are coming to him from the Unseen—he wants to tell us about it; he wants to awaken us!"

Until the wee hours, they watched this situation. The grammarian tore off all his clothes, threw them aside, and stood there naked. Everybody gathered around him and they sprinkled him with water and rosewater. When he cooled down a little, the judge grasped the man's hand, took him aside, and asked, "For the sake of my soul and heart, tell me the truth. From where did this state of love and joy come to you?"

The man answered, "How can I not go into such a state—losing my mind? Since the time of Noah, and the time of Abraham until the blessed era of Muhammad, the 'li' particle has made nouns genetive and is pronounced with a vowel point for 'i,' but this singer changed the case by pronouncing the word coming after the genetive with a vowel point indicating 'e'!"

Now, if a person, instead of spending so much effort for a meaningless aim, were to spend his strength to reach the land of Eternity, the Way of the Truth, how great that pleasure would be! That strength is your capital.

And if a person buys something that he doesn't need, he'll end up having to sell what he does need.

❊

Recognizing the Moment

A Sufi, a traveler on the way of Truth, endured a period of severe trials for years and served his shaikh and others, but the time for rain from the cloud of hope hadn't yet arrived.

> Until the apportioned time arrives,
> You can't benefit from the closeness of friends!

After the days of old age and despair had come, one day when he had been visiting the graveyard, he remembered his past hopes and he wept. He put a brick under his head and fell asleep. Within that sleep his work was completed and that for which he longed was attained. When he awoke, immediately he stood up and began to kiss the brick. He embraced it, and wherever he went he always kept it with him—when he visited people, in the mosque, the toilet, or the bath, in the country, during sema, in the bazaar—in short, the brick was always with him. If someone praised him, he told him to praise the brick first, or if someone offered their hand to him, he would tell them to give their hand to the brick first. They asked him, "Why don't you leave it aside; why do you keep it with you all the time?"

He answered, "It will also come with me to the grave. I had lost something—for thirty years I had been hopeless and waiting and waiting. My hopes would rise and then again I would fall into despair. Hundreds of thousands of times I had thrashed about in this uncertainty. One day I put my head upon this brick and found what I had been looking for."

Abu Bakr

It's just as the Prophet said, "Whoever has something that brings him blessing, let him keep it with him." Although there is another saying, "Visit me now and then," but we know that this *hadith* referred to Abu Hurayrah and those like him. During talks with the Prophet, they had gone beyond the limits of courtesy, and their continuous presence had begun to weary him. He did not intend this saying for everyone, especially not for Abu Bakr. He didn't want him to be away from him, and he didn't want him to go out into battle. One day during a battle, a warrior dashed into the field, and the Muslims wouldn't fight him. Nobody dared.

People asked, "Why aren't you fighting? Where are the volunteers, those who renounce their lives, those who seek death [2:94]? Where are those who sacrifice their lives, who seek death in the same way that poets search for rhymes, the sick seek medicine, the prisoner freedom, and school children a holiday? What is the reason for such fear, avoidance, and reluctance? Who are you afraid of?"

They answered, "It's not because we fear for our lives, but the warrior who has jumped into the field is Abu Bakr's son, the light of his eye. The Muslim warriors are ashamed to fight against him; this is the reason."

When these words reached Abu Bakr's ears, the Prophet Muhammad and he were sitting together. Abu Bakr asked the reason for the turmoil. "Your son has come forth," they said.

Immediately, Abu Bakr jumped from his place and went onto the battlefield. When his son saw his father's face, he immediately retreated. Abu Bakr retreated, too, and returned.

The Prophet put his hands onto Abu Bakr's hands and said, "O Siddiq![142] Keep your *nafs* for us!" That is, "According to you, your *nafs* has no value, but for us it has great worth. Protect it for us. Don't go into battle, don't go into the fighting; don't separate from our companionship."

How could the Prophet say to Abu Bakr, "Visit me from time to time?" For the other believers, combat was an obligation; for Abu Bakr it would have been separation. The good deeds of the devout are sins for those who have attained closeness with God.

❁

Restoring the Castle

When a castle falls into the hands of a rebel, it becomes permissible, even obligatory to destroy it, and you have to give the destroyers robes of honor. To repair the castle then would be a treacherous sin, but after the castle is taken back from the rebel and the flags of the sultan are raised, there is no longer any reason to destroy it. Then, it would be treason to destroy it, and to completely restore it becomes one's duty and rightful service.

---

142 Abu Bakr was known as the most sincere and truthful (*siddiq*) as he was the first man to attest to Muhammad's prophethood and continually he manifested a deep trust and devotion to God.

Piety is maintained through religion, prayer beads,
and mosques.
The clothes of a heretic, blasphemy, and the tavern
are for those whose love is strong.
But unless faith turns into blasphemy,
and blasphemy into faith,
The servant of God can't become a true Muslim.

✲

Seeing with the Light of Truth

To speak in the presence of the masters of spiritual conversation (*sohbet*) is discourteous, unless it is as an offering. For example, people take their money to an assayer and say, "If there are any counterfeit coins, separate them to one side." But if the assayer is a lover or friend of that person, or if he is a disciple, then even the ugliness of the friend seems beautiful, and his counterfeit appears to him as true coin. "The lover's eye is blind, and his ear is deaf." Well, one who is a friend also falls in love with the sweet words of the speaker.

In response to this we say, "All lovers aren't like this; every lover doesn't see the ugly as beautiful. There are lovers who see each thing just as it is, because they see with the light of the Truth, for 'The faithful see with the light of God.'[143] Those happy lovers never fall in love with faults. As Abraham said, '*I love not that which sets* [6:76].'"[144]

---

143 See *Surah az-Zumar*, The Throngs 39:22:

Could, then, one whose bosom God has opened wide with willingness towards self-surrender unto Him, so that he is illumined by a light [that flows] from his Sustainer, [be likened to the blind and deaf of heart]?

144 See *Surah al-An'am*, Cattle 6:75-79.

And thus We gave Abraham [his first] insight into [God's] mighty dominion over the heavens and the earth—and [this] to the end that he might become one of those who are inwardly sure.

Then, when the night overshadowed him with its darkness, he beheld a star; [and] he exclaimed, "This is my Sustainer!"—but when it went down, he said, "I love not the things that set."

Then, when he beheld the moon rising, he said, "This is my Sustainer!"—but when it went down, he said, "Indeed, if my Sustainer guide me not, I will most certainly become one of the people who go astray!" Then, when he beheld the sun rising, he said, "This is my Sustainer! This one is the greatest [of all]!"—but when it [too] went down, he exclaimed:

It is impossible for the mature ones to fasten their
hearts on beauty that will pass away.

Bound by Imitation

Every degeneration in the world is caused by people either believing out of imitation or denying out of imitation. Though a grief comes to a saint, they don't recognize that that person's sainthood is only through imitation. And so also, from imitation, appreciation of him is sometimes warm one moment and cold the next.

How is it possible to regard people of imitation as Muslims?[145]

How can it be possible that grief or pain can come to such a person if he is really a saint? According to himself, he is the "most elect of the elect," yet he causes the desolation of the universe, just as, *They rebelled against their Sustainer's apostles: and so He took them to task with a punishing grasp exceedingly severe* [69:10].[146]

Even if a person is a believer at first, imitation may envelop him in doubt. In the end he keeps removing veils, but until he renounces that conviction [of thinking he's truly a "saint of the saints"] the number of veils only increases, until it kills that conviction. However he doesn't openly reveal why this conviction died, because he doesn't want people to lose their high opinion of him. Yet if he doesn't reveal it, people will fall into heresy. But again he wonders, how can he reveal this? He has no self-confidence left. People of purity are those who can recognize the situation whether or not that person admits that his inner conviction is gone.

One of the dervishes said, "You see that what's gone is gone."

"O my people! Behold, far be it from me to ascribe divinity, as you do, to anything beside God! Behold, unto Him who brought into being the heavens and the earth have I turned my face, having turned away from all that is false; and I am not of those who ascribe divinity to anything beside Him."

145 One's journey of faith may begin in imitation, but to really be a "Muslim," one must surrender one's self to God. As Suleyman Dede, a Mevlevi shaikh, used to say, "May God make my imitation real."

146 The arrogant and pridefully rebellious draw God's wrath upon themselves, even as Pharaoh did. See *Surah al-Haqqah,* The Laying Bare of the Truth 69:9.

You keep talking in the gatherings—what kind of garbling is this!

You see that liberation and honesty are only outwardly with you, not within you, otherwise you would be my friend . . . if you were ready to sacrifice your head for this station. This station is a station of such a person of God that his community and his path is the best of all communities and paths.

The Blessings of Striving

I keep running to reach the Friend.
My life nears its end, but still I am asleep.
Let's say I will reach the Beloved in the end;
yet where will I find the days that have passed?

The Path that leads to the Truth is one of two possibilities: either it is through the opening up of the inner universe—and the Prophets and saints have walked upon this path—or through acquiring knowledge which is also a struggle and a clearing of inner impurities. Where else but Hell could be the place of those who leave aside both of these two ways?

Be as One

The creation of you all and the resurrection of you all is but as a single soul: for, truly, God is All-Hearing, All-Seeing [31:28]. A similar point is made in the *hadith*: "The faithful are like one body." When the prophets call communities to the way of the Truth, their call means, "O you who are estranged in form, you are a part of Me, why aren't you aware of this? O part! Come and don't live being unaware of the whole! Understand this and come closer to Me; get to know Me."

But they say: "No, I'd rather kill myself than come closer to you, or merge with you." In short, no matter how much they may progress, in their open retreating, their imagination only increases and illusions block their way.

On this way of wakefulness, as much as someone progresses, truth upon truth and vision upon vision opens.

❁

Protecting Health

It's easier to protect health than to restore health, and it's easier to avoid sin than to ask for forgiveness.

After you've strayed from your regimen and come down with a disease, then you set out for perseverance. "Why couldn't I be even a little patient?" you grumble to yourself. But what good is patience and perseverance then?

❁

Good Cooking

If you can see that I don't need to go on a journey but that this is for your own work, then when it comes to this journey that we make, it will be pleasing—I wasn't intending to order you to go on this journey.

"Let me do this by myself; let me set out to put your work in order," I said, "because separation cooks within separation."

One can ask, "What are all those commands and prohibitions? Why didn't I obey—why didn't I think about that which was easy as opposed to this difficulty of separation?"

In the words that I spoke, I was duplicitous and hypocritical. I was being kind to both sides and speaking enigmatically. But, now one has to speak openly. What value does this thing have?

Let me go on fifty journeys for you. And the journeys I will make will be for the sole purpose of completing your work. Otherwise, what difference does it make to me—from the land of Rum let me travel to Damascus, or let me be at the Kaaba or in Constantinople, it is all the same.

However, there is the fact that separation cooks a person; it improves him. Is it better today to arrive having improved and been cooked, or is it better to keep being cooked through separation? Where does the one who has been cooked within the state of union open his eye? How can the one who was left on the outside in every situation find a way beyond the veil? Can he be at all like those who are always sitting inside the veil? Of the things that you say, they don't listen to the definition of the lover and his testimony—that faults appear to him as rightful: "The lover is blind and deaf."

Is it ever possible for a human being to be a lover, yet still to have the capacity of sight and discrimination, not to completely lose himself and be overcome by love?

I said, "It is not possible to oppose 'the possible.' Let me tell you the ideas of the theologians: the first is 'the necessary'—this is the universe and the attributes of the Truth, Himself. The second is 'the impossible,' i.e. that which cannot be; like the two opposites that cannot unite. The third is 'the possible,' that is, the state of contingency which can turn either way; either it can be, or it can not be. Everybody who is included within this third group is liberated."

Even so, the Paradise from which Adam was exiled was an exalted forested place on the earth. This paradise is not the paradise promised to the faithful, which reveals its sign from the highest heaven.

I told him, "You are telling me that I am talking about philosophy all the time, but it's you who began the philosophizing."

Money Troubles

A peasant was plowing in a field.[147] The iron of the plow struck something and got stuck. When the oxen stopped, he began to beat them, but it wasn't possible to make them go forward. Wounded all over from the ox-goad, the oxen fell on their faces. The farmer felt the place again where the plow had gotten stuck. After taking out a few stones, he saw the iron and how it had become stuck on the edge of a large jug. He pulled on the end of the iron, but he couldn't move it from its place. No matter how much he tried to lift it from its place and move it, he couldn't manage it.

I told the man, "Since you can't pull the iron out, then find a way to break off its head!" He tried hard, but he couldn't do it.

"I wonder, if this is some plunder—perhaps it's a hidden treasure full of silver coins," he was saying to himself. Because he was a

147 M. 45.

villager, he never imagined it might be gold. At last he broke away the iron, and saw that the inside of the jug was full of gold. He took out a handful of coins, and holding them in his hand, he looked at them and said, "I swear it is gold!"

Until then the villager had been a man without concerns or worries. He used to just plow and do his work. But after that, the illusions and desires of the world swarmed around his head. He worried, "What is the best thing to do about this?" He struggled with ideas like, "Shall I take these to such and such a person, or to the sultan?" Just then he saw the sultan far away, returning from hunting. Very unhappily, he began to shout in order to yield the money.

When two of the sultan's bodyguards heard him they ran toward him. Then, the villager regretted his previous decision.

"Why did you call us?" the men asked. "And give us some water to drink!" they said.

The villager said, "I called you to ask the way to the city," because when they reached him, he had changed his mind. He just couldn't tell them.

The men laughed and said, "Are you asking us the way to the city? Well, the way to the city is over that way," and they pointed in the direction from which they had come. When the guards went away, the villager again felt regret.

"I've forgotten the way to the city that you showed me, so let me ask again: is it this direction or that?" he called.

One of the guards wanted to beat the villager, but the other stayed his hand. They returned to the sultan and sat down, but they kept laughing and looking at each other. They hadn't been able to make any sense out of the villager's confused words. The sultan became very angry at their behavior; he ordered both of the guards to be killed.

One of the two guards who was very gentle-tempered begged the sultan for forgiveness. "O king of the universe! Just give your command, so that they might ask us the reason for this laughter of ours. Then for God's sake, listen to us!" he said. And they told their whole story.

"If this is true, go and bring the villager here," the sultan said.

The guards ran back, but the villager became frightened when he saw them.

"By God, they must be coming after me," he said to himself.

The guards called, "Let's go, the sultan wants you."

The villager thought to himself, "If you don't have money, it's a problem; if you do have money, it's also a problem, but to gain gold and then have problems is better."

In my opinion, trouble without money is better, because one doesn't have the fear of losing one's soul.

These words came as a joke. It's better to joke with these people than to talk seriously with them. Even so, one whose greatness is manifest has a world and sanctity of his own.

> Honesty is a city, and I am the sultan of that city.
> Let me live there, die there, and find protection there.

If a man like this makes a joke, the joke causes a feeling of awe in those around him. A serious word doesn't bring forth such a feeling of awe, and certainly if the joke isn't sharp or threatening it's more agreeable.

❊

Being a Child of Adam

They were discussing, "How did each of the great masters of struggle accomplish their victories?" How was it when it came to Adam? How was it when it came to Abraham? What were the victories like of the greatest of the faithful, Ali?

Each one of them said something according to his capacity. When it came to my turn, no matter how much they insisted, I wouldn't speak. There was a dervish there who bowed his head and also said nothing. A desire to talk with him arose within me.

I said, "To be a child of Adam is to commit but a single error in one's life, and then spend the rest of one's life regretting it.[148] He

---

148 I.e., Only a human, not an animal, can feel lifelong remorse for a sin.

must follow the tradition of his father[149] and ask forgiveness from God. 'He who is like his father is not without mercy,'" and I spoke about the sin of Adam and how he repented.

True Victory

They asked me, "What was the reason for the revelation of *Surely, We have opened for thee . . .* [48:1]?"

I said, "When the Qur'anic verse, *I do not know what will be done with you or with me* [46:9][150] descended, they could not understand that this verse also has another meaning besides the outer meaning. They began to grumble, saying, 'You look towards someone who does not know what will become of him and his people?!' Well, just after this, *Surely We have opened for thee* [48:1] was sent down."[151]

They asked again, "What kind of an answer was this for them?"

"This is how the conversation flows," I said. "The words '*I don't know* [46:9]' within that verse are not a sign of ignorance or confusion. Instead they mean, 'I wonder in which royal robe the sultan will clothe me, or which property he will grant to me?'"

They asked once again, "We are still doubtful about this saying, too. Isn't it a defect for such a person not to know in what kind of a

---

149 "The tradition of his father" refers to the repentence of the Prophet Adam when he was exiled from Paradise.

150 [*Surah al-Ahqaf* (The Sand-Dunes), 46:9]: *Say: "I am not the first of [God's] apostles; and [like all of them,] I do not know what will be done with me or with you; I only follow what is revealed to me: for I am nothing but a plain warner."*

151 [*Surah al-Fath* (Victory), 48:1-5]: *In the Name of God the Infinitely Compassionate and Merciful, Surely, [O Muhammad,] We have opened for you a manifest victory, ('Innaa fatahnaa laka fatham-mubiinaa) so that God might show His forgiveness of all your faults, past as well as future, and [thus] bestow upon you the full measure of His blessings, and guide you on a straight way, and [show] that God will succour you with [His] mighty succour. It is He who from on high has bestowed inner peace upon the hearts of the faithful, so that—seeing that God's are all the forces of the heavens and the earth, and that God is all-knowing, truly wise—they might grow yet more firm in their faith, [and] that He might admit the faithful, both men and women, into gardens through which running waters flow, therein to abide, and that He might efface their [past bad] deeds: and that is, in the sight of God, indeed a triumph supreme!*

robe of honor he would be clothed? Since he has been given some robes and favors, how is it that he can't know the rest, because 'a portion is an indication of the whole.'"

"This isn't ignorance," I said. "Instead it indicates the greatness and infinity of the giving. Just as it was said in another place, And what could make you conceive what it is, that steep uphill road? [90:12][152] or also, And what could make you conceive what that Day of Reckoning will be [82:17]?"

The truth of these words doesn't reach them.

Listen with a Different Ear

They said, "Because of his poor education, he keeps repeating the same words all the time."

I told them, "This is only due to your poor education; my words are quite good, but it is difficult to make you understand them. Even if I say them a hundred times, you still understand a different meaning, and so that essential meaning remains untouched."

Well, he was saying: "The field of words is very wide."

I wanted to answer him and said, "Perhaps the field of meaning is very wide, but the field of words is very narrow." With him I was speaking only in a veiled way, so that he might realize that he doesn't know anything about veiling, either!

"Listen to this word with a different ear," I said. "Don't listen with the ear that has heard the words of the shaikhs! What place does Bayazid Bastami and his words, 'Glory be to me . . . ,' have in a place where these words are being spoken?"

---

152 [*Surah Balad* 90:6-17]: *He boasts, "I have spent wealth abundant!" Does he, then, think that no one sees him? Have We not given him two eyes, and a tongue, and a pair of lips, and shown him the two highways [of good and evil]? But he would not try to ascend the steep uphill road. . . . And what could make you conceive what it is, that steep uphill road? [It is] the freeing of one's neck [from the burden of sin], or the feeding, upon a day of [one's own] hunger, of an orphan near of kin, or of a needy [stranger] lying in the dust—and being, withal, of those who have attained to faith, and who enjoin upon one another patience in adversity, and enjoin upon one another compassion.*

❁

Real Surrender . . . Who Knows Who Is a Muslim?

A Muslim gave his heart to a girl who was an unbeliever; he begged and pleaded with her to be with him. The girl said, "I am not a Muslim, you are a Muslim; it's impossible. Follow my way." The man became an unbeliever. And after this, could they call him "unbeliever" or "Muslim"?

On the other hand, an unbeliever had fallen in love with a Muslim girl as beautiful as the moon. "If you want to marry me, become a Muslim," she said. The man became a Muslim. And whoever says, "He is not a Muslim," becomes an unbeliever. In other words, one who says, "He is an unbeliever" becomes himself an unbeliever, so why does he bother talking about somebody else?

❁

Transforming the Nafs

Now this world is like a beautiful young woman. When that unbeliever saw God's servant, she became a lover, she became a Muslim—she became the next world. She became "My Satan has become a Muslim" (*hadith*), and "The blessed property suits the blessed human being" was actualized.

The *nafs* says, "Let me become a Muslim gradually; I'll become a good human being." This is a difficult struggle (*cille*). The *nafs* has to get purified, there is no other way, but it is weak and begins to beat around the bush.

Even so, it was said in the *hadith* that *nafs-i-mutmainnah*, the *nafs* that has become contented with the Truth, is better and more saintly than the *nafs-i-lawwamah*, the *nafs* that blames itself. But, then, why does God swear by *nafs-i-lawwamah* and say, "*I swear by the nafs that blames itself* [75:2]," but does not swear by *nafs-i-mutmainnah* which is more exalted? He doesn't want to make it a point of conversation; He is keeping it secret because it is more exalted. In the same way, someone might say, "O king! For the sake of the dust under your feet!" Instead of speaking of his exalted soul, he points to something else.

Another interpretation of this is the Qur'anic verse, *He takes into His Mercy everyone who wills [to be admitted]; but as for the evildoers—for them has He readied grievous suffering* [76:31].

Why do they recite at funerals: "Glory be to that living one who never dies." People think that they are speaking about God. However, God is much greater than that they should mention his name with death. They are really speaking to the one who has died, saying, "Now you have come to such a life that you will never die again!"

> When the light of Day shines, we will be brought together.
> Which blessing is there that time has not blurred?

❁

A Dervish Cloak

He said, "A dervish had a cloak. This cloak used to speak with him. He used to consult with his cloak and ask it questions."

It is God's Divine law—if he wills, He makes other things than humans speak, too. The miracles of the prophets have been accepted as true by many different people.

Now, since you are a human being, how can it be that you don't speak—that your tongue doesn't start talking—but you just keep repeating some old wives' tales or Arabic poems! That's it! Now, where are your own words?

❁

Humility before God

The shaikh was saying, "Islam! Islam is necessary!" But he himself didn't really know anything about Islam; he didn't even know the outer form of Islam.

They say, "Such and such a person's manner of speaking is harsh." For a month, two months, one after the other, they listen to his words but can't grasp anything. And then that person of little understanding freely claims that, "God has given me something so great!" or "I have received such a great thing from God that neither those who came before nor those who have come later could understand it."

We say, "God has given us something infinitesimal," and we are occupied with it and manifest the proof of it.

He says to Mevlana, "I love you, and I love others for your sake." He offers the following poem of Majnun as proof:

> Out of love for her, I love all that is dark,
> Because of her love, I love even dogs that are black.

Are you saying this about someone other than Mevlana Shamsuddin Tabrizi? If you love me for his sake, that is better and more pleasing to me than if you love him for my sake.

Poverty Is My Pride

He said, "The shaikh is above the *fakir*, because of poverty; above the shaikh is the *qutb* [the spiritual pole of the era]; and above the *qutb*, is such and such."

I wanted to say, "Have you ever been able to convey anything about this poverty to anyone? Have you brought any news about this rank of poverty from those ignorant shaikhs? The greatest in the world, the Prophet of God, the lord of the universe and of Adam has said, 'Adam and everyone after him walk under my banner,' without pride, and 'I am the most eloquent among the Arabs and non-Arabs,' without pride, but 'Poverty is my pride (*hadith*).' What business do you have with this poverty that you are putting it beneath a shaikh?"

But I didn't say anything; the only way to answer him was silence.

Then he said, "If they are like thorns, you have to set them on fire."

"Are you going to follow Noah or Muhammad?" I asked. "Because the Prophet Noah begged, '*O Lord! Don't leave a single unbeliever upon the Earth* [71:26]!' while Muhammad said, 'My God, guide my people to the right path! Because they do not know.'"

Tasting of the Way

Those who undergo a period of severe trial (*cille*) are following Moses, because they haven't tasted the pleasure of following Muhammad.

God forbid! Maybe they don't know about following the way of Muhammad, but they don't have much of the taste of following the way of Moses, either.

You say, "The saint is all alone, everybody is paying attention to the world—nobody walks with him, or in front of him, or behind him." In the same way, some people look down upon the sultan's officers because they ride alone, but they look up to the captain of the guard because he has soldiers who walk with him, in front of and behind him.

❁

Pay Attention to Whose Shoes You Are Wearing

If you depart a little from a conclusion to which you had come by yourself, this doesn't mean that you are always fickle in your decisions. On a dark night, someone wanting to leave a crowded place may happen to mistakenly put on someone else's shoe and tear one side of it. Now, he doesn't need to leave wearing the wrong shoe. Here, to apologize makes sense—it was dark. But at such a time, each person should keep an eye on his own shoes.[153]

❁

Grasp the Whole

There are people who appreciate rhymed prose, rhymed words, and they always speak in that way. Some recite poetry all the time, while some always speak in prose. Each of them chooses a part, a branch of speech. But the *logos* of God is complete and whole. Grasp the whole so that all the parts might be yours. Don't desire anything other than that; don't reach for just a part, because then you risk losing the whole from your grasp.

At someone's door a tree appeared and grew. The owner of the house must care for the whole of the tree so that all of its branches may be his, and its trunk, too. If he grabs hold of just a branch, then

---

153 "If the shoe fits, wear it." If you recognize that it doesn't, don't wear it home just to cover your mistake—acknowledge your mistake. Be watchful, especially in moments of darkness.

the trunk of the tree will be lost to him. There is also the danger that that single branch may break; then having lost the branch, he will have lost his connection with the trunk.[154]

The Tongue of Truth

The meaning of Iblis existed before his form, just as the spirits of the children of Adam were created before their forms. The spirits are ranged in ranks. God said to the spirits, "*Am I not your Lord?*" [7:172][155] And they said, "*Yes, truly You are.*" This was before the spirits had each entered their bodily forms. Now, what does Muhammad say? "Satan circulates within the blood vessels of the children of Adam just like blood flows within their veins." (*hadith*). How can that ugly image with which they represent Satan circulate within the veins of human beings? Satan may enter the veins of the children of Adam, but he doesn't enter the words of the dervish, because it's not the dervish who is speaking. This dervish has been annihilated; the words are coming from the other side. It's like when you make a bagpipe out of a goatskin, and put it to your mouth and blow; then every sound that comes out of it is your sound, not the goat's voice. However, it comes through the goat's skin, but here the goat has perished, and the meaning that used to come through the goat's voice has also been annihilated.

Likewise, you can also turn that goatskin into a drum. You can play the drum; another sound comes from it. But if you had hit this skin when the animal was alive, you would only hear the voice of a goat.

> Only a person of wisdom knows
> how many years have passed between that voice and this.

---

154 Reach for God—embrace the Real, not branches of knowledge that may leave you hanging out on a limb, or let you fall when they are no longer able to support you.

155 Shams is referring to the *Day of Alast*, the Day of the covenant with God in pre-eternity.

It was necessary to give this example because the dervish who has become perfected speaks with the tongue of the Truth (*Al-Haqq*). So how can anyone object to the words of such a dervish?

❋

Seeing God

I told him, "The one with mature understanding knows that no incompleteness comes from God; any incompleteness or defect comes from one's own impatience."

In the end, this *You shall not be able to see me!* [7:143] was due to Moses' impatience. If he had behaved a little more patiently, he would have gotten an answer to his question, and found the One who answers.

If you don't listen for the answer, if it doesn't come, whom does the meaning reach? Patience gives strength to the one who listens. Then a different knowledge helps your knowledge, so that you may give an answer to every difficult question that is asked. After this, he gives hundreds of answers, and the gathering warms. Then to the eye of the dervish, the gathering seems to pass pleasantly; his interest in the gathering awakens, and that interest has its influence and bears fruit.

In actuality, this dervish has not learned anything from this side, his education was from beyond. Through God's abundance, to teach about the other side fell to this one's lot. How can you object to him with the tales of this side?

God said, "*Eyes cannot perceive Him* [6:103]." This is the side of despair. Then He said, "*He perceives*," and this is the side of hope. When the Truth of sight turned its face to Moses, it overwhelmed him, and he was drowned within this sight. "*Show Yourself to me*," he said, and received an answer in God's language.[156] "*You shall not be able to see me!*" That is, if you want to see Me like this—with the eye of the world—you can never see Me. This expression is an exaggerated rejection, and it is astonishing. Because you are already in a state

156 M. 50.

of having been drowned due to seeing Me, how can you still say, "Appear to me and let me look at You?" Otherwise, how can one fall into doubt about Moses? He is the darling of God, his Prophet. The Qur'an is full of places where he is mentioned, even as it's said, "If someone loves something very much, he speaks of it often."

After God told Moses, "*You shall not be able to see Me*," He said, "*Look at the mountain!*" That mountain is the self of Moses, and due to his greatness and unshakable perseverance, God called it a mountain. This means, "If you look at your own *nafs*, you will see Me." This is a word that is very close to, "The one who knows himself (his own *nafs*) knows his Lord." As Moses looked at himself, he saw his God, and as *He revealed His glory* [7:143], his self was annihilated—the "mountain" crumbled to dust. How could it be otherwise, for how could you consider it appropriate for God to reject the prayer of a prophet like Moses who speaks with Him, showing him a lifeless mountain? After that Moses said, "*O Lord! I turn to You in repentence* [7:143]!" That is, he meant, "I repent of the sin of asking to see You when already I was drowned in sight."

❊

The Sleep of the People of God

The sleep of the people of God is not sleep. Perhaps it is wakefulness itself. Because there are things that are not shown to a human being when he is awake. Because of his fragility and weakness, they are shown only during sleep, within dreams, so that he might endure them. And when the human being matures, then they are shown to him without a veil.

❊

How Long Is the Way

Someone asked, "How long is the way that goes from the servant to his Lord?"

I said, "It is as long as the way that goes from God to the servant." Even if one says "thirty thousand years," it won't be right, because it doesn't have a limit—it can't be measured. It is impossible to define something that has no measure; it is impossible to talk about the end of an endless thing—it would be false and meaningless. Know that an infinite thing is very distant from that which has an end, but this is the aspect of words that pertain to form which has no relationship to infinity. Yet wherever there are words, God is also there. And words will go on *until the Day the time whereof is known* [15:37].

When the dervish begins to speak, one should not oppose his words. Yes, the rule is this: that every word spoken at the *madrasah*, every thought studied at the *madrasah*, is very useful for debate and discussion. But those words are distant from this purpose; they have nothing to do with what I am talking about.

True Strength

A man had brought an Indian sword to a friend. "This is an Indian sword," he said to him.

His friend asked, "What's so special about an Indian sword?"

He answered, "It cuts everything it hits into two."

And the poor friend said, "A Sufi is the child of the moment. Let's strike the sword on that stone pillar over there; let's test it," and immediately he brought the sword and struck it against the stone. The sword broke into two.

He turned to his friend and said, "Now, didn't you say that this sword would cut everything it hits in two?"

His friend said, "Yes, the sword was a real Indian sword for sure, but the stone was more skillful."

Moses was more Pharoah than Pharaoh.

Brothers Beyond Time

Muhammad said, "Oh! how I miss my brothers!"

His companions asked, "O Messenger of God! Did you want us who are your brothers?"

"No, you are my friends," he said.

"Then your brothers are the prophets who have come before you and have now passed from the world?" they asked.

The Blessed Prophet said, "No, it is not those brothers of mine that I am missing, either. I am missing the graceful servants—the saints of God—who will come after me."

Just Be a Dervish

I was about to reach the age of puberty, but I hadn't yet completely matured. Thirty or forty days had passed, but because of this love [of God], I still didn't want to eat anything.

In the city of Hamadan there was a preacher who had begun to harangue the people, "Everybody compares God to somebody." The town preacher had gone to the pulpit and begun to quote the Qur'anic verses related to similitude. In front of the pulpit, the Qur'an reciters were reciting verses like, *The Most Gracious is seated on the throne of His Almightiness* [20:5], and then, *Can you ever feel secure that He who is in heaven will not cause the earth to swallow you up when, lo, it begins to quake?* [67:16] and, *Your Sustainer stands revealed, as well as the angels, rank upon rank* [89:22]; and *They fear their Sustainer high above them* [16:50].

The preacher was one of those who had fallen into the way of metaphoric belief, and he began to explain the meaning of these verses from the point of view of similitude. He also related *hadith* like: "You shall see your Lord as if you are seeing the full moon at night," "God created Adam in His own form," "I saw my Lord in a red robe." He was relating these beautiful traditions that have a number of meanings, and interpreting them from the point of view of similitude. He was saying, "Woe to anyone who doesn't construct a metaphor for God with these attributes of His and doesn't know Him through these forms! Even though they may worship Him, still they will go to Hell. Their worship won't be accepted, because they deny the form of God."

While he was conveying the verses and *hadith* related to this, other people were asserting the Absolute Being of God and His formlessness, and they were questioning him. They countered the preacher's words with verses like: *Wherever you are, He is together with you* [57:4] and *There isn't anything that is like Him* [42:11], but he interpreted them all by way of metaphor, uniting them all within the perspective of similitude. He would not acknowledge the perspective of the absoluteness of God and His incomparability, and made the people tremble with fear of it.

The people went home and told all of this to their spouses and their children and counseled: "Imagine that God is seated on a throne. In a very beautiful way, He has extended his two feet downwards to the footstool, and as the town preacher says, the angels have surrounded His throne. Whoever says that He doesn't have such forms, has no faith. Alas for his death, alas for his grave, alas for his end!"

The next week, a Sunni preacher who was a stranger arrived. The Qur'an reciters (*hafiz*) recited the verses of transcendance. This preacher began to speak about and interpret the verses, *There is nothing like Him* [42:11]; *He didn't give birth, nor was He born* [112:3]; *The heavens have been rolled with His hands . . .* [39:67].[157] He said that the people of similitude should be flayed. "Whoever speaks of such things is a blasphemer; whoever talks about forms for God, can't be saved from Hell. Alas for the religion and the grave of one who attributes a location to God!" he said. He explained away all the verses that related to similitude, interpreting them one by one, and he threatened people with Hell so intensely and frightened them so much that they came to the conclusion that whoever talks about similitude, his worship is not worship, and his faith is not faith.

"Alas for the poor one who says that God needs location! Alas for those who listen to such words!" he said. Those who heard these words of the Sunni preacher became very frightened and returned to their homes confused and saddened.

---

157 *. . . the heavens will be rolled up in His right hand: limitless is He in His glory, and sublimely exalted above anything to which they may ascribe a share in His divinity.* [*Surah az-Zumar*, The Throngs 39:67]

One of them, when he came home, didn't sit down to eat his dinner but went into a corner and sat with his head bent to his knees, and he began to weep like a child. All his children gathered around him, but he sent them away, shouting and yelling at them. The children ran to their mother.

The poor woman came to him: "Effendi! May you be well! Our food is getting cold. Aren't you going to eat? You are yelling at the children and sending them away; what's the matter? They are all crying," she said.

The man said, "Go away! Such a fire is burning me."

The woman asked him again, "Are you putting aside God, in Whom you have always placed your hope and trust? What's going on? You have always been a patient man; up until now, many troubles have come to you, but you have been patient through them all and passed through them easily. You have relied upon God; and God has rescued you from all those difficulties and made your heart content. Out of gratitude for those past blessings, turn this trouble, also, over to God, and don't pay attention to it, so that He might pour His Grace upon you."

Upon these words, the man's heart softened. "What am I to do? They have left us helpless; we are on the verge of death! Last week a preacher insisted, 'Know that God is seated on the throne; anyone who doesn't know Him on the throne is a blasphemer. If he dies, he dies a blasphemer.' And then this week, another preacher came and went up to the pulpit and said, 'Whoever believes that God is seated upon a throne and thinks of such things, like imagining Him to be in the heavens, that person's deeds and worship will not be accepted, because God is exempt from space.' Now, with these contradictory words, which side should we take? How will we live? How will we die? We are left helpless!" he said.

The woman replied, "Don't be bewildered; don't be confused! Whether God is upon the throne, or whether He is not on a throne, or whether He sits somewhere or He is without a place, let Him be wherever He is, and may He live long, and may His glory be eternal. Just think about being a dervish and pay attention to your own dervishhood."

The Most Important Questions

In Arabic, three letters are used for swearing: *Waw, Be, Te.* I swear by each of these, "*wa'llah,*" "*bi'llah,*" "*ta'llah*"[158] that those who get educated in the *madrasah* are all thinking, "Let me get a position as a state official or in a *madrasah.*" These people who study in the religious schools are doing so in order to gain recognition and teaching positions. They tell people one must do beautiful deeds; they talk about such things in the gatherings so that they might get positions.

Why are you learning for the sake of a worldly morsel?! This rope is for climbing out of the well, not for clinging to, and falling further into other wells!

Bind yourself to these questions: "Who am I and what is my essence? Why have I come here and where am I going? Where is my origin? What am I involved in right now and towards what must I turn my face?"

Don't Backbite

To talk about someone who is not present is gossip; and to remember that which is present, is estrangement. Now, the person who remembers God,[159] and talks about God is not beyond this state. He is either present or absent. If He is absent, the one who talks about Him has gossiped; if He is present, one who speaks about Him only adds distance. For instance, a person who sits in front of the sultan can say, "The sultan has said this . . . ," or "The sultan has done this . . . ," but if he backbites, it is one of the great sins.

---

158 These are the exclamations that begin with the letters *w*, *b* and *t*, meaning "By God," (Consider) "For God's sake," "O my God!" (How can you not see?! You will see!) Shams is emphasizing what he is stating.

159 The word used for "remembrance" of God is *dhikr*, which is also the word used for chanting God's name.

Backbiting is one of the four great sins that are counted apart from other sins because of their ugliness. Among these four great sins, the first is backbiting, the second is bearing false witness, the third is murder, and the fourth is torture. Unless the one harmed forgives them, there is no way to be saved from punishment.

For the one with whom the sultan shares his secrets, praise is the form of nourishment. The *nafs* waits, saying, "Our lot hasn't yet come; this is not our lot." It never leaves us. It holds us by the throat. Where will we go, how will we be saved? We have fallen into such an *ayran*—it is without end![160] It is not contained by any cup, and so it has no boundary.

He begins to move out of the *ayran*, but then slips back into it.

"It's the honey," he says.

The more he moves his wings to get free, the deeper into it he sinks.[161]

❊

A Shaikh May Be Watching

Abu Najib (May God bless his spirit) had entered into seclusion because of a difficult situation. Several times in his dreams he was told that this difficult thing could not be accomplished without him—that is, he ought to go to see a certain shaikh.

"Let me go and visit him, but I wonder where will I see him?" he said.

A voice came: "You cannot see him."

"Then, what will I do?"

The answer came: "Come out of your seclusion, and come to the mosque. Walk around among the rows with an entreating and peaceful heart! Maybe he will see you—his eye may discover you."

---

160 *Ayran* is a yogurt drink. The metaphor of a fly falling into *ayran* is often used to signify immersion in a difficulty.

161 This image reflects back to the swimmer in the Sea and remembrance of Abu Bakr—surrender, and the Sea will carry you.

Now, when the situation of Abu Najib is like this, even if I am left without a shaikh, I am not really left without a shaikh.

❊

Confused Comings and Goings

A man died. They brought a hired mourner. He asked the relatives of the dead person: "Tell me the skills of the deceased one. Was he knowledgeable?"

"No," they said.

"Was he religious, a pious worshipper?"

"No!"

The mourner turned his face towards the Kaaba and asked again, "Did he pay attention to the poor and those who need help, and did he help them?"

"No," they said.

In short, whatever he asked, he could get no answer other than "No," nor could he gain any hints from their answers, so he began to weep: "O the poor one, he came confused and left confused!"

❊

A Stranger in the Dergah

One day, at the dergah (*tekke*), the dervishes were unable to concentrate on the *sema* no matter how they tried.

The shaikh said, "Be careful! There is a stranger among our dervishes."

They searched around and said, "No, there is no stranger here."

"Then check the shoes," the shaikh responded.

"Yes, there is a strange pair of shoes," they answered.

"Put those shoes outside of the *dergah*," he said.

They put them out, and immediately the *sema* ritual settled into order.

The intellect can find a way to the *dergah*, but it can't come all the way inside. There, intellect is a veil, heart is a veil, even the secret (*sirr*)[162] is a veil.

❁

Grasp the Essence

A man said to a barber, "Pick these white hairs out of my beard."

The barber saw that the white hairs outnumbered the black. First, he cut the man's beard with scissors, and then he put it into his hand and said, "Now, you pick them out! I've got other things to do!"

Grasp the essence! What are those things that you choose as clothes, as food, and as protection from the enemy? How can you say, "They are looking down on me," or "So and so isn't paying any attention to me"? Leave the branch or the twig, and weep for your origin and the root. Think of the origin and weep for it![163] Moan and scream so that you might see those branches and twigs sprout and grow.

Let all the arrogant, majestic, kingly ones, and the illustrious masters of knowledge prostrate their heads on the floor in front of you. Don't even turn around to glance at them! Then, even if you try to get rid of them, they won't leave. But if you cling to these branches and twigs, you'll lose the origin and root, and you won't gain anything from the branches.

❁

Advice

I give advice, but no matter how many times I give advice, some benefit by it, while others have gotten hurt. Their getting hurt spreads to me, and affects me. I said, "If giving advice is not appropriate in a certain situation, then let's begin to pray for those who affirm that God is Most Great and for those who are helpless so that they might come closer."

---

162 The *sirr* is the inmost essence of the human being. Existence is a veil. All aspects of individual existence must be put aside in order to enter the Divine Presence.

163 Saddened that you have lost it, weep so that you may regain it.

You are weeping for every branch like the young sufi who prostrated himself at my feet and said, "After having followed so and so, I lost all my possessions. I have let go of all kinds of work," and he added, "Now my hope is in a single greeting from you. Speak it so that I may return home, or cast your glance upon me!"

"I cannot do what you ask. Why not be someone whom a thousand people like that would be ready to serve?"

"What must I do?" he said.

I answered: "You must unite with the origin; you must find the origin that everyone is seeking. You have to search for the origin of origins, the goal of all goals, not the root that will break off in your hand like a rotten branch one day. You have to work with all your might to search for the origin. You have to take everything that troubles your heart, and that causes you to drift away from the goal seriously into account. If you think that it is easy to attain, you will have underestimated the goal."

❊

Opening to the Light

There is no blame for the blind, and there is no blame for the lame, either. [48:17] If a person wants it, "advice" is for the one who has faith, because in comparison to the person of faith, everyone else is blind and lame. The one who sees, and the one who walks beautifully is such a person that Gabriel can't keep up with him. He says, "Come" to Gabriel, and Gabriel answers, "No, I cannot come; if I come even an inch closer, I'll get burned."[164]

In Reality, He is the one who is steadfast. Honest color and true temperament are His. Therefore He Himself speaks; He Himself listens. He is not speaking to anyone else.

What is the interpretation of this? All the time, the learned and educated ones burn in our Hell. This is how our Hell is. There is

164 These are the words that the Archangel Gabriel spoke in response to Muhammad when during the *Mi'raj* Muhammad was approaching the Presence of God. Muhammad continued alone into God's Presence.

a kind of person about whom Hell complains. "Hell has come," it moans. Hell complains, "He has come to Hell!" when Hell sees him.

Hell wishes the faithful well and tells them, "Pass on, O faithful one; your light will extinguish my fire!"

One of the great ones came to the grave of a saint. He saw that he had passed from the world veiled. He sat there for forty days and waited at the head of the grave so that his work might be completed.

❊

Investigate

Now, come and tell us how the rising of the sun and the turning of the skies is according to your way of thinking? How can one understand the things that astronomers relate, from the outer meaning of the Qur'an?

Come; let's investigate. "A believer is an investigator." Today, one has to accept the intelligent information about the stars.

Let's say I belong to the Shafi'i sect,[165] and I have found something in the Hanafi sect which would help my work and improve it. If I didn't accept it, it would be obstinacy.

The wise one is completely aware of a person's state, he smiles at every word he hears, and he knows from which rank it is spoken. He knows in which station that person is. He sees who is who, sees each one's station, and thanks God that He hasn't tied him to that rank, that it has passed from him.

God has many servants. He wants a meaning and a wisdom from each one of them. And each man of wisdom is aware of everyone's state and is familiar with them, too. And others who know this man of wisdom see him and don't see anybody other than God in him.

---

165 The Shafi'i sect is one of the four major schools of law within Islam, following the example of Imam as-Shafi'i. The other three are Hanafi, Maliki, and Hanbali.

This and That

God Most High did not withhold His secret from this servant of His. Which secret of His does He ever withhold? But He speaks about the secrets of the world in a veiled way; you need have no fear about that. Well, for this reason Muhammad said, "I know best about the matters of the next world, and you know better about the things of this world!"

There is a reason for that, and there is a reason for this, too: *A person cannot know beforehand what he will be earning tomorrow, and no soul knows in which land he will die* [31:34].

Whose Universe Are You Watching?

Someone said: "I was on a ship. A jewel like the sun shone over the ocean. Immediately I looked at the sea and that gem. It almost took away the light of my eyes; I covered my eyes with my hands." Then he talked about his spectacular observations and the strange wonders of the sea.

I said to him, "Do you want to see miraculous things? Come and watch my inside! You are always watching your own universe; you are only seeing what is inside of you. Come and watch my universe, see what is within me!"

God Knows Best

There is nothing superior to the Qur'an; there is no word above the Word of God. But, this Qur'an has come for the common people, and in its verses that guide people with commands and prohibitions, there is one kind of taste. There is a different pleasure in its words for the people of God who have attained realization. God knows best.

Guided by the Heart

A person binds himself to a shaikh, to a guide of deep heart.[166] Or, one day, a friend goes and begs something from those of the past, or from those that are living, or from someone whom he thinks has a heart. After that he doesn't forget about his *nafs*, but he turns his face to the direction of the heart, and withdraws into a corner.

In the middle of the night, he separates from his spouse and children and takes shelter in a corner of the house and weeps deeply. Like this he waits, until the time comes when a light appears from the land of the heart. Abruptly, remembering the joy of heart for which he had longed, he prostrates himself weeping, and God sweetens again his relationship with him.

Be a Friend

My wish is to improve human beings, that is, to guide them to the right path, and always to make possible that which is impossible. As it mentions in the Qur'an, just like Jesus, I want to heal the hopelessly blind and the leprous people. Let me choose the way of friendship, and let me direct friends towards friendship as well. Well, why don't you walk in this way, too!

The End is to Return to the Beginning

Now, when the state of the saints, the lovers and beloveds is like this, the answer of Junayd to the question, "What is the end?" was this: "The end, is to return to the beginning."

One of the outer meanings is that just as the traveler, the disciple, worships, chants, and prays openly in the beginning, also from now on because an awe has come to him, he can no longer worship in the same way.

---

166 M. 55.

The good deeds of the people of God correspond to the degree of useless deeds of the people who are close to them.

Whoever has become our friend, must worship more than he did before. I am not saying to friends, "What relationship do the words that we spoke yesterday have with the words of Bayazid, Junayd, or Hallaj, that master of disgrace?" But follow my words about worshipping! Because, the people whose names were just mentioned could never be even a hair on the beard of Muhammad.

Interpreting Truly

Joseph was a great prophet. He was proud that he knew how to interpret dreams, and at the same time he was thankful to God for it.[167] The prophets long to be in his presence.

Now I am saying this because Mevlana thinks well of him—and this is how I, also, consider him to be. I don't see a superiority in myself—I wonder why it is that words that please him come out of me? I wonder why—this is not my state. One day, though, when I became tired of words, I caught the collar of one of the words coming to me from I knew not where, from whom or which direction: "From where do I speak?" I asked.

"From God."

"Where and to whom do I speak?"

"To a great human being," and this is Mevlana.

The Truth Is Not Bound to Time

When it comes to talking about Muhammad, peace and blessings upon him, I can't say anything, because his work is so huge. When God dipped him into and took him out of the Sea of Beneficence, from each one of the drops of light sprinkling from his holy body an apostle, a prophet has come into existence. And from the drops that were left behind, the saints of God were created.

167 See *Surah Yusuf*, Joseph 12:101.

And so, how could I even speak about them with the same breath? I can only say, "The one who has come last is superior to those who came before." How could I compare another prophet with Muhammad? This knowledge came to me without my being educated in a particular science or expending intellectual effort or other work—this state is the abundance of my obedience to him.

And this was the first word that I spoke with him [Mevlana]: "How was it that Bayazid Bastami didn't grasp following him? Why didn't he also say, 'Glory be to You! We could not worship You as You ought to be worshipped!'"[168]

With his perfection, Mevlana understood the whole of these words and their unfolding. Where do these words lead? Where do they end? Because of the purity of his inner spirit, Mevlana became intoxicated. His drunkenness was a completely clean and pure drunkenness. I had known the pleasure and taste of these words, but through his drunkenness I realized a higher pleasure of these words of which I had been unaware.

These words are only my words; they are not my state. If they were my state, they couldn't be either inferior or superior. And these words came to an end in this way. At the same time, though, my words are also for someone else in another time. The Truth is not bound to time; the Truth doesn't die.

What role does time have? Yes, Truth doesn't die with the passing of time, but you are a being that has a name—did that name come to you from you?

❉

"My Shaikh"

A disciple needs to be very respectful towards his shaikh. This is why they say, "see him through his disciple."

---

168 In Arabic the word for "teacher" is "Rabb," often translated as "Lord," but having the meaning "the one who educates and raises up." The word for "serving" and "worshipping" is the same, so one who is a servant is also one who worships. Muhammad used to pray, "O my God, we have not worshipped You as You ought to be worshipped."

They asked a disciple, "Is your master better or Bayazid Bastami?"

"My master is better," he said.

"Well, then, is your master better or the Prophet, peace be upon him?"

"My master."

"Or, is your master better or God?"

"My master," he said, "because it is through him that I have found this secret of oneness and unity, through no one but him."

Well, this is how the understanding of unity is for those who remain at the level of metaphor, but it would be better to say:

> I have become my darling, and my darling
> has become me.
> We have become two spirits within one body.

This is a metaphor, a similitude, but it's different from the metaphor of that dervish. The path between that and the universe of Oneness is a long road.

What is appropriate for me is to protect the path upon which our friendship and the brotherhood of our outer life walk. Other than that, relationships like "shaikh and disciple" give me no pleasure. You know, some say, "Let shaikhhood and disciplehood vanish into the earth."[169]

Strive to Do the Good

They tell a story about Ali (may God be pleased with him). He had said, "We were in the Baqi cemetery and offering the funeral *salaat.* The Prophet came to us and said, 'There is no man or woman for whom God has not written whether he or she will go to Paradise or to Hell.'

"One of those who were there asked, 'I wonder, can we change this destiny?'

"He said, 'Endeavor—do good deeds. Each facilitates the work for which he or she is created; people created for Paradise make

169 Shams uses an expression resembling "let it go to hell."

easier the deeds of the people of Paradise; and those who were created for Hell make easier the work of the people of Hell.'

"After this, the Prophet recited the following verses from *Surah Layl* [92:5-7]: *And so, as for one who gives to others and is conscious of God, and believes in the truth of the ultimate good—for him shall we make easy the path towards ultimate ease.*"

Stay Fresh

There isn't a continuous insight from the beginning of the cloak of dervishhood until the end. I stayed clean and I also want those people who are concerned with desire and carnal passions, whom I don't like, to keep clean and clear.

Always keep yourself fresh, so that you don't meet with the saying of the Blessed Prophet to Abu Hurayrah: "Visit me now and then so that affection may grow!" If you hear this from him with the tongue of the heart, you should go into seclusion and weep: "What's happened to me, what has happened that I'm being spoken to in this way? These words are not said to close friends or even other friends."

Weep for this state of yours and perhaps you will come to some ease. Whether you pay attention to it or not, the words, "Visit me now and then," have come out of their mouths.

The reason for the *hadith* about this visiting is this: Abu Hurayrah used to carry the shoes of Blessed Mustafa. He used to touch them to his head and eyes, and then he would place them upon his head. But once, he hastily put the shoes in their place, without giving them so much attention. No one else has said this—this is a secret. This once, let me explain it:

Blessed Muhammad inwardly said, "He used to put the shoes upon his head and touch them to his eyes, and I would invoke God Most High. 'O My Lord,' I would say, 'have my shoes become so worthless as to be placed on his head and eyes?' Now, because you have darkened, to your eye I appear to have darkened. Don't look at me with darkened eyes!"

The purpose of the example of this "Visit me now and then" is this—look at me with such an eye that you might not weary of me; always see me as fresh and new, because I never grow old. Don't let yourself grow old, either. If there is a feeling of weariness in your glance, see to refreshing your sight—say, "I wonder, what is the reason for this?"

Say, "I wonder what has happened—have I been sitting with people of useless desires?" Look for the error within yourself.

To say, "Visit me now and then!" means, "Go and quickly see the truth within me." This seeing is beneficial for you. Renew yourself. I am already new. Prove yourself. I am constant and determined. If you cannot see me as persevering, it's because of your own lack of perseverance.

❊

Realize the Being of God

What use does saying that God exists, or trying to prove that He exists have for the being of God? Pay attention to making yourself exist so that the whole night the angels may praise you, and that about you they might say, "He has realized the Being of God."

Muhammad said, "Happy is the one who sees me, and happy is he who has seen the one who sees me." Even if he says this a hundred times, it isn't too much. "Whoever sees me, I see him, then he becomes like me." This speaker speaks words and looks carefully to see if he is understood. He doesn't intentionally make things complicated or confusing. His words end like they begin.

"Everyone who drinks wine, sooner or later gets drunk."

But if he keeps his wine within the jug, its quality strengthens.

❊

Disappearing in Friendship

I don't have the power to see Mevlana. Mevlana also says the same about me. But, according to me, friendship means to kill one's *nafs* after seeing Mevlana, so that they may say, "We couldn't find him anymore, he's dead." Today, consider this gathering of friends as a spoil of war and a gift of God, and a blessed opportunity.

❁

Entering Paradise

More and more one becomes satisfied (*nafs al-mutmainnah*)—one comes to a state of having faith in the Truth and having become more content with it—and after this, a trace of maturity, a continuous faith, and peace of consciousness remains within you. Well, then, that means you have reached the Truth.

After God Most High said, *O, soul that is content and has faith! Enter among my servants!* to the contented *nafs*, there may be those who perhaps think that there was no need to strengthen this honoring of His by also saying, *Enter my paradise*![170] However, the *nafs* by which one has to swear is the *nafs al-lawwamah*—the blaming self, not the contented self. One swears only by the repentant self (*nafs al-lawwamah*) because the contented self (*nafs al-mutmainnah*) is too dear.

Similarly, God gathered all the angels within His presence; it was impossible for them not to obey His command. And the inspiration that we have placed into anyone's heart has been put there by God—it is only God who has created it in that heart.

❁

May the Remembrance of Your Tongue Be the Remembrance of Your Heart

Someone said, "I want to call upon God."

Another responded, "May you not be separated from the One whose name you call." Then your calling becomes the remembrance of the heart; remembrance with only the tongue is not enough.

Bayazid Bastami used to chant with his heart. Why didn't he also chant with his tongue! Because he was spiritually drunk he said,

---

170 *[But unto the righteous God will say,] "O thou human being that hast attained to inner peace! Return thou unto thy Sustainer, well-pleased [and] pleasing [Him]: enter, then, together with My [other true] servants—yea, enter thou My paradise!"* [*Surah Fajr*, The Daybreak 89:27-30]

"Glory be to me!" In this state of drunkenness, he wasn't able to follow Blessed Mustafa, who was beyond drunkenness. Bayazid was so drunk that it was impossible for him to follow the sober ones.

Witnessing God's Beauty

Everyone knows the story of that scholar who taught the Qur'an—he used to teach seven kinds of recitation. He asked one gold coin for each verse. This was the contract he made with his students. His motto was: "Forms are many, but meaning is one."

For sixteen years, I have kept the parable that I learned from my master as a remembrance: he said, "People are like a cluster of grapes. From the point of view of form, the grapes are numerous. But if we squeeze this cluster into a cup, no trace of number remains." Put these words to use.

No other sight can kill the cluster of the desires of the commanding self, *nafs al-ammarah*, as well as its witnessing of the beauty within the universe of the heart. When it sees the universe of God's beauty, it immediately weakens. That commanding self is like the powerful sultan before whom everyone else is helpless—when a little bit of poison is given to him in a cup, his hands and feet lose their tenacity, and all of his aggressiveness disappears.

The Light of Muhammad

If the light of Muhammad were to fall upon a heart, it would burn both you and the master in whom you trust. The pearl radiates light—whether below or above, it illuminates every direction at once. Who are you in comparison to that benevolent Meccan?

If the light has appeared to someone and then hasn't reappeared, he doesn't deny it; he holds to that possibility. "It is a souvenir of harmony, it is a remembering," he says.

Can anybody ever be superior to Muhammad? He splits the moon in the heavens in two![171]

❋

There Is No Monasticism in Islam

"There is no monasticism in Islam," it was said. This does not mean, "Be with people all the time." Observe people from a distance, but speak words of Truth to them, and speak in a pleasant and subtle way.

If someone comes to you in the midst of your life and says, "The secret of the words is not like that," then ask him the difference between the words of the people and the word that has no letters or voice. If he answers you rightly, prostrate at his feet; if he says, "What is the secret of these words? That is for strangers," and if he shows you signs, and enlightens you about this matter, and if majesty, greatness, and the power of God is seen in him, then he is our younger brother. But he must be such a brave person with such a trouble, such a love within him that it burns away every delusion, imagination, or hesitation, and tears away the veils of doubt.

The *hadith* "I have such a moment with God that neither a prophet with a book nor an angel close to God can enter in between us" is an invitation, not just a state. This means, "Do something like this so that this state may also be yours."

❋

The Sun's Business is Shining

He says, "O Sun! don't radiate any more divine light, so that the hearts of the bats may not be hurt."

But this is the business of the sun; of course it will radiate light. Would it ever stop shining so that the eyes of the bats might not be hurt?

---

171 M. 60.

It is related that one memorable night in the Prophet's presence the moon appeared to split into two distinct parts. The splitting of the moon is also referred to in the Qur'an as a sign—a harbinger of the Day of Resurrection and the standing before God.

He said, "The sun isn't troubled by bats or those with weak eyes. It just keeps radiating light."

Only those who worship the sun have any fear. They think, "Perhaps the sun may feel sad, hide behind a cloud, or toy with us, and we might be left without its light."

Then he said, "Someone who worships the sun must believe in the sun like this—they mustn't show disrespect to the sun." But the belief of the faithful must be so strong in certainty that they are able to pass over the mountain, so that they may see the seven-headed lion and grab it by its ears, and so that they might not suffer, because of the strength of their faith and love of the light of day.

Faith and love turn human beings into heroes—they remove all fear.

I Have Such a Moment with God

"I have such a moment with God . . . ," is an invitation. Otherwise, if it were a state, as we said before, could the word "I" have a place within that state? Then where is "with"; what place could four different things like "nearness," "angels," "books" and "sent messengers" have there? These words have been spoken as words—they are each invitations.

There is never despair. If this state were to remain for two moments, within the first moment there is "hope," and within the second moment, cry out and lose yourself. Cry out so strongly that there may be hopes and laughter within it.

Words of Joy

Smiles and laughter certainly are not caused by grief, neither are boundless joys. Everybody has some joy. The pious ascetic, the worshipper, the scholar, the saint, and the prophet, each has his or her own joy.

In short, even if the secret of these words is ancient, the secret of the secret within the words is older. And so, they bow their heads, they surrender before the sword of these words. There is also a kind of speech that is beautiful, but endless, and brings with it despair.

"The best speech is brief but deep in meaning." Isn't the beauty in the words of the Prophet Muhammad because of this?

There are so many veils of darkness and light that cover the Self of God, that these thousands of obstacles rend the rope of hope. Even if a person reads books for a thousand years, he can never have the temperament of Blessed Muhammad, and that reading will have been no use to him. What use to a donkey is a sack of books loaded on its back?

☼

Rather than Debate, Prove the Truth!

Learn how to debate—if you are tired of truth and reality—get educated in the science of debate!

Discussion is the blending of different words and ideas—if someone's words are a lie, debate isn't necessary. If all his words are true, because there is no incompatibility or contradiction, again there's no need for debate or discussion.

You always say this is so; you never claim the contrary. If it is clearly understood that there is truth in something—this truth doesn't manifest by itself. Try to prove it through your self.

Whether it is truth or it is a lie, discussion, obstinacy, and inappropriate arguments aren't useful for you. If the claim is true, then God will hold accountable the one who thinks the opposite, even if the person busy with the debate is one of the saints!

☼

O Glorious Morning Light!

In the seventh verse of *Surah Dhuha* [The Glorious Morning Light 93:7], it is said, "*Didn't he find you having wandered from the way, and guide you*?" What does this mean? O Muhammad! God found you having lost your way; He showed you the true way—everybody has interpreted this as meaning that the Truth found him in a state where he had lost his way. Is He like a shepherd who loses a calf, and then runs this way and that way so that He may find it?"

Rather, Muhammad found that he himself had wandered. That is, he found his *self* that had wandered by means of his *Self*.

❊

Umar and Abu Bakr

Muhammad asked Gabriel, "What is Umar's rank with God?" Gabriel answered: "Even if I had a life four times longer than the life that was given to the Prophet Noah, and I began to tell you about his virtues, still I wouldn't be able to finish." Muhammad asked again, "And what would you say about Abu Bakr?" Gabriel gave this answer, "Even with all Umar's superior qualities, he is only one of the beautiful traits of Abu Bakr."

❊

Waking into Presence

It is necessary, from time to time, for the *nafs* to leave "the between," so that joy might show its face and a light might appear in it, and that the *nafs* might reach a point beyond which it cannot go.[172]

If that light were only temporarily in him, it would not be coming from the *nafs*, but, if you are on His way, one day it comes to you and decides to remain in you. We have spoken these words now so as not to leave things until the last minute. As the poet points out: "Let's say, I will reach union with God . . . "[173]

There seems to be a weakness here, but from the perspective of its fitting the situation it is very strong; because the fragrance of union is coming from that weakness:

> I am asleep, but this is wakefulness.
> How would those who sleep know that I am awake?

---

172 Shams seems to be referring here again to the *hadith*: "I have such a moment with God that neither a prophet with a book nor an angel close to God can enter in between," reminding us also of the moment of the Prophet's *Mi'raj* when even Gabriel could not go further with him.

173 See p.95 of this text.

❊

Playing Chess

He said, "If there is a thorn, you have to burn it."

I said, "That's following Noah, not Muhammad." With his prayer, "O Lord! Guide my people to the right way," he wasn't wanting to openly reveal the manifestation of those words. These people who go through severe trials are following Moses, because they have found a little taste in that. Now it is easy to be like this. If you become like this, my work will be easy.

I am a man who has two aspects. I move my hand from one piece to another and return the king to his own place and protect him from being checkmated. Without being checkmated outside, the king comes back to his place, and then this king is never checkmated. Though he can be compared with other kings who are checkmated, he's different from those kings who hide at home and become checkmated there.

He has spoken these words, but you aren't saying anything. In order to explain the Truth, it's possible to say just a few things and then bring forth hundreds of clear evidences for each word.

❊

Love Makes One Blind to All but the Beloved

He said, "God has given the staff of servanthood into the hands of the blind, because they are able to attain the real meaning of servanthood." Maybe by the help of that staff you can receive a fragrance from prayers and *salaat*. Why is this happening like this? Imagine the Prophet in front of your eyes with all his maturity. If a person believes that he can educate people by just teaching them how to read and write, he is a sweet little veiled one. Such a person has no authority nor any knowledge about anything. If he thinks he can educate them by love, this means that he has some wisdom.

The Blessed Prophet used to do *salaat* until his feet would swell. He would say, "*Allahu Akbar*"[174] and within that state, he would be absent from the world.

❋

Philosophers

Is the Resurrection with bodies or spirits? According to the philosopher, the spirits are gathered on the Day of Resurrection. He is a fool—he reads only what he himself writes and whatever he doesn't know, he thinks is impossible. According to him, things that are beyond his belief are disasters, and even if Bayazid Bastami were to hold his reins, it would make no difference.

❋

Towards That Universe

Sometimes my heart contracts. A moment comes when instead of answering, you keep silent. All of these inappropriate things come from this. People are talking, and you are not answering, but just keeping silent all the time. At least you know how at ease I am in my abode—you know my state. If somebody from the outside says something, you don't say, "I see this clearly—I see it with my eyes in a way that is brighter even than the sun."

You say, "Saints of God have signs."

Don't you know the sign within the self of the saints? When the saints are left helpless, due to that weakness of theirs, either a light of heart occurs in them or a blurriness comes to their spirits. Just as Satan was left in the darkness due to his weakness, the angels reached the light because of theirs. This is how a miracle happens. The signs of the Truth are also like this. When they are left helpless, immediately they bow down.

---

174 "God is Greater." This is the phrase that begins each cycle of prayer of the *salaat*.

"I can know a person at first glance," he was saying. He is greatly in error. First of all, he can't speak with the judge, and the vizier will be of no help to him either. First come over to the right side and sit down.

If he says, "I love others beside you also for your sake," then you should say something different than this—say, "My heart will return to its place when you long for Mevlana Shamsuddin. Love me because of him."

I say, "Whatever he says, answer him, even if he doesn't speak, still you should speak." You and I are in a terrible and stressful place together. In such and such a place, he killed thirty thieves and also captured thirty people. The man you see—his head has been cut, and he is covered with blood, but I am showing the world as very beautiful, serene, and safe. I am reciting poems that give joy to the heart. I have no fear of anything.

He is asking me, "What do you want? If thirty people come and cut your mother's throat, would you say, 'Go and let them slaughter you, too, so that your spirit may shine!'?"

"No, how can I go?" you say—so, don't go; sit down here.

What has God created me for? What I'm going to say is, "Don't ask for a son-in-law from me! That which was entrusted to me has come to pass."

When I was speaking those words, my face was towards this universe. Under this condition, if they say, "That universe is more pleasing," they have told the truth. So, where is that universe? If it is so, why aren't you going with them? I am asking.

❊

Yearning Opens the Heart

May a person whom God has guided and given food and beneficence show to those who have a doubt about the possibility of seeing God their blindness, in order that they may come to know both God and His servants! Even if a Tatar were to enter through this door, see us, believe in us and turn his face toward us, there is no doubt that he will benefit from us more than these shaikhs, because suddenly by himself he has become filled. What those like him have is yearning for God; a wind of the moment blows and shatters them to pieces.

❁

Being Filled with God

Shaikh Muhammad was laughing at the situation of Sayyid and his friends, and saying, "What kind of a thing to say is this, 'My whole body is filled with God'?" I was also laughing. He thought that I was laughing because I was agreeing with him, but I was laughing at his own situation: "You cannot see yourself!"

He was asleep, and he had a dream of Shihab of Nishabur who was one of the friends. This Shihab is superior to Shaikh Shihabuddin. He is the disciple of Shaikh Najib. . . .

In his dream, Shihab was running to the top of a mountain, and a woman was running after him; after he came to the top, he began to run down the other side. The woman put her fingers to her lips and said, "He has died!"[175]

Early in the morning, Shaikh Muhammad came to the *madrasah* and knocked at the door. They were all upset and said, "Shaikh Shihabuddin has died." Shaikh Muhammad went away. "That was the devil," they said.

When day came, he came back and saw that Shihabuddin had died smiling, with his head upon his hand among the books. Shaikh Muhammad kissed his eyes and beard, said "farewell," and left.

Those who had gathered said, "No, that was either Khidr or an angel who passed by and left!"

If he bore the signs of the present moment, one would be bewildered.

---

175 Shams is referring here to Muhammad Ibn al-Arabi who received intimation through his dream of the passing of Shihabuddin Suhrawardi.

❊

The Meanings of the Qur'an

It is said, "There are many reciters whom the Qur'an curses." The "reciters" mentioned here are referred to in connection with the word for "many" or "several," so it doesn't apply to all readers. There are "readers," *hafizes* [those who have memorized the whole Qur'an] who are experts in reciting the Qur'an. And the pure servants of God are familiar with the seven kinds of meanings of the Qur'an, because the Qur'an has seven levels of meanings such as the outer, the inner, and the inner of the inner. But the seven meanings aren't always in harmony with the customs and understanding of the people who are reading the Qur'an. Some people do know about meanings other than these seven levels and also meanings beyond even those. This is God's work. To be familiar with the seven kinds of meaning, or the hundred thousand kinds of meaning of the Qur'an, is each a different gift of the Truth; it is a grace.

How should those who look for the Truth, and who are His pure servants, put on coquettish airs in front of the Beloved when the time of union comes? Above this station[176] there is another station that is the station of the most elect servants. They are not mentioned in the Qur'an but there is an indication of them. People like them have no relation to the Qur'an "readers" just mentioned. They belong to neither the group who read badly nor those who read well. They are the special and chosen servants of God. I have spoken of them before.

❊

May Your Winter Turn to Spring

Winter is an appropriate opportunity to come together for friends who have fallen apart from each other. Then, you cannot create excuses like, "I am going to the seaside to wander around."

---

176 M. 65.
This rank of *naz*—putting on coquettish airs.

When you go out, you look and see that spring has turned to winter, but if a person knows me well, his winter turns into spring. Whoever behaves righteously and honestly towards me, increase of comfort and well-being reach him from me; he lives even more strongly than I do, and things that don't even occur to my mind, come to his.

❊

The Face of the Sun Is Turned towards Mevlana Because Mevlana's Face Is also Turned towards the Sun

In this endeavor, one has to follow hundreds of Abu Bakrs, instrument players, and Juhas; but without understanding what the degree of strength of these people is, and where they will take the work, why would I do this work?

May God Most High enlighten you with the bright lights that He radiates from the treasure of secrets that He hides from even His own pure servants.

The sun enlightens the whole universe, and the words that come out of my mouth, although they are under black veils, are very bright. This sun is hidden behind them. Their faces are turned towards the heavens, but *the light of the earth and of the heavens is from Him.*[177]

The face of the sun is turned towards Mevlana, because Mevlana's face is also turned towards the sun.

In the Qur'an, God Most High has said, "*Those who strive hard in Our cause—We shall most certainly guide them onto paths that lead unto Us* [29:69]." Well, this verse is an indication of this subtle point.

---

177 See *Surah an-Nur, Light* 24:35:

> *God is the Light of the heavens and the earth. The parable of His light is, as it were, that of a niche containing a lamp; the lamp is [enclosed] in glass, the glass [shining] like a radiant star: [a lamp] lit from a blessed tree—an olive-tree that is neither of the east nor of the west—the oil whereof [is so bright that it] would well-nigh give light [of itself] even though fire had not touched it: light upon light!*
>
> *God guides unto His light him that wills [to be guided]; and [to this end] God propounds parables unto men, since God [alone] has full knowledge of all things.*

The beginning and the end of this verse are related to each other in this way: they can be reversed. *We shall guide on Our ways those who struggle in Us.*

First, understand what the purpose of the question is and then according to it, arise to answer! Various easy questions seem to be difficult at first, but they are useful to remember later.

Who is "He" in the words that you recite, "There is no God but He"? Whom does it indicate?

Someone said, "This is a pulpit in a mosque, you can't speak so openly like this!"

Muhammad made several indications, but never spoke so openly and clearly. But this can never be spoken, because one of those who will understand the words is "I."

The Ascetic on the Mountain

An ascetic lived on a mountain, but he wasn't an ascetic inclined towards people; he had turned into a mountain man, otherwise he would have been living among people who have some understanding and imagination and who have a capacity for the knowledge of God. What was he doing on the mountain? He was earth, so he had turned towards stones. But what does a human being have to do with rocks—what relationship can he have?

Live among people, but in uncrowded places—always be together with God in seclusion; keep to yourself.[178] But don't

178 One feels Shams' alignment with the code of awareness and behavior formulated by 'Abd al-Khaliq Ghudjuvani in the 11th Century (the Laws of the Khwajagan):

Remember every breath. As we breathe we should place our attention on each successive breath and be aware of our own presence. Inattention is what separates us from God. The more that one is able to be conscious of one's breath, the stronger is one's inner life.

Watch each step. Remember where you came from and where you are going. You wish for freedom and you must never forget it. Keep your attention on the step you are taking at this moment.

forget that the Blessed Prophet has said, "There is no monasticism in Islam." From a certain point of view, this is a prohibition against separating oneself. People consider those who leave the mountain and return among human beings to be people of wisdom and miracles.

Another meaning of this *hadith* is that Muslims are prohibited from refraining from marriage and living a life separate from women.[179] Why marry and yet live as a bachelor—what would be the meaning of living apart from everything that is within the heart, everything that is pleasing?

Every year, all the people of the city and the sultan would go to visit the ascetic on the mountain. He liked the way the people showed such a love and regard for him. He would enter into such a state that he felt no desire towards anything anymore—he had even completely stopped eating and drinking.

Journey toward your homeland. You are traveling from the world of appearances to the world of reality. Man cannot know his destiny as long as he is in the subjective dream state.

Solitude in the crowd. Enter into the life of the outer world without losing one's inner freedom. Remember God and do not allow yourself to be identified with anything.

Remember your Friend. You may discover the Friend, i.e., God, through the *being* of your guide. Let the prayer of your tongue be the prayer of your heart.

Return to God. No aim but to attain Reality. We must be single-minded about our goal. The possibility of transformation is a gift to be valued above all other possessions.

Remain watchful. Struggle with alien thoughts. Keep your attention on what you are doing, whether outwardly or inwardly. Observe what captures your attention and why.

Be constantly aware of the Divine Presence. Accustom yourself to recognize the quality of the divine presence in your heart. The "loss of self" allows us to participate in a greater Being.

179 Another *hadith* of the Prophet Muhammad is: "Marriage is half of the faith." Being in partnership polishes the *nafs*, and marriage and family life and all its inherent responsibilities can help the soul to grow in faith, in compassion, in generosity, in all the qualities reflected from the Divine, in trust in the one Sustainer.

One day a strange dervish, a saint passed by, and asked him, "This isn't a holiday, or the spring festival; what is this gathering?"

He answered, "Are you a fool, or are you mad (*majnun*)?
What a pity, Layla doesn't understand the state of Majnun.
Only Majnun knows his state.
"Are you mad?" he said.

Then the dervish said, "Don't speak like that!"

Then he said, "I repent, forgive me," and he prostrated himself at the feet of the dervish.

The dervish said to him, "A fragrance of tasting has come to me from this word of yours." This was a pleasing taste that was caused by his repentance and modesty of heart.

"On this mountain, you know, there is a man of God. They are coming to visit him," he said.

Bright Silence

As Mevlana said, if we speak words with the maturity of our power, it will be received in a more pleasant way. Words spoken taking heed from the heart, spirit, and meaning are more pleasant, but sometimes they can be misleading. So let me be silent, that is better!

He answered, "If you are silent, your speech becomes brighter, because both the light of silence and the value of speech are hidden within silence."

Essential Breath

A dervish went into the presence of the sultan, greeted him, and said, "Listen to a word from me."

Upon the sweet words of the dervish, the sultan pulled back the reins of his horse. His heart was overcome, and he got down off his horse. He said to himself, "Whatever this dervish wants, let me give it to him—goods, buildings and land, even if he wants my daughter, I will sacrifice them all to him, and even if he wants my wife, let me divorce her and present her to him."

Then, immediately, he asked, "O dervish, what is your wish from me? Whatever you want, tell me and let me immediately give it to you for you have such a sweet breath."

"Yes," the dervish said, "sweet breath is essential for a dervish. You spoke a few words with me and my words sweetened your words so much that it got you off your horse, and thus you surrendered to me! If you don't withhold the honor of listening to me, within your own being the words will become complete."

Souls in Simplicity

O sultan! Even though you must be among people, at least for an hour leave them, so that they might say, "The king has gone to visit a dervish."

And then, let's go to such a house that it might not be apparent which is the king and which is the dervish.[180]

Everything Is Perishing Except the Face of God

This is not a story. This is a word, but I never want to speak it with you; even so, you are full of mercy. Remember that day you told me, "I regret that I've wanted anything from you—even just sitting on a sheepskin together with you is pleasant."[181] But this is a loan, not an obligation. Those days that have passed no longer exist.

---

180 In later years, sultan Selim was a follower of the Mevlevi Way. One evening he had gone to the tekke and told his retinue to wait for him. The hour grew late and at long last one of his courtiers went to the door and knocked. He asked, "Is sultan Selim here?" He was told, "No, there is no sultan here." "But we were told to await him here," his courtier replied, puzzled. The doorkeeper went to inquire further. The *Dede* (head of the *tekke*) responded, "O he is looking for Dervish Selim. Go and call Selim *Jan* and tell him his ride is here." Before God we are all simply souls (*janlar*).

181 M. 70.
I.e., not on a throne or seat of honor, but side by side in contemplation.

❁

Stop Complaining

Don't complain, "God has shown me more troubles than He gave the prophets and saints!" It's you who are at fault in your obedience of the command. You keep thinking that it is always going to be like this, but commandments have come because it's possible to obey them, and you are made for this. But if you don't have the strength to obey the commandment today, how can you complain? Under the weight of His command, even the Prophet said, "*Surah Hud* has made my hair white." If you are saying, "There was a great advantage for the Prophet in obeying these commandments," there is no harm for you, either. "Poor me," you say, but that complaint is worse than boasting.[182]

❁

Taking Warnings to Heart

How will I tell the story about the lion with seven heads, to lead them to the way? For whose destiny will these words be helpful in making a change?

Imaginary anxiety and fears come to you. "Mercy! Let it not be me," you say.

"No, it is not you," I am saying.

Besides you and me, someone who really needs advice is necessary so that the effect of that advice might become visible. Now, although these commandments are difficult for others, the best characteristic is that none of the commandments are difficult for you. Bayazid couldn't have the strength to bear it for five days or even one. But if my heart has turned towards a person and his companionship pleases me, I warn him. If you look carefully, you see the

---

182 *Surah Hud* 9-11: *And thus it is: if We let man taste some of Our grace, and then take it away from him—behold, he abandons all hope, forgetting all gratitude [for Our past favours]. And thus it is: if We let him taste ease and plenty after hardship has visited him, he is sure to say, "Gone is all affliction from me!"—for, behold, he is given to vain exultation, and glories only in himself. [And thus it is with most men—] save those who are patient in adversity and do righteous deeds: it is they whom forgiveness of sins awaits, and a great reward.*

root, and that sight pleases you. This is the reason for that. If you were a great man of the world, you wouldn't need help from others. Only if you are not like that does help become necessary for you—in this moment, you understand the secrets of the intercession of the Prophet. After the dark night I turned my face in this direction—like someone hopeless who finds hope, hope appeared within me.

You had said, "It is *haram* (religiously unlawful) for me to speak when I am with you." Yes, it is *haram* to speak in front of us if it is without permission, but if you have my permission, then it is rightful to speak.

Incomparability

For God's sake, a thousand people like Kezervani or Khojandi aren't equal to even a single hair of Mevlana. In all fields of knowledge, I swear by God that even Moses couldn't be his equal. By nature, Mevlana is quick witted. He stuns others into silence.

Just Say, "Yes!"

All these things that are happening have occurred because of me, and due to your silence. What a beautiful offense this is—brighter, more pleasant, and more illustrious than a thousand enlightening true words.

The subject of "the inside" (*batin*) is something other than all these discussions. I continue to remain in my own state; I never leave it.

How could it be that, from time to time, I wouldn't remember that joyfulness we shared? You, too, know that we are from the same city.

He told me: "There is no doubt that you came drunk from the Truth, but not like those who have become drunk from wine."

"Yes," I said, "it's true that I have drunk, but among people there are those who drink two glasses of wine and get drunk, and there are also human beings who although they have emptied thousands of glasses, who may drink until their faces are completely red, still remain sober, aware of their environment, and conscious of where they are."

I thought to myself, "In this matter the best thing for you to do is to stop all opposition; before the one in front of you says 'No,'—just say, 'Yes.'"

True Manliness

Ali has said that manliness becomes apparent in three places—in war, in bed when one is in the arms of a woman, and in the marketplace. There is not a treasure worth even five cents in comparison with the generosity of Blessed Ali. He offers this advice and goes on; I also summarize these words and go on. I speak openly. And I remember the spirits of the great ones of the past with longing.

Know Your Beloved

There is no seeker among those who look for God who has not matured on the Way. If the seeker is mature in his longing, but the beloved for whom he is searching hasn't yet matured in the aspect of being loved, then the outcome is uncertain. But, in the aspect of being loved, if the beloved has come to maturity, this means that both of them have understood each other well, and they have merged with each other. From this point of view, there is nothing superior to a man of wisdom, but according to another view, there is something superior.

Let's say that there is a vizier. He can understand all the states of the sultan—he knows his habits, temperament, what causes him to get angry and what he likes. He has grasped this without asking anybody. But although that vizier is so close, still despite all this closeness of the vizier to the sultan, he is not certain of the safety of his life, because the heads of many viziers have been chopped off.

However, Ayaz, the favorite friend of Sultan Mahmoud of Ghazna, was certain about the safety of his life; he was at ease and had no fear. Even when he made a mistake, if he fell and broke something, or when he spilled water or food on his clothes, despite his mistakes he would still entertain the sultan, lightening his heart throughout the day. And the sultan would tolerate all these mistakes, because Ayaz was very dear to him. Although the vizier knew about all these mistakes of his, how could he glare at him for even a moment, because the sultan could sacrifice thousands of heads for his sake.

When the sultan tells a secret to the vizier for safekeeping, he doesn't need to warn him not to reveal it to anyone; and the vizier behaves very carefully to keep this secret and takes it to his grave.

Finding Muhammad

When you're sitting together with Muhammad (peace and blessings upon him), you're making a mistake if you want to see Moses or to see Jesus. He has hunted the greatest of his prey. But if you had seen Moses, you would also find him in Muhammad. Whenever they tell you something about Moses and speak of his endeavors, the same has also been said by Muhammad.

If you were to read the Torah and listen to his characteristics from that book, you would see that Moses was longing for Muhammad and saying a thousand times, "O Lord! I wish you hadn't given prophethood to me," or "I wish you had delayed my sitting in my place for a little while, so that I might have seen him!"

So, come, you and I, let's sit together with Mevlana for six months and moan and cry out.

Beyond the Grave

Listen to *Surah Ya Sin* that opens hearts in this world, don't listen to the words coming from the world. I have left the city where I lived. I said to myself, "Walk! Look at your own universe!"

They asked me, "What is the work that you do? Did they give you news from this world? Did you see it?"

"Of course, I'll go and see," I said, when I came to this path.

"Well here's your world," they said.

"What did you understand from this universe? Didn't they give you any information about it?" And he added, "You are unworthy of that world, give up that bathhouse furnace."

"Here, I saw a land just like you have described to me."

"What work do you have to do there? Tell us!" he said.

"Don't you know about this universe?" I asked.

"How could I not know, if you know," he replied, "but I don't know."

"Then let's walk so that your eye and heart might be opened. What are we waiting for here?"

Sooner or later every community passes to the side of the grave. There is no doubt that the world is a grave around which a fire is burning. The grave softens them so that whatever they contain might burn away more easily.

Whose Letter Are You Reading?

Imagine a sheet of paper—one side is turned towards you and the other side is turned towards the Beloved, or each side is turned towards someone else. You can read the side of the paper turned towards you, but what is most essential is to read the side turned towards the Friend, the Beloved.

Have We Not Made the Mountains Pillars

This way is a very strange and secret way. The police chiefs are sitting there saying, "The way isn't this way; don't go this way." All of the six directions are enlightened with the Divine Light of God.

The poor philosopher was left outside of the seven heavens. In the space that seems to be empty everything certainly has a truth, a reality. Just as it was said in the Qur'an, "*Have We not made the mountains pillars* [78:7]?" The "pillars" mentioned in this verse, are neither the mountains nor the rocks, but they have been spoken about one by one. Don't you see that when these mountains stand in their places, the tent of the heavens is pitched. But if these were the pillars of the earth, how would that tent be pitched in heaven?

Let me say, "May God Most High give Mevlana a long life," and may you say, "Amin!" May God forgive and give him to us, and may He forgive and give us to him.[183] And may He give us all long lives! Amin!

For whomever they pray, "May God give them long lives!" you just also say, "Amin!"

❊

There Is No Doubt that the Lover Is Where the Beloved Is

My God Most High, from the East of the world to the West, has filled that earthenware jug with water. They asked, "Where will the one who prays and these prayers be contained, when this container is full of water?" He has sent the water . . . "Have you remembered me?"[184]

I swear that you haven't been able to understand me—if you had understood me, all the organs in your body would tremble, your heart would palpitate, and you would shake.[185] A voice from within you would shout at you, "This is a saint of God! This is the most powerful friend of God Most High who has created the earth and the sky and the creatures in between!" and it would cry, "This is a saint who is present here!"

This beloved friend is that person who is sitting there. There is no doubt that the lover is where the beloved is. There is a reason for not recognizing it, but I'm not really more terrible than you. I used to be ashamed before of the way you served me when we were together, but now I don't avoid it, because it is a pleasant thing to be together with a person of wisdom who is distant from the claims of I-ness.

---

183 I.e. May God forgive our sins for each other's sake, and not separate us from each other.

Shams indicates here how men/women of God are like mountains supporting the tent of Divine Presence, connecting earth with heaven.

184 *Remember Me and I will remember you.* [*Surah al-Baqarah* 2:152]

185 *The faithful are those whose hearts tremble with awe whenever God is mentioned, and whose faith is strengthened whenever His signs are conveyed to them . . .* [*Surah al-Anfal* 8:2-4].

The Blessed Prophet said, "O Lord! We couldn't worship You as You ought to be worshipped!" and Bayazid Bastami boasted, "Glory be to me; how great is my glory!" There is one single truth in every age.

The real disciple of the shaikh is the one who is always with him. The rest are like the dust that comes with the wind and is dispersed by the breeze. But don't be sad! Be that unique friend! Because, among those thousands of sinful ones, one can find only one real friend—he wouldn't be regarded as a stranger and he could be taken behind a veil. When the journey comes to an end, with the divine light of his bright reason, he is like an angel who burns the world with his wings. But, where is that real friend?

Where is that manly man who can distinguish the good from the bad within this mud of lusts?[186] Even if you pluck out his moustache, still he won't move his lips. He is a person who is worth speaking and joking with. Among the people his words are referred to: "These are so and so's words." Most of the time, people benefit from him, most of the time they find the right way through him.[187] In his words, there is a fragrance from the universe of the Truth. There is no doubt that the breath of such a person is the breath of Paradise, and perhaps it is the breath of the Truth. If you wish, please call him, "The dearest among the people." O brothers who are near the Truth! Please show respect to these attained ones!

Inner Capacity

Mevlana said, "One cannot make sense of three things: one of these is anxiety in the midst of joy of heart; the second is fear in the midst of peace of mind; and the third is not recognizing the appropriate benefit when it is essential."

A real man of God is respectful even in responding to the dog that passes by his door. Regarding the subject of majesty or great-

186 Where is that human being of heart—only with the eye of the heart can one see through the veils of desire.

187 They find the Way with his help.

ness, the will I have prevails over majesty. He behaves thoughtfully and in a dignified way—he protects both sides.

When the place is inappropriate and the people there have no capacity, to speak is torture. Books don't say anything about this; perhaps H. can, but he doesn't speak about this either—in my era, many people deny it. In my presence, he repented of smoking cannabis and telling lies, but now he has forgotten.

Those who have God-given knowledge are of two kinds. Knowledge comes to one group like a flood, leaving them bewildered. Among this group only one or two people can speak. "From the perspective of form and meaning, you have a proper state," they say, but I haven't seen that state in them. Another group passes beyond the water. All the friends of God, saints and prophets, long to meet them and see their faces.

When a person has become stuck in the belief that even a hundred saints (*velis*) couldn't be exchanged for the dust of the feet of a single prophet—a person who has arrived at this belief, where will he end up?

A person who clings to the belief that the Qur'an is the speech of God and the *hadith* are the words of the Prophet, what can one hope for from him? If his beginning is like this, where will he arrive in the end? He must have learned these things while a child, but he has remained in this very narrow place.

Those Who Possess the Kernel

The universe of the Truth is an infinitely wide expanse. According to some, it is extremely clear and simple. For some it is very difficult, while according to some it is very easy—yet because of this easiness they remain bewildered. Those who speak about such things, hesitate here.

In the *hadith* it has been said, "The Qur'an has seven levels of meaning of both the outer (*zahir*), the inner (*batin*), and the inner of the inner." Of these meanings, the scholars know the outer meanings, the saints know the inner meanings, and the prophets know the hidden meanings within the inner meanings, the fourth "none knows but God." So, how can the children of Adam benefit from this? There are many secrets within the *hadith* as there are in the Qur'an. As God Most High has said, "*His heart did not deny what he saw . . .*" [53:11].[188]

---

188 *Surah Najm* (The Unfolding " or "The Star") 53:10-18:

And thus did [God] reveal unto His servant whatever He deemed right to reveal.
[Lit., "whatever He revealed" . . . In its deeper sense the above phrase implies that even to His chosen prophets God does not *entirely* unveil the ultimate mysteries of existence, of life and death, of the purpose for which He has created the universe, or of the nature of the universe itself. ~ M. Asad]

The [servant's] heart did not give the lie to what he saw:
[Inasmuch as the Prophet was fully aware of the spiritual character of his experience, there was no conflict between his conscious mind and his intuitive perception (the "vision of the heart") of what is normally not perceptible. ~ M. Asad]

will you, then, contend with him as to what he saw?
[Thus the Qur'an makes it clear that the Prophet's vision . . . was not a delusion but a true spiritual experience: but precisely because it was purely *spiritual* in nature, it could be conveyed to others only by means of symbols and allegories, which sceptics all too readily dismiss as fancies, "contending with him as to what he saw." ~ M. Asad]

And, indeed, he saw it descend a second time by the lote-tree of the farthest limit,
[I.e., on the occasion of his mystic experience of the "Ascension" (*mi'raj*). Explaining the vision conveyed in the expression *sidrat al-muntaha,* Raghib suggests that owing to the abundance of its leafy shade, the *sidr* or *sidrah* (the Arabian lote-tree) appears in the Qur'an as well as in the Traditions relating to the Ascension as a symbol of the "shade—i.e., the spiritual peace and fulfilment—of paradise. One may assume that the qualifying term *al-muntaha* ("of the utmost [or "farthest"] limit") is indicative of the fact that God has set a definite limit to all knowledge accessible to created beings, as pointed out in the *Nihayah*: implying, in particular, that human knowledge, though potentially vast and penetrating, can never—not even in paradise (the "garden of promise" mentioned in the next verse)—attain to an understanding of the ultimate reality, which the Creator has reserved for Himself. ~ M. Asad]

near unto the garden of promise, with the lote-tree veiled in a veil of nameless splendor . . .
["when the lote-tree was veiled with whatever veiled [it]": a phrase deliberately vague (*mubham*), indicative of the inconceivable majesty and splendor attaching to this symbol of paradise "which no description can picture and no definition can embrace" (Zamakhshari). ~ M. Asad]

They also hesitate to speak about the meaning of the subtle point, "What no eye has seen and no ear has heard."[189]

Ali and Muhammad

Even though there were secrets in the Qur'an, even though he recited the pure verses of the Qur'an everyday, Ali didn't lose himself. But when he heard a single word of the secrets, he lost himself in ecstasy and all that trouble unfolded.[190]

And so, it seems that Bayazid, with his veiled words, wanted to tell secrets from his own self.

The Prophet didn't reveal secrets; he gave guidance. Within the guidance, he has conveyed mention of his companions, too, in a veiled way without explanation—*those endowed with insight* [2:179],[191] but he hasn't spoken about their states.

[And withal,] the eye did not waver, nor yet did it stray: truly did he see some of the most profound of his Sustainer's symbols.

M. 75.

189 *Hadith qudsi*: The Prophet said, "God says, 'I have readied for My righteous servants what no eye has ever seen, and no ear has ever heard, and no heart of man has ever conceived.'"

190 The Prophet Muhammad was given as *a guide and a mercy to all humankind*—to very few did he speak the secrets of his Lord. Once to Ali he confided secrets of the Way, but told him not to reveal them to anyone. Ali was so overcome with ecstasy that burning with such fire, he at last whispered the secrets into the water of a deep well. One day a shepherd paused to water his flock there, and from the reedbed that fed from that water he cut a reed. From it he crafted a reed flute, the first *ney*, which when he played it, voiced the longing for the Divine within the secrets that Ali had confided to the water. The *ney* is one of the primary instruments of Mevlevi music, and its voice begins Rumi's *Mathnawi*: "Every since they cut me from the reedbed, I have longed to return to that state of union. . . . "

191 This phrase is also translated as "O you of understanding." The word used for "insight" or "understanding" is *lubb* which has the meaning of "kernel" or "seed," and so it might also be translated as "O you possessors of the kernels."

See also *Surah al-An'am*, Cattle, 6:95: *You are the One who causes the seeds and kernels to split open and the plants to sprout forth.*

They have shown themselves openly and made themselves known, but the real saint, who is the friend of God, has remained hidden and secret. Muhammad burned with a great passion to see them—he did not have that opportunity, but he would speak about his longing for them.[192]

If Bayazid had been aware of this, he would never have said the word "I." As a matter of fact, in the end, he wanted a "rope girdle" [worn by Christians]. Were the last days of Hakim Sana'i better than Sayyid Burhannuddin or were the last days of Sayyid Burhannuddin better than my master? Sana'i had a good state and Burhannuddin had a vast knowledge. You see these people like Imad and others—those who have come, lived, and passed away are a hundred times greater. Just as a sample handful taken from a large sack of wheat will show the quality of the thousands of grains of wheat within the sack, even so, all of them are also like that.

Haste Is from the Devil

You are asking: "Does Satan reach that rank?" Yes, he does. Because Satan had reached the state of Moses, who had reached the rank of speaking with God—for that reason, Khidr had told Moses, "You can't be patient enough to be with me!" Moses was in a hurry to ask questions, and haste comes from Satan. But from another aspect, he (Satan) could never reach his rank, because hundreds like him couldn't reach the dust of the feet of Moses.

Pay Attention and a Secret May Be Revealed

Mevlana doesn't allow me to work. In the whole world, I have only one friend—let me not deprive him of what he wants. How could I listen to him, and not respond to his longing?

---

192 He would say, "O my brothers!" See the section "Brothers Beyond Time" p.109 of this text.

You are not my friends. Where are you in relation to friendship with me? It is only through the blessing of Mevlana that you hear a word from me. Those who do listen to me sometimes, must listen very carefully when I speak.

Since you are an Abraham,[193] you came with your book—you see me as a teacher, but many times it happens that someone will serve someone whom he doesn't recognize. How could service without recognition be the same as service with recognition?

Sometimes when I speak with people, if you listen carefully, you will understand that the words are all veiled—they are full of secrets. Those who discount these public words haven't understood anything—those who say, "This is easy," can't receive anything from me or my words. They can receive no benefit, no portion from me, for many secrets have been hidden within the words spoken in these public gatherings. And there may be a great secret that can only be spoken by hiding it within a joke, if one even tries to say it.

The appropriate thing is for you to come to visit because of your own longing, before others send you. Love is like this. If I leave this time, will you be able to find me? I am saying, "if"—I am not saying this with certainty. To speak of this "if" which is bound to conditions, is very difficult for the friend. Words like "if," "provided that," "I wish it were," and "I suppose" are all like this.

When a follower of Fakhruddin-i Razi was dying, he spoke this couplet about being reasonable:

> Intellect ends up in shackles,
> and the hard work of the scholars results in heresy.
> And then there is also the verse:
> Our spirits are scared of our bodies.

To those who escape from the *nafs* and its desires, a secret is revealed—at that very moment. They are not left deprived.

---

193 "Shaykh Ibrahim"—One of those participating in the conversations with Shams, possibly Qutb ad-Din Ibrahim who had been a disciple of Mevlana's father, Bahaeddin Weled, and was beloved by Shams as well as Mevlana as one of the finest dervishes.

❊

Mevlana Has No Equal

As for Mevlana, during this era, nowhere in the world is there anyone who is equal to him or who is like him. In all areas of knowledge, in theology, in the sciences of grammar, syntax, and logic, he speaks powerfully and discusses with the greatest experts. He is superior to them; he speaks more beautifully and he gives greater pleasure than they do. If it is necessary, if his heart wants it, if his sorrow doesn't impede it, if the tastelessness of the subject doesn't stand in the way, he speaks with more authority than any of them.

Even if I were to study these subjects for a hundred years, I couldn't attain a tenth of the knowledge and ability that he has, but he thinks that he doesn't know anything; he acts as though that's how it is. When he is in front of me, when he is listening to what I say—I don't know how to say it—it's discourteous to even say, but he passes into such a shy state it's as if he were a two-year-old child sitting in front of his father, or as though he were a new Muslim who hasn't yet heard anything about Islam.

One day early in the morning I was talking about the universe of meaning. He said, "Since this ear became an ear it hasn't heard such subtlety." He was very much affected.

❊

An Ocean of Love, a Mountain of Meaning

The house is empty, but nobody is coming. When I think of how they served me! When I was waking up from sleep, rose syrup was placed by my pillow. My friend sits next to me, but he is silent. And when he speaks, he doesn't just talk about the weather.

In anyone's opinion, he is a great man. If love and longing are predominant in you, when you look at him, you'll see an Ocean. If love prevails within you, you realize that God is also victorious within you. A great man like a mountain! I have beautiful things to say about you.

❁

Sharing the Salt

Abu Bakr used to interpret the meanings of words. Even if not only this interpretation but everything he said did not fit the meaning of the words he interpreted, God would make them true. Muhammad both used to interpret words and had the power to heal the blind and the lepers like Jesus.

Thousands tell stories about Muhammad. Earlier, Jesus put the salt in all the earthen pots, but later on it was Muhammad who added the salt, and he is the last of the Prophets. In other words, he is the person who closed the door of prophethood and who sealed it. Now, someone to sprinkle the salt is needed.[194]

❁

Becoming a Humble Servant

Only those who are humble can be friends with me. It is important that the feeling of humility and the feeling of servanthood might increase the inclination not to commit sins. If before today you were abstaining from the religiously forbidden (*haram*), from now on what is appropriate for you is to also abstain even from that which is religiously permitted (*halal*). But if this attitude brings you to the point of selling even your patched cloak, it won't be a good thing.

❁

Mevlana Is Enough for Me

When it comes to this world, there is nothing I want from anybody. I only wish to behave in accordance with the Prophet's custom of accepting gifts. If you have hundreds of thousands of gold and silver coins—a castle full of gold—and you give it to me, I'll look at your face, and if I can't see a divine light on your forehead, and a light of

---

194 It is salt that adds flavor and preserves; salt is essential for the proper functioning of the human being (these earthen pots) both physically and spiritually. The true spiritual teacher is the one who can "sprinkle the salt" in the right measure, in the right moment.

yearning in your heart, to me that gold and silver would be nothing but a pile of manure.

If I had any wants, Mevlana would be enough for me. Remember—you keep reading your own letter; at least, read a few things from the letter of the friend, too. That would be more useful for you. All these troubles of yours come from your reading of your letter all the time and not listening to the song of the Beloved. That imagination (*hayal*) is born from knowledge (*'ilm*) and understanding (*gnosis*). But after that imagination there is another knowledge and gnosis. And that knowledge and gnosis also have other imaginations. It becomes long.

There is another way that is shorter than these which is not like that, but they have given this shortcut a bad reputation; you have to find a different name for it. A good principle was established. One day you burn, and the next day you don't. But the best principle is not to ask for money from anybody, so that it might not attract your mind to the world. Don't turn in the direction of worldly things, or pay attention to them. But now, there is one thing that I regret: I wish I had thousands that I might have sacrificed them for his sake.

Open Your Eyes

It is as if the Resurrection has opened now, and the Unseen universe has been revealed. Yes, I swear that the Unseen is apparent, the veil has been removed, but for those whose eyes are open.

From What Level Are You Listening

When someone says, "That sofa is high," this "height" is not according to the ceiling but according to the floor.

I have openly told this to Mevlana: "When I speak to them, if they can't understand my words, then you tell it to them." Do I have a command from God to speak to them in such low metaphors?

I am talking about the origin and foundation of the work—it seems so difficult to them. But when as a metaphor I speak about another origin, I cover the words; I speak in such a veiled way that in the end every word hides another.

About the subject of the Truth,[195] Mevlana never speaks in a veiled way, because I dove very deeply with him—I have openly told him about everything in a clear way. When Mevlana begins to speak, people accept it, ask his forgiveness, and bow their heads like dervishes.

The Light of the Way of God

Thousands of useless words have been spoken about, "When poverty is complete, he is God." But if there is no blasphemy in the words, then it means that "when poverty *(fakr)* is completed, God appears; you find Him and see Him." If the meaning isn't that, then what difference can there be between you and a Christian? For Jesus was subtler than Mansur al-Hallaj, Bayazid, and others.

Why blame a Christian because he says that Jesus is God or he is God's son, when you are saying something similar. The meaning of the words, "When poverty is completed, God appears" is like the meaning in the words, "Whoever's *nafs* (commanding self) dies, his Satan also dies; having been cleared of harmful traits, he reaches God." But this attainment is not, God forbid, reaching the Self *(Dhat)* of God, but rather to enter upon His way. The servant understands that he has not attained God, but that he has only entered upon the way of God. Otherwise, he has strayed from the path of God, his *nafs* comes back to life and his satan, too! The one who can't distinguish the difference between the Light of the way of God and the Light of the Self of God, continues in darkness and is blind.

God Most High has seven hundred veils of light or seven hundred thousand coverings; when it is said that if one of these veils were opened it would burn both the world and those who are in it, then the question arises, "Which veil is it that when it is gradually removed, one can reach the Divine light of the Self, one can reach the Light that shines from the Essence?"

195 M. 80.

"Ablution upon ablution is light upon light" means light upon light pours down upon one who is birthed into a state of ablution who cleanses his self. It doesn't mean you should make the ablutions twice. . . .

God has a fragrance that comes to one's nose like the fragrance of musk and ambergris, but how could it every really be like ambergris and musk? When God wants to manifest Himself to His servant, that fragrance can be sensed—it makes one drunk to the point of fainting. These words never come to an end.

Coming Close to the Essence

Muhammad said, "O Christian! You couldn't know Jesus; at least know me. Then you will have known me, and him as well!"

Now, they know Muhammad as the Seal of the Prophets.

They ask about his sayings . . . whether he was too shy to say, "Whoever knows my self knows my Lord," and so instead he said, "He who knows himself knows his Lord."

Without awareness, people interpret his words. The perceptive said to themselves, "We know this poor, dirty, disobedient, and dark little *nafs* of ours, but can one obtain the ability to know God from this?" Those who have reached the secret, understood what he said.

Pulling Back from the Fire

I said, "What right do I have to eat, drink, and sleep? Did God Most High create me only for that? Until He speaks with me without any mediator, until I ask Him and he tells me what this eating and sleeping is—did I come to this universe to eat and drink blindly?"

If the work is like this, and I can speak and communicate face to face with Him, then I eat and drink because I understand how I came here, where I am going, where my safety lies, and what my end will be. So I live freely, without worries.

"How could this be understood with the intellect?" I asked, and I turned my face to Him.

It's like when a mother has but a single child in the whole universe, a very good and beautiful baby, who puts his hand into the fire. Just as the mother would jump to grab her baby, the fragrance of the Truth pulled me away from the fire.

❊

Aspiration

One of the beautiful names of God is the One Who Seeks (*Murid*).[196] And in the end, this seeker will have a wish (*murad*). And another one of His names is Aspirant (*talib*). He should have someone for whom he aspires (*matlub*).

Someone asked, "Is it like this for everyone? At least in the beginning, I was also an aspirant."

I said, "Everyone is not an aspirant. If a light from that aspiration were to fall upon the people of the world, nobody would be able to endure it, they would all burn and be utterly destroyed."

One of these aspirants is the Prophet Moses. He looked for a trace of God on the mountain—he passed beyond himself, and came back. So how could everybody randomly be the one who is searched for? There is no doubt about the subtle point in the couplet:

> If they drive us away from our city, so what?
> The countryside also belongs to us.

If God gives me success, I'll go to a place where no sound or echo might reach me. Let the winds blowing from different directions run after each other and let me recite something—let me whisper into the ears of the wind, bring your ears there, too.

> One who has a guarantee and support to lean on—
> his heart is joyful; his back is strong,
> and he doesn't grieve for anything.

---

196 The word *murid* comes from *irada* (will); *murid* means "one who wills," or "one who wishes" —"one who desires."

✲

Mevlana's Good Teaching

I had mentioned about the problem with my eye: "Now, this is not something within my power to do anything about, this is an obstacle that has come from the universe of the Unseen. Now, go! Only the letter of Mevlana is enough for me."

His son (sultan Veled), whom he sent to me said, "Then what would Mevlana say to me? Wouldn't he tell me, 'O stupid one, O Ass, O foolish one! I sent you to bring that person. And since you went, and you found him, and he told you that his eye was aching, then what was appropriate for you to do was to wait there, to serve him, and until he returned to health, to stay there."

From these words of the young man I understood that Mevlana had taught him those words, that humility. Those words, that gentleness, those subtle answers must all be due to Mevlana's teaching that he showed such an extraordinary interest in me about this matter.

If I give an example that is superior to these words, it won't fit into the minds of the ignorant people. He understood that as his wife hasn't held onto his words yet, his son couldn't hold onto them either! What beautiful attributes that none of them contradict each other; this one with that one, and that one with the other are in harmony. When that attribute increases this one, this one also increases the other. Even if an attribute passes further ahead than others for a time, still there is an order and justice among them.

✲

Look Ahead

Now you are saying, "No answer has come to the things that I asked, from these obscure words. What is this darkness at his door?"

It is also the place where the *nafs* lay in ambush. As Attar said, "Even if you pass through difficult trials (*cille*) day and night for a hundred years, even if you follow regimens and fasting, on that Day, they will ask you neither about this trial nor that seclusion. Think about what is further ahead, look there!

❊

Love of the Homeland is Part of the Faith

He says, "Why would such and such a person's son walk behind a stranger from Tabriz? Would the earth of Khorasan be a follower of the earth of Tabriz and be dependent on it?"

He claims to be a person of piety and joy, but he doesn't have enough intelligence to understand that the honoring of earth is not the point.

If someone from Istanbul says, "Mecca is of this world, from the universe of matter; and faith is from the other world, that is from the universe of meaning," here, what the one from Mecca should do is agree with the one from Istanbul. In the *hadith*, "Love of the homeland is part of the faith," how could the intention of Muhammad be love of Mecca? Mecca is of this world, but faith is not of this world.

Therefore, things related to faith are not of this universe—they are from the other universe. Just as in the *hadith*, "Islam began as a stranger, and it will return as a stranger"—the intention is the same. Since Islam is a stranger, this means it has come from a different universe. How can it be particular to Mecca? Those who say it belongs only to Mecca, are the ones who couldn't even reach the first step of love.

❊

The Stages of Drunkenness

It is very difficult to free oneself of this understanding—one has to run a long way to get free from this drunkenness of desire. And after this, the drunkenness of the universe of the Spirit comes. The Spirit has not appeared yet, but the drunkenness it brings is great, so that from drunkenness he looks neither upon the shaikhs nor the prophets.

When he begins to speak nothing comes to his mind of *ayats* or *hadith*. Conveying words heard from this one or that one makes him ashamed, unless the intention is to explain a particular subject to people.

To pass through this second stage of drunkenness is very difficult and tricky, and only if God Most High sends one of His dear servants whom He has uniquely created to show him the real truth of the Spirit—then he directs him to the way of the Truth and helps bring him to his purpose.

The drunkenness of the Way of God appears at the third stage. There is also a great drunkenness in this, but it is also closer to sobriety. Because God takes him out of that perplexity of what he thought it was.

And after this comes the fourth stage, and this is drunkenness directly through God. This stage is the stage of perfection.

And after this comes the stage of sobriety.

As for the interpretation of desire, first of all, we are not talking about things like women, gold, or love of the world. Some circle around the world out of fear that this drunkenness of desire might decrease. Many monks have this drunkenness of desire. It is this that they reveal.

Imad, and those like him, were people who were mature in the drunkenness of desire. There was also a fragrance from the drunkenness of Spirit in them; they had found a way to it. Awhad Kirmani was closer to the completion of desire. Pharoah's magicians had become complete in desire, but Pharaoh was not. He was a logician; he was a man of that way. The magicians had a skill that Pharaoh did not have. In Sayyid Burhanuddin there was much fragrance of the Spirit and the drunkenness of the Spirit, too. He had a great deal of knowledge, but he was not attached to anything.

Shaikh Abu Bakr Sellabaf's[197] drunkenness was from God, but he did not have the sobriety that comes after that drunkenness. This point was made known to me through the way of knowledge.

This servant's own happiness also became clear, but it was not near and certain. They sent one of His pure servants to teach him his happiness in a sure and certain way and to educate him gently.

---

197 Abu Bakr Sellabaf, the basket-weaver of Tabriz, was Shams' first spiritual teacher.

✲

Speaking Ill Only Distances the Speaker

When someone speaks ill of Him, he is only hurting himself. How can he hurt God? How can such words even come out of their mouths, unless they don't know God? This is like the saying of Sana'i:

> O poor one, whose gods hurt God!

In the *hadith* it has been said, "I have such a time with God that neither an angel close to God nor a prophet sent with a book can enter in between." The "angel" is his completely clean spirit, and "the prophet" is his completely purified body. Since the angel and the prophet cannot enter between, who would dare to open this veil? No one but this son of his from Tabriz can speak about this. [198]

This is not the station and the degree of the state of Muhammad; this is an invitation. Many words have been spoken about this—how could the meaning of it be expressed by the word "state"?

✲

The Resurrection Is Now

A human being who is looking for the Truth claims to aspire, to depart from the circle of desires, and to reach the fragrance of the spirit. Some of these claims may be true and some not. If we want to know, we investigate—if someone's inclination is turned more towards the deeds of this world, he is a liar and a phony.

Although these words are warm, when compared with the warmth of the words that I want to reveal, they seem cold and frozen. Today, you and we are here, and we consider the Day of Resurrection to have already arrived. In the dervish, in the servants of God, there is such a faith that it is as if this hour is the hour of the Resurrection, and this is the Last Day.

---

198 M. 85.

❁

Awe and Majesty

One day Abu Yazid[199] was speaking about this from the pulpit . . . I mean a gathering for spiritual conversation (*sohbet*), not a wooden pulpit.

Just then a woman stood up and turned her face toward him.

Immediately, he said, "Sit down, woman!"

Instead, she sprang forward: "O Shaikh! O phony! You know this isn't so with you! Although the words you speak are true, who are you in relation to them? These words are not your words; this work is not your work. The sign of the Resurrection is that out of awe and majesty it will be impossible to distinguish between a man and a woman."

Abu Yazid shut up.

❁

Witnessing

I have come to this world to observe and watch. I was listening to letterless and signless speech, to every silent word, and I was hearing words from this side, too.

I said, "O letterless speech! If you are speech, tell me, what are these?"

"According to me, this is a toy," it said.

"So, did you send me for a plaything?" I asked.

"No," it said, "you wanted everything; accordingly, you have a place in water and earth, and I do not know or see it."

Now, I hear every word, I can see in all directions, and I understand the level of each word spoken.

The Prophet said, "If one day a scholar of religion passes down a street, for forty days Satan cannot pass there." Here, our Prophet didn't say just "a scholar," but "a scholar of religion."

Those who call Jesus the son of God don't say that he broke off from God by means of copulation. Perhaps it is like several other

---

199 Abu Yazid is another way of expressing the name of Bayazid Bastami.

examples of "birth." Let's say that "this word" has been "born" from such and such a person. This does not mean "it was born" in the usual sense.

Religious Profiteers

There is no harm for me in seeing the sultan, and it is good for him, but harm comes to these shaikhs in speaking with princes. If they are real servants of God, I am not saying across a pool or a river, but even if they pass across an ocean, their skirts will not get wet.[200] But these aren't those. Not only their skirts will get wet, but they may well sink into the water from tip to toe and drown. Only harm comes to princes from seeing them, because whatever skill and longing to

---

200 See Mevlana's *Fihi ma Fihi*, translated by Wheeler Thackston as *Signs of the Unseen*, p.1-2 :

> The Prophet (peace be with him) said, "The worst scholar is one who visits princes, but the best prince is one who visits scholars. Happy the prince at a poor man's door; wretched the poor man at a prince's gate." People have taken this saying at its face value to mean that it is not fitting for a scholar to visit a prince lest he become a bad scholar. It does not, however, mean what people imagine. Its true meaning is that the worst scholar is one who receives support from princes, whom he must fear in order to gain his livelihood. Such a man's primary aim in the pursuit of learning is for princes to bestow gifts upon him, to hold him in high esteem, and to grant him official positions. Therefore, it is on their account that he betters himself and exchanges his ignorance for learning. When he becomes a scholar, he learns proper etiquette out of fear of them and their power to punish. So, willy-nilly, he conducts himself as they would have him do. Therefore, whether outwardly it be the prince who visits the scholar or the scholar who visits the prince, such a scholar must conduct himself as a guest while the prince acts as host. On the other hand, when a scholar dons the robe of learning, not for the sake of princes but rather first and foremost for God's sake, and when his conduct and comportment are along the path of rectitude, as his natural inclination should be, and for no other reason—like a fish, which can live only in water—then such a scholar is so ruled by reason that during his time all men stand in awe of his presence and are illuminated by his reflected radiance, whether they are aware of it or not. If such a scholar goes to a prince, it is he who acts as the host and the prince the guest, because the prince will be receiving assistance and will be dependent upon the scholar. The scholar is quite independent of the prince; he will shed light like the sun, whose only property is to give and bestow.

work they may have remains locked because of being with these religious profiteers.

❊

A Community of Spirit

Everybody who comes into this universe comes together with a comrade. Desires and appetite are the comrade for some, and for some the comrade is Love.

As it is said, Love has existed from the infinite beginning, but people have different ideas regarding the spirit. Some philosophers say that the spirit is of the eternal (*qadim*). And some put forth the view that it was created afterwards—that is, it did not exist in the beginning, but it came into being later. But in any case, the coming together of the spirits[201] came later. In the *hadith*, it was said, "Spirits are armies that have gathered." But there are different kinds of togetherness.[202] Those who are fond of taverns (*meydans*) form one community and the mischief makers another. We are talking about the community connected with spirit.

When we say, "God's knowledge encompasses all," God is also within this community, for *God is together with those who are conscious of Him (taqwa), those who avoid evil and do good deeds* [16:128], and *Surely, God is together with us* [9:40].

So, if the Tatar had known us within the same community in the first creation, today at this moment, he would also be together with us and Imad, too. Even so, God said, "In the universe that I created from water and clay I will create a representative (*khalif*), and I will multiply you from the creation of that representative, within that universe of water and clay."

---

201 Shams is referring to the Day of *Alast* when all the spirits were gathered before their creation in form and asked by the Creator, "Am I not your Lord?" to which we all replied, "Yes."

202 *It is He who has made you His representatives on earth: He has raised you in ranks, some above others, that He may test you with the gifts He has given for your Sustainer is swift with stringency, yet Ever Ready to Forgive, Infinitely Merciful.* [*Surah al-An'am*, Cattle 6:165].

They said, "O Sustainer! In this universe of togetherness with You, we are at ease and happy. We are afraid that we will be scattered and left far away from this happiness!"

God said, "I know that you aren't saying this out of disobedience or rudeness, but take refuge in Me. You are afraid that your community will break apart, however my power is sufficient for everything; there is no incompleteness to my power. I will gather you together again, together with each other, and in the same form!"[203]

A Kiosk for the Honored Guest

There is no doubt that there is a purpose and reason in the creation of this universe. There is someone for whom the inside and outside of this palace have been furnished. Whatever exists is in service to him. Everything is for him. The building of this universe was created for him; he was not created for its sake. It is just like when a rich person has a dear guest—he has a beautiful kiosk built in his honor and furnishes it for him.

Take the Hand of One Who Knows

There are travelers on the path of the way of God, but those who look for Him and want to find Him by means of the intellect can never find the way, unless that Self that he is looking for directly shows him the way. If he wishes, let this traveler search the whole universe, in all directions, let him take knowledge as a guide for himself and live with scholars who have greater authority than he and who are thirsty for the Truth, but if that Beloved for whom he is looking does not show Herself, there is no doubt that he cannot attain anything.

The knowledge of the Way of God cannot be obtained by effort. Even if a person were to try to move heaven and earth to attain this knowledge, still his hands will be left empty, and he will only sink

203 "In paradise we will be with those we love (*hadith*)."

into darkness, unless he grasps the hand of one of those who have attained the knowledge of God and works together with him. Isn't that what the Friend of God wants—to help him reach his aim?

Today, if I tell you that that man of God you are looking for is me, does this mean that Mevlana isn't? What a great happiness it is for him that he has found what he was looking for and has reached it; otherwise it would be misfortune upon misfortune.

Today, the advice I will give you is this: there is a day before us when they will call out, "*Return*." That is the Day of Gathering (*Qiyamat*). On that day to say, "O, what did we do?" will be of no use. But this "Day of the Standing Before God" is useful in this moment.[204]

Start Today, Asking God's Help

The Prophet said: "Remember the hue of the face of the person who will come to you. When there is grief, he gives me joy."

The community you are in has fallen into a deep sleep. They say, "Promises that are postponed are forgotten." A lover doesn't act like this. One has to start the work early. Today's work should not be left for tomorrow, and when beginning the work, one has to ask for God's help. Well, there can't be a clearer word than this. There can be no whiter yogurt than this. As a judge once said, "People don't eat thorns, and you can't eat them either."

Speaking Openly

Even the Blessed Prophet didn't speak as openly as this about these meanings. This wasn't because he couldn't, but perhaps because he didn't have enough time to speak longer or explain them; he was occupied with other things. But for me there's no obstacle to speaking about the meaning as it is and openly. Although I am pacifying myself with words, that meaning comes to me from this couplet:

---

204 Make your accounting now; be constantly ready to meet Your Sustainer—die before you die.

Because of the sin I've committed, I don't know
where to run,
but following every sin, forgiveness is in front of me.

Render thanks unto Him: [for your Sustainer has provided you with] a land most goodly, and a Sustainer much-forgiving [34:15], and *Truly, [O Muhammad,] We have opened before you a manifest victory, so that God might show His forgiveness of all your faults, past as well as future,*[205] *and bestow upon you the full measure of His blessings, and guide you on a straight way* [48:1-2] are all signs of this forgiveness. . . .

For some people, what they are searching for comes to them in the way that they long for it. To some, it shows its face only when they are dying. Some people spend their whole lives on the path searching for it, but on this way, to die with the longing to attain one's longing is also a great work.

✲

Forty Mornings

The blessed Prophet said, "From the heart of those who sincerely worship God Most Great for forty days, springs of wisdom flow"—wisdom pours out from their tongues. These forty mornings are the key to the opening of the heart of one who is sincerely faithful, otherwise even a hundred thousand mornings won't be of use to him.

✲

True Faith

The devil secretly prostrated himself in front of John the Baptist. What is this? "Faith out of fear and despair isn't worth much," they say. So which is true faith in God? True faith is the faith of those who see the embroideries of that world and hear the voices of that Divine universe without becoming dyed in the hues of this world.

---

205 Lit., "so that God might forgive you all that is past of your sins and all that is yet to come"—thus indicating elliptically that freedom from faults is an exclusive prerogative of God, and that every human being, however exalted, is bound to err on occasion. ~ M. Asad

Why wasn't it like this for Pharaoh? His faith should also be accepted since within the last breath, with a single word, you can die as one who is faithful. Pharaoh also had that possibility.[206]

In the Qur'an, it is said that this is accepted up to three times. *Those people who have faith at first and then become deniers, and then have faith again and then deny again, and they increase their blasphemy—God does not forgive them, nor lead them to the right path* [4:137]. God doesn't want the denier to persist and insist upon his denial. Perhaps because he has fallen away from faith twice, he has become a blasphemer a third time. His former denial has grown to such an extent that it has exceeded his faith; that is, his denial has become dominant over his faith. Such huge denial results in his being deprived of faith.

But if I were to speak about the other aspect of this matter, it would seem as though there is nothing to talk about. To say, "Act according to whichever you want of these—good news, warnings, and frightening statements in the Qur'an—whichever path or way you want to walk, walk that way and in the end, from the point of view of the religious law, if you utter the words of faith, you'll die as a believer," is to encourage people in the wrong way and to lead them to destruction. It's contrary to the Qur'an. Speaking like this isn't right, because the result is that it makes people go to sleep, leads them to ignorance, and keeps them from their work. People are already so lazy that you can't even describe it! When people hear someone say, "Do whatever you want to do!" they then trust in the saying that at the last breath, simply with a word one can become like a new-born baby and depart from this world as a believer.

Yes, it may seem that such and such a person has departed as a denier, but actually, he may have gone in faith. Even if that person had verbally denied the third time, from the perspective of the Truth, he or she might really be one of the faithful because in actuality, he/she is outside of the clear statement ". . . *they increase*

206 It is said that even with a person's last breath, at the moment of death, if he/she, attests to the Divine Unity then that person is considered as having died as a person of faith, and God may forgive him/her.

their blasphemy." But if someone says, "What kind of a religious law is this that it causes people's destruction?" we say: "to bring them to shelter away from such frightening advice is a hundred thousand times more terrible—it is like throwing them into the well. If you walk on this Way, if you struggle on this way and strive night and day, the way that you will go is right and real. But why don't you show this Way to someone else; why do you lull him into a rabbit's sleep, or are you just an imitator on this way? Or is warning them not the true way? Come, tell me how that's possible! What sense does it make to talk to such a person?[207]

If the praiseworthy glance of that Being whom people are seeking on this Way were to fall for a moment upon a fire-worshipper of seventy years, and if he shows a little love to him, no fire-worshipping will remain in him. All of his work will become *islam* [surrender].

Saintly Words

A person in the gathering said, "I am saying Shamsuddin is his saint."

"No," I said, "This is slander for me."

Whomever Shamsuddin swears at, and rebukes and speaks harsh words to, if that person hears it, well, that person turns into a saint. This isn't such a big deal.

What does a Shaikh Need?

I asked: "What does a Shaikh need? What does he not have? Do I have some deficiency in my Sufism?

"I don't even have a shirt! Yes, tell me, tell me! Have I ever neglected any courtesy, anything related to the good manners of Sufism? Today, I don't even have a shirt on my back—they have stolen it on the Way. But what insufficiency does this give to the Sufi, or to his joy of life?"

207 M. 90.

"Okay, here is not a Sufi, but the most honestly speaking man of the religion," he said.

"Think whatever you want," I said. "I speak the Truth."

❊

A Son of Adam

One day a doorman asked, "Who are you?"

"This is a bit of a difficult question, now let me think. Are you ready to sit and listen until your bottom gets sore, so that I might tell you who I am?" I said.

Some time ago, a great person came and passed on—his name was Adam. Well, I am one of his sons.

❊

Shaikh Abu'l Hasan Kharaqani and Sultan Mahmoud of Ghazna

"We were in the service of the Sultan of the Truth and the Law. We weren't of the time of that great person, Shaikh Abu'l Hasan Kharaqani, who was of the time of Sultan Mahmoud of Ghazna," they said and told the story of the Shaikh as follows:

Sultan Mahmoud was an awake and truth loving king. One day he had come into the presence of the shaikh to visit him and ask for his prayers, but the shaikh didn't pay much attention to him.

The sultan spoke: "In the Qur'an, aren't the counsels such as "*Obey God, the Messenger, and those among you who are in authority* [4:59] commandments of God?"

The shaikh answered: "O King of Islam! The first command of this verse, '*Obey God*!' has brought us such a pleasure and awe that we haven't been able to grasp yet whether there is a universe of the Messenger or not, so how could we pass to the third?"

When Sultan Mahmoud heard these words, he wept, and with trembling hands he held the hand of the shaikh and kissed it.

Sultan Mahmoud, Ayaz, and the Huma Bird

Another story they tell:

Sultan Mahmoud had seen a Huma bird [a mythical bird, a bird of paradise] flying in the sky. Immediately he gave an order and said, "Let the whole army march! Maybe it will light upon you and become yours." Everybody began running around. At that moment, Ayaz disappeared.

The sultan asked: "Didn't my Ayaz go? Maybe the shadow of the Huma will alight upon him."

As he was looking around, he saw Ayaz's horse with an empty saddle, and he heard a moaning. He got off of his horse to see the reason. And what does he see there? Ayaz is under his horse, without a hat on his head, moaning.

The sultan asked, "What are you doing there? Why didn't you go to look for the shadow of the Huma bird?"

Ayaz answered, "You are my Huma bird, and the shadow I am looking for is your shadow. I only look for the shadow of the Huma to reach your shadow. How could I leave you now, and look for it?"

Sultan Mahmoud embraced him with affection. Both of their shadows merged with each other in such a way that the shadow of thousands of Huma birds couldn't be equal to that shadow.

The sultan is the shadow of God, they say, but the universe of God is light within light, delight within delight, power within power, and fervor within fervor; this world of shadows that we see is just the world—it is totally bad, ugly, fleeting, and tasteless. How is it possible that it could be the shadow of God?

Yet, if there is a king clearly manifest, and if the meaning of kingship is shining in him, this is a very good thing. The concern and love felt for a tree is, in the end, for its fruit. A tree without fruit is only good for burning.

Sweet Water

A form may be very good, but only if it is together with the meaning. Otherwise, if the words spoken with form have no relation to the meaning, what is their use? Great attention is needed to be able to understand the words of Mevlana, because these have a fragrance of subtlety and humor. They are magical.

Let's say that two people are sitting next to each other. Their eyes are both open and bright. There is neither a hair, nor a crust of sleep nor of dust in their eyes. One of them sees something, but the other can't see anything.

Yes, the words of the people of heart who have attained are pleasant. Perhaps they don't teach something, but it is possible to learn many things from their words. That master of knowledge and wisdom says: "A human being who is full of his own knowledge and skills is like a jug full of water. Pour out that salty water within you, and let us fill you with this sweet, clean water."

He says, "Even a single drop of that life-giving water will make your cheeks rosy and bring you health and well-being. Whatever bile, black blood, phlegm, or traces of irritation you may have, it will clear them away. But in order to wash away those accumulations, in order to clear them, one must wash the jug seven times with clean water. It will never become clean if you wash it with foul water. Only with this sweet water will it become clean.

If the human being washes this earthen jug and fills it again with sweet water, those who see him will say, "No, I can no longer see that state he had when he was emptying, now while he is filling."

And that Owner of Beneficence says, "If you see me as the Owner of Beneficence, I am Forgiving, I am true to My Word." It is essential that he recognize this. Otherwise, if he delays in emptying what is in him, he will have waited too long. From lack of awareness of those meanings, without a doubt, such a person will remain full of his own I-ness.

A stomach already full of water has no appetite for drinking cool water. The feeling of I-ness in him has formed a hundred kinds of veils in front of his face and eye. How could these words affect him? How could he see me?

❁

Beyond the Lote Tree

Mevlana said, "I see trees, vineyards, and gardens in the palm of your hand. I see a clear and vast ocean of life-giving water. The trees aren't such that their roots descend low, and their branches pass beyond the Lote Tree (*Sidratul-Muntaha*) of the Seventh Heaven. Their shade and greenness is exceedingly beautiful." But no one sees this.

There is a secret and joy in love that those who are fond of lust are seeking. There are also lovers who are already absorbed within that secret. God says: "If people had known how I am, they would turn to Me from all directions, speak about Me, listen to Me, and be pleased with Me."

❁

Philosophy, Theology, and Truth

The easiest of these sciences is the science of the rituals of purification. Muslim religious law is more difficult, and the principles of the religious law are even more difficult than that. The principles of theology are also harder than those.

They say that philosophy and metaphysics are like trading blows with the prophets, except for fear of the sword. They try to prove their own way as right, but they speak rubbish—Plato and those who follow him say, "If everyone were like us, there would be no need for the prophets." This is rubbish!

If Plato heard that without any preparation, someone was turning earth into gold, "If you, also, do as he does, you will be his brother." But since you don't have the power to do this now, and you see that that person is superior to you, then why don't you see that it is necessary to follow him?[208]

---

208 Perhaps one might understand Shams to be saying, "When Muhammad was able to transform himself and through his way of surrender those around

❁

Taking the Medicine

If a sick person who comes to a doctor says, "O doctor! Give me a remedy for this disease that I have," he must not be looking for anything else. Let him seek only the cure. If they bring bread or sweet halvahs in front of a man who has come looking for water to drink, and if he eats them, the man is a liar in his claim of thirst. In the same way, if someone claims to be hungry—if they bring him clear water and he drinks, then he's a liar about being hungry.

❁

Completing Stories

You are speaking so sweetly, telling the story of the sultan and others. Let me also make a point. I'll tell you about Hajjaj. I turned to Mevlana and said, "One day Hajjaj, like a man sweating from the warmth, had gone out on a winter's day. The cold outside struck him so that he was about to freeze." I made a sign to Mevlana, "Now you should say something."

At that moment, Mevlana was plunged deep in reflection, but he listened to me, and began to speak. Just then the story of Hajjaj came to completion. Suddenly, his state changed—it is strange, but tears flew from his eyes.

I told the story of the sultan and the breaking of the pearl.

And in regard to the friends, I was occupied with nothing but praying, "O my God! Protect them." Let them follow the example of the Blessed Prophet! He asked for help from God, begging, "O Lord! Guide my people for they do not know."

❁

People of Paradise and People of Hell

Let me tell you about the qualities of the people of Paradise. Let me also tell you the sign of the people of Hell. Since the day God

---

him into shining lights, why do you not recognize that following his Way of Surrender would also help you in your own transformation?"

created this universe like an arrow shot from a bow, every day, every moment, He has been opening and closing doors. This takes place at such a limitless speed that one's mind stops.

Whomever you see who has a beautiful temperament and a beautiful face, if his/her words are straight forward, if he/she is open-hearted, and if he prays for good things for everyone, a joy of heart comes from the speech of such a person. He/she makes you forget the anxieties and tightness of this universe; your inside opens in such a way that even if he/she swears at you, you laugh. Maybe, when he speaks of unity, like Sirajuddin, you weep, but you feel a hundred thousand joys and laughter within yourself. Such a person is a being of paradise.

There is also a kind of person who drinks blood; there is a coldness on his face and in his words that only bring you anxiety. His words are repulsive, rather than warming like the speech of the joyful human being. Well, such a person is a devil, a person of Hell.

Now, whoever has realized such a secret behaves accordingly, and doesn't praise a hundred thousand shaikhs. Why would such a person be afraid of death—why should he value his head? An animal lives by its head, but the human being lives by his innermost secret (*sirr*) and intellect. Whoever lives only with his head, may death be upon him. But those who live according to their innermost secret and intellect are those human beings whom God created as people of Beneficence.[209] After all, how can that favor of God that is called "the secret" fit within a head and a conical hat?

❁

The Universe is Behind this Mirror

You are saying, "The universe is behind this mirror."

Yes, I see that *Jalal* Light of Power on the mirror. "I have no strength and power left, unless you give power and strength, O

---

209 *Now, truly, We have honored . . .* [*Surah al-Isra*, The Night Journey 17:70-72].

Sustainer!"[210] we are saying now, and God is saying, "Yes, but see to moving a little by yourself so that I may give you power and strength!" Yes, we are moving; with what difficulties we are moving our hands and feet to be liberated from this difficult place. O My God Most High!

In order to draw blood from small children, just as the cupper gives dried fruit like walnuts and raisins to them, and amuses and quiets them, in order to make them forget the pain they feel, just as he soothes them and then inserts his lancet, so, too, God who is the Most Great, busies His servant with these kinds of things and shows His Beauty first, and then He breaks the mirror. Then, the attained ones of the heart become the people of Truth; they remain in a strange bewilderment.

Mevlana's Adab

In order to one day be able to understand what his way is, one has to cast away from one's head shaikhood and fame. With all his heart and soul, he is the son of Muhammad, peace and blessings be upon him. He has become a shaikh whom God Most High has nourished and raised. The manners (*adab*) indicated in the *hadith*, "My God educated me with the most beautiful character," are his qualities. His distinguished sons are also like that.

Intensify Your Prayer

Yes, five times *salaat* a day is obligatory; sincerely do this. Even if your way is different, do it openly because it is obligatory. After the night prayer you can leave your spouse sleeping, amuse your son with raisins, quiet your daughter with walnuts, and do the *salaat* until morning; this is religiously allowed. The religion of Muhammad (peace and blessings upon him) is like this.

---

210 See *Surah Kahf*, The Cave: *Whatever God wills [shall come to pass, for] there is no power save with God* [18:39]*!*" . . . *For thus it is: all protective power belongs to God alone, the True One. He is the best to grant recompense, and the best to determine what is to be* [18:44].

You can also go to the place where they sing out the call to prayer and remain in seclusion there. If you haven't heard the voice of the muezzin because of spiritual absorption, it's more appropriate for you to take refuge within the shadow of God than to look for some hole to escape into. Then you will be secure from all cooling and death, and you will have become adorned with the attributes of the Truth. You will grasp the being of that Everliving One who keeps beings on their feet. Death dies if from a distance it sees you coming, because you have found divine life. One must walk quietly on this way, so that no one may hear.

✲

Real Knowing

Can this wisdom be gained in the *madrasah*? It can't be obtained there in six thousand years, in six times the length of the life of Noah. Hundreds of thousands of years of education are worth nothing compared to a servant's being in the presence of God for even one moment.

A single one of God's servants has the power to dissolve all the knowledge of Plato and show it as empty; in a moment he can do this. However, he will speak with him gently and say, "This man is a great philosopher!" Because Plato was both a philosopher and someone of knowledge. After all, he wrestled with the prophets, and that's not without meaning.

Sulayman-i Tirmidhi used to say, "At least convey the words of the people of religion." Now these people who give advice from the pulpits and sit on prayer-carpets are the highwaymen of the religion of Muhammad. They position themselves comfortably on the prayer rug of Bayazid, and speak from the pulpit of Shaqiq-i Balkhi! Who do they think they are advising? The community there? Where is the community? Go, stand up and whirl. . . .

Teaching and Learning

One day, someone said to me: "I benefit more from Mevlana's counsel than yours."

In response to this, I said: "Let's bring the community of friends together, let's discuss something so that they might understand."

The purpose for this is not to mislead the community, but to learn. It's just as in the Qur'an, when the prophet Joseph was yearning for God;He taught him this yearning. *O Sustainer! You have given me [something] of sovereignty and have taught me [something] of the interpretation of words and dreams* [12:101]. The words, "*Originator of the heavens and the earth*" were also taught to him in a special way.[211] In a broad way also, again in the next verse, it was said that only God, and those who are greatly advanced in knowledge, know how to interpret this.[212]

[Joseph] says, *Kill me as a muslim*! Isn't that strange! Considering this explanation, which "Islam" does Joseph want? And then he says, "*Join me with the community of the good and upright ones*!" Which good and upright ones?

In every prophet there is goodness and uprightness, but prophethood is not in every righteous one. He means, "My God! You did not leave me without a share of prophethood; don't leave me without a portion of the saints either; join my spirit with them!" If it were not so, would he want to persevere both in Islam and in joining the good and upright ones?

The Command cannot be ignored. There is no doubt that the commandments of this poor one (*fakir*) also have their usefulness.

---

211 *O my Sustainer! You have indeed bestowed upon me something of power, and have imparted to me some knowledge of the inner meaning of happenings. Originator of the heavens and the earth! You are near to me in this world and in the life to come: let me die as one who has surrendered himself to You (muslim), and make me one with the good and upright ones!* [*Surah Yusuf*, Joseph 12:101]

212 *Truly, my Sustainer is unfathomable in [the way He brings about] whatever He wills: truly, He alone is all-knowing, truly wise!* [*Surah Yusuf*, Joseph 12:100]

See also 12:76: *We do raise to [high] degrees [of knowledge] whomever We will—but above everyone who is endowed with knowledge there is One who knows all.*

By these commandments, the doors of spirituality are opened. The *poor one* doesn't fix his eye on the world, its favors or ornaments—he himself is good fortune beyond description.

The Great Turning (Tawba)

Without a doubt, the children of the wealthy and those who have benefited from the favors of the world don't need anything; they may not run after it, but in them there is a wish for softness and a great desire to get along easily with people. If they dive too much into the pleasures of the world, harmony is lost, and if they behave outrageously, or if they are frustrated, mischief occurs. Even those among them who feel some sadness about their desires, and those who anticipate something other than their own superiority, can't separate their desires (*nafs al-ammarah*) from the world.

They never try to approach repentance, but get drawn further into worldly desires. They have no relationship with the spiritual guidance of: *Did he not find you wandering, and guide you?* [*Surah Dhuha* 93:7]. Instead they all run in the direction of waywardness. When the devil makes you lose your way in your desires, can you ever find the right way by yourself? When he makes you lose control over your desires, your state then seems more pleasant to you than if Gabriel were to reach you. Perhaps only God, with His help and efforts towards His servant, can turn you away from this.

Tasting the Moment

My *nafs* shows such obedience to me that even if they were to bring hundreds of thousands of plates of halvah and kababs, and even if I had an appetite, I would never even turn around and look at the food that others crave. The barley bread that I give it in the right moment is more pleasant than the kabab that I might give it at the wrong moment.

Microcosm or Macrocosm

According to the scholars, the microcosm is hidden within the creation of the human being, and the macrocosm is this universe that surrounds us. But according to the prophets, this outer universe is the microcosm; the macrocosm is the human being. And so, this world is just an indication of the universe within the human being.[213]

> I won't let you become just a thought in this heart.
> I don't want you to be brought low by these eyes.
> I'm keeping you within my soul,
> not in my eye or my heart,
> so that with my last breath you might
> still be my beloved!

My Lord Gives Me Food

Yes, God gives lots of gold, and He gives it even if I am not wanting it. As you give to me you say, "With this money you can buy a mill. Buy it—let me turn it for you."

The mill is made of stones and iron, but this is made of flesh, skin, nerves, and veins. Besides that, it has a soul and life—if you don't give, I will turn, myself.

Because of this, everyday many times they reject me, saying, "It would be more useful if he earned three or five coins."

Well, it was these words that caused me to lose my appetite during my childhood. Although three or four days would pass, I wouldn't eat anything. Not because of the words of the people, but because I was in awe of the words of the Truth.

Without reason, I had lost any interest in eating and drinking. My father would say, "Eat, my son!" I was saying, "I can't eat any-

---

213 Shams reminds us here of the verse: *Truly, We did offer the trust to the heavens, and the earth, and the mountains: but they refused to bear it because they were afraid of it. Yet man took it up. . . .* [*Surah al-Ahzab*, The Confederates 33:72], and also the *hadith qudsi*, "The heavens and the earth could not encompass Me, but I am encompassed by the heart of My faithful servant." See also "Where is the Heart?" p.184 of this text.

thing. But I am not getting weak; my strength is such that if I want to I can fly like a bird out of the window."

"There is a wonder in this, but he doesn't want to reveal it to you," they said.

Miracles are shown to those who are deniers. If you are not a complete denier, it isn't revealed to you. It is revealed to one who asks for it, and it occurs within a community, not off in a corner somewhere. There is a community of people around us.

Signs

Now, let me say something about the matter of Mevlana saying I was hurt.

"Shams is benefiting a lot from Mevlana's words," I heard they had said. Yes, from this point of view it is beneficial for me, in this way he helps me—he indicates certain signs to me. But those signs are not for you. They are only for me. His speaking is not to you either.[214]

Well, you see how he found me as a poor stranger, and how he brought me into ease and peace! So whose Mevlana is Mevlana? If he gives a name to someone, he never abandons him.

Every dream that he would see at night would become true before the morning *salaat,* and its effect would last until the time of the second *salaat.* I worked strongly from the heart so that this might not turn into a habit.

Praising

Everybody in the *dergah* knows that even a lifeless being couldn't endure this for more than seven months. At the *madrasah,* those who listen to me go crazy, but why should one make sane people crazy—then the possibility of talking with them is lost. However, it is a fact that whether I am a Sufi or not, the *dergah* is a place for pure people. They don't have to worry about shopping or cooking.

---

214 M. 100.

Lifeless beings also experience separation and uniting. However, their moanings aren't often heard. As it says in the Qur'an: "*There is nothing that does not celebrate His immeasurable glory—but you fail to grasp the manner of their glorifying Him*! [17:44]."[215]

❊

Where Is the Heart?

Where is the heart? They give the shameful one advice, "Purify your self (*nafs*) from filth, stinginess, and bad habits so that you may be saved from hell," but they don't speak to him about the qualities of the heart.

God Most High has shown the rank of the heart: "The earth and heavens could not encompass Me, but I am encompassed within the heart of My faithful servant (*hadith qudsi*)," and "The heart of the believer is between the two fingers of the Infinitely Merciful (*hadith qudsi*)," and "He looks at your heart (*hadith*)."

He said, "So I thought a lot about this saying of Sanai, 'You will see a heart purified from all kinds of excessive desires and stinginess,' and I pushed my mind to find the proof of this meaning."

Then Mevlana recited the verse of Sanai:

> O Sanai! In this world, try to live
> like a poor wandering dervish—
> throw earth in the eyes of the pretenders to purity!

❊

Following Muhammad

How can one join the community of Muhammad? Where is Muhammad (upon him be peace)? Where is "following him" both in form and in meaning?

That light and brightness by which Muhammad's eye saw should become the living light of his eye. The eye of Muhammad should become his eye.

---

215 See "The Moaning Pillar" section p.51 of this text.

He should become adorned with patience and his other qualities. Leaving other attributes aside, he should become adorned with patience and even more beautiful characteristics.

❊

Being and Nothingness

What is a Shaikh? Being. What is a disciple? Isn't he only non-being? As a matter of fact, a disciple cannot be a disciple unless he becomes nothing.

❊

Intensifying Witnessing

One who sees us becomes either the Muslim of Muslims or the unbeliever of the unbelievers. Those who see insufficiency in our worship in respect to its outer appearance, are those who have not been able to reach our meaning and see only our outside. Those who think, "His help is so great, he doesn't need this worship," drift away from worship, which is the real cause of connection between worlds.

❊

God Is the Best Protector

The sect of the Mu'tazilites is close to philosophy. It is said, "The one who digs a well for his brother falls into it himself."

What kind of belief is this? I am coming from the side of dervishhood, and even though this way is full of many terrors and dangers, still one sees that God Most High protects you.

Now you are with a dervish. What kind of evil, fearful thought do these people have that they refer to God as "Ahmad, the oxherd"?[216] What will teach them manners?

---

216 I.e., As though God could lose someone and then need to find him . . . See "O Glorious Morning Light," p.130 of this text.

❊

Generosity Keeps Calling Us

Let's say I have worn a bad suit for a while—this is my own choice, because what God wishes for me is all blessing within blessing and generosity within generosity. And yet it is also a fact that what I deserve may be gentleness or stringency depending on the situation. How can I feel sad due to grace?

❊

A Stranger in a Strange Land

Every four days a weariness would come over me, but after a little while this state would pass. I could not swallow even a morsel.

"What's happened to you?" they would ask.

"Nothing has happened to me. Do I seem mad? Have I torn off my clothes? Have I struck you, or torn your clothes?"

"But you aren't eating anything," they would say.

"No, I am not eating today . . . tomorrow, the day after, another day."

What would a fellow villager know? Even my father didn't know anything of me! I was a stranger in my own town, and even my father was a stranger to me. My heart was frightened of him. I used to think that he might tear into me, and even though he was speaking gently to me, I used to think that he might beat me and kick me out of the house.

I would say, "If my spiritual being was born from his meaning, the meaning within me would have to be his offspring. It should be in harmony with him and become perfected, but I am like a duck's egg put under a hen." Tears would flow from his eyes.

❊

Make Use of the Light

Muhammad (May the Peace and Blessings of God be upon him) has said, "O My God Most High! We could not worship You as You ought to be worshipped." But Bayazid said, "Glory be to me; how great is my glory!" When things come to this, if someone looks at these words of Bayazid and thinks that his state is stronger than Muhammad's state, then he is an ignorant fool.

If you are looking for the reality of the Law, yes, there is the Law, and there is the Way, and the Truth. The Law is like a lamp, and the purpose of the lamp is to give you light when you journey. You can trust it simply—you put a wick into it and hang it up, and you can see the surrounding area by its light. But if you don't go anywhere, what is the use? How can you reach the Truth with a light that just stays put? It is essential that you reach the Truth! Journey on the Way!

The Entrancing Trap

Beyond this world of water and earth, beyond the mountain in the Unseen universe, like Gog and Magog[217] we were mixed together with each other. Suddenly, the call, "*Go down* [2:36]!" came to us. From there we came down to this lowly universe. From far away, in the distance within the universe of darkness and nothingness, existence emerged. Cities and trees could not yet be seen.

We were like children who had never seen this universe. As we came closer, gradually the problem of grains and traps began to appear in front of our eye. If the delight in the grain had not overcome the difficulties of falling into the trap, this universe and this being would not have come into existence.

They say Adam saw a stone far away coming towards him in its majesty. His love overflowed and he ran towards it.

The Door of Worship

There is a sultan in the palace. The way that leads to the sultan passes through the door. In other words, those who come to Him

---

217 M. 105.

Gog and Magog are symbolic of the peoples who greedily wrought destruction on the earth. See *Surah al-Kahf*, The Cave 18:94-110.

are respectful—they don't try to climb over the very high walls of the palace. *I take refuge in God!*[218] Those who want to jump over those walls fall down. And those disrespectful ones who think that everything is permissible get stuck at the door.

Some people are very confused about how to behave as servants of God. I said, "This is their incompleteness." There is another answer, but here words become dangerous. Listen to these words very carefully.

Those who come from outside of the door must enter the Sultan's palace through the door. But the Sultan also has some pure servants who are already inside. This is very difficult; there is great danger here.

Muhammad (peace and blessings upon him) was one of those pure servants, and yet he still performed his servanthood completely.

In answer we say, "Even when the Prophet gained complete strength and power, the meaning of servanthood never decreased in him; it only continued to increase." He knew the exalted pleasure of servanthood. When he was at the door, he saw himself as inside, and when he was inside, he also saw himself as inside.

But this aspect was weak in others, and that meaning was lessening in them. And so, Abu Sai'd (Ibn Abi al-Khayr) said, "What kind of a man is this?" about Avicenna (Ibn Sina). "He did a few things, but it is as if he didn't accomplish anything."

❁

The Moment of Prayer

Although sometimes Mevlana and I unintentionally miss the time of worship during the day, we aren't happy about it. Privately we make up for what we have missed. Especially on Fridays, if I don't go to

218 By taking refuge in God, the door is opened. See 19:18, 23:97, 40:56; see also *Surahs* 113 and 114.

Bow in worship and draw near [96:19].

the *salaat*,[219] my heart becomes constricted. I feel sad, and ask myself why I couldn't join its meaning with this meaning. Even though there is not a real sorrow, still I feel sad. The divine guidance can suddenly draw a servant in while he is worshipping.

Right Speech, Right Action

First of all, remember this advice: there is no repetition of my words; I never say the same thing twice. What's appropriate is not to repeat my words but to put them into action. Whatever has happened has all happened because of the repeating of our words. Never repeat them.

If someone insists, "Please tell us those life-giving and sweet words so that we may listen!"

Say, "I cannot repeat what was said. If it is necessary for you, go and listen!"

When it is the right time to speak, I know it; then I will speak. But if I don't see it as appropriate, I won't speak.

Everyday He Is about Some New Endeavor

There is a *hadith*: "God Most High has completed creating the creatures and their qualities and determining the measure of their sustenances and their lives." This is true, but there is also a verse that says, *Everyday He is about some new endeavor* [55:29],[220] and this needs to be explained in relation to this *hadith*.

---

219 The friday gathering for prayer in the mosque is a special time for the community to come together in worship.

220 *All that is on earth will perish; but forever will abide the Face of your Sustainer, Full of Majesty and Abundant Honor.*

Then which of your Sustainer's blessings will you deny?

Every creature in the heavens and on earth depends on Him: every day He manifests in wondrous new ways!

Then which of your Sustainer's blessings will you deny? [Surah ar-Rahman, The Most Compassionate *55:26-30].*

In other words, everyday, He is interested in the state of His servant and never separates from him—this is so from the infinite past to the infinite future.

❊

Wordless as a Wall

In order to benefit from a shaikh, I asked two questions. He didn't answer. I wonder if he saw us as unable to benefit from the answer he would give? Or did he think that we were not capable of understanding it? Or that it was not our portion to know it?

He said: "It is not his custom; he doesn't give answers to such questions. Only when the moment comes, if he becomes joyful he begins the conversation (*sohbet*) and speaks."

But you see, what the shaikh says is all conveyed from this or that one, artificial things. He relates either a *hadith*, or a story, or the poem of a poet. He doesn't speak a word from himself. "Tell something from your own births, give an answer," I am saying!

But he is speaking with the language of his state. Just as that wall tells you, "What voice do you expect from me?" Does anybody hope that a voice will emerge from this wall?

❊

The Helper

"What is the place of knowledge or books here! Have you killed your *nafs*?" I said, "Because 'to die' means not to fall into darkness again." That pleasure must be continuous within you, complete. Consider the *nafs* as dead, so that slowly it may die.[221]

Now, this is dependent upon someone's help. God has bound that to a cause—if a person turns toward God, this is the first cause. So a person comes. Even if there is a wall from earth to heaven in front of you, that helper removes that wall that blocks your way—with a single kick, he knocks it down. He also teaches you how he tore down other walls! Now, when you become bound to his help,

221 M. 110.

your work continues until it is completed. With his help, the attraction of God comes.

What use is it to surrender to God's decree? One must be content with his deeds; no matter what he does or says—you surrender. Don't do anything that might cause that helper to cut off that help! Respect and love towards him causes that help to increase.

Divine Wine

We drank and drank; we emptied cups, carafes, and jugs! So that even the pourer and the cup got tired of our hand! The cupbearer makes everyone weary, but this one made that cupbearer weary and helpless in his hands.

Continuous wine makes the reason depart—if you don't get drunk with ten cups, you get drunk with twelve, or let's say you have to drink a large jug full of wine and finish it, and you drink another jug, and then you drink the whole barrel, and you consume whatever there is.

Then the tavern-keeper tells you, "If this tavern has been emptied, there are still many other taverns in the city; go there."

Are these words that we are speaking? Who can drink a whole barrel full of wine? Not one in a hundred can do that.

But, in this world, no one has ever heard of a man who is fond of chugging his wine becoming more and more sober—one who the more he drinks, filled to the throat, becomes more sober—who is that sober sane one who makes a world and a universe sanely sober, too? Well, that would be amazing!

But don't you see that hero who is saturated with Divine wine, who holds the wine in his hand! From tip to toe his being has become the wine. That hero has come. Don't you see that grand shaikh who turned the wine upside down! But that falling is a thousand times better than the standing.

I swear by God that God will again, in the end, grab from us that hero whom we grabbed and stood upon his feet. Veils were placed in front of you on the way. But if that devil has come from someone other than God, it means he doesn't exist. The devil cannot stand in front of you. Know this well!

You see how I grabbed you—I remembered one of our friends. I am not saying "one of our enemies," because he would become one of the friends.

☼

In the Dyeing Vat of Hu

Mevlana's words are exactly to the point. He said, "Whomever he swears at, he turns into a saint."

Just then a thought passed through his mind that when you came, we were saying, "He came". . ."—It is not right for him to stop our conversation.

I said, "There is so much strength here—let's dye them with a single hue."[222]

Even without the obligatories of "standing" (*qiyam*) and "bowing" (*ruku*),[223] if you are together with God, strength comes to your soul. Your flesh disappears and your eyes melt into flowing water.

☼

Clear Words

"Too many words are like a donkey's burden," they say. True, but still, one understands things by means of words. However, words should be both instructive and clear. When one is speaking, one should speak sweetly, beautifully, and aesthetically. Words shouldn't be dry and tasteless; the clearer your speech, the brighter it is.

---

222 See *Mathnawi* II, 1345-1347:

> The baptism of God is the dyeing vat of Hu,
> God's absoluteness, in which all colors become one.
> When the contemplative falls into that vat—
> and you say, "Come out."
> He says, "I am the vat . . . The red-hot iron has taken on the color of fire.

223 I.e., If you are together with God, even without the obligatory postures of the ritual prayer (*salaat*), your soul strengthens.

Sometimes, even when people speak the opposite of words that are enjoyable, still we can't call them tasteless words. There is a word that you can pull and turn in all directions. Just as when you say, "When he was jumping down from the minaret, half way down he regretted it!"

I am not interfering with your words. I am not saying, "Go ahead, say it, but it's not realistic."

"If you have power," he said, "the words you speak seem very attractive to me."

I asked him, "From now on, what attraction are you looking for?" Whatever you say, I will listen to it—I am pulling it in the direction of the Truth. I am enjoying it.

❊

Show Us Things as They Really Are

Those who don't understand the inner meaning of the prayer of the Blessed Prophet, "O Instructor! Show us things as they really are,"[224] live comfortably in this universe of stones and lumps of manure. Only those whose eyes are open become spectators of the universe of God. And yet, aren't your ear and mind also on this path?

"Yes, yes!" he said.

❊

Becoming a True Muslim

They say: "One has to become a Muslim."

Yes, if Islam is necessary, one has to work for it, otherwise what can one gain from a deceiving mind? Meaningless words, aren't they?

"Yes," I said. "And Islam was born from careful thought, it is very good. Aren't there also the elect servants of God, who have been educated among Muslims and yet have a fear of that Islam? From a very young age, all of them have worked for nothing but

---

224 *Hadith*: O God, show us the truth as the truth and give us the blessing of following it; show us falsehood as falsehood and give us the blessing of avoiding it.

surrender, and they don't either. No matter how much they avoid Islam and being a Muslim, Islam[225] is clearly seen on their faces."[226]

An Open Secret

I am reciting the words of the Great Master (*Sultan ul-Ulama*, the father of Mevlana Jalaluddin). He says: "If you cannot see the Truth, how can you prostrate? Are you prostrating yourself in front of someone other than God?"

After all, is there any inconsistency in these words which if you wrote them down some would say are blasphemy? In the Qur'an it was said, *Say: "If all the sea were ink for my Sustainer's words, the sea would indeed be exhausted before my Sustainer's words are exhausted! Even if We were to add to it sea upon sea* [18:109]." Some people have fearlessly spoken very clearly about this.

How can there be a secret in the story of Joseph and Zuleikha? However, if the owner of that secret wants it to be revealed, he reveals it. Otherwise, as long as the secret exists, it remains a secret.

According to those who don't know, there is no secret. According to them, everything is manifest. Where is that human being who does not have a secret within himself?

A secret that has come to the Jews and the fire worshippers, and has reached their children, how can it be a secret? Yes, something may be a secret, but how can something that the Qur'an says is

---

225 I.e., surrender and the peace that comes with surrender. *Witness—the only true religion in the sight of God is self-surrender to Him/Her* [*Surah al 'Imran*, The House of Imran, 3:16-19].

226 See *Surah al-Fath*, 48: 28-29:

It is He Who has sent His Messenger with guidance and the Way of Truth, so that it might prevail over all false ways; and God is sufficient as witness. Muhammad is the Messenger of God; and those who are with him stand firm when facing those who deny the Truth, and are compassionate with each other.

You can see them bow and prostrate themselves in prayer, seeking grace from God and His good pleasure. On their faces are their marks, traced by prostration.

This is their parable in the Torah, and their parable in the Gospel: like a seed which sends forth its shoot, which grows strong, so that it becomes thick, and then stands firm on its stem, delighting those who sow with wonder.

obligatory, remain a secret? Yes, there may be a secret, but a thing that the Qur'an openly commands as "obligatory" is not a secret. It cannot be in varied hues, either. How can the secret be in varied colors? Especially if the spiritual help within the words is continuous.

Moving Slowly towards Clarity

Come, O clear spirit!

Let's say we are like water that flows beneath straw. The water slowly moves under the straw, but the straw isn't aware of it until suddenly it is thrown into the air. *All scattered dust* [25:23] it flies away, but the water remains, flowing on.

In the place where you are, the Friend is apparent. In order to hunt a lion, they show him a smaller animal, a bobcat. Unless he sees the prey, you cannot hunt a lion. The Sufi also matures by moving slowly.

Shihabuddin Suhrawardi spoke about the Self of God and the Transcendent Self. My heart wants Nasiruddin.

He spoke to Ziya, saying, "My wife is not going along the way of God."

And he answered, "They are sleeping—they are asleep; we must wake them up."

Happiness

I swear that seeing your face is happiness for us. If someone wants to see Muhammad easily, let him go and see Mevlana. Like grass waving in the wind, without forcing oneself, bow in front of him. If someone wants to behave otherwise, let him live as he wills.

But how happy is the one who has found Mevlana!

Who am I? I have found once, and I am happy.

If you have any doubts, he will show you a shortcut out of your confusion. But due to your doubt, you may enjoy it for a time, and for a time a coldness comes to you. That is not a way to work, that is not a way to make friends either. This way is the way that goes to the other side.

Day and Night

"May your days pass in goodness, may your nights pass in felicity!"—what is the meaning of saying this to Mevlana?

One day someone asked, "What is the meaning of the verse, *Chant the name of God in the early mornings and the evening* [33:42],[227] and *Glorify Him through the long nights* [76:26]?"

I answered, "When a child is learning how to write, he only understands the words literally. In the same way, you are also understanding only the basic meaning of the words. So what is the difference? Since you can't reach that reality, you cannot reach that station, either. What is the difference, I wonder?"

He said, "'The night' means that a cloud comes and draws a veil in front of you. How is it possible that the disciple of a saint could see Him seventy times a day? Even a prophet sent with a book hasn't been able to reach that station.

"All the scholars understand that a specific characteristic has been given to each prophet—the honor of friendship to Abraham, speech to Moses, and vision—the seeing of the Face of God, to Muhammad.

"But if a person says, 'Sainthood and prophethood are in perception,' this is just to preserve the place of the ordinary person. They express it through other words—even though they don't openly speak about the overflowing of divine lights, births, and unveilings, that is the Reality.[228]

---

227 See *Surah al-Ahzab*, The Confederates, 33:41-43:

> *O you who have attained to faith! Remember God with unceasing remembrance, and extol His limitless glory from morn to evening. He it is who bestows His blessings upon you, with His angels [echoing Him], so that He might take you out of the depths of darkness into the light. And, indeed, a dispenser of grace is He unto the faithful.*

228 M. 115.

"Now a point upon which all the scholars agree is that a saint cannot reach the station of a prophet. How would that which a saint or a saint's disciple sees, be hidden from a prophet? *Whoever is blind in this world will also be blind in the next world* [17:72]."

These words that Mevlana wrote in his letter are stimulating; they are exciting. Even a stone, within its stoniness, would begin to move.

Breathings from Your Lord

The Prophet said: "In your time there are breathings that will come to you from your Lord, so open yourself to receive them." You should speak about this tradition and its meaning, and interpret it.

It seems that these beautiful breathings are the breath of a servant who has attained such a closeness to God that he has become the alchemy of happiness. Neither that book, nor alchemy, nor happiness could be compared with it—if one particle of this elixir were put into a hundred million storehouses full of copper, all of them would become pure gold.

So they ask, "Where is that breath of that man of God?"

> Last night, in my dream a shaikh told me,
> "The trouble of the way of love is all because of
> 'I' and 'we.'
> I said to him, "Then which one is 'I' and
> which one 'we'?
> "The remedy for all difficulties is within You,"
> He said, "Anything that is not the Truth is all
> 'I' and 'we'
> —that is the source of every error."

The word is one of the attributes of God. God enters into words—He veils Himself so that words may reach people, that He may not remain outside the veil. Otherwise how could He make His words heard by people? It is all within His Power—if He wishes, He draws the veil in front of Him; if He wishes, He throws it back. It is not they who remove the cover of the things that He has veiled. This is why I say that when I speak, I descend into a weaker state.

The attributes of God don't separate from Him. Miracles and wonders are the attributes of the servant—God doesn't have miracles. The elect servants are guided by the attributes of God.[229]

❊

Within the Presence

Even without being in retreat, a state of continuous seclusion comes to you when you are in the presence of the shaikh, when you are serving a real shaikh. Such a state comes to you that it is as if you are always in seclusion. God has such servants that someone who serves them finds himself constantly within seclusion.[230]

❊

Welcoming the Festival of Eagerness

We had heard that lots of semas and invitations were happening in Konya, but I haven't seen them—I mean they don't have anything of the state or words.[231]

He said, "You will see."[232]

---

229 See *Surah as-Shura*, Consultation, 42:51-53:

And it is not given to mortal man that God should speak unto him otherwise than through sudden inspiration, or from behind a veil, or by sending an apostle to reveal, by His leave, whatever He wills: for, truly, He is exalted, wise.

And thus, too, have We revealed unto you a life-giving message, at Our behest. You did not know what revelation is, nor what faith [implies]: but [now] We have caused this [message] to be a light, whereby We guide whom We will of Our servants: and, truly, [on the strength thereof] you, too, shall guide onto the straight way—the way that leads to God, to whom all that is in the heavens and all that is on earth belongs. Oh, truly, with God is the beginning and the end of all things!

230 Shams is referring to the state when one's mind and heart are continuously fixed within the Presence of God.

231 "State and speech" (*hal wa kal*) are important terms in the Sufi glossary. A person's state and his words reveal his spiritual development.

232 By their fruits you will know them . . . . And as God says in a number of places in the Qur'an, on Resurrection Day all will become clear, "You will see." You will see the Truth by means of the Truth.

See Mevlana's *ghazal* in *The Pocket Rumi Reader*, "Love is a Stranger," translated by Kabir Helminski, Shambhala Publications, 2001, p.23.

Since the day I saw your beauty, an interest and love for you placed itself in my heart. If you didn't know how to write, I would have taught you how to write. But you knew how already.

I want a person who knows nothing, but who is eager to learn.

In this moment, as soon as I say this, you manifest humility. You feel sad that this interest was not shown to you, and you don't hear what I say.

Heart came on solid footing with breath refined
to warn the best of communities.
Heart placed your head
like a pen on the page of love.

We are joyous pennants in your just wind.
Master, to where do you dance?
Toward the land of liberation,
toward the plain of non-existence.

Master, tell us which non-existence you mean.
The ear of eternity knows the letter of eternity.

Love is a stranger with a strange language,
like an Arab in Persia. I have brought a story;
it is strange, like the one who tells it.
Listen to your servant.

Joseph's face enlightened the well in which he hung.
His imprisonment became a palace
with orchards and meadows, a paradise,
a royal hall, and a chamber of sanctity.

Just as you toss a stone into the water,
the water at that very moment parts to receive it.
Just as a cloudy night is dispelled by a clear dawn,
from his humiliation and loss he views high heaven.

Reason, do not envy my mouth.
God witnesses the blessings.
Though the tree drinks from hidden roots,
we see the display of its branches.
Whatever the earth took from heaven,
it yields up honestly in spring.

Whether you have stolen a bead or a jewel,
whether you have raised a flag or a pen,
the night is gone and day has arrived,
and the sleeper shall see what he has dreamed.

He found himself by means of his self (nafs) [93:7]—God forbid, may you not say, "He lost his way," about the Prophet, or attribute "losing and then finding him again," to God. Don't get confused by the many interpretations! Although this saying has an obvious meaning, a hundred million secrets are revealed here for the seeker of the Truth. Through it, obstacles that surround the names of God are removed, and it also teaches how to dissolve other walls and obstacles.

Didn't they designate the word *nafs* as "feminine"? If I can hide the secret here, let me keep it hidden.

❋

Beyond Obligation

Someone said, "He dove deeply."

Someone else said, "This must be due to remembrance (*zhikr*)."

I said, "No, it happened due to the One who is remembered, that is, God."

One who sacrifices his self, without a doubt remains alive [with real life], because he sees his life in that sacrifice, and he clearly understands where he is going in the end. But how can one who recognizes life give this life to sensuality—unless he is crazy and considers death [living absorbed with the ego] superior to life. The one who clearly sees it organizes his life accordingly.

Once that divine bird within you flies out of the well of the body, from then on it is freed from the thought of fasting or the obligation of prayer. Because when the spirit has flown, the body is dead. Who can say to the dead, "Stand up and do *salaat*!" Just as such an invitation would be unnecessary then, for the same reason, one doesn't demand such things of the living dead either.[233]

---

233 See the reference to Abu Bakr on p.82 of this text.

❊

Whirling to the Beat of Alif

When that woman teacher was teaching the Arabic alphabet to the children, she was singing a melody, "*Alif*, dot, *alif* for I,"[234] and clapping her hands. A state came to me, and I began to whirl.

I said, "I have nothing covering me, but "*alif*, dot, *alif*." Even on a winter's day, I have no sheepskin cloak!"[235]

❊

Let the Cotton Fall Away

When we are speaking to someone, if we can't see his interest in this work, we tell him, "Go away," because it creates difficulties on the path; so we avoid it.

We are waiting for the moment when nothing is left of the *nafs* within him. Then, just as when a wound of the body heals, the cotton bandage falls away.

❊

A Merging

Mevlana kissed me on my forehead: "I am I, but now I have become you. Don't you see it exactly like that?" Assume this oneness to be a merging.

---

234 The arabic letters "alif" (a straight line), "nun" (a semicircle with a dot above), followed by another "alif" form the word "ana" which means I.

235 The sheepskin is a symbol of the *nafs*, the animal nature. And so it has become traditional for dervishes to sit upon sheepskins in gatherings for worship, symbolic of the subduing of the ego. *Inshallah* (God willing), when self surrenders completely to the Beloved, the lover is merged with the Beloved until "nothing remains but my name." See *Mathnawi* V:2020-2024 (*The Pocket Rumi Reader*, p.190.)

At breakfast tea a beloved asked her lover,
"Who do you love more, yourself or me?"
"From my head to my foot I have become you.
Nothing remains of me but my name.
You have your wish. Only you exist.
I've disappeared like a drop of vinegar in an ocean of honey."

Stand up, and let's go. Where have you been my friend? In which mosque did you and I make *salaat*? Now it is time for weeping, but I am not weeping. But Perir was weeping. I made him sit down by the fountain, and he became quiet. I gave him a few windings of turban—pull his ear so that he might weep.

You and I are pleased, you see! God has created me for you; for you, I sacrificed the whole world.

Go and search—I could not see that Shams; is he in Aleppo? —I wonder?

It must be due to the sadness of those disciples who have lost their way that he is like that—they take a few steps and then they cool like ice.[236] But if he had seen me, he would serve me devotedly; he wouldn't have let me come, and these silver coins would stay with me. For goodness sake! You are staring in a strange way! Yes, what are you saying?

O Lord! There isn't even a single day when the respect and love in my heart towards him decreases! God willing, don't ever think of leaving.[237]

---

236 I.e., They lose their love and affection for the path and their guide.

237 See Mevlana's *ghazal*: "You and I," *The Pocket Rumi Reader*, p.41:

> A moment of happiness,
> you and I sitting on the verandah,
> apparently two, but one in soul, you and I.
>
> We feel the flowing water of life here,
> you and I, with the garden's beauty,
> the birds singing.
>
> The stars will be watching us,
> and we will show them
> how it is to be the thinnest crescent moon.
>
> You and I unselfed, will be together,
> indifferent to idle speculation, you and I.
> The parrots of heaven will be cracking sugar
> as we laugh together, you and I.
>
> And what is even more amazing
> is that while here together, you and I

Making the Impossible Possible

Troublesome imaginations are not necessarily bad. A clean, beautiful, and bright image can also become a veil for you. Where does it lead? It is yours, but even if that provision was given today, next week it will be something different. That provision reaches you today, because it belongs to you!

Even if it were not yours, if you hadn't earned it, if God wanted it to be so, still it would reach you. This is how the work of God is. He makes impossible things possible. He makes even the congenitally blind to see. When a complete whiteness comes to the eye, the philosophers' minds deny that this eye could ever see again, but to the mind of the Prophets it could. The philosopher who recognizes it says, "This is not my work, I don't have that power."[238] But if he were to speak like this, he would be a Muslim.

The servant is then left in such a situation that he falls down, prostrating himself upon his face, but if the help of God takes his hand, he stands up again.

Love Remembers

The human being remembers often the one whom he/she loves. Especially if that beloved is God! But who is able to remember Him as He deserves to be remembered?

We are remembering You all the time; we are filled with Your love.

La illaha illallah

"Don't drink wine in front of me," I told them.

---

are at this very moment in Iraq and Khorasan.
In one form upon this earth,
and in another form in a timeless sweet land.

238 M. 120.

They said, "We are religious scholars of the madrasahs and the mosques. We aren't afraid!"

But you are doing something that will make you sad—what does it matter if you get rebuked from time to time?

Their words didn't scare me. Even if I were to sit down inside the barrel, my clothes wouldn't be sullied for prayer; what harm does it have for me?

Ever since I was a child I have been far from it. If I saw a drunkard even at a distance, I would be repelled, concerned that it might fall upon me.

❊

Drinking La illaha illallah

Today by saying, "*La illaha illallah*," that is, "There is no god, but only God," first you deny God, then you begin to remember God. The unbelievers begin to prove His oneness only after saying, "*La illaha illallah*," completely. Then they throw dark delusions from their minds—those delusions leave and pass away, and after this, the brightest light begins, after this unifying (*tawhid*). This is the foundation of the work. But what the hoja and the one who supposes himself to be a scholar drink is not this.

❊

Burning the Past

What is passing through my mind? If you forget the tasteless, unpleasant memories that passed between us, or if you cover them over, then I, too, regard them as though they never happened. Yet, wherever you are, you are still considered incomplete.

I thought, "I wonder what there is between this son of Mevlana Jaluluddin and me? —God knows."[239]

"Perplexing," he said.

---

239 Shams is referring here to Mevlana's second son Alaeddin who struggled with Shams' presence in the family and his father's devotion to him. Alaeddin was not receptive to his mystical teachings and unlike his older brother Weled, would treat Shams with disrespect and animosity.

I am surprised to see that you are still dwelling on this event. There is no doubt that during the first year, you and we were in a state of disagreement, but I never made this clear to you. And because I hid this, day by day the disagreement increased. There is no doubt that this word of mine is like a burning fire.

During the first year, I was also roasted by this fire. I told lots of stories. But from now on, what has passed has passed, and I have also given up on it.

In any case, how long will you keep talking of these things? They are all stories that have been told again and again.

A time came when I was completely on fire.

Moses and Khidr

If a person claims that he really loves someone, evidence is asked from him. And that evidence is the giving away of possessions, the granting of favors. Just as when Mevlana claimed that he loved me, when I came he granted me thousands of favors and protected me. I regard these all as a grace from God.

Moses said, "My God! Would you give me a friend who would serve me without my asking him?"

"I wonder if He gave him or not," I said. "Did He also give success to him from this companion that He gave?"

"See," he said.

He asked a second time, and Khidr answered him with anger, "*Didn't I tell you that you will never be able to have patience with me* [18:75]?"

This anger was not from the *nafs*. How could there be anger that comes from the ego in the pure servants of God? *We take refuge in God*. It was a divine anger. One has to be careful to avoid it.

Work Hard to Avoid Obstacles

Work and endeavor so that there may be no obstacle, no veil. I have taught you the Way. Beg God, "O My God Most High! You gave this good fortune to us. We had no means to obtain this. Your beneficence became a light for us, be generous to us again! Do not take this good fortune away from us!"

Here, it is not the devil who will waylay you, but the jealousy of God. Because if you cannot guard the beneficence that He showed you, His jealousy will take it back from you. If a separation of a few days comes to you, strive hard to reach Him again.

Among the words spoken where I was, perhaps you have heard it from me: neither a son, a daughter, nor anyone else can be an obstacle between you. Your longing must become so heated that the power and warmth within that longing overcomes whomever it encounters, and he or she becomes your friend. Even within the coldest people, that coldness disappears. If a state reaches you from that happening, what a happy event it is.

The Presence of the Beloved Is Most Sweet

In spring, if I am parted from the beloved's cheek,
What care do I have for the garden? What use
is that greenness?
Or if thorns grow instead of fruit?
From the clouds, let stones fall instead of rain.

It is much more pleasant for me to be with you than where they would give me property and positions. If I were to go to Tabriz they would give me a position and acclaim. But being together with you is much more pleasant for me than these. If those who promise wealth and positions don't listen to my words and can't understand them, what pleasure would it bring? It's pleasant to be with someone who can understand.[240]

Where the Two Seas Meet

Now, one's longing, one's seeking for the beneficence of God must be so strong and hot that like that of Moses, it allows nothing to get in the way.

---

240 M. 125. Here, Shams is apparently speaking to Mevlana.

The Prophet Moses asked, "Is there anyone in the whole world more knowledgeable than I am?"

His friend, Joshua, answered: "There is someone in the world more knowledgeable than you."

Now, Moses didn't get angry at this answer, he didn't get offended by him. He didn't say, "What kind of a thing to say is this!" Instead, by saying, "Oh, why did you say that?" he asked for information, because he was searching.

Joshua was also a prophet, but he didn't have the authority in the outer world. In that age, the authority to judge belonged to the Prophet Moses.

This is also what I would do: if there were someone for whom I was searching, I would pay attention. I would question, "Should I do this like this; should I do this like that?" so that no obstacle might arise to keep us from coming together.

Moses had told his friend, "*I shall not give up until I reach the meeting place of the two seas, even if I spend untold years* [18:60].

"*I will search for years* (*Aw amziya huquba*)." This *huquba* is forty years according to some, and forty thousand years according to another interpretation, and eighty years or eighty thousand years according to others. This story of Moses is so hot that it sets the heavens aflame, but they tell it in such a cold manner.

Moses and his friend came to where the two seas meet.[241] According to some, near Aleppo or Antioch he was making the *salaat*

---

241 See *Surah al-Kahf*, The Cave 18:60-70:

> *And behold! [In the course of his wanderings,] Moses said to his servant: "I shall not give up until I reach the junction of the two seas, even if I spend untold years [in my quest]!*
>
> *But when they reached the junction between the two [seas], they forgot all about their fish, and it took its way into the sea and disappeared from sight.*
>
> *And after the two had walked some distance, [Moses] said to his servant: "Bring us our mid-day meal; we have indeed suffered hardship on this [day of] our journey!"*
>
> *Said [the servant]: "Wouldst thou believe it? When we betook ourselves to that rock for a rest, behold, I forgot about the fish—and none but Satan made me thus forget it!—and it took its way into the sea! How strange!"*
>
> *[Moses] exclaimed: "That [was the place] which we were seeking!"*

on the top of a hill, and according to others, Khidr was riding on a white horse across the sea, when they saw him from far away.

Now, God Most High praises Khidr, He said: *One of Our servants, on whom We had bestowed grace from Ourselves* [18:65]. This has not been said of any other servant. And besides this, *And unto whom We imparted knowledge from Ourselves* [18:65]. That wisdom is not taught at the *madrasah*; it is not learned at the *khanaqah*, through reading books, nor from a teacher; it cannot be obtained from any creature.

Now Joshua told Moses, "I know the subtlety of the work of Khidr. I am not strong enough to travel with him; I cannot come with you. But when he leaves you, let us meet again as friends; go." Joshua turned back, and Moses and Khidr remained together.

They began to talk with each other. He asked him some questions.

"*May I follow you* [18:66]?" he asked. "Whatever you tell me to do, I'll listen to you and obey."

See the longing within that great prophet who had already found the Truth, who had already reached the honor of talking with God.

Khidr told him, "*I will tell you* [18:78]," that is, "I will awaken you." Moses was a great prophet who awakened people to the Truth; now Khidr was awakening the awakener; he was waking him up to the Reality of the Truth. Now, it has become a debt for me to tell about the rest of the story, but I will tell it another time.

And the two turned back, retracing their footsteps, and found one of Our servants, on whom We had bestowed grace from Ourselves and unto whom We had imparted knowledge from Ourselves.

Moses said unto him: "May I follow you on the understanding that you will impart to me something of that consciousness of what is right which has been imparted to you?"

[The other] answered: "Witness, you will never be able to have patience with me—for how could you be patient about something that you cannot comprehend within the compass of [your] experience?

Replied [Moses]: "You will find me patient, if God so wills: and I shall not disobey you in anything!"

Said [the sage]: "Well, then, if you are to follow me, do not question me about anything [that I may do] until I myself give you an account of it!"

Happy is he who keeps the story of Khidr and Moses in his heart when he meets a servant of God and takes him as his guide.[242]

The Joy of Salaat

I swear by God Most High that the days I do the *salaat* I become very joyful. The Prophet manifested the completion of dervishhood with a subtle saying: "Poverty is my pride." Isn't it a happiness to follow that dervish?

He doesn't see it as suitable for him to follow. And not only does he not do the prayer, he would insult those who do the *salaat* and ridicule them. After all, the reason Rashid was sent away was due to this; I kept myself distant from him because of this.

I was saying, "Every now and then, he used to make an insulting remark, 'Doesn't this *salaat* ever become an obstacle for you?'"

And I responded, "Every now and then, do you have intercourse with that concubine?"

"Yes, yes, but that's not an obstacle," he said. "This is an effort for God—you are putting your face upon the ground in an unsightly act."

"Ask the disciple, 'For the sake of the love of God who has created you, tell me! Is there anything more beautiful and sweet than this—is there anything more pleasing than making love face to face?'"[243]

---

242 In the *Menaqib-al-arifin*, *The Accounts of the Mevlevi Dervishes* #170, Mevlana is quoted as saying:

"Our Shamsuddin Tabrizi is beloved by Khidr (blessings on both of them)." On the door of the retreat cell at the tekke, our Master wrote with his blessed hand: "This is the lodging of one beloved by Khidr."

243 It is understood that within the *salaat*, when one makes the prostration, one is deepening in the presence of God—it is said that the *salaat* is the *mir'aj* (ascension into the Presence of God) of the faithful. *Prostrate yourself and draw near* [*Surah al-Alaq*, The Connecting Cell 96:19]. As one bows more and more fully, one enters more and more fully into the Divine Presence, opening the possibility of meeting God "face to face." This is an offering of Love, a journey of Love.

❁

The Sweetness of the Command

"*Bismillah*,"[244] I said, "just sew this; it will be a good deed for you."

So many times I have read the *Qulhuwallah*[245] for you. I read it ten times, and it will be enough. Now, I am feeling compassionate because of his misfortune.

He says, "It is not in our capacity to endure the difficulties in your service."

If an order comes, it is a courtesy to follow it. Coming without an order is a distancing, so to come without being ordered becomes going away. Going without an order would be, also. But there is a blurriness and defect in him so that he cannot see the command.

Ayaz didn't have such defective thought. As soon as he saw the command, he would understand the sweetness of it. But they are not of such illumined heart. They could not even see the command.

If Mevlana wants to listen to words for a while, I know that the desire to speak has awakened in his and my heart. If in a moment I see a subtlety in Mevlana, I understand it and begin to tell stories, and I speak no other words.

Since you are being free and easy, and the visitors are not leaving, I am leaving.

❁

The Salaat of the Inside

What we need is to leave aside that *salaat* of the outside that is sometimes done or sometimes cannot be done because of some excuse or forgetfulness—a very sober and a very sad person both do it. Sometimes a person doesn't talk about doing the *salaat*, but a time

---

244 *Bismillah* is the beginning of the phrase *Bismillah arRahman arRahim*, "In the Name of God, the most Compassionate and Most Merciful," which begins each of the *surahs* of the Qur'an and which Muslims recite at the beginning of every endeavor.

245 Shams is referring to *Surah al-Ihklas*, Purity, *surah* 112, which is considered one of the most important *surahs* of the Qur'an, and a protection, the *surah* of God's incomparable oneness. *Qulhuwallah* is the first line: *Say, "He is God."*

comes when he declares that he is in a state of continuous *salaat.* If he is a man, he swears that he will divorce his wife if this isn't true; if she is a woman, she swears by putting her hand on the Qur'an fifty times that what she says is the truth. Because there is a *salaat* of the outside and of the inside, just like everything that has an inside has an outside.

The *salaat* of the inside is peace of heart. If he or she is within this state, the person has sworn truly. Especially in regard to giving away possessions and giving alms, if one does a good deed without telling anybody about it, without even passing it through one's own mind and without thinking, "I did a good deed," one is on the right path. If he is one of those, when he is giving alms, you would think that he himself is being given the alms. Within this, a pride is hidden that even the one who gives the alms is not aware of, but certainly it is well-regarded.

Who Has a Heart?

This heart of mine has never told a lie. I don't have to verify my heart—it has never proved me false. The heart is a beautiful indicator. Even a little beauty of heart manifests as trustworthiness. People don't refer to a trustworthy man as "one who has a spirit" or "one who is wise"—they say, "He has a heart."

Would I ever experience troubles if my beloved were like me? Especially if she were very wakeful and wise, she would be like a kingdom and fortune for me. Even if I were injured by a hundred thousand blows or spears, still I would not worry or feel pain.

Ali Is the Gate

The meaning of the words that I spoke today are a reminder that although Ali never claimed such a thing, the Prophet Muhammad said, "I am the city of knowledge and Ali is its gate (*hadith*)." He praised him.[246]

---

246 Ali was one of the most devoted to his Lord, a man of true heart who by his example showed a way into the Divine Presence.

Let a Woman Be

"Shaikhood is not necessary for a woman," I said.

"Yes, it feels cool," he said.

"But the meaning of this word 'it feels cool' hasn't been understood," I said. In other words, this means that it is also appropriate for a woman, but it has more taste for a man. However, it is not necessary for a woman, whether it feels cool or warm. If Fatima and Aisha had acted as shaikhs, I would have changed my belief in the Prophet. But they didn't.

If God Most High wishes to open the door for a woman, he keeps her silent and hidden. It is best for a woman to do her own work, to spin her own thread.[247]

A Real Shaikh

Since the day I left my own city I haven't seen a single shaikh. If anyone were to be a shaikh, Mevlana would be fit to be one. But he doesn't convey a cloak.[248] If someone comes and tries to force him and persists saying, "Give us a cloak," and keeps on hanging around saying, "Cut off our hair—then he will give it," then in this respect, to give a cloak is one thing. Mevlana's saying, "Come and be my disciple," is something else.

See *Mathnawi* I 3763-3765:

Since you are the gate of the city of knowledge, since you are the beams of the sun of clemency,

Be open O gate, to the one who seeks the gate, so that by means of you, the husks may reach the core,

Be open unto everlasting, O gate of mercy, O entrance-hall to *None is like unto Him.*

247 M. 130.

"*Nafs*" (soul) has a feminine gender. On the spiritual journey, it is best for the dervish to remain to the side, quietly in devotion, burying his/her secret (*sirr*) in the earth, until the Sun brings forth strong growth and flowering.

248 "Conveying a cloak" refers to the bestowal of the robe of dervishhood, and when the student has ripened, the robe of shaikhhood.

Shaikh Abu Bakr Sellabaf didn't have the custom of giving a cloak either. I never met his shaikh, so I don't know whether he did so or not. But I left Tabriz with this wish [of finding someone worthy of being a shaikh], but I couldn't find anyone. However, the world is not empty—there is a shaikh somewhere. . . .

I've never seen a person of this position who has this attribute.[249] It is a journey of a hundred thousand years. I haven't found anyone but Mevlana with this attribute. Now, when I returned again from Aleppo, it was due to this.

If they told me, "Your father has missed you so much—he stood up from his grave, and at a place just a step away from the village of Tel Basher, he is waiting to see you. Come, so that he might see you and then return to his grave. Come now, to see your father!"

I would say, "No, let it be! What can I do?" I wouldn't go even a step out of Aleppo. I came only for Mevlana.

Come Willingly

As a matter of fact, someone who does things because of being forced to do them can't be saved even when dogs are saved. It is because of this that the dog of the friends of the Cave [18:18] will ascend to the Throne of God. There is no doubt about this. Listen well to this word and ignore the rest.

In the universe there are both the people of this world and of the next world, and also there are the people of the Truth. Shibli is of the people of the next world. Mevlana is of the people of the Truth.

---

249 Shams says in another moment of his *Maqalat*, "I've never seen someone who is filling the role of shaikh who really has the attribute of shaikhood. [So and so] has prostrated a hundred times and has made promises and has requested a cloak (*khirqa*) from me and Mevlana has said, "The *khirqa* is not my way, my *khirqa* is my companionship and that which you obtain from me. My *khirqa* is that. When the time for that comes I will place your *khirqa* over your head and you will place my *khirqa* over mine."

Humility

Last night I was again looking out for the friends. Each of them, one by one, I visualized in front of me—each one's faith, longing, and understanding.

He came and I said, "Why is he like this?" I felt pity for his states. He belongs to us, yet this is how he is.

"Why don't you keep within this joy of heart since you are ours," I say.

That's why I gave that greeting. I always act like this to those whom I greet: first, I correct his deeds, and then I ask how he is.

Maybe I have said it a thousand times—when we love someone, we are harsh with him; when we see that he has slipped a little, we give him a hundred thousand kinds of reckonings. The others we don't take to task for a mountain of error!

If someone turns towards the desert, it's out of ignorance and estrangement. Let's show respect to him, let's serve him, even though he has remained a stranger to us and distant. Don't you see how far we are willing to go to show respect and to be kind to a person who isn't even worthy of carrying your old shoes! How many times we have closed our eyes to their bad behavior! Don't you see that the troubles that came to the prophets and the saints were also like that—because they were His pure servants.

Yesterday, so and so acted humbly. I am pleased when someone can be humble like this, because His is the greatest compassion for all friends, enemies, believers and unbelievers. I wish that God might show them the right way.

A Friend of the Friend

I begged God: "O Lord! Introduce me to Your saints, Your friends, make me companions with them!" In my dream, it was said, "We will give you the companionship of one saint."

I asked, "Where is that saint?"

The next night it was told to me, "This saint is in the land of Rum (Anatolia). After a time, in another dream, it was told to me, "The time hasn't come yet. There is a time for everything."

Clear Water

Happily I speak. There is brightness within me. I had become a stagnant pool, twisting in upon itself. Then Mevlana's essence struck mine and made the water flow, so that now it pours happily, fresh, and flourishing.

Are You Going To Speak or Listen?

I have a habit of asking those who come to me, "Sir! Are you going to speak or listen?"

If someone says, "I will speak," I can listen to him for three days and nights one after the other, unless he runs away and I am liberated. If he says, "I will listen," then I speak. Only then do I begin to speak, if he won't be interrupting.

The Blessing of the Moment

They asked a Sufi: "Would you like a slap in cash or in credit?"

"Hit and go away!" he said.

In the leaving is a blessing. He was afraid of the painful regret of losing the blessing of that moment.[250]

Dancing with the Beauty

Mevlana says, "So and so was dancing yesterday."

---

250 See *Mathnawi* I:133-134:

> O friend, the Sufi is "the son of the moment"
> It is not the rule of his way to say, "To-morrow."
> Can it be that you art not a true Sufi?
> Ready money is lost by giving credit.

However, at other times, because it can be a discourteous behavior, this state of his didn't please me. But last night, because I knew the reason for it, I was very pleased and was at ease.

And I am relying upon prayers. You act slowly; they act slowly. You hurry up; they hurry up.

Don't you like this Mary? Don't you see the beauty of this baby, don't you fall in love with him?

Wandering

Mevlana says that he doesn't like my going alone, but this is how it is—by myself I can wander around anywhere, I can sit down in any shop. But he is a dignified person—I can't make the *mufti* of a city wander around with me in that way from shop to shop, from place to place; I can't make him stroll into every hovel so that they may know we are together.

I've never acted with you with that care-free callous manner of the shaikhs—"If you want to belong to me, come with me."

Instead, whatever you see as difficult is unnecessary for you.

Your sitting there like this is only temporary. My heart is apprehensive.

"I See God . . ."

A disciple said, "I see God clearly seventy times a day."

His shaikh told him, "If you were to see Bayazid Bastami once, it would be better than your seeing God seventy times."

When Bayazid was coming out of the oak grove, the disciple saw him and immediately fell down and died, because he was a lover. He was seeking. He died. That is, of his *nafs* only a little remained, and it was purified.

The disciple, with his limited sight and incomplete discernment had seen only the form of his own imagination. He hadn't seen God with the power of Bayazid. And a hundred thousand "Bayazids" don't approach even the dust of the sandals of Moses.

In imitation you keep repeating, "Thousands of saints can't reach the dust of the feet of a prophet." Then how do you see it as possible that a bum should see Him a thousand times a day, and that Moses, who spoke with God, couldn't see Him?

If someone wants to interpret the words of God to mean, "It is possible to see God," one has to ask for a *fatwa*.[251] If words can be pulled in two different directions, they are spoken together with explanations. True words need no explanation.

Because naked and inappropriate words like "I am the Truth"[252] don't stand up to explanation—of course the one who spoke them lost his head.

❉

Eyes Cannot Perceive Him, but He Perceives All Vision

Since you can't elucidate the meaning of the Qur'anic verse, "*Eyes cannot perceive Him, but He perceives all vision* [6:103]," at least give me nine kisses so that I might. What is your highest desire? To find and reach the One who is sought. God always tells the truth, and I swear by His Divine Being that this verse is true.

May the Peace and Compassion of God be upon you. I have given up any thought of fattening my neck and belly. The friends have been renewed, but I haven't been able to find my old body. The bad side of the thing is that all the time you are reading your own letter; you aren't reading the letter of the Friend. At least, read a little from the letter of the Friend, too.[253]

---

251 A *fatwa* is a legal ruling made by a religious authority.

252 Shams is referring to Mansur al-Hallaj, who in a state of ecstasy said, "*Ana'l Haqq* (I am the Truth)," and was hung on the gallows as a heretic.

253 M. 135.

Everything is Perishing Except His Face

In my dream Mevlana and I were together and I was reciting, "*Everything is perishing except His Face* [28:88]." In other words, all that will remain from this existence is the face of the friends.

> So many darlings, drunk and dizzy
> With eyes full of tears, come to this door.

You shall not be able to see Me [7:143]! He is in front of your eyes, but you can't see Him. If you want to see Him like this, then *You will not be able to see Me*. He is so subtle that He cannot be seen by eyes. *Eyes cannot perceive Him, but He perceives all vision* [6:103]. The meaning here charges beyond the previous one many times. As for the wisdom in having been told, *You cannot see Him, but look at the mountain* [7:143]—that mountain is your own self existence. Listen well to the Prophet Muhammad—in the end, "The one who knows himself knows his Lord." Because of this, his wish to see his Lord was different from that of Moses. Evidence of this is the words: "*O Lord! I have repented* [7:143] of asking for such a thing. *I am the first of those who have faith* [7:143]."[254]

---

254 See *Surah al-A'raf*, The Faculty of Discernment, 7:142-144:

> *And [then] We appointed for Moses thirty nights [on Mount Sinai]; and We added to them ten, whereby the term of forty nights set by his Sustainer was fulfilled. And Moses said to his brother Aaron: "Take my place among my people; and act righteously, and follow not the path of the spreaders of corruption."*
>
> *And when Moses came [to Mount Sinai] at the time set by Us, and his Sustainer spoke to him, he said: "O my Sustainer! Show [Yourself] to me, so that I might behold You!"*
>
> *Said [God]: "Never can you see Me. However, behold this mountain: if it remains firm in its place, then—only then—will you see Me."*
>
> *And as soon as his Sustainer revealed His glory to the mountain, He caused it to crumble to dust; and Moses fell down in a swoon. And when he came to himself, he said: "Limitless are You in Your glory! Unto You do I turn in repentance; and I shall be the first to have faith in You!*
>
> *Said [God]: "O Moses! Behold, I have raised you above all people by virtue of the messages which I have entrusted to you, and by virtue of My speaking [to you]: hold fast, therefore, to that with which I have entrusted you, and be among the grateful!"*

☼

The Welcoming Water

Since water lets dirt enter it, and doesn't cast it out, how can He send away someone who is longing for Him, someone who is thirsty? There is a kind of water that can't take dirt without becoming foul, so it casts the dirt away from itself out of concern that it might become unclean. But there is another water which even if you throw all the filth of the world into it, it never changes or becomes foul.

☼

Surely, the Truth Is All That Is

Well, those words, "I am the Truth (*Ana'l Haqq*)," are not without an interpretation. And things become muddy, because if you are saying "I," then who is "the Truth?" If you are saying "the Truth," what is the word "I" but a naked, lowly, and deathly dry word?

The muftis of the time wanted the death of Hallaj. The muftis of investigation and the muftis of the law helped them, too, so that they might share God's reward for the pious act.

Still, he was left stuck between doubt and certainty. He couldn't reach the rank of certainty and was asking, "I wonder if I exist?"

The way of the seekers of Truth passes through the rank of certainty. Only after this station do they reach their final destination. And that which is really sought is that final station.

☼

The Unique Pearl

Let me go and see Mevlana. He did not come to the world to ask for anything, nor to complete a sign. It is an indication of the state of the beloved who has no sign in the world. Visible signs are for the seeker, not for the one who is sought. These words belong to the seeker. Nothing is seen except through seekers. The real seeker of Truth is the one on whose forehead a light from the Beloved shines. By means of that light, whoever's face he/she looks upon, he/she sees whether that person is in felicity or misery.

The seeker of Truth has come to witness, to see if there are some who have already established a relationship with the Beloved whom they were seeking.

He sees those seekers who have lost their comfort and are grieving. He says, "Well, I am the unique pearl. I have come to witness the Beloved who is searched for within the universe.

They say, "Now we have found ease, so let's settle here."

The other one says, "Is this a place to settle?"

"Then let's go," they say.

And he says, "At least for a few days, let's stop and observe."

Now, with my light, each day we'll watch this universe. Since we have become friends, let's watch this universe with my light, as seekers of Truth. One who seeks the Truth, out of exuberance, may begin to speak early like Jesus. The Beloved who is sought, either gives him the authority to speak after forty days, or he can see the face of the Friend he is seeking after sixteen years have passed, and after fifteen years He makes him speak warm words.

Doubt, Imitation, and Verification

Even with all of that, I am saying that doubt has become mixed with the dust of his shoe. Nearness (certainty) and doubt in nearness are the beginning of the way with God. Even a hundred thousand of them haven't been able to reach this point. It's not fitting, especially for shaikhhood and guidance, that with all that hair and beard he should remain at the door.[255] People like this can never save themselves from doubt.

Only very few of them are other than imitators. An imitator doesn't understand anything about either this one's or that one's poetry or anything about the word of God. God forbid that he might become a heretic, in other words, that he might accept the Truth by means of nearness with the Truth, not through imitation. He will

255 I.e., Despite all those outer signs of shaikhhood, beard etc., he hasn't been able to pass through the door.

understand the real Truth, the inner meaning of the Qur'an—that the inside of the inside has been a veil for him—not through imitation, but only through verification.

Is someone else's poem more moving or your own words, your own light of verification?

A Priceless Pearl

The power within you is like wool in a big sack. But if it lays a wager with the pearl within and says, "Am I more valuable or that sack of cotton?" the pearl replies, "Let's ask the mad ones, not the sober."

And the mad who hear this respond, "There is a gem that is even more valuable than many sacks filled with Berber gold. The value of that pearl within is itself."

As for the sober one, he says, "Don't pay attention to his words, he's crazy."

That incomparable pearl is priceless.

Stop, O My Camel, with Joy

All words in the whole world belong to seekers, to those who search. And what is the sign of the one they are seeking? I am listening; you are listening.

When weighing "The Truth Sought" with "God" one has to know the right moment to be able to reach that universe. In the end, where are you going? My graceful friend! What more can one say after this discussion? "May God be with you," I say. But this is not a wish for separation—it is a prayer that the favor and help of God, and the friendship of the Master and the Truth who knows the secrets, might protect you.

Stop, O my camel! Joy has come to its last degree; the work is finished; the way has come to an end. The earth has turned into a beautiful paradise. The time of celebration has come again, and things have been set right.

It Is in God's Hands

If a human being intends to awaken, whether he has only fallen asleep or is dead, he needs the breath of Jesus. If the Prophet Jesus breathes into him and if He wants him to come back to life, he awakens with just a little shaking, but if He doesn't really intend to awaken him, what happens then? Then, that person begins to resist. Just as God Most High has said to the Prophet Muhammad, "*You cannot bring the one whom you love to the right way* [28:56]!" [256]

He said, "You see, don't you, how hard the work is. Brave young men have sheered off these mountains at their roots, yet they have still remained backward in religion and deeds. How Muhammad moaned due to the command that came to him, *Walk straight forward as you have been commanded* [11:112]! He expressed his difficulty exclaiming, "*Surah Hud* and others like it have made my hair turn white."

For Ayaz, the command wasn't heavy; for him it was easy.

So I said, "After all, it was Ayaz's aspiration that made the command easy."

"Yes," he said. "Ayaz was loving and affectionate even towards dogs. How could he not love the light of his eye?"

Recognizing Need

Sultan Mahmoud of Ghazna didn't allow into his presence a discourteous man who had not bathed, whose body was stinking with sweat and filth. So how could the Prophet Muhammad, who one might say has many times the capacity of Mahmoud[257] and is of a much higher rank, how could he accept such people? In the end, the

---

256 I.e., You may love a person, but this doesn't necessarily mean that you'll be able to guide this person. It is in God's hands.

257 "Muhammad" is a more intensive form of the word *hamd* (to praise) than Mahmoud. Mahmoud is "one who is praiseworthy," but Muhammad is "one who is created to be praised." Shams refers to their inner reality as well as their outer station—the strength and receptivity of Muhammad's spirit was much greater. God willing, the higher one's station, the more one is able to be of help.

spirits of the great attained ones are ready. They recognize the living ones and help them.

❊

See with His Eye

How can a person act discourteously and say things about Muhammad that aren't worthy of his station? You keep reading your own letter—you aren't reading the letter of that divine one. In other words, you are looking at him with your own *nafs*—you are not adapting your state to his.

He said, "My outer self has been created from that of which others' insides are created." Well, what he means by "others" are the saints and the prophets. He means, "That which they know as inner knowledge of the heart is for me outer knowledge." What they see within (*batin*), the Prophet saw everywhere, outside himself. That one who speaks words from himself has come outside of himself—he has come out of his own home to call others to remember.

"O God Most High who turns hearts and eyes wherever You want! Keep my heart fixed upon my religion!" This is a prayer for others' sake—it means, "If you come face to face with such an event, beg God like this." If you don't look at it like this, you begin to wrongly think that the greatest prophet of God sent with a Book was caught by his *nafs*, and crying out because of the rebellion of his ego. No police force wanders around the house of his heart. Even a heretic knows that there is no fear in him. If he had spoken the words just for himself, they wouldn't have gone anywhere else.

> I am content with myself—
> from now on, I will be with I.

This is one more secret that Muhammad spoke, but kept hidden from Umar, not because he was withholding something from him, but because its time hadn't yet come. If he had revealed it to Umar then, Umar would have become bewildered and his being a caliph would have been difficult. He wouldn't have been able to manage the outward law or to disperse it through the world.

What I want from you is for you to express the boiling of deep feelings within you, to reveal them outwardly, so that both drunkenness and sobriety might be openly manifest. Do you have the state I want? Where is it? Right in front of you. I am doing these things myself, so that you might see and reveal that secret! Let me pick you up like a water jug and carry you around, and take you there, and let you do those things with that new capacious cloak, so that your inside may also remain strong.

First, let me teach you to sit around a tandir oven. The first day, you sit a little to the side, and then gradually you come close to the fire.[258]

Good Character

Mevlana and I were talking about your prayers. I was saying a few things, and speaking about what it means to say "I." Because of the outcome of your prayers and your inner cleanliness, tears flew from my eyes. Yes, our Prophet has said that a teacher, a guide is necessary for this *adab* of good manners. By saying, "My Lord has taught me about good character," he manifested something very great. With these words of his, he praised the dervish.

It isn't necessary for us to talk together, because they can't understand it, but I will speak in order that the one person who asked me a very difficult question might benefit. Because by his question, a benefit is sought, and in this way, the states of the shaikh who guides and the disciple who is guided can become clear.

Witnessing the Real

I asked Mevlana, "What have you witnessed in this universe?"

---

258 M. 140.

He answered, "Someone who talks about something with everybody is either lacking in witnessing or is only falsely claiming to have observed. If his witnessing keeps him from speaking with everybody, that is something else."

Let's say, my stomach is full, but I need water. How can I eat bread? If I eat it, my situation only gets worse.

The Work of a Fakir

The work of the fakir of God is not futile. You saw what lights appeared on that first day. Just think how things might have been if that joy had continued until now.

Considering that, everything that has happened was not because of that work.

It was not your business to go to Damascus, it was my work.

Mevlana glanced at me and said, "He is looking for God in such a person!"

"I have strong faith in him," I said. "But first what he said is wrong. I am not looking for God in him. I am looking for him in God."

Cleanse Your Eye

Nothing harms a human being as much as his/her own eye. That is, many times he/she becomes the object of the evil eye. You look and see that nobody is aware of this. But I know it. The evil eye touched and passed by like a sip of water.

Swimming in the Sea

When you do the ablution, your whole body seems so bright and beautiful that when you place your head in prostration, such a state comes to you that even a drink couldn't harm you. But if he, himself, doesn't have this rank, if he doesn't have the power to move his arms and legs in this sea, it's useless.

❁

In Which Direction Are You Turning

He was of the seekers. He was searching—to speak of what he is seeking doesn't harm him.

If I were to lie down here and sleep until Resurrection Day, it wouldn't harm me; perhaps every day would be even better for me.

Nevertheless, on the days I miss the *salaat*, I feel sad; I feel uneasy all night until the morning. And the days I am with it, I am happy and joyful.

> Within the Kaaba, there is no *qiblah*
> (direction of prayer),
> Outside of the Kaaba, one must find the *qiblah*.

❁

With You Alone

> Come and take the tablecloth away, and give me water.
> Tonight, if you were to sleep apart from me,
> I couldn't be comfortable—I would struggle.
> But if you cover me, it doesn't matter
> if winter is coming.[259]

❁

Burning Bright

My body is very delicate—when even a little sickness finds its way to me, I become sick night and day. But I am preventing the attacks of illness with hunger. I burn them with the fire of hunger and fasting.

❁

Standing Strong

How pleasing it is when Mevlana gets cross with someone. When he gets angry at someone, he hits his shoes on the floor.

"To speak about fright, is frightful," they say.

Well, I keep them strong.

---

259 It seems Shams is speaking here to his beloved wife, Kimya.

❊

Burning Words that Heal

My state is so full of fire nobody can endure it. But my words become a salve for the one who listens to them. The more they accept them the stronger they get.

A man of this work must have the capacity to work and to not become bothered by suffering or sorrow. When he sets out, every moment he must walk carefully so that his foot may not slip. The tradition of his father [Adam] is once. When he makes a mistake, immediately he regrets it, and then he is watchful and wakeful so as not to make that mistake again. Even if he does make a mistake, he doesn't give importance to it, he doesn't dwell on it. Because time is passing, and he understands that to feel sad and to wallow in suffering isn't useful.

Let's say, in a war, a man's hand is injured. At first he may feel a lot of pain and sadness about it, but what use is it to weep? Instead, he runs to a surgeon, to a doctor for healing, or he gives money to a practitioner and has it bound with a bandage, and as a result of the ease that bandage brings, he considers himself healed.

There are words from God's knowledge in Mevlana's speech—when he speaks he doesn't pay attention to whether his words are useful for someone or not. But, ever since my childhood, I have been inspired by God to teach *adab* through words so that a person might be liberated from his *nafs*, and proceed further. This shaikh is real.

❊

Words and Deeds

Some of the servants of God are men of words, and some are men of action. "You need a man of action as your leader more than a man of words." When the person who has the power to be a man of action speaks, his speech joins together with that power. It acts.

I go to the tekke in order to catch him. If I catch him there, if he greets me and shows the greatest respect, I return another time in order to catch him again. I am free to call to the way of Truth. But because the Prophet was assigned to this mission, he has said, "*Surah Hud* has made my hair white." Because I am not obligated in this matter, the command of God, "*Be steadfast as you were commanded*," only renews me. . . .

There is no difficulty in the deeds of God; from His perspective nothing is difficult.

You Are My Spring Festival

What can I tell you, what can I tell him? As long as the world and the next world remain, there is a love that is far removed from the feelings of lust, and nothing can be an obstacle for this.

O please! Tell us, one by one.
O please, will you?
Are you longing for a friend or a cupbearer
who will bring you to bright mornings?
O soul, today you are all my hope!
There are other beloveds,
 but it is you who burns this heart!
With the spring festival the people of the world
 rejoice.
But you are my festival and my spring, both!

Abstinence

If you want to know whether a man is really thirsty,[260] put halvah and candy in front of him. If he turns around and looks at it, thirst is not really his concern.

Yesterday, I drank a little soup and didn't eat anything else. If I didn't continually restrict my diet, I would get sick. My body is frail, but I keep it clear with the fire of abstinence. Alas for the day when my heart doesn't want to eat carefully, when God causes that disease to appear so lovely to my heart that I don't want it to be remedied.

---

260 M. 145.

God Sees

"On these days, God protects and sees His servants more than He does on other days,"—these people speak like this. But since God is God, He sees and hears everything. So, why do you say, "He sees during Ramadan. Don't commit a sin! He also sees in the month of Sha'ban. Fast!" [261] Yet when the month of Shawwal arrives you get busy with mischief and sins.

With the tongue of the heart you're saying, "Ramadan is over; until next Ramadan God will not see or know what we are doing! So bring those entertainments and goblets of wine, let's drink now!"

One of the lesser known *hadith* is: "If a person repents of all his sins until a certain day, but then he returns to sinning, he becomes the plaything of Satan."

Good Behavior

Shaikh Ibrahim knows the oneness between us. When I speak, it is as though the words belong to Mevlana. We both say it. In any case, Mevlana never wants to say something different. . . .

He said, "They apologized, 'When Mevlana was with us, he used to laugh; he never rebuked us. He didn't force us to do things—"Do that right away!" He didn't shout at us; he didn't order us around or threaten us, so we made great efforts without any problem. If Shams acted like that, it wouldn't stop us from coming.'"

He is saying, "There is a Sufi saying: 'If I find something, you are liberated, otherwise you are in my hands.'"

This was my understanding, and I came with this purpose. If the disciples are faithful, OK. Otherwise, nothing is possible.

---

261 Ramadan is the month of fasting observed by Muslims and Sha'ban is the month preceeding it. Shawwal is the month that follows Ramadan.

The Whole Gold

Now you must see me completely so that certainty might come to you. Since you say, "The Truth, the right way is as I have done it,"—since you answer this way, isn't it understood by these words that you haven't yet seen me completely? I can't see the signs of it, either.

If half of the gold is left behind, or if the container is only half filled, the gold can't be considered to be complete. Don't they say, "One shouldn't return home without the cash." That means you must annihilate your own being—that is the completion of the gold.

A Cold Breath

Now, first of all, this separation is due to Alaeddin.[262] I wish he were just a scholarly enemy to us. Sir! No commandment or prohibition is an issue for us. We need neither his friendship nor his enmity. We have worn our "cloak" by Him, and we make hundreds of prostrations to Him.

Every day, he talks about enmity and leaving our friendship. I would like to send him away and then draw him to myself again. But

262 Shams is referring to Mevlana's younger, conservative son Alaeddin who was jealous of Shams and banding together with other conservatives and disgruntled students of Mevlana was opposing Shams and his friendship with Mevlana. Shams describes Alaeddin as one of cold breath—without love and the warmth it brings. The foment grew so strong that, after less than two years of being together with Mevlana (from November of 1244 to March of 1246), Shams disappeared. Shams is describing some of the difficulties of his journey. Mevlana was distraught to lose his friend and sent his older son Sultan Weled in search of him. He found Shams in Damascus and brought him back to Konya in May of 1247. For a while the atmosphere was better—to make Mevlana happy, his students welcomed Shams back to Konya. Shams indicates that part of the reason he had disappeared was that Mevlana also might be cooked within that separation, and that then he was even better able to receive what Shams had to give. However, it wasn't long before discontent surfaced again and Alaeddin was in the midst of the conflict. Shams is indicating that the time may be coming once again for him to disappear. It was Love that brought him back, and it was Love that took him further.

how cold—he is like the ice house of Abdul Aziz! I swear that it is difficult to set out at this time, but whether one likes it or not, it will be.

One remembers . . . such severe pains attacked me that for two years the fatigue of that traveling hasn't left me. I traveled and I returned; I had such pains that if they had filled all of Konya with gold, it wouldn't be worth those troubles, but your love outweighed everything. One can't leave a man of God because of a child. I've talked about all of this before, but I want to speak of it in this moment, too. With just one breath, an ill-omened one with a cold breath spoils a well-done work—he turns it upside down.

Traveling is very difficult for me. This time if I go, it won't be like the last time! Now I can neither go on a long journey nor even to Aksaray. However, if it is needed, I will withdraw to a corner that won't trouble me here and sit there. For two years now, I've had no tolerance for traveling. I was exhausted from the pains I had, but unless there are intimate meaningful conversations and the gatherings of the proper friends. . . . And if I set out this time, don't try to stop me like you did before! Don't oppose what I do!

A man of action has to weigh his actions carefully.

❊

Be a Friend

May God give Mevlana long life; may He give such a long life that his life may be a long and happy life infinitely and eternally.

Even if you are bound with chains, be a friend,[263] in such a way that you might know Solomon as living. When his love begins to overflow, for a moment he says, "You did well," and then he loses himself. Who is the one who gives him love? If you go further on the Way of Love, you begin feeling the fragrance of the universe of the Spirit, and you reach the universe of the Truth.

---

263 M. 150.

❊

Only Paradise Remains

Where is the one who will go to Hell? Will Hell remain infinitely in the end or Paradise? Then where is the servant bound for Hell? In the whole universe, there isn't a single person who will go to Hell, because Paradise is their Hell.

❊

Multiplication and Division

A constellation is born by the meeting of one planet with another planet. It is like the birth of a human being through the union of man and woman; just as heat develops through clothes upon the human body, something results from two things uniting. If you take the string away from the bow, what can it do?

❊

You Are Satan; You Are Gabriel

Someone asked: "Who is Satan?"

"Satan is you!" I said. If he had asked, "Who is Gabriel?" I would have also said, "It is you."

You must learn an art or a craft so that by means of it you may earn your living. Why are you living in poverty?

Whoever speaks ill of a friend to you—whether he does this openly or secretly—if he says, "Your friend is jealous of you," know that he is really the one who is jealous. Such a person may be burning with jealousy.

When someone asked me, "Who is Satan (Iblis)?" I said, "You, for at this moment, I am saturated with Idris.[264] If you are not Iblis, then

---

264 Shams is referring to the Prophet Idris—who some consider to be the same as the Biblical Enoch mentioned in Genesis, and others consider to be another name for Ilyas, the Biblical Elijah (See *Surah Maryam*, Mary 19:56-57 *Behold, he was a man of truth, a prophet, whom We exalted unto a lofty station,* and also *Surah al-Anbiya*, The Prophets 21:85). Shams is playing with the similar sound and opposite meaning of Idris and Iblis. There is no room for thought of the Devil

why aren't you also immersed in Idris? If you had any sign of Idris in you, what business would you have with the Devil?"

If you had asked, "Who is Gabriel?" I would have also said, "You."

I am saying that this question of yours is like the question of the man who asks, "Is this imam's *salaat* correct according to the law of the religion?" when during the *salaat* he sees that while the imam is leading the *salaat* he isn't looking at the place of prostration but is looking around to his right and left.

I say, "Both of these peoples's *salaat* becomes invalid."

"But what about the *salaat* of the imam," he said, "how can that be the same?"

I said, "One is the imam, and he is looking all around during the *salaat*, he isn't aware of being in God's presence. The other one is supposed to be following him, but he is watching over the eye of the imam—so, for sure, neither is focused on the *qiblah*.[265]

Praising and Cursing

Whoever says to you "Such and such person has praised you," tell him, "It's you who is praising me—you are using him as a pretext!" Whoever says to you that such and such person speaks ill of you, say to him, "It's you who are speaking ill of me—you are using him as an excuse!"

They say, "The one who tells you about someone cursing you is the one who is cursing you," because maybe [the other person]

(Iblis) if one is within the state of remembrance of a prophet, united with his being—immersed in remembrance of God.

265 During the *salaat*, whether leading the prayer or following, one's eyes are meant to be focused on the place of prostration, the place of meeting God face to face. One resides in that Presence, merging one's own presence in the Presence of the Divine. Here, neither the imam nor the person supposedly following his leadership in the prayer is focused on the place of prostration, but rather, their attention is wandering. Shams reminds us again of *Surah Dhuha: Didn't he find you wandering and guide you?*

didn't really say that, or perhaps he said it with a different intention or meaning.

If he comes and says, "So and so has said you are jealous," say "There are two kinds of jealousy. One is the jealousy that takes you to Paradise—this is the jealousy that urges one to move further in doing the good: "Why should I fall behind him in virtue?" he says.

Lady Kirra[266] is jealous; Mevlana is also jealous. But this jealousy carries one to Paradise. The whole day, my conversations are all about this jealousy.

But another person's jealousy takes him to Hell: "I am serving, but because of that, he is jealous of me—he wants me to give it up, so that I might be left behind."

The House Is Yours

Master, this house is yours. Don't go. I will go, while offering you a Qaf mountain of gratitude.

Let me leave the conversation of Mevlana in a state in which I carry his honor upon my shoulders, and let me express my gratitude again. Let me remain free. My foolishness has reached such a degree that even if the Prophet Moses were to come and say, "Show me that community I was longing for," I would show him—"Well, that is it."

I made a vow—if I am delivered from this state, let me give everything I have, hidden or clearly manifest, as alms.[267] Now,

---

266 M. 155

Lady Kirra was Mevlana's saintly wife. She was the spiritual teacher of many women in the community, as was their daughter, Melike.

267 According to the Mevlevi tradition, Shams had been so afire with longing that he begged God to show him one of the real, hidden friends of God.

He received the answer, "Your request is a serious one and your desire, intense. What will you give?"

He answered, "My head."

Divine Beauty granted him this favour, and with great joy he found himself in Mevlana's company.

(*Menaqib al-arifin, Accounts of the Mevlevi Dervishes* by Aflaki, #545.)

enemies, you won't be able to trick me with the trap that you will set for me. If you were to pick up Qaf Mountain and load it upon my shoulders, and if you added another like it, and if you never took these away, still my soul would be at ease.

He Carries Qaf Mountain upon His Back

Those who bear feelings of enmity towards the saints of God imagine that they are doing them harm. Actually, this is wrong—instead they are even doing them good, because they make the saints' hearts cold toward them. The saints carry the burden of the world's grief. Their love and protection for a person increases that burden—it is as though Qaf Mountain were placed on their necks and shoulders. If a person does something to increase their love, it makes it heavier—they share that person's troubles more. But then that person forgets about their love and thoughts—well, this lightens the burden of the saint and brings ease to his soul.

No, this is true. God also spoke like this—He gave me all kinds of skills and knowledge.

He raised his finger to his ear[268]—"There is no god but God," he said.

Sharing Food of the Other World

They are calling me in the garden, I wonder why! Come, and let me whisper it into your ear.

You ask, "What are these bloody tears for?"

"Since you are asking, come—let me tell you!"

Have you understood now? I am telling all of this for you, but don't let anybody hear this and understand that I am telling it for you—the times are bad.

---

268 Shams refers again to the Prophet Muhammad who was strong enough to pull "the bow" to its full extension so as to let the arrow of remembrance fly with full force—into the Presence of God.

There was a young man—I told him the whole story of Zaynab. I had given a great deal of importance to his work. For several days, he wanted to repeat those words over and over again.

I saw that and said, "No. Why did you believe that I told all of this for you, and yet you don't want to understand?"

He said, "Yes. I understood."

"Tell it again."

He said, "Let me tell it to Mevlana, and let him repeat it to you."

I said, "But why are you repeating something that I have told you to Mevlana? Why are you repeating it to him? Let's say, you have heard this from me, but can I trust in how others will hear this from you?"

It was said, "The one who eats together with one who is forgiven, is also forgiven," But what is meant by this is not bread and provisions, it means, "those who eat of the spiritual food that he eats,"—the food of the other world.

❁

The Preserved Tablet

There have been so many things said about *Ta Ha* [20:1]. According to some interpretations, *Ta Ha* is one of the names of Muhammad, or it means: "O Man!" Or they say that these letters with dots and curves are like the marks of the astronomers. Now, we know that one must read the interpretations of it only from the Preserved Tablet.[269]

---

269 The letters "Ta, Ha" are the opening of *Surah 20* known as *Surah TaHa*. The Preserved Tablet (*lawh mahfuz*) is the Book of God upon which the destiny of beings and the sacred books are written. See *Surah al-Buruj*, The Great Constellations 85:22. Rather than listening to interpretations about the Qur'an from others, one must look to the Book of God, the completed human being, for real knowing, and find the meaning within oneself.

See *Mathnawi* V, 3128-3130:

Ask the meaning of the Qur'an from the Qur'an alone,
and from that one who has set fire to his idle fancy and extinguished it,
and has become a sacrifice to the Qur'an, bowing low in humbleness,
so that the Qur'an has become the essence of his spirit.
That essential oil that has wholly devoted itself to the rose—
smell either that oil or the rose, as you please.

❁

The Ghazali Brothers

May God's compassion be upon them, Ahmad Ghazali and his two brothers were from a pure lineage. Each one of them was without equal in his own field of knowledge. Muhammad Ghazali was especially unique in a number of sciences. The books he wrote are brighter than the sun. Mevlana knows this. His brother, Ahmad Ghazali, had become the sultan of those eminent in gnosis.

The third brother, Umar Ghazali, was a wealthy and well-known merchant. In generosity and beneficence nobody could equal him.

Someone said to Muhammad Ghazali, "About that brother of yours, Ahmad, they are saying, 'He speaks, but he doesn't really know much.'" Muhammad Ghazali sent his book *Dhakhira* to his brother and warned the man who would take the book, "Go, enter in courteously, and whatever he does, pay attention. Notice if he smiles—do not lose sight of any movement he makes, of head or hand! Be very careful in the moment when your eye meets his eye. Try to observe all his attitudes and gestures—pay attention to his hands and even his feet."

When the man who brought the book went inside, he saw that Ahmad was sitting contentedly in the *khanaqah*. When his eye met his eye, the master smiled and asked, "Did you bring us books?"

The man began to tremble.

Then, he began to speak—the master said, "I am illiterate, but being illiterate (*ummi*) is one thing and being ignorant (*'ammi*) is something else. One who is ignorant is blind, but a person who is illiterate simply can't read." Then, he said, "Now, you read the book, so that I may listen."

That poor man, shaking all the while, read some from each part of the book.

Then Ahmad told him, "Now, at the beginning of the book, write these lines that I will recite to you:

> My heart has become kabab from the fire of Love.
> My face is flushed with the liver's blood.
> The moisture of the Beloved's lips is my wine.

Don't blame me now—what good is giving me advice?
Why would I need the apparent,
 what will I do with a book?
When the darling has such lips,
 what would I do with wine?"

❊

What Will I Do with Words?

"Satan is a pretext, Adam is the point. Satan is darkness, Adam is light. Satan is lowly, Adam is exalted."

I was speaking in this way, yesterday—I was talking to myself and walking around the moat. It was as if the words were pouring upon me and I was overcome. The words were completely overwhelming me. "What will I do," I was saying, "if words overcome me like this on the pulpit?"

I won't go up to the pulpit anymore. Master, it is a lie—I am not preaching at all. Words are within me. Whoever wants to hear my words must come into my inner universe, but there is a doorkeeper.

❊

Secrets of the Heart

Yes there are also other doors, and there are also other doorkeepers. There are also others on the way. It is a long road to reach the universe of the heart.

The person taken to the universe of the heart is one who has a secret. People get him drunk, so that he might reveal that secret, so that he might tell everything within that drunkenness. But the one who listens to him has to understand which among those drunkard's words is the secret. There are little things that had never been spoken but some of which escaped from his mouth, and then were covered over again.

Even an expert of religious law who is hard of hearing becomes amazed at my words. How can just anyone relate my words; how can they convey them to others? I swear by the Majestic Self of God the Most Great that when Mevlana wants to convey my words to others, he conveys them better than I do. He embellishes them with more beautiful subtleties and meanings, but even so, Mevlana will not have conveyed my words. When Mevlana writes it, with the divine light of God he will find it, or he won't find it. Let's see.

Wherever You Are, He is with You

One has to observe within all these different states to witness the wonders of His work. Within one moment, your state is like this, in another moment, it is like that. Like this, He keeps your eyes closed, and then He makes you open your eyes, like that!

The human being is greater than all created beings, because his vision is wide enough to contain the Throne, the Highest Heaven, the heavens and the earth, and all the creatures that are in between.

The vision of this creature, who shares the attributes of God, is greater than all vision other than His. Why should it be strange if with all His attributes God manifests Himself through this creature? *Wherever you are, He is with you* [57:4].

By means of this power of sight and understanding, God has shown a direction to each one, in such a way that they see no other direction. One sees the work of goldsmithing, and to another He shows the subtleties of jewelry, of alchemy, of sorcery, or of explanations. Someone else strives on the way of logic and debate; he sees the fine points of jurisprudence and theology. And others, filled with ease and the pleasure of the other universe, see the Divine Light of God, while someone else sees desire, attraction, beauty, and love, the other sees only foolishness and buffoonery. And someone else sees angels, *houris*, the Throne and the Highest Heaven, and is drawn to these.[270] For each of them, a window of sight is opened in this kiosk, and they watch the universe from a different balcony. This one is not aware of that one's state, and that one doesn't understand anything about the state of this one.

Balconies have been opened for hundreds of thousands—an infinite number—of living beings, for animals, insects, and angels. A

270 M. 160.

doctor or an astronomer, or whoever goes higher, will see still more balconies open.

The Beautiful Face of God

Some people don't know about it, but Ahmad Ghazali had a difficulty which was a veil for him—no one was able to help him remove that veil, but he was very courageous. He was such a human being that if he turned his eye to the heavens and looked in the direction of the angels, he could see and read the wisdom of, *He utterly turned it over* and the divine understanding of *When the sky is split asunder* [84:1].[271] People had no idea of the secret suffering through which he was passing.

Whatever they say about his asceticism and retreats is all lies. He never remained sitting in seclusion for these forty-day retreats; that is an innovation (*bida*), it is a tradition invented later in the religion of Muhammad. The Prophet Muhammad never remained in seclusion for forty days.[272] That's in the story of Moses. Read and reflect on *And when We appointed for Moses forty nights* [2:51].

Don't these blind ones see that Moses, despite such greatness and closeness to God, pleaded, "O Lord! Make me one of the community of Muhammad!" In other words, "My God Most High! Make me one of your servants who see Your Beauty!" This is the secret of this saying. Otherwise, why would Moses wish to be with you and me. His intention was either this secret or another. This may seem to be a criticism of Moses, God forbid, but the Prophet Moses knew that the community among the communities that would see the Beautiful Face of God would be the community of Muhammad.

---

271 See *Surah al-Inshiqaq*, The Splitting Asunder, 84:1-6: *In the Name of God, the Most Compassionate and Merciful, When the sky is split asunder, obeying its Sustainer, as in truth it must; and when the earth is levelled, and casts forth whatever is in it, and becomes utterly void, obeying its Sustainer, as in truth it must: then, O man—you that have, truly, been toiling towards your Sustainer in painful toil—then shall you meet Him!*

272 Muhammad took regular retreats, but he never remained in seclusion. He returned to the community and took on all the responsibilities of human life, in a continuous state of remembrance. See "The Ease of Burning," p.398 of this text.

While Ahmad Ghazali was trying hard to dissolve that veil, a voice came to him, or the light of inspiration shone in his heart: "The Shaikh of Sangan will remove the veil from your eye." Ghazali immediately got up and went. The day that he arrived, he went to see him and found him in *sama*—during that *sama* his difficulty came to an end.

❂

This Isn't a Pigsty

One day, Mevlana was counseling the dervishes, and he began speaking to them about my qualities. The friends were moved to sympathy by these words. Mevlana said: "If you show even a little dislike or a sign of unkindness to Master Shamsuddin-i Tabrizi—may God increase his greatness—the counsel that I have given you and your sensitivity will remain closed for you. The devil, the wolf inside you, will throw snow in your eyes again."

The friends said, "No! Let's go and apologize to him. Let us ask his forgiveness, and from now on, let's not behave discourteously to Mevlana Shamsuddin."

They came to the door of the house, but couldn't find the way to enter. Right away their feelings completely changed.

The reason for our not letting them in was this: I was saying to myself, "This is not some pigsty where everyone who feels a little regret can come in, and then when he feels a little stress, can just run back out."

❂

Be Present in Need

Reflect on what happened with his brother, that great one, and Ahmad Ghazali. His brother, Muhammad, sent him books, so that he might avoid the condemnation of those who thought badly about him. Muhammad had told him, "Now and then, if you quote something from this book, you'll stop the wagging tongues of those who think ill of you." Because of that, Ahmad wouldn't let his brother in his *khanaqah*. According to one tradition, for seven years, and according to another story, for fifteen years he was forced to journey. Ahmad was saying to him: "Is this a pigsty, so that whenever you find yourself overwhelmed, you run here?"[273]

After all, I don't expect anything from these friends. First, I gain no knowledge from you. Instead, if you prepare yourselves by being completely present in need, you might understand my words—if you empty yourself of your own knowledge and imaginings. Even so, you may not comprehend my words.

Jurist or Fakir

They ask us about such and such a friend, "Is he a jurist or a fakir?"

He said, "He is both a jurist and a fakir."

"Then why does he only talk about jurisprudence?"

He answered, "His poverty is not like the fakirhood of those people who have such a coldness—one shouldn't talk about it with this group. It would be a pity to speak of it with these people.

He speaks words of knowledge, and he tells secrets through signs, so that his own words might not be spoken.

It Is for Your Benefit

Whatever I order you to do, it is only for your benefit. If someone speaks with you with the words of the dervishes, listen to him faithfully. When you listen, don't become deniers. If you do, after having listened, then formal apologies are useless. You ruin yourself in a thousand different ways, and then with your belly stuck out, you proudly say, "O Lord! *We have wronged our own souls* [7:23], now we have purified our heart!" For that you need the help of a friend.

---

273 Muhammad Ghazali was a great theologian, from a sufi lineage. After this, he left his post and wandered for many years, searching his soul until, "I arrived at Truth, not by systematic reasoning and accumulation of proofs, but by a flash of light which God sent into my soul."

❊

Patience and Practice

A rope dancer would walk on the rope with eyes blindfolded, with wooden clogs on his feet, a water jug on his head and holding four things in his hands. He would walk forward on the rope making creaking sounds with his feet, and return again, then suddenly he would throw himself down, hold the rope with his feet and under his armpits, then hang himself by a single finger, and then jump back onto the rope again.

Meanwhile, his heavy friend kept falling. All the time he was on the rope, his friend would keep shouting at him, "I've brought you here in the name of . . . such and such a teacher," and he would begin to weep. Then quickly people would gather up the sticks and blankets and offer loads of advice.

They practice tightrope walking at the seaside, so that if they fall off the rope they fall into the water. In this way, after long practice, they become master tightrope walkers. And after that, they practice on land. Gradually they raise their rope and learn about the best ways to stand and walk on it. Just as patience is needed for the crescent moon to become full, for the rain on the rocks to turn them into rubies, and for the drops that rain onto the sea to become pearls, these, too, would slowly become expert tightrope walkers through patience and practice.

With time, from unripe grapes you can make halvah.

❊

Be Steadfast

Whenever they swear at me, I am pleased, and when they praise me, I feel sad. Because "praising" must be such that "cursing" doesn't follow it. Otherwise, that praising is just hypocrisy. In the end, the hypocrite is worse than an unbeliever. *Truly, the hypocrites shall be in the lowest depth of the fire* [4:145].[274]

Give Now

In order to motivate a miserly rich man who was in the gathering, a preacher, at the most heated point of his talk, said, "O community! A divine inspiration has come to me![275] At this moment, it is passing through the beautiful, gentle, and honored mind of this master who is sitting here, 'Right this minute, let me go, and for God's sake, let me pour a hundred coins upon the head of this scholar who is the Imam of the age.'"

The miserly rich man said, "O Imam! That inspiration that has come to you is in relation to the joy of your own heart, the good will within you. But, may a hundred thousand curses of God be upon my mind—such a thought has never entered it."

This is how it happened. . . . Let's see how each one will cross this river.

The Truth Is the Mirror of the Servant

Islam [the peace that comes with surrender] is in opposing one's desires. It is in not obeying one's self (*nafs*). And unbelief is the obeying of one's desires. Let's say, someone has become a believer. The meaning of this is: " From now on, I will not follow my desires, my *nafs*—I give my word."

---

274 See *Surah an-Nisa*, Women 4:144-147:

O you who have attained to faith! Do not take the deniers of the truth for your allies in preference to the faithful! Do you want to place before God a manifest proof of your guilt?

Truly, the hypocrites shall be in the lowest depth of the fire, and you will find none who could succour them. But excepted shall be they who repent, and live righteously, and hold fast to God, and grow sincere in their faith in God alone: for these shall be one with the faithful—and in time God will grant to all the faithful a mighty reward.

Why would God cause you to suffer [for your past sins] if you are grateful and attain to faith—seeing that God is always responsive to gratitude, all-knowing?

275 M. 165.

And someone else said, "This isn't my work. I cannot do this—I will just pay the tax and live the way I want."

And the Prophet agreed with this and accepted it; he gave a guarantee paper to the non-muslim and said, "Whoever hurts a Zimmi, a non-Muslim, it is as if he has hurt me."

Someone else said, "I am a Muslim, and from now on, I repent of lust and sensuality." But he neither wants to pay the tax nor give up his desires. "I am a believer, a Muslim," he says, but he has no faith. He says, "I am an honest man," but, actually, he is not honest.

He says to you, "I am your friend. I am your servant," but he isn't. "I am pure," he says, but he is impure. "I am the falcon," he says. No, he is a crow. You have to thank the believer because he is not an unbeliever. You also have to thank the unbeliever because he is not a hypocrite.

Based upon one of the less common *hadith*, they say that when the people of Hell empty out, when all its most shallow and deepest corners are emptied and its doors are closed, when Hell is a ruined and abandoned abode, the screams of the hypocrites will still be heard. They will ask them, "What kind of a community are you that although everyone else has left, you are still here?"

"We are the hypocrites. Neither hope of liberation nor the opportunity to stay here is left to us."

Shamsuddin Khu'i, the Judge, spoke about this *hadith* during the lesson, but it is not widely known. Only one who is familiar with meaning, one who knows the inner meaning of things, receives a share from this.

Now there is an open hypocrisy and a hidden hypocrisy. We and our friends are far from that open hypocrisy, but one has to work harder to remove the secret hypocrisy within the children of Adam. It was said (*hadith*): "The believer is the mirror of the believer." More important is the meaning, "the Truth is the mirror of the servant, and the servant is the mirror of the Truth." Perfected words are full of meaning like this.

Sweet Words

Someone was opposing Shamsuddin Khu'i and began a discussion with the intention of humiliating that man of religion. He was saying: "Such and such person has memorized so many poems, he has learned something about every science, as well as things about the state and the parliament. And this other person has no information about anything; he knows nothing about official things!"

You are saying, "In short, he doesn't have anything in his memory, nor has he written a book." But he is a man of the word—he has experience. Don't you see how he speaks when necessary. No matter how vast the knowledge of the other is, if he doesn't have experience, see how he is incapable of speaking in the moment when it's needed."

Now, the difference between these is in relation to the knowledge of the outer feelings and thoughts—it is of the intellect of this world and the feeling of this world.

But if I were to describe the degrees of intelligence of the other world, it would be deceptive. Am I not telling you to take the cotton out of your ear and not to be a slave to empty words? Don't be misled by open hypocrisy—open your eyes and ears, and grasp the inner meaning of the work.

How can you convey a secret to a person of war? Is it any use to tell him, "Come, give up this war, give up this opposition?" He is in love with war. Wherever he sees a fight, he follows his inclination and leaps forward.

And the one who wants peace behaves accordingly, speaks accordingly, and works accordingly, so that he may come closer to peace. He says: "I am so ashamed. I repent of everything I did or said; it was the encouragement of the devil, the devil's trick. O Lord! What a wrongful deed I have done! What a deed I did."

Yet it was only an imagined fear that I said something that broke his heart. Let him express regret through beautiful words and behavior, so that he might prove that he is a lover of peace.

Love is your master. When you arrive there,
With the tongue of that state,
she will tell you about her subtleties.

The Prophet said, "Shall I tell you about a magical art that is religiously permitted and by which, without having to spend anything, you can turn free men into slaves?"

His companions said, "O Messenger of God, tell us."

He said, "It is good behavior, and a sweet tongue."

The Loving Mind

The heart is greater, more expansive, more pleasant and more illumined than the heavens; why would one narrow it with useless words? How could it be appropriate to constrict a very pleasant universe into a prison for oneself? What is the purpose of turning a universe like a fruitful garden into a tight prison, wasting time with delusions and ugly imaginings and throwing oneself into a dark universe and sleeping in ignorance all the time, wrapped up in a cocoon like a silkworm? We are of the people who turn the prison into a fruitful garden. If our prison turns into a fruitful garden, imagine what our fruitful garden might become? Just watch, and see!

None of the gracious words of the Prophet have surprised me; only one *hadith* has bewildered me: "The world is the prison of the believer." I don't see the world as a prison at all. "Where is the prison?" I'm asking. But that blessed one said, "the prison of the believers," he didn't say, "the prison of the servants." The servants are a different community.

One doesn't have to fit one's own meaning into that narrow thought. Whatever comes from the Friend, quickly say, "It's just like that," and keep going.

The Persian Shaikh

There was a scholar of religion who was referred to as "the man with the black breeches." Malik Adil[276] used to have a great deal of faith in him. This shaikh started arguing with the owner of the donkey he was riding.

He was saying, in Persian, "This donkey isn't walking well; he keeps falling on his face. But, the other day you showed me a good donkey, and then you gave the good donkeys to the others—you gave me the lame one."

They said to him, "This man doesn't understand Persian; speak in Arabic!"

The Persian thought for a while; he prepared the words that he would say in Arabic. The owner of the donkey had gone a little ways away. So as not to forget the Arabic words, the shaikh called out to him.

The donkey-owner asked, "What are you saying?"

The shaikh stuttered the Arabic words he had put together, "Tomorrow, I, a worthy donkey . . . "

The donkey-man said, "Today, also, O Shaikh!"

The other jurists, who envied him, all asked him to lead the night *salaat*. They knew that he couldn't recite the *Fatiha*,[277] and so, they thought that in this way, Malik Adil would come to see it, too. After this was agreed, they kept him busy talking, so that he would miss the right moment for the prayer. But he sensed the plan. He turned towards Malik Adil, "O Great King," he said, "Do you know how to walk stammeringly?"

"No," the king said.

The Hoja signaled to the servant with his eyes to bring his shoes. He put them on and jumped up from his place. He stepped on one foot, dragging the other one, and then pausing, in the same way,

---

276 Malik Adil (Mahmoud ibn Zangi) was the "Just King" who ruled in Damascus.

277 The *Fatiha* is the opening chapter of the Qur'an. It is recited in Arabic at the beginning of every cycle of prayer.

he stepped on the other foot and dragging it, he demonstrated crippledness as he went to lead the prayer.

The Waters of Truth

One of those who were in the gathering of the shaikh, was saying, "Now, neither blasphemy nor faith remains in me. I can find neither blasphemy nor faith within myself. I've come into your presence. Nothing of Judaism, or Fire-worshipping, or the beliefs I inherited from my mother or father remain in me. Even though formerly I believed in them and had faith, gradually I gave up those early beliefs."

This path is very difficult. Its beginning and end are not clear. Of course, it is not easy; even as he cannot remember his early beliefs, he can't find a way back to them either. It's like this: beside a river, a man takes off his clothes to bathe and jumps into the water.[278] The water is flowing very vigorously; it grabs hold of him and drags him downstream. He tries to leap towards the place where his clothes are so that he may take them and put them back on. But what can he do—the water that was flowing so strongly has grabbed him and taken him away.

Contemplation

The worship and work of Muhammad, may the Peace and Blessing of God be upon him, was immersion in Divine contemplation (*istighraq*). He said, "The work is the work of the heart, service is the service of the heart, and servanthood is servanthood of the heart." But one can reach that universe of Divine contemplation and witnessing only through annihilating oneself in the Greatness of God. Muhammad knew that not everyone had a way to

278 M. 170.

engage in the real work and worship. To very few of God's servants has the happiness of immersion been given. So he gave the commandments to his community to do the five times a day *salaat* and thirty days of fasting a year, and the rituals of the pilgrimage, so that the community might not be deprived of that witnessing of the miraculous manifestations of God in the hidden realm. This was so that they might be liberated and understand their place of benefit in relation to other communities, and so that perhaps the fragrance from that happiness of divine contemplation might also reach them. If this were not the case, what relationship would there be between hunger in fasting and servanthood before God? Of what use would be these open invitations of religion and worship?

❊

Rats and Cats

Many shaikhs are the waylayers of the religion of Muhammad. Like rats, they work to turn the house of this religion upside down. But there are also cats among the dear servants of God who work to clear away these rats. Even if hundreds of thousands of rats were to come together, they could not muster enough courage to even look at a single cat, because the majesty of the cat prevents them from being able to gather together. And cats are a community among themselves. If rats had the courage to gather, if they could join together and if a few self-sacrificing rats were among them, then the cat could catch one of them, and while he was occupied with it, the others could scratch the cat's eyes out, jump onto his head, and certainly could kill him. Or at least, they could escape. But the fear within them prevents them from gathering together. A rat is the symbol of dispersion, and a cat is the symbol of gathering.

The Sanctuary of the Heart

It was said, "*The one who enters into it finds peace* [3:97]."[279] There is no doubt that "it" is the heart. *Are they, then, not aware that We have set up a secure sanctuary,*[280] *while all around them people are being carried away* [29:67]? Outside the heart's sanctuary, the devil lurks — *he whispers in the breasts of men* [114:5]. A hundred thousand times he carries them away with fears and doubts and despair. But the Truth nurtured the Prophet Abraham in the midst of the fire, the Truth completed him. The Prophet Moses was brought up and nurtured at the hand of the enemy through God's grace.

Yes, the Prophet knew this about the favor and guidance of God, so he said, "First the Friend and then the Path."

Humility before the Truth

They tell me, "Some people are talking about you—'He is a heretic, he is occupied with innovations.'" They find fault with me.[281]

And I said, "They are telling the truth. I am an innovator."

---

279 See *Surah Imran*, 3:96-97: *Behold, the first House of worship ever set up for humankind was indeed the one at Mecca: rich in blessing, and a guidance unto all the worlds, full of clear messages—the place where Abraham once stood. And whoever enters it finds inner peace. And so, pilgrimage unto the House is a duty owed to God by all people who are able to undertake it. And as for those who deny the truth—truly, God does not stand in need of anything in all the worlds.*

280 The "sanctuary secure" indicates the inner peace and sense of spiritual fulfillment within the heart which God bestows on those of faith.

281 Within the more conservative Islamic community, innovation (*bida*), or anything that is "new" and might not be done just as the prophet did it, is looked upon as heretical. Shams is saying he is keeping the religion "new," fresh, filled with life.

In another passage of the *Maqalat*, he describes how someone was calling him an innovator, and he says they are speaking the truth, because he wasn't keeping up with their tempo in the performing of the *salaat*. He was moving much more slowly, immersed in prayer.

In a passage of the *Menaqib al-arifin* (#143), Mevlana's wife, Kirra, describes Mevlana praying slowly, also: One evening our Master was saying the

Now tell me, what is the truth, the inner meaning of this *salaat*? First of all, some of the philosophers say, "It is shameful, improper, and an imperfection full of fault to put one's head on the ground—keep your body on your feet."

He fell on his face—that was my purpose, this was what I wanted. I quoted from the philosophers and said that they are not of the faithful. Now give me permission to say one more thing. Even Muhammad is saying, "Stop, let me listen to what he is saying."

If you do something improper, you should know it—the real man of his word is the person who can say, "This was the reason." Since you are that person now, this is also appropriate for you.

I cannot say of anybody, "He is impious; he is full of sins." I don't see anyone as connected to bad things, nor do I think badly about anyone. And I ask for God's forgiveness, so that bad thoughts might be cleared from within me.

But I am saying that the devil is the source of that miracle—it has become an obstacle that keeps you from that which you seek. You need to empty yourself of that miracle, so that it doesn't stand in your way.

---

evening prayer in our house. He recited the *Fatiha*, word for word, so slowly that those present had time to recite ten chapters of the Qur'an.

During the prayer, tears fell from his blessed eyes so profusely that we could hear them falling. I kissed his blessed feet and wept and cried, "O protector of the unfortunate, the hope of the servants of God is in your hands, when your ecstasy takes this form where do all your lamentations go?"

He answered, "*Allahu Akbar* (God is greater)! My efforts are very limited and insufficient, but I ask forgiveness of our great and glorious Sustainer and pray: 'O great Lord, unlike mine, Your power is without limit; forgive me.' When Our Prophet (Blessings and Peace be upon Him) heard these words: *'God will manifest his forgiveness of all thy faults, past as well as future and thus bestow upon thee the full measure of His blessings, and guide thee on a straight way'* [*Surah al-Fath*, Victory 48:2], he answered, 'Am I not your grateful servant?'"

❊

Pure Trust

Those people who are not of the inside, even if you show hundreds of thousands of miracles to them, they won't have faith.

Abu Bakr (May God be pleased with him) never demanded any miracles. He would say, "Whatever the Prophet says, we have faith in it and accept it as true."

❊

Increase Your Capacity

O Master! People see things according to their own capacity.

He said, "By making comparisons among themselves, the community has broken apart."

Far away from the mosque, we are calling to them: "Which group is responsible for fragmenting the community in this way? It is their obligation to gather them back together." What kind of helplessness is this? Because of their helplessness they go further astray, and openness of heart is in others, not in them.

I am saying that for me poison is an antidote. May your sins be upon my throat, because I am swallowing this. Bear witness! Don't accuse me of others' sins. Even if I were blameworthy before, I have no sins left now—Hell is afraid of me. Finally, it is as it was said in the *hadith*—it calls to me, "Pass by, O faithful one! Your light will extinguish my fire!"

❊

Listen to the Command, "Be!"

Go out through the gate of intellect—does the veil drop away? They don't have the courage to take even a single step.

He said, "He knows nothing about grammar."

The one who knows the rules of language, is the one who has himself become the rules of language. By God! Unless a human being turns completely into syntax, he will never have any inkling of this knowledge.

❁

The Pains of Love

I only cause trouble for those whom I love, but sometimes the trouble I cause isn't fitting. Within the wish to make things easy, there is both mercy and wrath. But in the universe of solitude, it is all favor—there is only grace and tasting.

Such a strange suspicion came to me due to this, that she doesn't want to come back. It is useless to return to the vineyard. Because he will not be able to see her in the vineyard, he will even be afraid of Chelebi, of his revealing this secret there. He can't see her there either.

They said, "She went to Bedr."

"Why did she go to Bedr?"

She said, "Then give me permission, too, let me go. Why are you keeping me?"

As she was saying, "Let me go," I was saying, "No, never, never!"

She smiled at me. That smile means, "God has given me a blessing, how will I ever be able to give thanks enough?" In addition, this also meant, "What are you saying? How can I live without you?"

May God give you goodness!

This woman, I don't want you—this time, if she goes and leaves, it's not my concern. Let me bring a witness; let me set her free before she comes. The main thing that makes me sad, that binds my hands and feet is her leaving her heart in me and leaving her eyes behind. This would be a shame.

What does he know of the state of a helpless woman? This woman has come into my marriage, and a closeness has occurred between us. Even if she behaves like this, she is a good woman. Don't look at her with her own eyes.[282]

---

282 In another passage of the *Maqalat*, Shams seems to be referring to Mevlana's conservative son, Alaeddin when he says, "Let me call him either a flea or a grasshopper, because he is jumpy, jumping, jumpily." Then he says, "It is due to this sinless Kimya. But we must be her mine, so that she may not see herself as stony." It seems that Alaeddin may have been attracted to Shams' beautiful and saintly young wife, Kimya, who had been part of Mevlana's household

She would never be proud of the fact that my glance has fallen upon her, or that my skin has touched hers. She never would regard herself as a saint.

"What is she doing in Bedr?" I said.

"Just sightseeing—it is an outing," she said.

"How can she become friends with these people? How can she go on an excursion? How can she sit together with them? It is as if she is your wife—how can that ill-tempered wife go away without getting my permission? What kind of mischief has she done? Give Mevlana my respects and beg him to come by for a moment to speak a few words with me, because my mind is bewildered."

"Let him come sometime," I said.

"The confused mind of the friend passes to his friend's, too," he said.

He begged me. "Give her a break of ten days; let her rent a house and then go."

"Tell her, she can stay for two months, she can stay for two years, but let her not hurt us. Tell her not to make a scandal; let her stay."[283]

---

before Shams' arrival. When Mevlana suggested that she marry Shams and she happily did so, this added to Alaeddin's jealousy of Shams. Alaeddin's behavior may have been the cause of deepening Shams' displeasure with Kimya when she went on an outing to the vineyards without his permission. Kimya loved Shams deeply and he loved her.

283 Mevlana came to Shams and saw him speaking with Kimya. Thinking Kimya had returned, he went away for a while to give them privacy and then after a while came back to find Shams was alone. Mevlana asked where Kimya had gone. Shams replied, "My Lord loves me so much that He appears to me in all the forms that I love." (See *Menaqib al-arifin* #511)

When Kimya did return, Shams became angry with her. It seems she caught cold on the outing, and became quite ill. Not long after, she died, leaving Shams beside himself.

Leaving Aside Ego

Some people recite the Throne Verse at the head of the sick, and there are also some who become the Throne Verse themselves.[284]

A creative word makes people sleepy, but awakened hearts work even while sleeping. For Goodness sake! Say it again—what was the beginning of this verse?

The companions of Muhammad never opposed him. Because of their faith in him, while they were listening to him, they would become intoxicated. Of those beautiful words, Abu Bakr conveyed no more than seven *hadith*. If people had only asked they could have received many benefits—many secrets would have been revealed. The fragrance of our words comes from this.

The saying of Hallaj, "I am the Truth," is without restraint. Bayazid's words, "Glory be to me," are a bit more veiled. There is no human being who does not have at least a little egoism.

When Moses (may the greeting of God be upon him) showed a sign of egoism, saying "I am more knowledgeable than any other human being on earth," Allah sent him Khidr so that he might journey with him for a few days, and he might lose that egoism.[285]

Muhammad (May the Peace and blessings of God be upon him) said to Ali, "Why did you follow me in continuous fasting? You have become so thin and weak. I am not like one of you. I pass the night with my Lord—*He gives me to eat and to drink* [26:79]." Some say that this was the reason for the verse, *Say* [*O Prophet*]: "*I am but a mortal man*

---

284 When a person is sick in bed, verses from the Qur'an are read to help the patient recover. Shams refers here to the "Throne verse" *Surah al-Baqarah*, 2:255:

God—there is no deity but Hu, the Ever-Living, the Self-Subsisting Source of all Being. No slumber can seize Him/Her nor sleep. All things in heaven and on earth belong to Hu. Who could intercede in His/Her Presence without His/Her permission? He/She knows what appears in front of and behind His/Her creatures. Nor can they encompass any knowledge of Him/Her except what He/She wills. His/Her throne extends over the heavens and the earth, and He/She feels no fatigue in guarding and preserving them, for He/She is the Highest and Most Exalted.

285 M. 180.

like all of you [18:110]." In other words, "O My Representative! Put aside all ego, and speak in this way." But God Most High, in order not to beat down the heart of His dear prophet, also added to the end of the verse: *It has been revealed to me. Your God is One God.*[286] And *Hence, he who looks forward to meeting his Sustainer, let him do righteous deeds* [18:110] is similar to that and to "I am not like one of you."

And let him not ascribe unto anyone or anything a share in the worship due to his Sustainer [18:110]—this also is the same as that.

❊

Worship and Reason

Good servants cultivate the earth of this world by means of worship and reason. The two worlds have been bound together by these two—worship and reason. In every era, people are ignorant of the power of the command in both worlds. Your hands and your feet move and strengthen through imitation. There is no fear of being left in deprivation, but first He makes you turn away—then when you come to yourself, He makes you vigorous, full of life.

Everybody is in love with this word: "Well done!" They die for the sake of "Well done!"

Your seeing is by means of His attributes. Don't ask for anything other than what you need! Everything you are asking for is there.

To pay attention to filth, darkness, and gluttony, and the veils that belong to this world, and to live within blurriness and difficulties is like busying yourself with children's toys. Some disappear within the Seen and awaken from the sleep of ignorance.

❊

Conveying the Word

We have to preach tomorrow. It is difficult, but a door has been opened. There is no other way—if you close the door, screams, complaints, and criticisms begin. I wish it had at least been useful for them.

---

286 In other words, "I am also a mortal like you, but I receive revelations: Your God is One."

Everything that needs to be said has been said. It has been spoken about either openly or in a veiled way. But they behave as if they have never heard any advice. They grasp neither the open meaning of the words, nor do they understand their purpose and deeper meaning. Since they don't understand, how can they follow the advice?

Deeds without knowledge take people further astray. I wonder what they gain from the ascetic trials (*cille*) that they undertake? What are they doing there? The words, "There is no god besides God, there is only Allah," are not the business of the tongue but a matter of practice. One has to apply it. I don't know what he gets from this.

The word belongs only to Him. Wherever He wants, He turns it in that direction. In the end, God also has servants who become the state of that state. I don't know—am I the master of your words or not? "There are such servants . . . ," I am saying.[287]

> Yes, when the sun departs from someone,
> for light, instead of the sun, that poor
> one burns chips of pine.

OK, these things will be OK. This is God's business.

When you realize that you can't retain my words, you occupy yourself with other words. You aren't doing the *salaat*. You used to do it before. To be occupied with *salaat* and worship is a sign of happiness. Your doubts have made me grow old.[288] If anything were the cause of your separation that is it.

The Joy of True Knowledge

With all this craziness of mine, I have plunged so many sane ones into vats of wine. With all this absent-mindedness of mine, I have

---

287 See p.412 of this text: "God has such servants—nobody could stand the troubles they suffer. The ones who drink from the pitcher that is continually refilled cannot return to themselves. Others get drunk and leave, but they stay near the barrel of wine."

288 Shams resonates again with *Surah Hud*, see p.142 of this text.

carried away so many cunning ones under my arm. There was a joy of good news within me—it was as if I was flying through the heavens, I wasn't on the earth.[289]

You are getting an education, but according to me, you aren't. That would be the outcome if you read only one verse a day. Your father's intention in sending you to be educated was this. People these days are bad, they lead children astray. They have no fear of God.

In this moment, be grateful to God! The knowledge that you have received is enough.

On the way, I began to speak about different kinds of knowledge. I was saying: "The path is not like a house." Like a scholar who is an authority in many areas of knowledge, I was speaking about important topics. We have become more beneficial than many manuscripts. But, Mevlana is greater than we are, because, whatever there is, he is a thousand times that. Unless you give yourself completely to him, he won't become yours.

Be Careful What You Eat

God Most High says in the *hadith qudsi*: "When my servant comes close to me by a span, I come close to him by a cubit."[290]

Exaltedness and greatness is Mevlana's; I am saying this openly.

Will you look well upon me today? Would it ever be compatible with generosity that I should look at you only from the aspect of intellect, when you have such knowledge and such excellent qualities?

The Prophet has said: "When My servant is thirsty, clouds of wisdom cause rain to fall within his heart."

---

289 One of Shams' nicknames mentioned in the *Menaqib al-arifin* was "Shams the Flyer," some say because he would rise in the air, and because he would "fly" above the ground, not lingering anywhere for very long in his search for a true human being. Another of his nicknames was "Kamil of Tabriz" (the perfected one from Tabriz).

290 *Hadith qudsi*: "When someone approaches Me by a span, I approach him by a cubit; when he approaches Me by a cubit, I approach him by a fathom; and when he comes to Me walking, I come to him running." (A span is the distance between the thumb and the smallest finger when the palm is opened . . .)

The abode of those whose *qiblah* is the kitchen today,
Know that it will be Hell tomorrow.

O throat that has been cut by the command of God,
eat and drink!
But ask, "O throat, are you a throat,
or are you a sword?"

Self-Control for God's Sake

Restricting food increases the power within you; abundant food decreases the power of wisdom and thought.

Because everybody can adorn himself with it, listen to this advice: If you find something to eat in this world, but you don't eat it here, you will eat it in the next world.

"This is a place where I can begin," you say.[291]

Learn this so that you may gain openness of heart and rewards for your good deeds and so that the darling you are seeking might show her face to you often.

It's like this—two people fast; one remains hungry because he hasn't found anything to eat, and the other, although he has found everything, fasts for the sake of God's acceptance, only for gaining the reward of that good deed from God.

Let me give you another example: if the chief eunuch in a palace and a brave young man both avoid sex; or if a sick man and a powerfully healthy man both abstain from sex, are they ever equal to each other? In the same way, all animals also remain patient when they can't find or see a mate, but they all also have a weakness.

---

291 See *Mathnawi* V, 295-298 (*Jewels of Remembrance* p.90):

You who are kept in pawn to food,
you can be free if you suffer yourself to be weaned.
Truly in hunger there is abundant nourishment:
search after it diligently and cherish the hope of finding it.
Feed on the Light, be like the eye,
be in harmony with the angels, O best of humankind.
Like the Angel, make glorification of God your sustenance.

O faithful ones who are like Layla!
May God increase your number!

Those who generously sacrifice their souls for the sake of those who are thirsty for love, they are like Layla.

Can You See Us Waving?

"If someone approaches me by the span of a hand, I come near to him by a yard." There are so many words and subtle points waving within a human being who is a man of the word. But if he can't find anyone who has the ability to understand him, what use is it?

I became a man of the tavern, and I was
freed from troubles,
Neither piety nor concern about the Qur'an
remained in me.
On the way to serve those free human beings,
I fastened His strong belt around my belly.[292]
"Three things bring joy to the gathering," they say;
I have the wine, that beautiful one, and the light.

We showed you our servanthood, but what use is it?
Your ugly manners had no idea how to buy a slave!

How can a person who is digging a well avoid water?

What Is of Value?

Of her nurse who praised her and said that she was beautiful, a child asked, "If my face is beautiful to you, whose is the ugly face that is displeasing?"

Who is the one who claims to know me?

There is nothing ugly in the world, except according to some criterion.[293] Even blasphemy by itself is not ugly, but when it is com-

292 Here "the belt" refers to a special belt worn to indicate devotion and service. To wear it "around the belly" also indicates abstinence and control of bodily pleasures.

293 M. 185.

pared with faith, then it appears ugly. Otherwise, to its own self it is beautiful, but when it comes next to faith, it seems ugly and flawed. Iron in itself is iron—it is hard. It is useful for people; it is strong, but in comparison with copper it is less valuable, because copper is more maleable—it can be molded into any form. In chemistry it is more useful than iron, and because of this quality of copper, it is considered better than iron. Until the turn of silver comes, it seems very beautiful, but gold, jewels, and rare precious pearls are even better, one beyond the other.

Just once, ask the ruby, "Why have you become so red? Was it the sun that brought you this state?"

If words belittle it, devalue it, and try to break it, or in other words, if they find fault with it and speak of it like that, what difference does it make?

☼

At Home in the Water

The sign of a fish, we know, is that it lives in water.[294] If you see that any animal is running away from water, or that it has died out of fear of water, it is not a fish. When one speaks of God to it, out of sorrow and fear it dies, and because of this it wants to jump out of the water. But there's no need for witnesses and evidence to prove that a fish lives in water; it lives in the water, and it never leaves it. Or even if it comes out of it every now and then, the essential thing is that its home is in the water.

☼

No Bones about It

We have to remember this song that Juha sang while playing his lute when his arm was crippled.

> In your village, I keep picking up bones,
> So that dogs might not go there.

---

294 Shams is also referring here to the people of God who live in the Water of the Divine—the completed ones.

✲

What Do You Want?

A shaikh, one day, received an apple in his hand. He asked Zeyneddin Kelusi, "I have seen God, I wanted an apple from Him, and He gave it to me. What do you want from God? Bayazid Bastami wanted God from God; so and so wanted such and such."

Zeyneddin answered, "I also want God from God."

"Then you are of the station of Bayazid," he said.

I was a child when He asked me; and I made a gesture with my head, "I want You," I said.

He nodded His head, and from then on I couldn't say anything anymore. My mouth did not open, but my whole inside was completely filled with words, expressions, and meanings. I arrived at such a strange state—very few people have had such a thing happen to them in their childhood.

Whatever God Most High places in front of you, accept it as your greatest happiness.

✲

The Joy of Proximity

If two friends are speaking together, sitting next to each other or face to face, is the pleasure within that sweet conversation ever the same as the experience of watching them from a distance? If distance is not an obstacle, and joy of heart is with you, still how can that joy be compared to the joy of closeness. If a person is in presence and respect even when he is far away, imagine how it will be when he is near.

✲

The Dance of the People of God

The dance of the people of God is subtle and light. They walk like a leaf on the water. Inwardly, they are like a mountain; they are weighty like a hundred thousand mountains, but outwardly they appear as light as a straw.

Grasping the Reins

The Truth is within my hand—it is not "with me." All the attributes of God that you spoke about during the Friday sermon, *Nothing on earth or in the heavens is hidden from God* [3:5], or *Indeed, He keeps all things in His sight* [67:19], or *Does he, then, not know that God sees* [96:14]? Yes, I see all these attributes also as my attributes.

> Aren't you tired of these malicious dogs?
> Aren't you ashamed of these unbridled asses?
> He is the "Ornament of the religion,"
> but the color and smell of blasphemy;
> the "Pride of the kingdom,"
> but the disgrace and shame of the country!

One must grasp the reins and pull them with care. The difference between one who knows and one who is ignorant is just this: one pulls in the reins, but the other let's them loose.

Now, where is that reining in?

Will You Hold out Your Hand?

From the point of view of appearances, it seems that I am forbidding him to eat and drink. I am reflecting a lot; he must not be a hindrance for me—let me not be concerned about his food, drink, or the trouble of clothing and laundry. In other words, don't be occupied with him, but let's be together—let him serve for a while.

You say, "Well, this is ugly, it's doubtful." Is there a better shelter for the servant of God than to reach out his hand to the hands of the people of God—then would he ever not reach liberation?

"The face of the dervish is dark in both worlds," he said. If you are telling the truth, then what is it that you are inviting people to? To dark-facedness? If you are lying, then your slap means nothing at all.[295]

Someone else says, "Endure!" This word is the word of God, the word of those beloved of God.

---

295 See "The Blessing of the Moment" p.215 of this text.

Don't buy a chessboard for Alaeddin! If you are a friend of Mevlana's, don't do this. Because this is the time for his education, and he doesn't have much time. *He doesn't sleep at night. He can sleep only during one third of the night or less* [73:20].[296] Everyday he has to read some; even if it is a single line, he must do this.[297] But if he hears about this, he'll be hurt by me. He'll say, "He is trying to teach me my business!"

And so, they see the Truth as an enemy, they don't listen to the truthful words that aren't pleasing to them. When the scent of benefit comes to them, they get scared. This is a very strange thing. Some people enjoy wasting time. "One who walks in the dark loses his way," they say.

His whole body has turned into a tongue. Whether asking questions or answering them, he was behaving discourteously—he wasn't ever aware of the universe of the Truth.

If I could have spoken to them of the ecstasy that the prophets and saints seek, they would all become drunk and full of joy. The Truth would shine on their faces and bodies, and would be clearly manifest in them.

---

296 See *Surah al-Muzzammil*, O Thou Enwrapped One 73:1-8 and 20:

O thou enwrapped one! Keep awake [in prayer] at night, all but a small part of one-half thereof—or make it a little less than that, or add to it; and recite the Qur'an calmly and distinctly, with thy mind attuned to its meaning.

Behold, We shall bestow upon you a weighty message—truly, the hours of night impress the mind most strongly and speak with the clearest voice, whereas by day a long chain of doings is your portion. But [whether by night or by day,] remember your Sustainer's name, and devote yourself to Him with utter devotion. . . .

Behold, [O Prophet,] your Sustainer knows that you keep awake [in prayer] nearly two-thirds of the night, or one-half of it, or a third of it, together with some of those who follow you. And God, who determines the measure of night and day, is aware that you would never grudge it: and therefore He turns towards you in His grace.

Recite, then, as much of the Qur'an as you may do with ease. He knows that in time there will be among you sick people, and others who will go about the land in search of God's bounty, and others who will struggle in God's cause. Recite, then, as much of it as you may do with ease, and be constant in prayer, and spend in charity, and lend unto God a goodly loan: for whatever good deed you may offer up in your own behalf, you shall truly find it with God—yea, better, and richer in reward.

And seek God's forgiveness: behold, God is much-forgiving, a dispenser of grace!

297 M. 190.

❁

Cry Out

"I am burning up with this pain, I can't stand it," they say.

God says, "It is this for which I am holding on to you."

And the dervish is saying, "O Lord! I am burning up—what do you want of this servant of yours?"

"This burning of yours."

It is like the story of the breaking of the pearl—the lover asks his beloved, "Why did you break the pearl?"

The beloved answers, "I broke the pearl so that you might ask me about it."

The secret wisdom of this is that the Sea of Compassion wants to rise and overflow. And the cause of that is your yearning, weeping, and crying out. If the clouds of your anguish don't arise, the Sea of the divine mercy and knowledge doesn't surge forth.

> Does a mother nurse her baby, tell me,
> Unless, from hunger, the baby cries?[298]

❁

Finding the Source

A person who can't see the changes that go on inside and outside of himself, who doesn't understand the wisdom in hearing and seeing and intellect, and who has doubts about how the universe is run, and those who understand the miracles of all the prophets, the wonders of the saints, and their bringing of revelations and inspirations, and yet still are in doubt, say, "I wonder why my portion has been delayed?" or, "Why are things happening like this?" If such a disabled one witnesses that God is Compassionate, Knowing, and All-powerful, then he accepts it.

---

298 The story of the halvah boy in the *Mathnawi* is a beautiful example of Mevlana's elaboration of this theme. See *Mathnawi* II:376-444. See also *Surah Maryam*, 19:22-33.

Some people journeyed to find the source of the Euphrates (Firat) river. They walked for two years. At last, they saw that the river was emerging from the top of a mountain.

"How beautiful!" one of them said, and turned and jumped into the water. And another jumped in after him.

Someone thought that they had been pulled down: "God knows what has happened to them! What else can it be?"

And some of them returned and brought the news. They said: "We went as far as that place, but some friends who arrived there just before us, we don't know, but they made a sound like that of a frog falling into the water."

The mothers and siblings of the men gathered. They couldn't accept it. It is like when geese emerge from eggs upon which chickens have sat—when their mothers walk around on the land, they also walk with them, but when their mothers go into the water, they go into the water, too. And the others who come to the edge of the water and see them say, "Alas! The babies have gone and gotten drowned!"

Don't Break the Jug with Gossiping

A jug is helpless in front of a rock. It is quite an obvious truth that a jar should always avoid stones. If it gets broken, the pieces remain, but that which is inside gets spoiled—it spills and spreads everywhere. In other words, secret gossiping is that which breaks the jar. One must reply clearly in a way that will silence them, because they don't understand a silent answer. They understand clearly spoken words like, "Welcome," "Goodbye," "You have brought us joy." And what of the meaning of the verse, *See how your Lord has extended the shadow* [25:45], or *Allah is the light of the heavens and the earth* [24:35]?

La illaha illallah

If you want to benefit from me, don't behave humbly towards me and then secretly, like Pharaoh, when you are alone say, "O My God—you are my idol, and I am your servant!" to yourself. Don't say to everybody else, "*I am your Lord Most Great* [79:24]!" One must say "No!" (*La illaha illallah*) both on the outside (*zahir*) and on the inside (*batin*).[299]

❊

Haste is the Business of the Devil

Let me think for a while before answering so that I might not fall into a mistake like that vizier. Haste is the business of the Devil. Those who hurry can't see anything but the glossy surface of things. Because they are only looking at the outer appearance all the time, they see only the outer decoration and the form.

And they don't repent and ask for forgiveness for their sins. Repentance is the attribute of Adam and his offspring. And to insist on continuing in mistakes and sins is the attribute of the Devil and his children.

❊

Ripening

With loving caresses they make candy from sugar cane;
With time, from silkworms they make satin.
The work that you are doing, do it slowly—
    be a little patient.
With time, from unripe grapes you can make halvah.

❊

What News

O breeze of dawn! Do you bring news?
What news do you bring of the cheeks
    of that moon-faced one?
Are there days that you play and sing,
    or that you make zhikr of "Hayy and Hu?"
O wind! Blow more slowly—your fragrance
    is so pleasing!

---

299 M. 195.

Noah

I was working as a teacher, and one of the viziers had been fired from his job, and was working as a teacher, too. They sent a message from the sultan.

The sultan grabbed him by the skirt of his robe and asked: "During the time of the Prophet Noah, the world had become so developed and prosperous that in order to go from one city to another they would have to walk a distance of less than a day. If the length of the way were ever longer than a day, they would be quite astonished and would say that it was very far away indeed. For a thousand years, less fifty, the Prophet Noah was inviting his tribe to faith, and every day he would visit several places. How can this be?"

They were discussing: "How can one live for close to a thousand years?" Philosophers say that it is surely not possible to live more than a hundred and twenty years. I am not saying that I accept their words. They made lots of interpretations like, "For a thousand years he invited people to faith; everyday he would walk around an area five times—they would beat him up, and then, when Gabriel would touch him with his wing, his wounds would heal."

Noah certainly never gave up inviting them, but on the other hand, not more than seventy people became *muslims*. There are several stories, but among them, the truest one is this.

Yes, the invitation is true, but what would be the benefit of my accepting it? The treasury of my heart belongs to nobody—it belongs only to the Truth.

What Are You Planting?

Someone who plants thorns instead of roses,
Is fit for the gallows, not the pulpit.

The purpose of the creation of the world is the union of two friends, face to face, far from lust and sensuality and desires and ambitions, focused only on the way of God. What they seek is not the bread, the baker, or the butcher and the butcher-shop. It is just as I am now—at ease with Mevlana.

❊

Breaking Fast

Some people invited me [to break my fast with them]. Many times I offered excuses.

Instead, I would go to the church. There were some non-Muslims there who were my friends. Though they seemed to be non-Muslim on the outside, really, inwardly they were muslims.

I would say, "Bring me something, so that I may eat."

They would thank me a thousand times, and break their fast with me. Though they were fasting, they would eat.

❊

What Troubles Your Heart Troubles Mine

O Exalted Master, there's no need to praise you!

And you, too, give up praise! I'm saying this because to really praise Mevlana would be to care for that which brings him ease—let him be pleased and completely at ease. Be careful not to do anything that might disturb his mind, or hurt him. In reality, whatever troubles me, troubles Mevlana's heart, too.

❊

The Sultan and the Miller

Sultan Mahmoud (of Ghazna) had become separated from his army, and had gotten very hungry. Along the way he came by a miller's and said, "Peace be with you! Do you have anything to eat?"

The miller thought to himself as he went to look, "Let me be careful! Where has such a heavy and lively man come from?" He called out, "Today we have only leftover bread, will you eat that?"

"Bring it," the sultan said.

While the miller was going to bring it, he thought better of it and turned around, "If a loaf were left, we would eat it, too, but nothing's left—there's no bread, but we have flour, would you eat that?"

"Yes, bring it; bring whatever you have!"

The man went away, saying to himself, "Too bad—this guy is so hungry he's going to eat even the flour." This time, he returned saying, "But, it's mixed with millet." Then again he came and said, "The flour that's been ground actually belongs to orphans."

At last he brought a dusty sheepskin and shook it in the face of the sultan saying, "This is the only food that's left." He wanted to make him believe it. "I thought there was something," he said.

The sultan's eyes were hurt, so he went to the river's edge to wash them. He sat for a while with his hands over his eyes. Then he went on.

As he continued on the way, he came across a Turkish boy. "Do you have anything to eat?" he asked.

The boy answered, "Yes, but first greet me and then ask me, 'Would you like a guest?'"

"I swear, this boy is right," said Mahmoud to himself. Slowly he pulled the reins of his horse back, and then returned. He said, "May the peace of God be upon you (*As-Salaam Alaikum*)."

"And peace be unto you!"

"Would you like a guest?"

"Come, and be our guest—let me quickly bring you honeycomb, yogurt, milk, cheese, or whatever we have," he said.

The sultan ate these, and said to the boy, "Take this ring, because I am one of those who are close to the king—I may get something for you from the king with this. If they don't give you anything, I'll get it and give it to you."

When the boy looked at the ring, he thought to himself, "Alas! What a pity that I didn't butcher a sheep! What have I done?!"

As the sultan thought about him, his deed increased in value, and his status rose. Finally, the sultan caught up with his soldiers.

The boy arrived, and he showed his ring to them. All of them prostrated themselves in front of him and welcomed him with respect. And what does the boy see? All the lords and ministers lined up in a row, and the cavalrymen and commanders standing at attention. He looked around, wondering, "Which one is the sultan?"

When the boy saw the sultan dressed [in his royal robes], he was astonished, "O my God!" When he looked again, he realized that this was the sultan. He exclaimed to himself, "Oh! What did I do!"

The sultan began to speak, and the boy said to himself, "By God, he is the sultan!"

The sultan commanded, "Let forty slaves with golden belts come to serve him!" Just imagine the rest and those varied dishes of food!

Then he commanded, "Bring that miller—let me please his heart, too!"

A hundred armed cavalrymen set out. He had described the village to them and the mill. From a distance, they looked and saw him near a hill. One of them asked, "Is that the miller?"

"Yes, it is," they said.

Poor man, he said, "Alas! They have come." He ran and locked the door. When they knocked at the door, he made no sound.

"I am dead," he said.

"How can you be dead if you are speaking?"

The miller said, "This is my last breath, and it is about to come to an end—now, I am dead."

"Get up!" they said.

He didn't get up, and so they broke down the door, and went in. Again they said, "Get up! The sultan wants you!"

The miller began to plead, "O honorable men! What business would the king have with me? I am a poor miller. If the sultan has wheat, then bring the wheat here, and I will grind it into flour!"

"Cut it out," they said, "Get up, be quick! The sultan wants you."

"But I can grind it very well."

"Enough talking!" they said.

The miller said, "Let me give you bread and yogurt." He wouldn't give the sultan anything, and now he's welcoming a hundred people as his guest!

"Get up, what ridiculous things are you saying? Get up!" they said. Again he wouldn't get up, so they tied a rope around his neck and pulled him there.

The poor man looked all around trying to locate that royal master, but he couldn't see him. At last, with difficulty, he saw the sultan. "Ah! Even if I had a thousand heads, I couldn't save even one of them."

The sultan said, "Poor man! I have brought you here so that you may find my ring that has fallen into the tank."

"I am at your service," he said.

Secretly, the sultan gave orders to the others to tightly lock the man up there, and not to let him go for three days: "Let him learn what hunger means."

The poor man used to eat five maunds of bread a day. He had a hellish appetite. Left without bread for three days, he began awaiting death.

When the three days had passed, he said, "Bring him!"

"Get up and come out!" they called.

"What else do you want from me?" the miller said. "Nothing but a single breath is left to me—leave me so that I may die!"

"No," they said. "Do you think you are such a man that you will be able to save yourself by dying?"

"Alas!" he cried. "Woe is me!"

They took him into the presence of the sultan.

"O poor one," the sultan said, "tell me, would you eat plain rice?"

"Ah! Yes."

"I'd eat it, too, if we had it," he said. "Would you eat stew cooked with cumin and onions, or would you eat sugar cane or dates?"

"Oh! Where are they?" he asked.

"Would you also eat rice pudding, especially if it were well cooked with sugar?"

"Oh! How could I not eat it?"

"If we had it, we would eat it, too!"

In the same way, he described a number of delicious dishes.

At last, the miller began to beg, "O great Sultan! Kill me!"

Then the king's compassion was aroused. Because of that feeling of compassion, he remembered this couplet of Khayyam:

> I have done harm and you return harm;
> So tell me, what is the difference between you and I!

The king began to laugh. He ordered them to give him a thousand silver coins, a robe of honor, and send him happily on his way.

Then he commanded, "Call him back."

They ran after him and called him to come.

The miller thought, "Ah! He deceived me—perhaps now he'll throw me into a worse situation."

He began to beg those who had called him, "Here, take this gold of mine, and grant me my life!"

"Come along, give your answer there!" they said. They took him back into the presence of the sultan.

The king said, "Now, you must promise me![300] From now on, even if you don't give anything to anyone because of your greedy gullet, at least don't ever shake a sheepskin full of flour into anybody's face again! You almost blinded me."

The miller fell down on his face and wept deeply. He said, "And let me tell you that I will never again neglect showing hospitality to anyone, nor will I ever look down upon anyone again."

❋

We Will Show Them Our Signs on the Farthest Horizons And within Themselves

We will show them Our signs on the farthest horizons [41:53].[301] What is He telling us by this? *The horizons*? "The seasons of winter and summer." Then, *and in themselves*? He says: "Disease or health." What interpretations these are, O interpreters!

According to another interpretation *the signs on the horizons* are the splitting into two of the moon, and miracles! *In themselves* is the opening of the heart. *That He is the Truth* means that God is the Truth; Muhammad is also true. What a beautiful interpretation this is!

---

300 M. 200.

301 *We will show them Our signs on the farthest horizon and within themselves until it becomes manifest to them that He is the Truth* [*Surah al-Fussilat*, Clearly Spelled-Out, 41:53].

But for the travelers on the way of Truth, for them there is a beautiful message in every verse—it is like a love-letter! They know the Qur'an. The beauty of the Qur'an reveals its face to them.

What does *He is the Truth* mean? It is an interpretation to say, "*He is the Truth* means that everyone knows who God is."

There is Qudsi's; what would one do with Tusi's? *The Most Compassionate taught the Qur'an* [55:1-2]: you must listen to the commentary on the Qur'an from God, not from anybody else but the Truth. The commentaries of the interpreters are commentaries on their own state, not a commentary on the Qur'an. A literal version of the Qur'an—even a five year old child can relate that.

❋

A Pot Leaks Whatever Is in It

A blasphemer speaks of blasphemy—what else can he speak about but blasphemy? The faithful one speaks of faith, and the blasphemer speaks of blasphemy.

> A pot leaks whatever is in it.

❋

You Can Show Someone the Path, but You Can't Make Them Take It

There is no contradiction in the words of God, the Almighty: *You cannot guide those whom you love to the right path. Only God can guide the one whom He wills, to the right path* [28:56], and *You can guide to the true way* [42:52][302]—if the words are true, that is impossible.

You show a way; you say, "Here, this is the right way," but you cannot do more.

---

302 *Surah ash-Shura*, Consultation: 42:52-53: *And thus, too, We have caused this [message] to be a light, whereby We guide whom We will of Our servants: and, truly, you, too, shall guide onto the straight way—the way that leads to God, to whom all that is in the heavens and all that is on earth belongs.*

Oh, truly, with God is the beginning and the end of all things!

"It is I who lead him astray," says God, the Almighty. What we need to do is to be able to see the subtlety and the difference between these.

The Moment

Mevlana speaks just like this—he doesn't want anything else. "It's my nature," he says.[303]

"Life is but a moment," was written on a gravestone. One moment or three moments—finally, life has an end. The Sufi, they say, is the child of the moment. In other words, the human being is bound to his time. And our portion of life is but this one moment. Because we are in the gathering of Mevlana, we are serving him.

I was like an insect that landed on his sheepskin. It wasn't granted to me to speak clearly and eloquently. So, I prayed, "May God grant fruitfulness to Mevlana." He became the go-between for a good endeavor.

Keeping Water at Hand

They called someone to make music. He was slow in coming.

"Come," they said to him, "or don't you want to?"

He said, "Some water is needed; let me get some water for the pot."

A man of wisdom always keeps water with him in fiery things—this is a rule. If the water isn't ready at hand, the pot overflows, its oil evaporates, and neither is oil left in it, nor does the pot remain. If he forgets about it, the meat being cooked is lost, and he's also left without a pot.[304]

---

303 M. 205.

304 Likewise, the human being should always be in remembrance of God, ready to meet his Sustainer.

You Can Take him away from Me, but How Can You Keep Me away from him?

The Prophet Adam was forgetful.

He kept begging for forgiveness, "*O Lord! We have wronged our own selves* [7:23]. If you don't forgive our sins, if you don't have pity on us, we will be in loss, we will be among the helpless," and this was all he said. He wasn't occupied with any other words.

Satan kept insisting, "*I am better than he* [38:76]." He knew that the righteous must apologize, but his excuse was worse than his fault. He denied the Creator, the Exalted: "Don't you know that I know better."

When the devil said, "*For the sake of Your glory, I'll make them all lose their way* [38:82], these words include the prophets, the saints and the folk of God, because he doesn't neglect his job—how can the devil give up his own work?

God, the Most Great put His help on one side and the devil on the other to see what he would do.

He said, "You can take him away from Me, but how can you keep Me away from him?"[305]

Take a Lesson from the Master

If a tailor does the work of a blacksmith, his beard will get burnt. He should do his own work. On the other hand, if he comes to the blacksmith and begs, "O blacksmith! Teach me how to become a blacksmith!" and learns the craft from him, then neither his beard nor his hair will get burnt, just like the blacksmith's beard doesn't get burnt.

305 God is saying to Satan (the fallen Iblis), "You can lead him astray, but I will still be with him . . . with each one who wanders, just as with Adam." *We are nearer to him than his jugular vein* [*Surah Qaf* 50:16].

If he spends a hundred dirhems, and doesn't add salt to the food, it's useless. When he tries to eat it, he will spit it out. But if he adds just a bit of salt, whatever he shares will be salty.[306]

Even though someone may say something is "salt," unless according to its state and meaning it is salt, you can't call it "salt." If it isn't, he will get no benefit from fasting, austerities, or regimens, and perhaps he will even fall into a darker state.

The Prophet Muhammad didn't come to give good news to one without it. He only gives news to those who have it, "You also have it." *We have sent you as a herald of glad tidings and a warner* [17:105]. It becomes clear who has it and who doesn't.

O God Most High! O Master! O Great Sovereign! O Lord of all the worlds!

❊

Surely, with Every Difficulty Comes Ease

O bad tempered and hard headed man! You can't understand my outside; how could you know my inside? How can you give any news of it? O ass! O ass!

No, no—try to keep any belief that makes you warm! And stay away from any belief that makes you cold!

A real human being is one who is happy in the midst of difficulty; he feels joy even in the midst of grief. He knows that the thing for which he is longing and the lack of it are intertwined. Within the

---

306 In the Mevlevi tradition, the value of salt is especially recognized. When one visits the tomb of the saintly Atesh Baz, Mevlana's cook, one finds a dish of salt there beside his sarcophagus. One may help oneself to some for healing and blessing, and further conveyance to friends.

Since the time of Mevlana, as Mevlevi tekkes developed, the head cook was the main instructor of the dervishes. Much of the teaching took place in the kitchen, including the beginning instruction in whirling. There are many metaphors in Mevlana's writings about the human being who is cooked by God. As Mevlana himself said, "First I was raw, then I was cooked, then I was burnt." One who is well-cooked is able to flavor the food, of life experience and of prayer, with Spirit so that it might be truly nourishing, of good taste, and real benefit.

lack, there is still the hope of having it, and within having it, is the worry for its loss.

The day it was the turn of my malaria, I was happy that health would be coming the next day. And when I was feeling strong, I was sad that the following day the fever would return.

You say, "Yesterday, if I hadn't eaten that, I would not have this pain today"—you have to be careful about how you put your self into it.

The brave one is the one who makes everyone Self-sufficient—his maturity is recognized by means of this. Then he becomes a great man.

Abundance

"One person's food is enough for two (*hadith*)." But who is that person? If he is Muhammad, his food, his abundance is enough for all of the two worlds.[307]

Flying Like a Falcon

Among the friends here, there is a dear dervish with such a living heart that if Mevlana had known about his state, he wouldn't glance at him with anything but honor and respect. For more than ten years, this one who prays for you here experienced sincerity and closeness in his circle, and when we went to Damascus he openly showed his friendship to us as well. . . . Among the dervishes and saints such a dervish is very rare and it is difficult to have even one dervish like him. This one who prays for you is not an imitator. Those who are within this circle have also heard the words of this purified servant.

I've seen lots of so-called saints and dervishes, and have had conversations with them. I can distinguish the difference between the pseudo and real people of God by both their words and behavior. I have also encountered some whom I admire and who are

307 This section is near the end of the first volume of the *Maqalat*, and it is noted that Shamsuddin Lahawari, Sharif Lahawari, Najib Muallim, and Fakhruddin Malik were the transcribers of this first volume.

outstanding. My heart doesn't bow in front of just everyone it sees. This bird of the heart doesn't bow to every grain. The Simurgh watches all of the other birds from above. He sees their lack of effort and self-indulgence, but he sees a different endeavor on the part of the falcon. He finds a jewel, a modesty of heart within him. He treats him with kindness and affection. The others fly for just an hour and then land in low places. Although the falcon doesn't have enough power to see the Simurgh, still through the influence of the glance of the Simurgh, the falcon can recognize some of the finer qualities within himself.[308]

Seeing the Meaning

A hunter used to hunt lions and the dogs would bark. The hunter had to shout at the dogs so that they might not scare the lion and cause him to escape into the forest. Now, you've also come close to the lion; what a headache they are causing from a distance! They are not worth even a single slap, and they are neglecting the *salaat.*

Rabia al-Adawiyye said, "I sent my heart to this world so that it might see this world. Then I told it, 'Go to the world of meaning, and see the meaning, too.' It didn't return to me."

A Morsel of Meaning

I wanted to make those words reach them, so that I might speak of secrets to them. But during the talk you were moved, and a state came over you.

I have often stated objections to the words of the great ones, but I've never objected to the words of Muhammad.

This is such a circle that its gate or entrance is this. If you walk around the circle from the inside, it's as if you have walked around it outside. If you find the way out, you return.

---

308 M. 210. Shams refers to the parable of *The Conference of the Birds* by Attar.

You are walking around the circle by yourself—if you give up, then you make the way much longer. If you pass by that point of liberation, you keep falling back into the desert, and you move into the direction of nothingness and death.

I'm telling you these things so that you may put them into your mouth like a morsel.

❊

Be Determined

Let your mind be determined. You say, "The mother of Abraham, that mature woman, turned her face up to the heavens and begged God." She was the mother of Abraham. If you also have good intentions, God will correct your deeds. Only one out of seven hundred thousand people can radiate light and not receive abundant blessing from your circle.

This is how the tradition has gone on since long ago; the decree is like this. The words of God are true, they are an unchanging law. Everyday, the Beloved comes before you.

Instead of welcoming Him you run away, so that He runs away, too.

We have spoken about the plea of Moses, "*O Lord! Show yourself to me* [7:143]!" in relation to something else, not in order to be able to say that separation is possible. If someone is hunting, and the lion senses the smell of a human being, he hides.

What do the children of a sultan do when they are alone? Although they live apart from the people of their country, it is when they appear among people that they understand more clearly the meaning of the exalted rank that people give to them.

❊

Seeking the Water

There is a time when grapes are harmed by winter, but later on, no fear remains. Then if the grape-vine is covered by snow, still it receives nourishment, even then.

There are no beggars in the land of Anatolia. You are eating the wrong food; you are eating nothing but bread. "Of course, it is heavy," you say, "but it's very cheap."

At first fish used to go just to the water's edge, but now wherever a fish goes, water flows there, too.

The value of meat, wine, and watermelon varies according to whether the body is healthy or sick. If the body is healthy these are useful; if it is sick, they are sometimes harmful. For this reason, they recommend to the sick that they should abstain from meat.

They have called the hawk a "sturdy fellow"[309] for this reason—when he flies to the side of the unclean, he doesn't remain there, but returns to the king. If he doesn't return and remains near a carcass he has found, they don't call him a "hawk." Here the "hawk" is the symbol of life and watchfulness. "The Glory is in him," he said. Either we do or we don't have help. The eye of surrender is focused on you.

Ahh

Someone came to the gathering late. "Has the *salaat* been done?" he asked.

"Yes," they said.

He uttered a loud sigh, "AH!"

A man of God who was present also sighed, "AH! Let me give you all the *salaat* I have done throughout my entire life to you in exchange for that one "AH!"

He said, "Now that is what I also needed."

Look and see what a sign this is. It is the friend who says it.[310]

---

309 The word "baz" means both "hawk" and "sturdy fellow." Shams is making a play on words, as he often does.

310 M. 215. See *Mathnawi* II 2771-2779 and surrounding verses.

❊

Make the Mir'aj

There is no doubt that this world and the next world are like two sisters who don't get along. There is no sisterhood left in the world, she changed her state. When that sisterhood is only outward, no real sisterhood remains—the connection is severed.

Again, it was said, "People are asleep; when they die, they wake up." Following Muhammad is really called following him if you also follow him in making the *mir'aj*. Work and persevere, worship, do good to others, and strive so that you may establish an abode in the heart. If you want the world, you'll be at a loss—you'll look for its reasons and causes and not discover anything. Worship, look for the Truth, and set out on the way by serving the people of God! Seek God through serving them.

> Take as your companion one who is more advanced,
> So that your situation might improve.

❊

Reaching for a Hand

In his dream, Sultan Weled had fallen into murky water, and had cried, "Help, hold my hand!" And I hadn't held his hand, and he sank and went under.

When he woke up, he said to himself, "Before I tell him about the dream I saw, I'll see if he tells me about it and interprets it. If he does, this dream belongs to his station. If he doesn't speak about it, it must belong to me."

I was very close to speaking about it, but I didn't say anything. . . .

The community of Muhammad must be broken-hearted. The body of former communities that came before passed away—it was broken, and then it reached hard-heartedness through worldly problems related to the body, and then spiritual problems.

Hallaj, who said, "I am the Truth," could not save himself. He was a Muslim whose heart was broken. To say, "My Teacher, my Lord is Most Great," wasn't enough for him. He wasn't satisfied.

❁

Be of the Firmly-rooted

There are no shoes left like the shoes of Ayaz. No skin is left from the skin of which he was made. All his pleas became coquetries, because he sensed the fragrance of the Beloved who is both delicate and beautiful. Her qualities are beyond skin and outer flesh.

Alaeddin! My heart wants to let me explain these words to you. Let me interpret them, as I am speaking with symbols and signs. Maybe what I am doing is not good manners, but since you forgive this due to my brazenness, let me speak of it now: "There is one source of water, though it has separated into many streams, rivers, and canals. Sometimes it flows one way, and sometimes it flows another. A time comes when the water that flows along this way, empties out the other way until it passes into its own channel. Sometimes the water that comes from that channel flows in this direction. Those who pass through the various waterways to the source of the water, drink from it, dive into it and get wet. From then on, they have been liberated from the branches, and they reach the root of their source.

Those who catch hold of a branch, will break it and fall, but those who take hold of the trunk of the tree will gain all the branches. They are content with the abode of the Beloved. Others eat and drink; they pass beyond intellect and reasoning but still cannot find a way to the abode of the Beloved.[311] How could it be that those who have a great capacity for reasoning and a strong intellect wouldn't want everyone else to have such a strong intellect and capacity? A philosopher says that he is speaking in accordance with intellect and reason, yet he has no knowledge about the divine intellect. . . .

After twelve years, someone saw the Prophet (may the greeting and peace of God be upon him) in his dream again and said, "O Messenger

311 Shams was still trying to encourage Alaeddin to deepen in his real connection to his Lord. Unfortunately, Alaeddin was not open to Shams' help. Rather than grasping the trunk of the fruitful tree, he held tight to a dry and brittle branch.

of God! Why have you not come? Every Thursday night you used to show yourself to me. Then you left me like a fish without water!"

The Prophet said, "I was occupied with grieving."

"What grieving?" I asked the representative of Allah.

"Grieving for my own community (the people of Islam). During these twelve years only seven people have turned their faces to the true *qiblah* and come towards me—no one else. All the rest have turned away from the *qiblah*."

Now, there is a hidden meaning in these words. This is a clear example of *None but God and the firmly-rooted knows its meaning* [3:7].[312]

Worship Beyond Fear

Beware of whatever you are afraid of! The self (*nafs*) must pass through the stage of the broken-heart. Even if that doesn't consume it, it passes through suffering. But how can one know? One has to gain it through awareness, union, and mutual understanding. That's enough now. You have clarified it; you have seen it openly.

If you want to understand the meaning in the words of the great prophet who says, "The learned are the inheritors of the prophets (*hadith*)," I won't explain anything about him—you have seen the pleasure of worship. It's as if you are finding your own worth.

If you had not seen or grasped it, you might have dived and gone into the Divine universe. May you seek higher and higher—may you say, "*Allahu Akbar*" (God is Greater than all else.) Worship consists in this. See to ridding yourself of the thoughts and groundless fears that come into your imagination, and turn your eye to higher universes,

---

312 See *Surah al-'Imran* 3:7-9:

> *None save God knows its final meaning. Hence, those who are deeply rooted in knowledge say:*
>
> *"We believe in it; the whole [of the divine writ] is from our Sustainer—even though none takes this to heart except those who are endowed with insight.*
>
> *"O our Sustainer! Do not let our hearts swerve from the truth after You have guided us; and bestow upon us the gift of Your grace: truly, You are the Giver of Gifts.*
>
> *"O our Sustainer! Truly, You will gather humankind together to witness the Day about which there is no doubt: truly, God never fails to fulfill His promise."*

because He is more exalted than anything that comes to the mind and its imaginings. Even the ideas and imagination of the prophets and heavenly messengers—He cannot even be contained within those. He is even Greater.

❊

Truth and Words

Sometimes they say, "Everything is the Truth (*Haqq*); there is no creation (*khalq*)." But if there were no creation, speech would have no letters or voices; there are no letters or voices where the Truth is.

❊

Kimya

Now they gave Kimya to me. They sent Kimya to me and it's you who knows about the rest. He taught her about remembrance (*zhikr*); he told her about how it is done. How else could I take care of her?

❊

Secrets No Ear Has Heard

The hearts of the people of God are very wide and open. They are as boundless and limitless as the heavens. All of these heavens turn under his heart.

There is good news in the holy tradition (*hadith qudsi*), "I have prepared such a thing for My good servants that no eye has seen, and no ear has heard, nor has it been revealed to the heart of any human being." That is stronger than *His heart didn't lie about what he saw* [53:11]. Pass beyond this.

There He mentioned lying—this is evidence of a veil. This was indicated in the Qur'an and that in the *hadith*. In the Qur'an, very little was said about this secret.

❊

Don't Drink from Every Spring

It came to my mind that one should not drink from every spring.

He said, "There can't be separation between us—how can he go?"

I didn't like it that he didn't say, "God willing (*Inshallah*)." Yes, because he didn't say that, I said, "You are fit for Shaikh Muhammad."[313]

Friendship was his, but the real reason was something else. When he came to me I filled a goblet, but he could neither drink it nor pour it out. My heart wouldn't let me leave him, it wouldn't let me just pass by and go. I couldn't behave with him as I did with others.

I said, "Repent, give up this habit!"

Metaphor is a bridge to the Truth, and the Truth is a bridge to metaphor. Tonight, if I hadn't come, something would have been lost between us.

Metaphor is a Bridge to the Truth

> Metaphor is a bridge to the Truth,
> and the Truth is a bridge to metaphor.

Keep the dervish's words in your mind, even though he doesn't explain them to you. On the way of God, he freely gives his heart and his possessions. Because the world is only a bridge, but while the bridge is falling down and on fire, one who makes buildings on such a bridge can never be safe.

Don't Waste Your Life

Look for one who is beautiful so that you may be a lover! If you do not become completely a lover with this one, then find a different lovely one. There are beautiful ones who have remained hidden behind a veil. There is another one who can receive you; become his servant.

So you are comfortable, you are independent, you are living without difficulty—are you free? You need bread, you need clothes, but this servant doesn't have such concerns. His Lord provides both his clothing and his food. How could love of bread be his concern?

---

313 M. 220.

In the Qur'an it says, *The squanderers are the siblings of Satan* [17:27].[314] Those who squander are not only those who go to taverns and waste a lot of money there—what value can that have? The real squanderers spend their worthy lives, that treasure which is the capital of infinite felicity, in vain. Even if they have no fear of punishment, how could they smash such a pearl into pieces under a stone and destroy it? Don't you regret it? While all the evidence is telling you that one day the sun will set, why are you letting yourself be distracted by sensuality; why are you sleeping in ignorance? Were you brought here to sleep?

Surely this pearl is not within everyone; otherwise, when giving counsel, it would appear, and everyone would act accordingly. Invite everyone . . . but some have no feet with which to walk, and some have no idea even about such a thing as feet. Their feet have become numb, but when suddenly everyone moves, they also receive a share from it. Of course, those who behave appropriately benefit.

Just as the Prophet (peace and blessings be upon him) said: "There is no doubt that those whom this divine light has reached become enlightened by it. But it doesn't reach a whole society . . . What happiness it is for those who walk upon my way. . . ."

Get Clean before You Go Home

I want to go to the bath often, but in order to benefit from it, one must come out and right away go where one has been invited. In my opinion, one has to sit for a long time in a bath so that the business may be completed, because then the dirt softens. How can I return home bringing that dirt back with me? What I need to do is to take the dirt of the body to the bath—what is the point

314 *Your Sustainer is fully aware of what is in your hearts. If you are righteous, [He will forgive you your errors]: for, behold, He is much-forgiving to those who turn unto Him again and again.*

And give his due to the near of kin, as well as to the needy and the wayfarer, but do not squander [your substance] senselessly. Behold, the squanderers are, indeed, of the siblings of Satan—inasmuch as Satan has indeed proved most ungrateful to his Sustainer. [*Surah al-Isra,* The Night Journey 17:25-27]

of leaving the bath still dirty?

If they let me, this is what I do—my work is like this.[315] Even though it isn't tasteful to speak about these things, at least I am giving you clues.

Halvah of the Moment

A Jew, a Christian, and a Muslim had become friends. On the way, they found some money and used it to buy halvah. "But now, it is too soon," they said, "let's eat it tomorrow, and besides there isn't much of it. The one who has the sweetest sleep shall eat the halvah." Their intention was not to let the Muslim eat any of it. But the Muslim got up in the middle of the night—does he ever sleep? He is a lover and a poor one.

"One can sleep anytime," he said, then he ate all of the halvah.

Towards morning, the Christian awoke and said, "Jesus came down from the heavens and pulled me up to heaven."

And the Jew said, "Moses brought me to wander about in Paradise; he showed me miraculous things there."

And the Muslim said, "Muhammad came to me and said, 'Poor fellow! Jesus elevated one of them to the fourth heaven, and Moses took the other to wander in Paradise. And you, poor deprived one! At least, get up and eat the halvah!' When he spoke to me like that, I jumped up and ate the halvah."

His companions said, "We swear that the best dream is your dream. We see that ours were all illusion."

Now what scent comes to you from this story? What share did you catch from this tale?

Prostrating in the Direction of the Heart

Being religious is such a sweet thing when as a favor, a grace from God, one is gifted with subtly seeing Him, and one comes to faith;

315 I.e., to enter Shams' presence is like entering a bath.

then there are also those who have faith who have not seen.

Eventually, He commanded him to do the *salaat* in the direction of the *qiblah*.[316] No matter where you are, *salaat* should be done in the direction of the Kaaba. All around the world, they have unanimously agreed that from every horizon, this turning is obligatory. Believers form a circle around the Kaaba and prostrate themselves. If you remove the Kaaba from the middle, are they prostrating to each other all the time? Each has become prostrated in front of his or her own heart.

❈

Awake at Night with the Beloved

During the day you sleep until evening comes so that you might remain awake at night together with the Beloved. There was a time when I wanted to be alone with the Beloved at night. Let there be nights of union. With the Beloved, I did not sleep during the day either. When useless sleep comes, and images are overthrown, wandering might not be apparent to others.

❈

Standing at the Threshold

Around noon, I was walking quickly. There was no one around. It was as if the angels had kept the people very busy—they had been so occupied with them that there was a deep silence as if two lovers were whispering secrets to each other.

After that hurried walk, I hesitated to enter the door, and I turned my face toward the house.[317] He saw me from upstairs, and he opened the window, realizing that I didn't know the way. He was such a strong young man that if he had put his hand on that wall he could have shaken it.

---

316 Muhammad received a revelation of the Qur'an indicating a change in the direction of prayer from the original focus on Jerusalem to establishing the Kaaba in Mecca as the direction of prayer (*qiblah*).

317 M. 225.

He had accepted to live happily at the threshold of his Beloved. He swore on seven books and said, "I will never be hurt, tell me!"

"Thanks be to God," he said. In the end, that young man has not become a bloody drunkard. Over the last two or three days, he has become my disciple. He is in great delight and joy, but he has a little sorrow. That sorrow is insignificant from my point of view, though others may see it as great.

"Beware, lest it come to my mind on the way," I was saying. That goodness, good behavior, and maturity of yours is clear to us. It is not possible to turn back now. He used to listen to my wishes there, and he would express his longing to me here.

God Is Greater

You are saying, "God is greater (*Allahu Akbar*)." So what is it that is less? In other words, if a person thinks to himself of a being who is the Creator of the Heavens, who has created the Footstool, the Throne, the Divine Lights, and Paradise, He is still greater. Don't stop there, go further so that you may find greatness, that you might live at ease together with the Truth.

Trembling for Union with You

O Beloved, the satisfied of this world thirst for union
with you!
The heroes of the world tremble in fear of separation
from you.
What are the eyes of a gazelle compared to your eyes?
O Beauty, the feet of all these lions are bound by your
curls.

It may be that the one who sings this poem knows nothing of it, and is not a person of that state. Perhaps he is a farmer or a villager and understands neither poetry nor prose. But, is it just Hakim Sanai, Nizami, Khaqani, and Attar who say such things? The poor ones also have a share in those words.

A leopard eats cheese; it also drinks milk. A lion tears out hearts, rips out livers, and eats them. Each has its own provision.

❁

Colors of Interpretation

If a love is strong, no matter how much the beloved may make her perfection and beauty appear to be greater than it is, to the lover she will appear even more pleasing.

What do these words mean? Everybody understands something from words, but each understands according to his or her own state. Pay attention: each person's interpretation is the expression of his or her own state.[318]

❁

Remember Your Purpose

Remember God has said in the Qur'an, "*Do you think that I have created you in mere idle play* [23:115]?"[319] This means that your creation is not by chance nor is it in vain; it is for the purpose of return.

❁

Sugar and Vinegar

If you are in the midst of praising someone, what business do you have with speaking ill of someone? Suppose your mouth is full of sugar—then why would you put vinegar into it?[320]

---

318 As Mevlana says in his *Mathnawi* V:3125, "The interpretation of a sacred text is true if it stirs you to hope, activity, and awe."

319 *Surah Mu'minun* 23:114-116: *He will say: "You have spent there but a short while: had you but known! Did you, then, think that We created you in mere idle play, and that you would not return to Us?" Know, then, God is sublimely exalted, the Ultimate Sovereign, the Ultimate Truth: there is no deity save Him, the Sustainer, in bountiful almightiness enthroned!*

320 If you are really occupied with praising God, and absorbed in that sweetness, how could you speak ill of someone else and destroy that sweetness with such vinegar?

If your mouth is full of vinegar, it's no shame for you not to do the *salaat*—why would it be? Since that is the place of the purified, what business does bad-mouthing have there?

The Peace that Comes with Friendship

A man was thinking bad thoughts about someone. The other one also had the same thoughts about him. There was a third man in between who was a friend of both of them. He said, "Now these two enemies will meet one another; let's see what will happen."

From there he went to a place where they would encounter one another and waited for his friends to pass. When his eyes met with those of the first friend, he prostrated in front of him. When the other friend saw this, he threw his knife on the ground and threw himself at the feet of that friend.

"Alas!" he said, "This means that you are my friend's friend—how could I kill the friend of my friend?"

The All-Compassionate Sat upon the Throne

For whom has the Blessed Prophet, the Messenger to all the worlds, said this prayer, "My God, kill me as 'poor,' resurrect me as 'poor,' and gather me together with 'the poor' in the life hereafter"? Why can't you save yourself from I-ness? If you were liberated from that claim of I-ness, you could improve.

"Explain it to me," he said.

One day, when the Prophet was going along the way, he had passed beyond himself, and a dervish who was walking behind him became enraptured and murmured these words, "My God, you are my servant, and I am your benevolent lord." A Companion who heard this, immediately wanted to kill the poor man.

The All-Compassionate sat upon the Throne [20:5], it says in the Qur'an. The station referred to as the "Throne" is the heart of the Prophet Muhammad. Did this station not exist before him—what was it like in his moment?

He tells Muhammad his story: *Taha*: "*Don't suffer; We have not revealed this Qur'an to cause you difficulty* [20:2]."[321] And in another verse it says, *Unto Him belongs all that is in the heavens and all that is on earth* [20:6]. Here, the "heavens" is his mind, and what is indicated by "the earth" is his body. It is all his story, and "sitting on the Throne" is his state.

It has been said, "The one who walks in darkness goes astray"—whoever looks at that great prophet from the point of view of outer form, but not from the viewpoint of meaning, goes astray.

How Could the Truth Be So Amazed?

The one who said, "Glory be to me, how great is my glory!" went astray.[322] Could this be the Truth speaking? How could the Truth be so amazed? How could the Reality be amazed and astonished at His own dominion? It was his self who said this. God did not withhold this drunkenness from him, but when he came to himself, in the state of sobriety, immediately he asked for forgiveness from God.

It Is the Work of the Carver

When I saw how completely straight the letter "*alif*" is, my back bent in two.

The letter "*lam*" said, "I am completely straight like *alif*, too."

"Beware," he said, "Don't say such things! Don't speak that way! You are *lam*. Know yourself as *lam*!"[323]

---

321 *We did not bestow the Qur'an on you from on high to make you unhappy* [*Surah TaHa* 20:2]. (I.e., the ethical discipline imposed upon man by the teachings of the Qur'an is not meant to narrow down his feel of life, but, on the contrary, to enhance it by deepening his consciousness of right and wrong. ~ M. Asad)

322 Shams refers again to Bayazid Bastami. See note # 60 of this text.

323 In Arabic and Persian script, the letter "*alif*" is a straight line, but the letter "*lam*" is a line that is bent. *Alif* begins the word Allah, and it is said that *alif* stands in witness to the Oneness of Reality. The letter "*lam*" begins the particle "*la*" which expresses negation. *Lam* must bow in humility for its self-existence before the Unseen.

It's more difficult to recognize these people than to recognize the Truth. You can know about the Truth through the evidence. If you see a piece of carved wood, you know that someone has carved it. It didn't carve itself.

In appearance, you think that these people are like you, but their inner aspect is different. They are very different from what you think they might be. Now, there is nothing surprising in recognizing a tree that has been carved. But who is the One who carved it, and what is His rank of greatness? And how is His infinity?

Only these people know this, but they don't reveal it.

Turning Grace

Since you have opened this door for yourself, there's nothing else to do; if there is, tell me—how can you close this door? That door will not close by itself. It's you who have caused this difficulty!

Day and night I am occupied with praying for you, because there are accidents on the way. One kind of accident is an accident that may occur in the future; the other is the accident that is already occurring. An accident that is already happening can't be avoided through prayers, but through prayer you can turn around one that may still be distant.

Some say, "Our God is kind, our God is good, but not for others."

With such a strong partiality, they find a god and make the mistake of thinking that what they imagine to be "God" is God. *God grants abundant grace to his servants* [42:23].[324] But it says "servants"—where are those servants?

Shihab the Philospher

In Damascus, Shihab was saying, "For me, the most reasonable truth is that God has bound Himself. He doesn't just do whatever He wants," but Fakhruddin Razi, for the sake of fatty morsels, rich

324 M. 230.

robes, and golden coins would tell the Khwarazmshah that God is the *Doer of whatever He wills* [11:107].

Shihab said, "Life for me is a heavy burden that hangs like a heavy pack on the back of someone's neck. That person's feet are in the mud, and he is old and weak. Then suddenly someone comes and cuts that rope, so that the heavy burden may fall from his neck and he might be liberated."

They came to Shihab and listened to thousands of truthful words. They benefited from him and prostrated before him. When they went out, they said, "This is a philosopher! The philospher is he who has knowledge of everything."

I erased that from the book. I said, "God is the One who knows everything." Instead I wrote, "A philosopher is one who knows many things."

Fakhruddin-i Razi's Adventures

Fakhruddin-i Razi was a philosopher, or was regarded as being one of them. When he happened to meet the Khwarazmshah, Fakhruddin began, "I have examined all the branches of knowledge, I have scrutinized all the books of the writers of the past and the writers of the present. I have examined every worthy book from the time of Plato until now. Having read each one of them, I then scrutinized every minute detail, clarified them, and memorized their points. I've gone through the notebooks of all the past scholars and learned the capacity of each of them. I have also lain bare the scholars of these times, so that I might understand the extent of each one's knowledge. I learned such and such a science, and the other, and I pursued each to its *n*th degree."

One of the renowned emirs of the palace, in order to discredit him said, "You may know even more than that, but we know that you are one of the blasphemers!"

He said, "I saw a crowd of frightened people fleeing. As I came closer, they tried to scare me, too: 'Beware! There is a dragon who could swallow the world like a morsel!' But I wasn't afraid.

"I went a little further. I saw a huge iron gate, of a width and height that cannot be expressed—it was closed. A huge lock had been placed on it that weighed maybe a thousand pounds.

"'The seven-headed dragon was here,' they said. 'Beware, don't go near this door!'

"My valiant temperament rebelled. I struck and broke the lock and went inside. I saw a worm. Right away I struck it down and squished it under my foot."

God knows best. . . .

But one wonders why all his words are about that worm, and all his books and writings are filled with that worm.

Bowing before Alif

When *alif* is known as *alif*, there is no need for explanation. But when it is not known, it is necessary to explain it. Then *ba*, and *ta* and all the letters need explaining. There was someone else who didn't understand, and the Qur'an explained it.

The letter "*alif*" is independent. It sits in front of "Allah." The letter "*ba*" carries his love in his heart—he has placed his head at the feet of *alif*.[325]

Now you! Have pity! Who has the strength to live like that? When I show humility to someone, he becomes frightened of me and runs away.

Birthing

Now what I need is to speak about how the gathering will be on the Day of Standing before God. As long as this skin, this body, exists—

325 Within the Islamic tradition, letters of the Arabic alphabet have numerical values attributed to them (*abjad*). An "*alif*" with the numerical value of one, stands for a true human being, a representative and servant of God, who witnesses to the Oneness. The letter "*alif*," the first letter of the alphabet, begins the word "Allah." "*Ba*," the second letter of the alphabet, is formed by a line that is curved with a dot underneath—the prostrating head beneath the feet of *alif*.

what use is it? Whoever dies, his day of resurrection has come—it means that essence is then eternal together with God—they are born.

❊

Be all Wakefulness and Sobriety

Even if they strike me a thousand times, it doesn't have any effect, except to make me more powerful. I can go to hell, to paradise, and the bazaar, too; but you are gentle and delicate, you cannot go!

I can translate any branch of knowledge from Arabic or another language into Persian. Say it, so that I may say it! That is Persian and this is Arabic. I speak for his sake. It is real Arabic when it is high Arabic, when it is spoken correctly, when it doesn't put one to sleep.

Your sleep is like wakefulness, but still, don't sleep. How can it be that the master is awake and the servant is asleep? Let your sleep be like that—let it be all wakefulness and sobriety.

❊

Shuayb and Job

We must be satisfied with God's Decree. God created the Prophet Shuayb blind. Shuayb accepted it. He couldn't see the faces of the dear servants with his eyes, but he could see them in the world of meaning. The outer seeing would have been pleasing, too, but even though he couldn't have that, he was satisfied. Real acceptance is when a human being is sober and still, and doesn't occupy his mind with the sorrow of lack.

The Prophet Job accepted those worms that wounded his body. He gave his whole heart to acceptance. He wasn't thinking, "When will this end?" He wasn't saying, "O Lord! O Lord! Let me know how long this pain will continue!"

❊

When Intentions Become Manifest

There are noble recorders, who know what you do [82:11-12]. If you intend to do a good deed, there is an angel watching on your right side and an angel on your left. The angel on your right side has received the command: "When he puts that thought and intention into practice, write it seven hundred times, or *even beyond reckoning* [2:212].[326]

Another indication is the verse, *Whoever hopes to meet his Sustainer, let him do righteous deeds, and let him not ascribe unto anyone or anything a share in the worship due to his Sustainer* [18:110]! . . . He is that "one"—he should not give his own existence a share.

God guides to His Light whom He wills [24:35]. The promises and punishments in the Qur'an have been measured out, and God Most High who is the Absolute Measurer is also forgiving.

He said, "Why don't you do the *salaat*?"

He said, "Because God ordered it."

"Where did He order this?"

He said, "Hasn't it been commanded, *Don't go near salaat when you are drunk* [4:43]? Read it yourself."

He said, "Everybody has his own work. For each it is different. One verse in the Qur'an is for the believers—it has come down for them. And after that, a different verse is for the blasphemers."

But in the universe of love, there is always grace and favor, there is no stringency or chastisement. We emerged from stringency a long time ago. But it is near here. Hell is on this side. If you pass beyond Hell, beyond the narrow path is Paradise. It is infinite and limitless. That is the universe of grace and happiness.

For Whom Are You Waiting?

There was a shoemaker who sewed a pair of beautiful shoes for the Prophet. The Prophet liked them. He said, "You have sewn them very beautifully."

---

326 M. 235.

And yet, truly, there are ever-watchful forces over you, noble, recording, aware of whatever you do. [*Surah al-Infitar,* the Cleaving Asunder, 82:10-12].

If beyond intending it, we actually accomplish a good deed, the angel to our right notes seven hundred good deeds or an infinite number of good deeds for that one act.

The man couldn't contain himself. He said, "I have sewn even better than this, O Messenger of God! I could."

He replied, "So who are you keeping that pair for? For whom are you going to sew those better shoes? Since you haven't sewn them for me, for whom are you sewing them?"

Infinite Moments

Up until the age of forty, Muhammad (peace and blessings upon him) didn't call people. Then for a full twenty-three years, he invited people to Islam. So many things happened. Yes, although the time was short. . . . You know that each moment that passes together with God is everlasting and infinite. Even if I am eating such a tasteless pilaf, it's all from His hand—O Sustainer!

The Mouse and the Camel

A mouse grabbed the halter of a camel and began to pull it. Because of his easy-goingness, modesty, and dignity, the camel walked behind the mouse.

Even as it has been said, "The faithful are patient, like easy-going camels." Some attribute this easy-going nature of the camel to its being gentle-tempered and modest, and some to its low degree of intelligence, despite the fact that it is taller than most other animals. The secret of this is something else.

The mouse had the camel walk until it reached the water's edge. That animal, with its swift walk and long body, couldn't just remain helpless—it asked the mouse, "Why did you halt here now? Why don't you cross over? Didn't you know that grabbing the halter of someone like me wouldn't suit you? Now, since you have taken the halter, keep walking ahead!"

"But the water is very vast and deep," the mouse said.

The camel, who had stepped into the water said, "Come, come! It's easy to pass across the water—at most, it's at the level of the knees."

"But," the mouse said, "there are differences between knees."

"Now repent, so that you may not do anything brazen like this again. Climb up onto my saddle and sit! What is the weight of even hundreds of thousands of mice like you on my saddle? In a single moment, we can pass across the water."

I came, I took hold of your hand, and we moved forward.

Winning the Heart of the Watchman

When you've won the heart of the watchman, then the whole garden belongs to you—gather fruit from whichever tree you want.

Because you are speaking at this moment, no one else can speak; he can't say whether I speak the truth. Just listen to the wise ones.

Being with you is a great blessing. Alas, one's life is not enough—I would need a whole world full of gold to scatter at your feet for the honor of being together with you.

We have a living God; what would we do with dead ones? The meaning of that unique God never changes. God's promise is never broken; but these pseudo gods are soon utterly ruined. God always endures.

The Wedding of the Nafs

Someone asked, "Who is Satan?"

The other person said, "It's you, because I am God, and you are my opposite—so who else can it be?"

There isn't just one kind of wedding. And this is the wedding of the *nafs*.

First Measure the Cloth

Don't eat randomly so that in the end you don't say, "It would have been better if I hadn't eaten it," or "If only I had never eaten it!"

"First, measure the cloth, and then cut it." Let's always take beautiful precautions in our endeavors.

❊

Astonishing Fish

We have made your sleep rest and made the night a cloak. And We made the day for your living [78:9-11]. *I have made your sleep rest and made the night a cloak* points to the state of sobriety. And *We have made the day for one's living* [78:11] points to the state of drunkenness.

A big fish lives by eating small fish. It is drunk with gratitude for being able to maintain its life by eating little fish.

In the ocean, a light appeared in the water. I asked the captain about it, but he made no sound—he didn't answer.

For a day, we sailed on and then another bright light appeared. Then immediately after that, the captain prostrated.

"This is a prostration of gratitude," he said. "If I had said anything about that first one, your liver would have burst from fear. That was one of the eyes of a fish, and this was the other one. If I had slept for a single moment, it could have destroyed us. The other fish are small. In the sea, the fish are always perplexed, but by this fish, the sea itself is amazed: "How can there be such a great one within me? What is it that is within me?" It is astonished.[327]

❊

Doing One's Work

The best work for a woman is to spin her thread in the corner of her home, and that which suits the dervish is dervishhood and silence.

What is the most beautiful thing for those who sell figs, do you know? To sell figs, to sell figs, O brother![328]

---

327 M. 240.

328 The *nafs* is feminine—the role of the dervish is to be receptive. The role of the one who sells figs (the mystic master) is to sell figs (to pass on mystic knowledge of the Truth). See *Mathnawi*, VI:760.

❊

A Unique Beauty

Sa'id Mussayyib was one of the professors in Baghdad. He had a daughter who was so unique in beauty and gentleness that her fame had reached the caliph. In order to marry this beauty, the caliph tried everything; he set many traps, but he wasn't successful.

Sa'id also had a student of theology who was poor and humble. At the *madrasah*, he used to sit in the back row by the shoes—his mother was poor.

One day, the eye of the master fell upon this student—when the class was over, he called him near. After greeting him, he said, "I will give my daughter to you, and you will be my representative."

The student told his mother about it. She became very frightened by the news, and felt an ill omen in it. "He's gone crazy! My baby!" she said, "Did you see this in a dream? I wonder what has happened to you—what will I do now? I don't have money to take you to a doctor."

The boy answered, "Mother, this is neither a dream nor imagination, nor sleep-talking, fever, or delirium. It really happened."

The next day his mother got worse; she began to share her trouble with the women of the neighborhood: "This boy will be the cause of our death—at least warn him and let him give up this imagining. Let him not say such things any more. If others ever hear this, they will interpret these things as madness, and they'll swear that he's raving mad."

When he went to his lesson the following day, the master called him again, and showed a deep interest in him.

After this the student, the poor lover of knowledge, rubbed his eyes, and he said to himself, "I wonder, is this an illusion or a dream? My mother and the neighborhood women are all saying, 'Because of all that thinking and reasoning, you have begun talking rubbish. Melancholy has overcome you.'"

Then he looked around again. Everything was in order and in place; the *madrasah*, himself, and the professor—nothing had changed at all. "No," he said, "I swear to God that this is not imagination; it's not melancholy or madness."

Again, he went home and told what had happened to his mother. This time, his mother and the neighborhood women said, "It's possible that the boy has fallen into a deep dark melancholy. He will be the cause of his own death and ours, too!" In short, whatever the young man said, they wouldn't believe a word of it.

At last, when the wedding-night approached, the young man put on beautiful clothes and came home—he had brought gold and silver to his mother. She was still suspicious, and her doubt wouldn't ease.

Then, that night, they brought the girl to her home. The mother and the neighborhood women looked at one another in astonishment.

A number of the women who knew the girl well went to her. They exclaimed to her, "O Lord! How can this be?"

The girl forcefully declared, "What is so astonishing? He is a man of knowledge and virtue, and we are also like that. But actually he is better than we are, because we are people of the world, and he pays no attention to it. So, he is more virtuous than we are. He is nobler than we are. We must also renounce the world, so that we might be like him."

The special servants of God are hard on their bodies. Yes, they feel agony—they've fallen into a great trouble of love, but this is not anybody else's business. And so their names are remembered—because of this, people remember their names. I wonder how this work will end.

❊

Efforts

Learn this from me. Be patient in front of food; carefully control your eating. The first thing you must do is this.[329]

---

329 M. 245.

Mevlana echoes this often. In the *Menaqib* he is quoted as saying, "There are many advantages to eating little: if a person does so, he will have better physical

If you are sleeping, what will you find? Exalted ranks are obtained in proportion to the effort exerted. Those who want to reach high ranks need to sleep wakefully at night. In other words, they don't sleep as they might wish.

Even though the Prophet had such an exalted station and such power, he didn't even have a room of his own, even though he deserved not two hundred, but four hundred. Those who follow Jesus know that he also was a Messenger of God who was very poor.

❊

A Lasting Love

It's not in my power to cry out—this sound comes only from the *ney*. Now it's not surprising that the salamander should fall in love with the fire. Each being is always in love with something. Would I turn my face away from a lover?

You have strong support. You are the exalted leader of the way of Truth! The promise is yours!

They brought a poor one to Muhammad and said, "He doesn't do *salaat*."

"Yes," the poor man said, "I cannot make any effort. All I can do is love God and His prophet. Surely in the end, this friendship will not leave me stranded on the way."

---

health, a better memory, clearer comprehension, a lighter heart and soul, a more penetrating glance, greater consolation, and a more generous character; he will need less sleep and less abundant provisions." *Menaqib* #189.

See for instance *Mathnawi* II, 1083-1086:

Man's original food is the light of God; material food is not for him;
but from disease, his mind has fallen into the delusion
that day and night he should eat only this food.
He is pale, weak, and faint:
where is the food of *by heaven which has starry tracks?*
That is the food of the chosen, food eaten without fork or throat.

❊

What is the Soul Worth

What is the soul? Has the one who amuses himself with his possessions seen anything better than his own soul? A single hair's value is greater than a hundred thousand pieces of gold. I am speaking to the intellect, to those who have intellect: "Leave those crazy ones, they are throwing their souls to the wind for the sake of their possessions. Have they seen anything more worthy than their own being that they have sacrificed their souls? What have they seen more worthy than the soul?"

And most certainly We shall test you with fear, and hunger, and loss of possessions and life, and with the lack of fruitfulness, but give good tidings to those who patiently persevere [2:155].

This is also a test. Give good news—see how their glances have turned to watch your patience, to see whether you are pleased with your situation.

To pass beyond the desert is something else, and to gain the pleasure of the pilgrimage is also something else again. We are also making the call to prayer with a secret sign. A single sign is enough for the man or woman of intelligence.

❊

The Other Side

If a jurist hasn't reached the universe of God yet, say whatever you want to say outwardly, but inwardly close your mouth with your hand. The tongue causes a sad wound. God understands every maturity. He pays for the cost of the blood of Gabriel from His treasury of Wisdom.

When they drink, they become more sober. The immature drink wine and become intoxicated with the pleasure of drunkenness and numbness, but these are clever sober drunkards! Die under their feet! For each of those playthings, he said, "What a strange plaything this is!" Go beyond the veil.

Every moment, from that side to this existence, they are calling, "There is separation." Every moment they are saying, "Come, leave."

On that side are the unchanging colors, the unchanging forms. The universe of the Truth is a pleasant universe.

Someone said, "We can't speak."

He says, "God is upon the Empyrean."

This one says, "He is spaceless."

We also became bewildered.

Wherever they say, "Live! May your life be long! May your time pass pleasantly!"—they regard this kind of talking as shameful.

For a while I was a jurist. I had read *Tanbih*, the religious law of the Shafi'i's, and other books of law. But now, none of them come to my mind.

To be together with friends is sweeter
than the years of youth.[330]

Remember to Ask

For the sake of His pure and exalted Existence, for God Most High's pure Self—those people also learned about that at the *madrasah*:

"Let's learn about wisdom. Let's establish ourselves at such and such *madrasah*," they said.

One should weigh such moments carefully. In this group, they are always talking about this. They say, "Let's gain such and such post—let's quickly become famous."

Why should one seek knowledge for the sake of a morsel from this world? What is the use of an education that doesn't teach who I am, what my essence is, why I have come here, where I will go, and where I have come from?

These people who study in the religious schools do so for the sake of fame and teaching positions. They say that one must do beautiful deeds; they declare this in these gatherings to gain status.[331]

---

330 M. 250.

331 See also *Mathnawi* II 2429-2435:

Knowledge is conventional and borrowed
when its owner is annoyed by people who aren't fascinated by it.

Why do you learn for the sake of a worldly morsel?! This rope is for the sake of climbing out of this well, not for the sake of falling from this well into another! Bind yourself to these questions: "Who am I and what is my essence? Why have I come here and where am I going? Where am I rooted? And what am I involved in right now and towards what must I turn my face?"

Water without the Jug

If these meanings are like water in a jug, I'm looking for water without a jug—jugless water.

The meanings in the language of Arabic have worn Arabic clothes. I am willing to endure difficulties to understand them well. The purpose is not learning Arabic.

> You are my goal, due to the Kaaba
> and the pagan temple!

What I mean by the pagan temple is the image of Your cheek and Your beauty. If the words of this poem, from the viewpoint of conveying those meanings I want, are not dear to my heart, for sure, they will be a burden.

Where can we go now? How can we save ourselves? We have fallen into an *ayran*, a limitless yoghurt, not contained by any cup that might allow us to climb out of it. Or, we are within honey—the more we move our wings, the more we stick.

Understanding God's Language

They said to Abu Najib (Suhrawardi), "Since you cannot see God, since you have not been favored by this, break your retreat, and

---

> Since it was learned as a bait for popularity,
> and not for enlightenment,
> the seeker of religious knowledge
> is no better than the seeker of worldly knowledge.
> He seeks to please the vulgar and noble,
> rather than to attain freedom from this world.

wander about. It's possible that He may see you, and that His glance might fall upon you, and your hard work might become easy."

These words are true. Who is capable of knowing God's words and language? The servant of God. Be the servant of God so that you might understand His language and words. I am not telling you, "Be God!" I am not speaking blasphemy.

Living creatures, and inanimate things, and the beauty of the void in space—they don't possess the characteristics that human beings have, but all of these are contained within the human being.

You are the exalted universe, the truth is this! Just as God has said: "My heaven and earth could not contain Me, only the heart of My faithful servant can contain Me."

❖

From Ahmad to Ahad

There is nothing more than an "m" from Ahmad to *Ahad*. And this "m" is the veil of meaning. You assume that "m" which comes in between is the world! But *how honored are the children of Adam* [17:70]! He is worth all the seven heavens and all creatures. And what a happiness it is for human beings who are of the community of Muhammad! Isn't the eye of Muhammad, Muhammad? Because you have become one of his community, Muhammad's eye is a light.

When you become one of his community, the Prophet becomes pleased with you and holds your hand. He introduces you to Moses and Jesus. He is pleased with you: "This man is of my community," he says. Presenting you to the residents of the ninth heaven and above, the Messenger says, "Please come look, and see!"[332]

---

332 Ahmad is another name for Muhammad. From "Ahmad" to "*Ahad*" (God the One) there is only an "m." Shams indicates that with the help of the light of Muhammad, the human being is brought through the heavens into the Presence of God.

❊

Dancing with Joy

I was only a child, and hadn't yet reached the age of maturity, when because of this love, for thirty or forty days I hadn't wanted to eat anything. When someone would speak of food to me, immediately I would pull back my hands and head. When the time for a meal came, I would accept it if they gave me food, but I would take it and hide it in my sleeve.

I was turning in *sema* within such a state of love—with His heated state, the Friend caught me. He kept turning me, like a baby bird. Like a young man who hasn't eaten for three days grabs a piece of bread and breaks it quickly into pieces—I was like that in His hand. He was turning me. My eyes became like two bowls full of blood.

I heard a voice. "He is still raw. Leave him in his own corner for a while—let him burn within himself," it said.[333]

Now, God forbid, but if you had brought a prostitute from a tavern—I was dancing with a hundred times more life and subtlety.

When a real one begins to dance, the seven heavens, the earth, and all their inhabitants all begin to dance. If a faithful follower of Muhammad begins to dance in the east, and there is a follower of Muhammad in the west, he also starts to dance with joy.

❊

The Camel and an Ant

A camel had become a friend to an ant. They came to the edge of the water. Immediately the ant withdrew its foot. The camel asked, "What's the matter with you?"

The ant answered, "It's the water."

The camel put its foot into the water. "Come, come," it said, "one can cross easily. The water isn't higher than one's knees."

"But," the ant said, "there are differences between knees—the water which is knee deep for you, is well over my head."

---

333 Hear the echo of "Doing One's Work" of this text, p.302

❊

Untying Knots

O brave one who dies trying to untie knots![334]

The human being was created for a purpose—that he might know where he came from, and where he will return. His internal and external senses were given in order to know this. These are each necessary tools for his seeking. When he or she uses them for something else, neither is his or her life joyful, nor does he or she reach security, nor does he or she become aware of his or her beginning or end.

To be occupied with knowledge—which is the best work in the world—loses time, and drags one far away. At the end of their days, the best have said, "What is left to us from this world is suffering and disease." This is advice for the whole world. Consider that they are not forced to say this, but it is their very sincere expression.

> Our spirits are frightened by our bodies,
> because the gain of the world is only trouble and pain.

The world answered and said: "Yes, safety is not gained here. The way of safety doesn't come from this place."

❊

Taming Our Self

If you are going to be regretful here, you should be full of regret in the beginning. Perhaps I could claim that a handful of soil from

---

334 See *Mathnawi* II:3733-3738:

> We're quite addicted to subtle discussions; we're very fond of solving problems. So that we may tie knots and then undo them, we constantly make rules for posing the difficulty and for answering the questions it raises.
>
> We're like a bird which loosens a snare and then ties it tighter again in order to perfect its skill.
>
> It deprives itself of open country; it leaves behind the meadowland, while its life is spent dealing with knots.
>
> Even then the snare is not mastered, but its wings are broken again and again.
>
> Don't struggle with knots, so your wings won't be broken.
>
> Don't risk ruining your feathers to display your proud efforts.

this meeting is better than the gold of togetherness with others, but you don't recognize the value of this coming together. One has to educate you. In whose hand do you see this oneness?

You have birth in common with all animals; if you have only the one birth, you aren't any different from them.

Love of God never delays one, but no one who is not born twice can ascend to the kingdom of heaven.

❊

A True Servant

The seeker said, "O Lord! Do not entrust me with a task—let me serve you many times over out of love rather than the task you propose for me. The order is frightening; the task is heavy."

God said, "Accomplishing just a little of what you are asked is a million times better than what you do on your own without the command. A coin that you give for the sake of the Sought is better than a thousand coins that you spend according to your own desire."

No true understanding of God do they have [6:91].[335]

---

335 See *Surah al-A'nam*, The Cattle, 6:82-92:

Those who have attained to faith, and who have not obscured their faith by wrongdoing—it is they who shall be secure, since it is they who have found the right path!

And this was Our argument which We vouchsafed unto Abraham against his people: We do raise by degrees whom We will. Truly, your Sustainer is Wise, All-knowing.

And We bestowed upon him Isaac and Jacob; and We guided each of them as We had guided Noah before. And out of his offspring, [We bestowed prophethood upon] David, and Solomon, and Job, and Joseph, and Moses, and Aaron: for thus do We reward the doers of good; and [upon] Zachariah, and John, and Jesus, and Elijah: every one of them was of the righteous; and [upon] Ishmael, and Elisha, and Jonah, and Lot. And every one of them did We favour above other people; and some of their forefathers and their offspring and their brethren: We elected them, and guided them onto a straight way.

Such is God's guidance: He guides therewith whomever He wills of His servants. And had they ascribed divinity to anything beside Him—in vain, indeed, would have been all [the good] that they ever did: [but] it was to them that We gave revelation, and sound judgment, and prophethood.

And now, although the unbelievers may choose to deny these truths, [know that] We have entrusted them to people who will never refuse to acknowledge them—to those whom God has guided. Follow, then, their guidance, [and] say, "No reward do I ask of you for this [truth]: behold, it is but an admonition unto all mankind!"

They value the favors of the world, and don't appreciate the million pieces of wisdom that could bring them close to everlasting life. If they find even a single coin, they rejoice, are amazed, regard it as a blessing, and kiss the ground. They waste themselves in the dust.

"Come! So that all we do might be correct—even what we eat and drink is through consultation among us. Even in eating let there be no separation or hypocrisy among us."

For the seeker said, "I've asked my self about piety and servanthood, but due to forgetfulness or enmity, she didn't answer."

❊

Earthquakes

While one city is turned upside down, another remains in safety. Listen to the words of the Truth. The power is in the hand of God. The sign in *Read!* [96:1] is a light—so that you may emanate it with ease. In other words, "O discourteous child! Pay Attention," and "O you who have grown old! Don't be childish!"

"O seeker of truth! Know the conditions for seeking." In the Qur'an it was said, "*When the earth shakes* . . . [99:1]." If they move it a little bit more, do you know what will happen? Rather than being ugly, it turns into a subtle power that can't be seen by the eye. This is a beautiful response. . . .

You are speaking about the heart. He said, "It is the Kaaba . . ."

For no true understanding of God have they when they say, "Never has God revealed anything unto man." Say: "Who has bestowed from on high the divine writ which Moses brought unto men as a light and a guidance, [and] which you treat as [mere] leaves of paper, making a show of them the while you conceal [so] much—although you have been taught [by it] what neither you nor your forefathers had ever known?" Say: "God [has revealed that divine writ]!"—and then leave them to play at their vain talk.

And this, too, is a divine writ which We have bestowed from on high—blessed, confirming the truth of whatever there still remains [of earlier revelations]—and [this] in order that you may warn the mother of cities and all who dwell around her. And those who believe in the life to come do believe in this; and it is they who are ever-mindful of their prayers.

May Revelation Dawn within You

Muhammad said, "The one who makes things expansive, finds expansion himself.[336] Someone who doesn't follow him, but who doesn't become a denier or a blasphemer—what does he become? He becomes a Christian, or a Jew. How would he know that there's power here? Mevlana is here.

Come, let's withdraw to the side—we were wishing so much for this meeting. One counsel isn't sufficient, but what is the rest? It is so that your spirit may be nourished and your deeds may be strong.

Now I am speaking the words of the Sufi. Perhaps we heard it on Tuesday or on Friday—both are possible. This Zahra and she—both of them have attempted to begin a quarrel. I don't know what their purpose is.

Even if the whole world would hang me by my beard, still if something needs to be said, I will say it. But without a doubt, even after a thousand years, these words will be heard by those whom I want to hear.

A few people became the Prophet's scribes for the revelation—those who wrote down the divine commands—and a few people became the place where the revelation descends, that is, the place of its effect. Work hard so that you may be both! In other words, be both the object of the revelation and the scribe of the revelation that comes to the heart.[337]

Journeys

The times when sleep doesn't come are the most beautiful times. Let me speak, or until sleep comes, write what I put in front of you to write. After all, I told him, "You are the human being whom I was wishing for; the others are none of my business!" From now on, write what I speak.

---

336 M. 255.

337 See *Mathnawi* I:3228-3297.

I'll go as far as Mosul. I haven't been there. I'll go to Tabriz, too. There I was preaching upon such and such a pulpit—I saw that community and their seclusions. After that, I'll go to Baghdad, and then to Damascus. I'll be gone at least two years, then I'll return.

For another two or three days endure these headaches I give, for

Only a single page is left in the book of my life.

How I Am Longing!

Our prophet said, "How I am longing for the meeting with my brothers."

The Companions of our Prophet said, "O Messenger of God! Are we those brothers?"

"No, you are my Companions."

They asked, "Are they the prophets?"

"No," he said, "they are dear servants who will come after me."[338]

Don't You Hear the Echo

Sleepily they asked a few questions, and then they went back to sleep again. Those words were the echo of wakefulness. Now how can it be that such an echo comes and still they don't awaken, they don't echo back? It is because of their lack of capacity.

Let all the people of the universe go to one side, and let me go to the other side. Whatever difficulties they have, let them question me

---

338 After Mevlana's passing, some visitors arrived from Medina, descendents of the Prophet and keepers of the Prophet's tomb. When they came to see Sultan Weled, they were each astonished to see that they tied their turbans in the same unusual way with the end of the winding hanging down to the heart. He inquired how they came to wear their turbans in that way which was the way his father had tied his turban and following his example all Mevlevis tied theirs. They said that during his *Mir'aj* the Prophet Muhammad had had a vision of a beautiful being and had asked Gabriel who this being was. Gabriel told him that he was one of the saints who would come after him and renew his religion. From that moment, the Prophet tied his turban in the same way as the being whom he saw, the winding connecting to the heart.

about them—let me answer all of them; I won't run away. I am not afraid of speaking. I don't jump from one branch to another.

☼

Only One Heart

God has not put two hearts within anyone [33:4]; He created only one heart in each. "Whatever we have, all belongs to Him." Both of these sayings have the same meaning.

The Truth never says, "I am the Truth (*Ana'l Haqq*)."[339] Nor does God ever say, "Glory be to Me!" "Glory be to Me,"[340] are words that express astonishment and wonder. It might be appropriate for a servant to use these words, "Glory be (*Subhana*) . . ." as an expression of wonder.

☼

True Speech

A quarter of the earth is inhabited by people. The other three-fourths burns under the heat of the sun and people can't live there. Those who have settled down in this one quarter, no matter what difficult questions they ask me, I will give them answers so that they might advance. They have written answers within answers, records within records and commentaries within commentaries for the questions that seem very difficult for them. But in my words, there are ten answers for each. She, with that Beauty and sweet manner, hasn't been written about in any book. This is why Mevlana has said to me: "Since the moment I met you, from my point of view, these books have had no taste."[341]

---

339 These are the words of the mystic Mansur al-Hallaj, declaring his unity with the Truth that earned him execution as a heretic.

340 Shams mentions again the words of Bayazid al-Bastami. See p.33 of this text. Shams is indicating that these words are more appropriately used by the servant in amazement of the Divine, rather than about oneself as unified with the Divine.

341 M. 260. "She," that Divine Beloved, has not been truly conveyed by any book.

❁

Much More Could Have Been Said

Yesterday, I brought your image in front of me; I began to discuss with him. "Why don't you openly answer these people like they are?" I said.

Your image gave this answer to me: "I'm ashamed in front of them, and I don't want them to be hurt."

And I answered that, and the discussion went on and on. What's left that I have not said? No, what was it that I did say? It's as if we haven't spoken about anything! That is, in comparison to the words of people who don't have much wisdom we have told a lot, but in relation to what I myself could tell we have said nothing.

❁

Only for God's Sake

The Blessed Prophet (may the greetings and peace of God be upon him) said, "For forty mornings, if a person completely devotes himself to God with all his or her soul and heart, springs of wisdom begin to flow from his heart to his tongue."

While our Prophet was explaining these words to his Companions, one of the friends went and occupied himself with prayers for forty days. Then he complained to the Prophet, "O Messenger of God!" he said, "Such a state has come to such and such friend that his eye, word, and hue have changed. And while you were declaring this state of his, you said, 'For forty mornings. . . .' I went and made as great an effort as I could for forty days. As it has been said in the Qur'an: *God offers a burden in proportion to one's capacity* [2:286]. There can't be any lies, God forbid, in your words."

The Prophet responded, "I said, 'If he serves with all his soul and heart.' The condition for 'serving with all one's heart and soul,' is to do it only for God. Otherwise, it's not real service or worship if it's for the sake of other wishes or desires. You wanted those wonderful words that you heard from that companion to appear in you, too. That's what you were seeking."

Forbidden Food

I have said to a group who have faith in us, "God has created you as very fortunate, because such people have fallen among you, and you have understood the value of being together with them. The ways of those who have been created as fortunate are a light—the light of the moon shines through their doors."

> Let me make a rule regarding the way of love—
> those who are unaware of it should not step
> onto this way.

The companionship of those with little feeling is very harmful—it is *haram*—and companionship with the ignorant is completely forbidden. What they eat is also forbidden. The forbidden food comes from ignorance—that morsel doesn't pass down this throat. If I were to eat his food, it would be as if a rock were catapulted into the shop of a glasswareman filled to the ceiling with glassware and bottles; everything would be broken into pieces.

God Most High has said, "Every sin of yours may be forgiven, except the sin of separation from Me."[342]

The Long and Short of It

First, what is *alif*? Tell me, and then afterwards, if I speak of *ba*, the matter lengthens. Now, long or short, all are the same for us. If we are long, so what? If we are short, so what? Long and short are the attributes of objects, of matter. Attributes and space were created afterwards. The first, the last, the beginning and the end appeared from God. There was neither the first nor the last without God, neither outside nor inside. In other words, there was neither the open nor the hidden.

342 See also *Surah an-Nisa*, Women 4:48 and 116.

O Human Beings! Go Beyond This Home of Phenomena!

"O people! Go beyond this home of phenomena!"

These are not just words, but a warning. It is an invitation, a call to that other universe. He is saying, "There is a universe, run there. If you get busy with this *salaat*, *salaat* leads you there. If you occupy yourself with steadfastness, steadfastness leads there."

How happy I am with your friendship, that God has given me such a friendship. This heart of mine gives itself to you; for me-that universe or this universe—what does it matter!

In Truth There Is No High or Low

For me the bottom of the earth or higher than the heavens are the same—there is no such thing as "low" or "high."

Muhammad said, "Don't see me as superior to Jonah, the son of Amittai, because he lived his *mi'raj* (ascension) at the bottom of the sea, within the belly of the fish, while I made my *mi'raj* beyond the seven heavens. Never see me as superior to him because of this!"

To consider Truth as bound to heights or depths is to assume that Truth could be bound to a location.

Perfection

There [in the Garden] silk will be their clothing [22:23].[343] I am wearing silk here, too, but you can't see it because of its subtlety. This thin skin has become like silk, but how could the value of the softness of silk be compared to this silk skin? How far that is from this!

---

343 *Surah Hajj*, Pilgrimage 22:23-24: *Behold, God will admit those who attain to faith and do righteous deeds into gardens through which running waters flow, wherein they will be adorned with bracelets of gold and pearls, and where silk will be their raiment: for they were [willing to be] guided towards the best of all tenets, and so they were guided onto the way that leads to the One unto whom all praise is due.*

Today I have completed your religion for you, I have completed My Grace upon you [5:3].[344] This means, "The soul has reached perfection within Your patterning."

> Be careful to be honest and brave!
> Otherwise, you'll find yourself disgraced
> in a thousand ways.

❊

Being with the Friend

When you know me, if you see me, why are you remembering those sorrows? If reaching ease is within my hand and ability, why are you getting stressed out? If you are with me, why are you preoccupied with yourself? If you are my friend, why are you befriending your self? Years pass, and with but a single person do we become true friends and reach peace of mind.

> Years are needed so that a stone, under the sun,
> may turn into a ruby in Bedahshan or a carnelian
> in Yemen;
> Months are needed so that a cotton seed,
> under the soil,
> May become clothing for one who is naked or a
> martyr's shroud.

If you see me, why do you keep looking at your self? If you are remembering me, why do you keep remembering your self (*nafs*)? Words of advice, and the business of remembering them indicates you are remembering your self—you are remembering being. If there is ease somewhere, then God is there—then what place could there be for advice or words?

---

344 *Surah Maida*, The Feast 5:3: *Today have I perfected your religion for you, and have bestowed upon you the full measure of My blessings, and willed that self-surrender (islam) be your religion.*

Reaching Contentment

There were seven Sufi friends who had sat together for several days. They were in need of food and drink, but due to the taste of the talk among them, they couldn't leave their places to go to get food.

A nobleman heard about their state. He came from a distance, and prostrated his face on the ground before them. He said, "What does your soul want?"

One among them said, "Go and prepare lots of food, enough for us. Empty the house and let none of the old or young ones remain. Leave the house yourself, too. Let no one knock at the door."

The nobleman did so. "These are seven people," he said, "as a precaution let me prepare a table enough for twenty and then send the people of the house to their relatives' houses." In addition, he told them, "Let no one wander around this house today."

He filled the cups, placed the bread on the table, welcomed them in and seated them at their places. "Now, with your permission, tonight, until morning I am taking leave of you," he said. He closed the door and went out.

He made it seem to them as if he had left the house, but he withdrew to a room upstairs, and secretly, through a hole, began watching how they ate. One by one, they put the bowls in front of themselves and began to eat. When the bowls were emptied, they would refill them. Suddenly, one among them fell away from the table. He reached the *seat of Truth* [54:55].[345] According to the law that everything returns to its origin, he heard the command, "*Return to your Lord* [89:28]!" He had already been sitting in righteousness, both there and here. Only a thin veil remained so that by means of that veil he could be seen here.

The six people who remained went on eating. Another hour passed and another friend also passed away after him. In this way,

---

345 *Surah al-Qamar*, The Moon 54:54-55: *Behold, the God-conscious will find themselves in [a paradise of] gardens and running waters, in a seat of truth, in the presence of a Sovereign who determines all things. . . .*

until the seventh, all of them passed away. Only one among them remained alive.

The nobleman lost his patience. He came as though from outside the house and asked, "How was it my Shaikh? Was the food enough? Did you eat as you wanted?"

"No," the Shaikh said, "if it had been enough, would I still be alive?"

As long as "wants" remain, food can't be considered to be "enough."

A completely fulfilling answer leaves neither question nor answers in any direction. As long as the desire to ask questions and find answers continues, as long as other questions and answers remain, it is not enough. If someone keeps talking, wanting more answers, it's proof that doubt remains within, in need of an answer.

Why Are You Talking about That which You Don't Know?

One day Shaikh Hamid was speaking about unbelief and faith. I looked at him and saw that even in a hundred years, he wouldn't come close to catching a whiff of the meaning of unbelief and faith. If he had understood this, out of wisdom and courtesy, he would have covered his own thoughts and said, "I see my words have come to an end—perhaps it's someone else's turn to speak?" These words would have been better and more complete than the others.

And so the Sufi says, "If I had found someone else better than you, you would have been saved from me, and I would have been saved from you. Otherwise, it's you who is in my hand," and he hides the bread in the sleeve of his cloak. So, they say, "Keep your departure, your gold, and your way hidden." The Prophet said, "Whoever keeps his secret hidden, masters his own work."

Mevlana Shamsuddin Tabrizi says, "The one who reveals his secret, masters his work." But, where is that servant? "O darling! How long are you going to talk about one whom you haven't seen?"

Angels, Prophets, and Miracles

One group of philosophers sees the angels as superior to the prophets—because Muhammad and the prophets were occupied with the people, they see them as, God forbid, flawed. They say the angels turned the prophets' faces toward the world—out of jealousy. They gave guidance to people, but this doesn't mean the prophets became distant from the Truth or were veiled from Him.

Of the miracles of the Prophets, they say, "We accept the ones which are in accordance with reason, and we don't accept the ones that are not. Because reason is the evidence of God, and God's proofs cannot contradict each other."

But one could say that a miracle is something that your intellect cannot perceive. Intellect is a proof from God within the human being, but if you don't use it appropriately, it misleads you. And so, intellects differ among the "seventy-two" sects.[346] Each intellect disagrees with the other.

For example, you ask two people, "How much is two times two?" Both of them give the same answer. About this, there's no disagreement between them, because it is easy to think about this simple question of arithmetic.[347] But if you ask them how much seven times seven is, or seventeen times seventeen, the answers of two intelligent people may be different, because this is a more difficult, more complicated question.

If they don't pause and make proper use of the intellect, it is like looking into a bent mirror. Otherwise, a hundred thousand true mirrors will all say the same thing: *confirming the truth of whatever there*

---

346 See *Surah ar-Rum*, The Byzantines 30:30-32: *So set your face steadily and truly to the faith, turning away from all that is false, according to the pattern with which He has made humankind; do not allow to be corrupted that which God has made.*

That is the true way, but most people do not understand.

Turn in repentance to Him and remain conscious of Him: be constant in prayer and do not be among those who join gods with God, those who split apart their religion and become sects—each group celebrating alone that which is with itself!

347 M. 265.

still remains of earlier revelations, and guarding over it [5:48].[348] Divine lights are all friends of each other.

❊

Let the Sun of the Intellect Help You to See

Let's say a hundred people are standing under the sun, and somebody is coming towards them from a distance looking at them with his eyes full of light, playing a drum and dancing. No disagreement arises among the people—they all see him in the same way.

But if this sound of drumming comes in a dark night or when it is foggy or cloudy, a hundred different ideas arise among those who hear it.

One person says, "It is a soldier who is coming."

Another says, "It is a circumcision celebration." In short, each of them forms a different idea.

❊

Who Receives the Nourishment?

Bayazid Bastami (may God glorify his spirit), whenever he would visit a city, would first visit the graveyards of that city and wander there.

Someone had asked Ibn Abbas, "O cousin of the Prophet! Where should I go when my heart wants ease?"

Ibn Abbas said, "During the day, wander in the graveyards and at night, wander through the heavens."[349]

---

348 *Surah Maida,* The Repast, *5:48: And unto you [O Prophet] have We vouchsafed this divine writ, setting forth the truth, confirming the truth of whatever there still remains of earlier revelations and determining what is true therein. Judge, then, between the followers of earlier revelation in accordance with what God has bestowed from on high, and do not follow errant views, forsaking the truth that has come unto you.*

Unto every one of you have We appointed a [different] law and way of life. And if God had so willed, He could surely have made you all one single community: but [He willed it otherwise] in order to test you by means of what He has vouchsafed unto you. Vie, then, with one another in doing good works! Unto God you all must return; and then He will make you truly understand all that on which you were wont to differ.

349 One day Sultan Weled (may God bless his tomb) said: "My grandfather, Behaeddin, lived to be eighty-five years old. He would often walk in the cemeteries and pray in this way: 'Oh Allah, help us to accept our burdens. You have

Bayazid was in the cemetery. He was wandering around, and he came across some human skulls that had turned up in the mud. An inspiration came to his heart: "Pick them up, and look at them carefully."

He looked at the skulls and saw that some of the ears were plugged, while in some the ears were open clear through from one ear to the other, and some were open from the ear to the throat.

"Lord!" he said, "People saw all of these as equals, but You have shown them to me as different! Now, why have they appeared with these different attributes?"

The inspiration came to Bayazid: "The heads in whose ears there are no holes, whose ears are blocked, are the ones who have not heard Our words. And the heads with holes from one ear to the other, are the ones whom Our words have entered through one ear and gone out through the other. But the heads that have an opening from the ear to the throat are the ones who have accepted Our words."

Return to Your Origin

It's possible that a man of heart may want someone to die, but not without a purpose—it's not his body that he wants to die, but his *nafs*.

Someone asked, "Why didn't you go to visit that dervish? Didn't you hear God saying, 'I became ill, and you didn't come to see Me.'"

The other answered, "My heart is very sensitive, and I wasn't inspired to go."

The Prophet of God (may the greeting and Peace of God be upon him) with his completely gentle and graceful heart, held in high regard the greeting of the dervishes of God. He would sit down on the floor together with them and listen to their words. Those who

---

commanded us to visit the graves of the dead during the day and at night to contemplate the brilliant stars in the heavens. The Prophet, peace and blessings upon him, advised us also to witness the marvels of Your creation.'"(*Menaqib al-arifin*, #49)

don't know the worth of dervishes invent excuses, "If we were to hold them in high regard, it would be hypocrisy."

"Don't let your face darken," they say to a sinful person, but a sinless, righteous person they kick aside.

He claims, "Without a doubt, I am good, without a doubt, I am perfect. My face is bright and my forehead is clear."

He neglects his origin, but in order to strengthen his branch he lowers himself. Like that, he is never going to be a saint.

❊

Grief and Joy

A sheep sees his head as worth two hundred thousand pieces of gold, but he doesn't see the door of the stable he sleeps in. He has neglected that—it is the origin—the way to be liberated from grief. To be proud of this being is just grief and sorrow. Right now you are grieving, even though you are saying you are not!

Grief has no more than one branch. It is just this. However, joy is pure and subtle like water—it spreads everywhere. It doesn't keep a flower that is about to bloom from opening.

❊

Untying Lovelocks

What the human being can know is, "There is no God but God." This could be his capacity. What does the child of Adam see? He constructs metaphors—of lovelocks and moles, but where are curls and moles in relation to God?

> If one can grab your curls in Hell, I would be ashamed
> of the beauties of Paradise.

What are curls doing in Hell? They must be untangled on the way of God—the eye and the ear must be opened. He must join with the attained ones of God and give up self-worship, because to worship God means to give up worshipping oneself.

Milk for the Spirit

There was a madman who used to convey messages from the Unseen. Whenever they would lock him up at home, later they would find him outside.

One day, my father had turned away from me and he was talking with some people. The crazy one walked up to my father in anger, raising his fists he said, "If it weren't for this child," pointing at me, then to me he said, "May you be happy," and went away respectfully.

I've never wasted my time playing dice, but I couldn't tolerate much hard work either. I couldn't stick with regular jobs—I kept going to wherever there was a spiritual conversation or talk. I came to the world for that work.

It was like the Prophet Jesus who during the first days he sucked milk, spoke just once, and then didn't speak again, because his first words were not by his own will.[350] Like an arrow shot without an archer. . . . He then embraced his mother's breast, because he had tasted that milk first. As it says, "*We caused him to refuse other nurses . . . and thus we restored [Moses] to his mother* [28:12-13]."[351]

---

350 See *Surah Maryam* 19:30-33.

351 *Surah al-Qasas*, The Story 28:7-13:

> *So We sent this inspiration to the mother of Moses:*
>
> *"Nurse, but when you fear for him cast him into the river, and do not be afraid or grieve: for We shall restore him to you, and We shall make him one of Our messengers."*
>
> *Then Pharaoh's people caught him up: it was intended that he should be an adversary and a cause of sorrow to them, for Pharaoh and Haman and their hosts were erring people.*
>
> *Pharaoh's wife said: "Here is a joy of the eye for me and for you: do not slay him. It may be that he will be of use to us, or we may adopt him as a son."*
>
> *And they did not perceive what was happening!*
>
> *But an emptiness came to the heart of Moses' mother: she was about to disclose him had We not strengthened her heart so that she might remain one of faith.*
>
> *And she said to his sister, "Follow him." So his sister watched him in the guise of a stranger, and they did not know.*
>
> *And We ordained that at first he should refuse to nurse until she said: "Shall I point out to you the people of a house that will nourish and raise him for you and be sincerely devoted to him?"*

But to one whose mother has died, they give just any woman of the neighborhood. The child sucks the milk of this random woman, but it gains her nature from her, too.

> A temperament that passes from the milk to the baby
> comes from the soul through the body.

Children of human beings suck milk from their mother's breasts; animal babies suck it from between their mother's legs.

In between, there are those who are afraid of milk and these, as I've said before, are the ones whose mothers have died. Actually, it's just the opposite . . . it's not the mothers who have died, but they themselves have died.

A mother says, "My milk has dried." However, she really is saying the opposite. Her milk hasn't dried—what has dried is the form of the milk. It arises from capacity.

❊

Eat What Is Food for the Spirit

Even if you throw a baby bird into a dark well, when its time comes, it sings, because it knows it's the moment. There are some whom we have taken out of the well, taught and raised, and what they eat is absolutely permitted (*halal*). In other words, what they eat is earned "from the labor of the hand and the sweat of the brow." This is the food of the spirit. "Eat through the labor of your hand and the sweat of your brow," that is, "Eat what is food for your own spirit!"

What would the others know about the meaning of the Qur'an and the Hadith? The Qur'an covers itself with a hundred kinds of veils. *None but the pure [of heart] can touch it* [56:79].[352] How can they open the bridal veil of that beautiful face of the Qur'an?

And so We restored him to his mother that her eye might be comforted, that she might not grieve, and that she might know that the promise of God is true; but most of them do not understand.

352 *Surah al-Waqiah*, That Which Comes to Pass, 56:75-80: *No, I call to witness the coming-down in parts [of this Qur'an]—and, behold, this is indeed a most solemn affirmation, if you but knew it! Behold, it is a truly noble discourse, [conveyed unto man] in a well-guarded*

❋

Seeing Obedience

Moses (may the greeting of God be upon him) was a prophet. I am not asking about the difference between a messenger (a prophet with a book—*nabi*) and a prophet of high station (*rasul*). I am speaking about "obedience" which is something other than that difference about which the scholars of form (*zahir*) have become confused.

He became bewildered, turning in so many directions. "Obedience" came to the door of his house, but he couldn't recognize it.

Moses gave an earthen jug to him and said, "Go, and bring some water." Moses went to the meeting with Khidr, but he couldn't see "obedience."

Muhammad recognized obedience. When he saw the dervish, he gazed well upon him, and spoke suitable words to him: "Are you hungry? Are you finding joy? Are you cleaning the mirror and holding it up to the faces of the friends so that they might see themselves?"

But, if the mirror is dirty and covered heavily with dust, what use would it be for you to hold it up in front of the friends?

The moment isn't right; otherwise, I would interpret "lending good things to God," and tell you about what a good loan is.

❋

Obedience and Trust

Even when you see the shaikh as disagreeable and cloudy, stay bound to him! Stay attached to him so that he may help you to become sweet, mature fruit. Because your maturing and your nourishment is through the abundance of that cloud.

A person may be good, but ignorant. A good man says, "I put my trust in God," but he may not have the knowledge to understand where the place of putting one's trust in God is. In short, "obedience" should be in accord with the indication, "Trust in God, but tether your camel first (*hadith*)." The Prophet didn't just give up and only trust in

---

divine writ which none but the pure [of heart] can touch: a revelation from the Sustainer of all the worlds!

God—he fought many battles and struggled mightily. Wasn't he wise? Wasn't he a man of knowledge? Wasn't he the best of men?[353]

☼

Spending for Goodness

One small coin in the hand of a real man of God is worth more than a hundred coins you give to others, because that coin is spent in the way of goodness. *Lend to God . . .* [73:20]. They say, "The Truth has a hand; before alms fall into the hand of the poor, they fall into the hand of God." And in the same way, a coin in the hand of those who have turned their faces toward service to the People of God is also worth more, because they will also spend it for goodness. Goodness is the servant of God. Goodness is God, and God is good.

☼

First the Friend, then the Path

"First the friend, and then the Path."[354] Friends are needed on this path. This whole universe is made of veils and coverings. When the child of Adam stepped upon the earth, the Empyrean, the Throne, the Seven Heavens, the sky and the mold of his own body became his covering, and the animal spirit, the holy spirit, too—he is hidden cover within cover, veil within veil, until the point when there is knowing. The knower, too, is a covering in relation to the Beloved. Where the Beloved is, even the knower near to Him is insignificant.

☼

Who is the Beloved? Who is the Lover?

What a Beloved He is that the man of wisdom and gnosis falls into poverty in front of him! Such and such a shaikh was in retreat. He

---

353 M. 270.

354 I.e., First *refik* (*rafiq*) and then *tarik* (*tariq*). The "friend" Shams refers to here is a spiritual friend or guide who is able to assist in removing veils on the spiritual journey, the "*tariqat –allah*," the "Way of God." When Muhammad was dying, as he was leaving this world for the Presence of the Divine, his last words were, ". . .to the highest Friend."

was meditating deeply, inquiring, "Who is the man of wisdom, and who is the beloved?" He saw himself walking on a vast desert, a desert that had no water or rain. He saw another shaikh approaching from the other side [of the desert]. When he got close to the shaikh, he asked: "Who is the beloved? Who is the lover?"

The shaikh answered, "The lover is coming from this side; and the beloved is coming from the other world."

It Is God Who Washes You Clean

When you wash your face, without a doubt, the one who washes it is God. He said, "Ablution upon ablution is Light upon Light." Ablution is you; ablution upon ablution is again you!

Hasan and Huseyn[355] were walking behind the companions of the Prophet, and along the way, the Prophet and all of them gathered at an aqueduct. They refreshed their ablutions with the water.

The Prophet asked them, "How is the ablution renewed?"

"O Messenger of God," they said, "You have told us that "Ablution upon ablution is light upon light."

"Even so, you were doing the ablutions, but already you were in a state of rapture!"

May God make your life happy, keep this counsel.

Don't Listen to Hurtful Words

I am speaking these words and advice for the blind, because they walk in darkness in a half-dead state. But if they have a stick in their hands, then they won't fall into a hole and break their backs. This advice isn't necessary for those who can partially see, because at least they can see a little.

355 Hasan and Huseyn were the grandchildren of the Prophet Muhammad, the children of Fatima and Ali.

Now whenever someone conveys something hurtful that someone has said, be hurt by the one who has told you—if you show your anger and hurt to him, it might be useful.

Know that learning from them is a heavy veil—one is diminshed by it, as though one has fallen into a well or a moat.

Then, in the end, he regrets having been occupied in licking this one's or that one's bowl—he loses the everlasting and eternal nourishment. After all, words and voices are bowls.

One shouldn't listen to hurtful things that people convey.

Ask with Adab

Yesterday, someone came; they had told him some things I had said. He jumped in my face, "Why did you speak about me like that? I have served the great ones; they all liked me and watched over me; none of them wanted me to leave them," he said.

"Ask your question more courteously (with more *adab*) so that I may give you the answer you need," I said.

Then he said, "I need to sit for an hour, so that I might calm down in order to speak more courteously."

I answered, "Then wait for two hours so that your *nafs* can cool down."

He sat for an hour and immediately began speaking: "I was appreciated by everyone and had a good reputation; everyone was referring to me with such beautiful names. Why have I fallen into such a bad position with you?" Then he added, "What are you going to call me; tell me, which name are you going to give me now?"

I said to him, "If you become a Muslim, I'll call you a Muslim; otherwise, 'a blasphemer,' 'an apostate,' or worse. Now, if you can speak without following your *nafs*, speak. Otherwise, there is nothing more I can say."

❊

Open the Door of the Heart

Glory be to God! Everything is a sacrifice for the human being, and the human being is a sacrifice for himself. Has God said, "We have honored the heavens," or "We have honored the Throne"?[356] Ascending to the Throne is useless; whether you ascend to the Throne or descend through the seven layers of the earth, it's of no use—one must open the door of the heart. This is what all the prophets, saints, and the attained ones were striving for. This is what they were seeking.

❊

Be Whole

The whole universe is within one human being. When he knows himself, he knows everything. The Tatar is within you—the attribute of stringency of the Tatar is within you.

"Guide my people for they do not know (*hadith*)," means "Guide my parts to wholeness." Though they were unbelievers, still they were part of [Muhammad]—if they hadn't been part of him, if they were separate, then how could he be the whole?

You were saying, "The universe exists through the whole, not the parts." When one says "the whole," which part could be excluded?

❊

A Moon-Faced Mirror

From her face, a masterpiece
    was left upon the moon—
A trace was left from that angel-face
    upon the moon.

No, no! What is the moon in comparison?!
The soul became her servant,
    and only she remains.

The moon, last night, fell down upon her pillow.

---

356 Instead, God said, "*We have honored the children of Adam* [17:70]."

Out of jealousy, I struggled desperately.
I beat my hands and feet upon the floor.

Who is the moon to deserve to sit with you?!
You are the beauty who has wandered the world,
whom everyone admires.

❊

Why Cry When the Prison Wall is Broken?

Someone was weeping: "The Tatars killed my brother, what a man of knowledge he was!"

I said to him, "If you had a trace of knowledge, you would know that the Tatars have given him eternal life with the blow of that sword."

How can the preachers know about that life? They stand up at the pulpit and begin to lament. They say, "The world is the prison of the believer (*hadith*)." If someone has escaped from prison, then one weeps for him?

"What a pity! He has escaped from prison!" they say, feeling sad. The Tatars opened a hole in the prison; or if he escaped in a different manner, he has only emigrated from one abode to another abode. Yet you are weeping and saying, "Why have they struck that pick-axe against the wall of that prison? Why have they hit that stone?"

One shouldn't pity them. Maybe that beautiful marble was keeping that person's feet bound, and now it has been broken away, and he has rushed out. But you are crying, you are striking your head and face with your fists, saying, "What a pity that they have cut it away!"

Or if they demolish the cage you've fallen into, you moan, "Alas! Why did they break this cage into pieces; why did they let this bird free?" Or they are lancing an abscess so that the pus and filth might come out, and right away you scream, "Why are they letting the pus flow away?"

❋

Mines of Gold

"Don't neglect to visit the attained ones of the Truth," means "Serve a person of wisdom, serve one who is perfected." "Beware! Give offerings to the poor," doesn't mean to the ignorant ones; it doesn't mean to those of limited understanding. People are like mines; they are like mines of gold.

❋

Tall Tales

They say that Hamza and Abdurrahman had gone on a long journey together. They wished to see the miraculous things on earth and to explore. But, where they went, some ants appeared. Each one of them was, may God protect us, as terrible as several elephants. Their custom during the time of war then was not to attack the whole front line, but to attack only one person at a time. First, Hamza sprang forth, he shot an arrow at the ants. Then another lion came; he shot at him, too. In this way, he shot down ten of them and then ran back and took refuge in the ship. And then, he struggled to save the life of Abdurrahman. He had just placed his arrow on his bow when two ants attacked from the side, and his arrow was of no use. Hamza shouted: "Run back! This is not your work." Abdurrahman retreated and took refuge in the ship. It was a strange journey on the land, but the most important part of this journey was on the sea.

I have a tall hat, and at night I tell tall tales.

❋

Real Kismet

A dervish was asking for alms from the owner of a shop. In order to get rid of him, the shopkeeper said, "I have nothing at hand."

I said to the shopkeeper, "This is a saintly dervish, why didn't you give him anything."

He answered, "God hadn't made it his portion (*kismet*)."

So I said to the shopkeeper, "God had made it his portion, but you became the obstacle. How can I confirm something I haven't seen with my own eyes? If you had put your hand into your purse and if the opening of the purse had squeezed your hand and wounded it, and if I saw that with my own eyes, then I would agree, 'Yes. God didn't want it.'"

❊

I Am with Those Who Are Broken

If two people are struggling, if they are fighting; whichever of them is overcome, God is with him. He is with the one who is broken, not with the one who overcomes. Because He said, "I am with those who are broken (*hadith qudsi*)."

> Where are those vows, where are those promises?
> You were slow to love, but you escaped so quickly!
> With your love, you bound me.
> I see that only I am in love with you;
> you left love to me.
>
> Now I'll sit upon the way
> and wear the clothes of the oppressed,
> I'll sue you—you've tortured me!
> Maybe, when I'm saved from separation and reach you,
> You'll feel pity for me;
> Or you'll clearly understand all the trouble
> you've caused me![357]

What you have sometimes wanted you have gotten now, so what has become of your vow? What has been the outcome of the words we spoke? Our words have come and gone like that!

❊

Let Me Hear Your Voice

He is a great man, he reads commentaries about the Qur'an, but whoever becomes completely a scholar is completely emptied of God, and completely filled with himself.

Suppose a Greek becomes a Muslim—he caught the fragrance of God. But when someone is full, a hundred thousand prophets

---

357 M. 275.

cannot empty his heart. Many a weeping becomes a veil and takes the servant further away from God.

"Speak openly now," he said, "what did you do about the matter about which we spoke?"

I said to him, "What is the indication of the words that you are speaking? How are they answering?"

This ear can't hear well. Come, speak into my ear!

> When the friend began to speak,
> I pretended I was deaf.
> Because of the sweetness of her words,
> lions go ahunting.
> I'm not really hard of hearing—
> I just wanted to listen once more to her words.

It is said that the angels begged God, "Such and such a faithful servant of yours is calling out to You so much; he is weeping and asking for help. You accept even the prayers of those who are estranged! Why won't You also accept his request?"

God Most High responded, "Leave Me with My servant. I am not less compassionate than you. I love him/her and I love his/her voice." The delayed response to some servants' pleas, is because of that affection and love.

Sometimes praising is a difficulty and a veil, and the words bounce back. Sometimes, if he doesn't praise, it tears him to pieces.

Sometimes weeping is pleasing to Him, and other times weeping troubles Him. Likewise with laughter.

It's You, Who Needs the Tears!

Shamsuddin of Khujandi was weeping for the People of the House.[358] We were weeping for him: "You are weeping for them! Someone joins with God, and you weep for them, but not for yourself! If you became aware of your own state, you would weep for yourself. And then, you

358 *Ahl-al Bayt*: the people of the House (the House of God, the Kaaba in Mecca) refers to the family of the Prophet Muhammad.

would call all the members of your family, gather all your relatives and everyone you know, and weep and moan for your own self!"

❊

Steadfast with the Truth

There is no change in the Truth; you are the one who has changed. In the same way, sometimes you like bread and yearn for it, and sometimes you get tired of it and turn away. Sometimes you feel affection towards a friend, and he or she seems very lovely to you—you say, "I love him"—and then after a while your feelings change, and you say, "I hate him." If you were steadfast within that state, he would always be sought after and beloved.

They call that state "maturity." I wonder what is understood by maturity? Well, maturity means clearly seeing the Truth.

❊

Shall We Reach Aksaray?

The one who has matured, doesn't know that he has matured; he reaches Aksaray, but he does not know that he has arrived in Aksaray, until he reaches it—he is full of fear and longing. He remains in doubt, "I wonder if I will be able to arrive or not?"

They say to him: "Let's not run after what we don't see."

But That which is not seen says, "Unless they run after Me and exhaust themselves, let Me not show Myself."

When things are like this, unless they act first from themselves, it won't happen.

If they have to imitate something, at least let them imitate the Qur'an.

❊

There is No Prayer without Presence

"To meditate for an hour is better than sixty years of worship (*hadith*)." What is meant by that "meditation" is the presence of a dervish who is sincere—that there might not be any falseness in that worship. Truly, that worship is far better than prayer in form made without presence of heart.

The *salaat* can be made up later, but one can't make up for lack of presence. The poor ones strive hard in this. "There is no *salaat* without presence (*hadith*)." Just as it has also been said, "Without the *Fatiha*, *salaat* is incomplete (*hadith*)."

According to them, the *Fatiha* is that presence of heart. It is such a presence that even if Gabriel comes, he can't approach. When the Prophet called Gabriel to come, Gabriel said, "No, if I approach an inch more, I will be burnt."

One Day, He May Be of the Faithful

I think positively about friends. I can't think otherwise, even if I haven't seen something with my own eyes. Even about blasphemers one cannot at first think badly. What I am saying is, "In reality, who can claim that in the end they will not be muslims, too?"

Umar,[359] May God be pleased with him, served idols for forty years. He made his supplications to the idol; he called upon it, "O Idol!"

But God answered him, "Here I am!"

Pride

A poor man entered a gathering of the Prophet Muhammad. A rich man proudly spread the skirt of his robe over the robe of that poor one. The Blessed Prophet became angry and glared at him.

The rich man said, "O Prophet of God! Let me give half of my possessions to him and remove this from me."

He forgave him.

I wouldn't trade even the slightest indication from Muhammad for a hundred thousand works of Qurayshi, Qushayri, and others.

---

359 Not long after his conversion to Islam, Umar became the greatest champion of the faith, and after the death of the Prophet Muhammad he became the second *caliph*, leader of the Muslim community.

They are tasteless and have no sense of beauty. There is no taste of meaning in them.

They don't give even a sip to those who worship their own *nafs*.

☼

Devotion

In our gathering, there was a boy who used to listen to our words. He was still small, but everyday he would run away from his father and mother and would come to us. He was very devoted and would say, "So that I may serve you, I need to be near you always."

But his father and mother were weeping, and he was afraid that I would find out about it and make him leave. It continued until all day long the child would stay with his head on his knees. His mother and his father didn't dare object.

Sometimes, I put my ear to the door. I heard this verse through the opening:

Near you, lovers come and fly away—
blood flows from their eyes.
Like the earth, I remain at your door,
while others pass by like the wind.

"What are you saying, my son?" I said, "Say it again."

"No," he said and wouldn't speak.

He died at the age of eighteen. How can I describe the bright capacity, intelligence, subtlety and power of his nature?

☼

Three Kinds of Hearts

If the friends knew what purity and good fortune we wish for them, they would give their lives to us. I never think badly about them.

What does a mind pure of the devil and fearful whisperings think about? The devil cannot enter into such a heart. Only angels dwell in this heart. God has said: "I have made this heart a home for My compassion; please leave."

There are three kinds of hearts. One is always the nest of the devil. The second kind is the house for both the devil and the angel. Sometimes the angel leaves and the devil enters, and sometimes the angel comes and makes the devil leave.

A third kind of heart is the home only of the angel. The devil can't enter there. This is because of what is written on the Preserved Tablets—they never turn their eyes from the Preserved Tablets—they are always before them.

It is like when a table is set with a tablecloth of silken thread, and there are golden plates and golden platters adorned with jewels, but there is no trace of food to be seen. One would rather have wooden plates with food on them.

Within the Heart of My Faithful Servant

See all within yourself: Moses, Jesus, Abraham, Noah, Adam, Eve, Asiya (Pharoah's wife), Khidr, Elias, Pharaoh and Nimrod, are all within you. You are an infinite universe; what are the earth and the skies in comparison? Didn't God say: "My heavens and My earth cannot contain Me, but I can be contained within the heart of a faithful servant of Mine" and "You will not find Me in the heavens; you will not find Me on the Throne!"?

The Journey to the Simurgh

All of those birds journeyed to serve the Simurgh (the Huma bird).[360] They had to cross seven seas. Some died from the cold and some fell down because of the strong scent of the sea until out of all of them, only two birds remained. They became proud: "Everyone else has fallen; only we will reach the Simurgh." But as soon as they saw the Simurgh, two drops of blood dripped from their beaks and they, too, gave up their lives.

---

360 M. 280.

Shams is referring again to the story of *The Conference of the Birds* by Attar.

After all, this Simurgh lives beyond Qaf Mountain, but where it flies from there only God knows. All of these birds gave up their lives to reach just the dust of Qaf Mountain.

They claimed to have a certain state, but if during their lives even a whiff of that state had reached them, they wouldn't have remained in the state they were.

True States

It is said that the antichrist (*dajjal*) will kill goats and sheep, and kill birds. He will pull out their wings and feathers, then he will rub them with his hand, and they will become whole and alive again. And he will place hands on a dry sheep, and it will give milk. He will cut a goat in half, then rub his hands over it, and it will become whole. The servants of the Truth who follow in the footsteps of Muhammad won't be deceived by that even though he (the *dajjal*) seems to manifest miracles.

They never become proud of their miraculous states. Even though they are imitators, God's attentiveness is their protector. From time to time, the effect of that attentiveness, though remaining veiled and secret, reaches the faithful one's soul, and that imitation gathers such strength that even a thousand times the manifestations of the antichrist couldn't even come close to it.

Now, the person who is connected to that state is never severed from it—neither when eating, nor when sleeping, nor in the toilet. He is sitting on the toilet and still the state is firmly established in him. It stays with him.

"What is his state like? After all, his body is on the toilet!" Some people estimate spiritual manliness by a person's beard. Say, we'll show them the measure of the spiritual virility of the truthful *murid*. Now, since they don't make the inner work, they focus on the outer.

❊

Sema of the Soul

Someone said: "You've given a bad name to the people of Knowledge with this sema."

I said, "Don't you know that except through them good from bad and *muslim* from *kafir* doesn't become manifest?"

He was saying, "You reach God through dancing?"

I said, "You, too, dance; you'll reach God."

Two steps and he arrived.[361]

❊

Moses and the Devil

One day I was alluding to a meaning of the *ayat*: *This is from the act of Satan* [28:15]. I said: "The Prophet of God used to say, "The devil circulates within the children of Adam like blood running through their veins." So, this devil isn't in the form of a Turk with a turban so you could easily recognize him. Such a heat arose in Moses that he struck the Egyptian with his fist; that heat was Satan.

❊

Crowing is the Rooster's Business, and the Morning is God's

Crowing is the rooster's business, and the morning is God's. Moses indicated this very thing when he asked, "O Lord, what's the use since Pharaoh isn't going to accept my invitation?" And He said, "Don't quit because of that; just speak."

God has servants who listen to their words and understand.

❊

True Charity

The giving of alms in secret is true charity—when because of the extent of immersion in sincerity and from keeping that sincerity in view, you take no pleasure in the giving of that free offering, because

---

361 Shams is referring here again to the Prophet's *mir'aj*, reaching into the Presence of God. He also reminds us, *Wherever you turn there is the Face of God* [2:115].

you are busy regretting that it wasn't better or more than it was.

Most of the time, Bayazid Bastami used to make the pilgrimage on foot. He had made the hajj seventy times. Then one day he saw that the travelers on the pilgrimage because of lack of water in the desert were extremely distressed and were about to die. He saw a dog near the well at whose edge the pilgrims had crowded to drink. Exhausted, it was looking at him. An inspiration came to Bayazid. "Be quick! Give water to this dog."

He cried out, "Who will buy a blessed worthy hajj for the price of a cup of water?" Nobody paid any attention to him. He increased his offer, "Five worthy hajjs completed on foot . . . , six . . . , seven . . . ?," until he reached seventy hajjs. At last, someone called out, "I will." It flashed through Abu Yazid's mind, "Haven't I done well! For the sake of a dog I've sold seventy pilgrimages made on foot." But when he put the water into a bowl and placed it in front of the dog, the dog turned its face away. Abu Yazid fell prostrate and repented.

A voice came, "How many times because of a deed you've done are you going to say to yourself, 'I did this and I did that'; do you see that even a dog doesn't accept this?"

Immediately, Bayazid cried out, "O God! I've repented. From now on, I won't think such thoughts." At that instant the dog plunged his mouth into the water and began to drink.

> What a Beloved!—even if with a hundred pleadings
> I were to beg,
> "Let me kiss your foot," you wouldn't let me.

❁

Let's Follow One Who Sees

Imaginings like Awhad's[362] before attaining knowledge lead one

---

362 Awhaduddin Kirmani was a friend of Ibn Arabi. Shams takes him to task for his lack of real seeing. He encountered him in Baghdad when he was gazing into a bucket of water. Shams asked him what he was doing. He replied, "Gazing at the moon." Shams said, "Why don't you turn around and look at the moon itself in the sky, unless you have some boil on your neck—then go find a doctor."

astray. After there is knowledge, images come that are correct and extremely beneficial; after that is the opening of the eye.

A truthful imitator is better than someone who with his own cleverness wants to carve a path and a way. I saw a blind man who had placed his hands on the back of a seeing man and was going along to Aksaray. And then that blind man pulled his hand away from the back of the seeing man, and blindly started traveling without a guide. Such a person is going towards non-existence. He lives in non-existence and dies in non-existence; either he dies of hunger or thirst, or a wild beast attacks him and eats him.

❊

What is Obligatory?

The common people pray five times a day to find deliverance from chastisement. But woe upon the ones who have let go of following Muhammad!

A bedouin asked, "O Messenger of God! What is obligatory?"

He answered, "Prayer five times a day."

He asked, "And fasting?"

He said, "Thirty fast-days."

"And alms?"

"Also."

He said, "Must I do anything else?"

He said, "No."

"Then let me not add anything more than this," he said and left.

After he left, the Blessed Prophet said, "If he does these things he will find deliverance."

And the others said: "Oh! If that's true, let's also be content with this much." And they gave up following the Prophet—they couldn't see.

❊

Burning with Light

One who has been born within the sun itself, has opened his eye within the sun and so from birth has become accustomed to its light.

They say, "Speak of the moon, speak of Mercury."

How can I speak of them? The sun isn't concerned with whether there is a moon in the cosmos or not. The moon and the planets are helpless, but everyone sees the moon and gazes at it, even though there is no comparison between the light of the moon and that of the sun. No one is able to look straight at the sun—the eye isn't strong enough to bear it.

What a strange creature the salamander is! It isn't burned by fire, but it drowns in water. The duck doesn't drown in the sea—it suffers no loss there, but fire burns it. A creature which neither fire can burn nor water can drown is extremely rare.

❊

Know! There Is No god but God

Know! There is no god except He [47:19] is a command to seek knowledge and in the same verse, *and seek forgiveness for your sins* is also a command to repent of this existence for it is only newly created! How can this existence that is newly arrived, how can it see the Knower of Eternity? Your body itself only came to be yesterday. Consider the spirit to be two or three days old, or consider it a thousand years old—still it is young.

❊

Umar

Umar (may God be pleased with him) was such a hero that with a single crack of his whip he would make a lion flee, the earth would give milk, and out of fear of him, wine would turn into vinegar.

Someone asked him: "What's in your hand?"

"It's vinegar," he said.

A trace of sunlight grazed his shoulder, and when he turned and glared at the sun out of the corner of his eye, the sun darkened. I believe this; what can I do if the philosophers don't!

This same Umar came to the mosque one day. The Prophet was speaking quietly with someone. Because of this, Umar didn't dare approach the Prophet, but he was thinking to himself, "Why am I not included in this confidence? But let me not go nearer."

The Prophet became aware of his thoughts. *The All-knowing, the All-Aware told me* [66:3]. He said, "O Umar! Did you hear what I was saying to that friend? Did you understand my words?"

Umar said, "No! O Messenger of God! I just saw your holy lips moving."

The Prophet said, "Then you've seen quite a bit, as by seeing the way letters were formed by our lips you could have seen what we were saying."

Umar fell prostrate in repentence.

❁

The Work Demands Stringency

Whomever I love, I treat harshly. If he accepts it, I become like a ball in his lap. Gentleness is such that if you are gentle to even a five-year old child, he has faith in you and loves you, but the work demands stringency. [363]

---

363 See *Mathnawi* III, 4008-4012 (*Jewels of Remembrance*, p.41):

I am amazed at the seeker of purity
who when it's time to be polished
complains of rough-handling.
Love is like a lawsuit:
to suffer harsh treatment is the evidence:
when you have no evidence, the lawsuit is lost.
Don't grieve when the Judge demands your evidence;
kiss the snake so that you may gain the treasure.
That harshness isn't towards you, O son,
but towards the harmful qualities within you.
When someone beats a rug,
the blows are not against the rug,
but against the dust within it.

A True Qiblah

I wanted someone of my own kind, so that I could make him my *qiblah* and turn my face toward him, because I was bored with myself. What do you understand of these words? Now that one whom I have made my *qiblah* will understand and grasp what I am saying.

Come! So that we might investigate the most difficult and most profound sayings of the Prophet and show their purpose, like a well examined palm of the hand. For example, we will look at the words, the meaning, the syntax, and the vocalization. For example the particle "*la*" has no interpretation; it is absolute negation. But the particle "*ma*" can be negative, declarative, as well as other aspects. If I had started thinking about these fine points, I would have seen what he had seen through struggle. If I had wanted to have a conversation with Muhammad, the Messenger of God, I would have had to see all the fine points of the words and interactions and would have spoken to him in a measured way.

But I stepped into friendship with you brazenly and boldly, I never thought about these words I speak, or whether I should be cautious, or that from this connection thoughts might arise because of which I should be careful. I have entered with boldness, brazenly.

May God Increase Us in Knowledge

"*This is separation* [18:78]," I spoke the words—not the reality.[364] Even if I wanted to, I can't leave. No, one must not be overconfident about this. *None feels secure from God's deep devising save people who are* [*already*] *lost* [7:99].[365]

---

364 This is a reference to the story of Moses and Khidr, in *Surah Kahf.* When Moses was unable to refrain from questioning Khidr's behavior, the sage answered: "*This is the parting of ways between me and you.* [*And now*] *I shall let you know the real meaning of all* [*those events*] *that you were unable to bear with patience* [18:78].

365 M. 285.

I complained to a learned man of my bad memory.
He pointed me towards abandoning sins—
towards abandoning existence.
For, knowledge is a blessing from God,
and the bounty of God doesn't flow to sinners.

So it was as if he said, "Real memory is in the giving up of memory."

And seek God's bounty [62:10]. This bounty is continually increasing. Seek to become more. Don't be satisfied with the jurists—say, "I want more!"[366] More than being a sufi, more than a gnostic (*arif*)—no matter what comes to you, more than that, more than the heavens. . . . It is said that whatever is in the entire cosmos is in the human being. But where are the seven heavens inside the human being? In which part of the human being are these stars, the sun, the moon?

✲

Come to Know Your Own Beauty

I separated from Qadi Shamsuddin because he wouldn't teach me.

He said. "I don't want to be ashamed in front of God. God has created you—he has made you beautiful. I can't make the creation of God ugly. I see a jewel that is extremely noble; I can't engrave anything upon it."

What business of yours is the eternity of the cosmos? Come to know your own eternity—whether you are eternal or newly created. As much life as you have, spend it in investigating your own situation. Why are you spending it on investigating the eternity of the cosmos?

You say, "Coming to know God is profound." O fool! It's you who are profound! If there is something profound, it's you! What kind of a friend are you that you don't know as clearly as the palm of your hand the secret of your Friend who has entered even within your own veins! What kind of a servant of God are you if you don't know His secrets and their inner meaning!

---

366 *O God, increase me in knowledge* [20:114].

Even with my shaikh I haven't spoken these words that I have spoken with you. I left him in sorrow and went. But he was saying, "I am the shaikh."

Mevlana says something different. He says, "Yes! He is our shaikh; through him our eye opened."

Dispelling Robbers on the Way

He said, "There are robbers on the way; there is no light in that direction. I fear for you if you go."

How can you know me? I have gone into the depths of the forest where even lions wouldn't dare to go. The wind was rattling the trees. A huge young man came towards me crying, "Woe upon you."

I paid no attention to him; I didn't even look at him. He shouted several times to frighten me, but I still paid no attention. He had such an axe in his hand that even if he had hit a boulder he could have shattered it. Again he said, "Woe upon you!"

I turned towards him. I hadn't even reached for a weapon when he fell down on his back. Motioning with his hand, he said, "Go, I have no business with you."

The Light of Zhikr

That Sufi Arshad was saying to his disciple, "While chanting, bring the *zhikr* out from within the belly."

"No," I said, "Bring the *zhikr* out not from the belly but from the center of your soul." These words of mine bewildered him.

Whenever I turn my face towards a person, he turns his face away from the whole world. I may show him my face, even if I don't show him myself.

Similarly, to those who asked about the sign of the truly faithful, the Prophet said, "It is turning away from this deceiving world."

We have a pearl within. When we turn someone's face towards that, he becomes estranged from all beloveds and friends. It's another subtlety—not prophethood, not messengerhood. About sainthood or gnosis what can I say?

The secret saints of God say: "In what way will we reveal ourselves or speak about who we are?"

He said: "Raise your head from Muhammad's collar, for we are following him!"

Otherwise, how can you call it following?

The radiance of their light reached Muhammad, so that he became almost selfless.

What a following this is! Mevlana was sitting when Khawajagi (a *murid* of Rumi's father) said, "It's time for prayer." Mevlana was absorbed within himself. We got up, and stood for prayers. Several times I glanced and saw that the imam[367] and all had turned their backs to the *qiblah*—"We let go of prayer and turned our faces away from the *qiblah*!"[368]

The Sun Is Shining!

I arrived in the midst of blood-letters, and this thought came to me, "What heedless people!" A sun has come up, beginningless and endless. What is this beginninglessness and endlessness? Both of these are qualities that became manifest just yesterday. The head has been named "beginningless" and its tail "endless"! But what are beginninglessness and endlessness in relation to that? A sun has come out, the entire cosmos has been illumined. What a sun! And these people are in darkness, and they have no news of it.

They called Muhammad a magician, but wherever the name of God is chanted, magic is dispelled. In a place where the inside is completely divine light—how can magic reside there? When it begins to rain, magic instantly departs. When so much rain of life

367 The imam is the person among the community who is leading the ritual prayer.

368 In that moment, Mevlana, in his absorption was the true direction of prayer.

and elixir of life and waters of life are raining and pouring forth from him, how can magic find a place within him?

Prostrations of the Heart

The followers of Muhammad should be like this, and Muhammad is like this. After all, you are saying bad things about the stone worshipper because he turns his face towards a stone or a picture on a wall, but you are also turning your face towards a wall! So, this is an allusion that Muhammad gave, but you do not understand—the Kaaba is within the world. The whole world turns their faces towards it. But if you were to remove this Kaaba from the middle, their prostrations would all be towards each others hearts. The prostration of that one beomes for this one, the prostration of this one towards the heart of that one!

Words of Truth

Don't you know, every word that I take in, I bring forward and set right? The speaker is strong—no weakness is appropriate for him. I have never had the habit of writing. Since I don't write the words they remain inside me, and every instant they show me a different face. Words are a pretext; the Truth (*Haqq*) has thrown off her veil and is revealing her beauty.

The Alif of Being

From the exuberance of the ocean of the words of the Truth, an "*alif*" was engraved on the Divine Tablet. The command came: "O spiritual Gabriel! Read this holy word!"

I hadn't yet completed my words when Shahab fled.

"I didn't have the strength to look at your face anymore," he said and left.

I said, "What is it?"

He was fleeing and was saying, "An extraordinary thing, a strange thing . . . !"

That Shahab, even though he spoke words of unbelief, he was spiritual and pure. He had become essential spirit and left food behind.

One day I was giving a hint and unveiling it. I didn't want the meaning to remain veiled from him. I said to him, "You are saying, 'He doesn't know the particulars, He knows universals.' What do you mean by these 'universals'?"

He said, "When I say, 'universal,' I don't know any part that is outside of that whole."

Yes, if one says "part," the whole is not inside it. One cannot speak of an orchard without including trees, but you can say the opposite. But if there are no trees, such a place is not an orchard; it's just an enclosed space.

❋

The Beauty of Persian

Now, I don't know the Hindi language, but not from inability. But what about Arabic? If that Indian were to hear it, "This is a very pleasant language," he would say. And what about the Persian language, with all its beauty and subtlety? These meanings and subtleties that have come out in Persian don't come out in Arabic.

❋

Becoming a Muslim

In front of us, no one is able to become a Muslim all at once. He or she becomes a Muslim, and then he or she becomes a blasphemer, and then again a Muslim. Each time, something departs from that person until the moment when he or she becomes perfected (*kamil*).

❋

Surrendering

He said, "Come with us, so we may stay awake all night together."

I said, "Tonight I am going to visit the Christian, because I have promised him to come tonight."

"We are Muslims; he is an unbeliever. Come with us!" they said.

I said, "No, he is Muslim in the depths of his heart, because he is surrendered. But there is no surrendering within you—to be a Muslim is to surrender."

They said, "Come, because surrendering is made possible through companionship (*sohbet*)."

I said, "There is no veil from my side and no curtain, go ahead in the name of God, test me!"

One of them began, "*We have honored the children of Adam; we have carried them on the land and on the sea* [17:70]."

Words leaped from my mouth, "Silence! You have no portion from this verse! Where is *We have carried them on land* and where are you?"

He wanted to ask a question. I said, "What will you ask from me? And what will your objections be?" I don't take disciples. They kept insisting, "Let us be your disciples; give us robes (*khirqa*)." I fled; they followed me until I stopped at the inn. They spread out the gifts they had brought, "Take these, all of these and accept us." But it was no use; I left.

I don't take murids. I take shaikhs, and not every shaikh, the perfect shaikh!

✲

Knowing the Self

"The one who knows himself knows his Lord," he said. What grief remains when that self whose name is *ammarah*, the commanding self, has come to a contented state? He no longer has any fear of anything in the world.

> You ask, "Why are your eyes the color of roses?"
> Since you have asked, let me tell you openly.
> Into this heart, the bloody tears of love pour—
> There they heat up and from these eyes overflow.

❊

Knowing We Do Not Know

> O you who ignorantly serve your own self!
> How long are you going to race about at its call?

They say that this line belongs to al-Ma'arri (Abu'l Ala Ma'arri). His words aren't much—they aren't like words of other strong ones, not like those of Hakim Sanai:

> My knowing has reached such a rank
> That now I understand I have no knowledge.[369]

One catches a fragrance from these words of his because they showed him something. He came to know, "From the beginning to the end, all that I have said is nothing."

The Face of the Truth is a light for humanity, for those who look for it. Well, such people come and see only themselves, and they wonder what's happening! They look at themselves, but they see by means of a servant. Moses—peace be upon him—fainted and fell down with that light.

He said, "We have not known You."[370] In other words, "I haven't known myself." "We have not worshipped You," in other words, "I have not worshipped myself."

❊

Finding the Treasure

The map of a treasure had come into someone's hands. It said, "Go out to the graveyard, and turn your back to that big dome[371]—you will turn your face to the East, and you'll place the arrow on the

---

369 M. 290.

370 This is a *hadith* of Muhammad, speaking of the Real: "We have not known You as You truly ought to be known; we have not worshipped You as You ought to be worshipped." See note # 60 of this text.

371 I.e., Turn away from your self. Within the clothing of the Mevlevi *sema* there is much symbolism. The tall, conical felt hat is representative of the tombstone of the ego.

bow and let it loose. In the place where the arrow falls, a treasure is hidden." The man went and shot the arrow, but no matter how he searched for it, he couldn't find the treasure. The news reached the sultan. He gathered all the bowmen who could shoot the furthest. They tested their arrows. But again nothing was found. They returned to the sultan.

Suddenly the man was inspired: "We didn't tell you to pull the string." He came, placed the arrow on the bow, and the arrow immediately fell in front of him. When the help of God arrives, with a single step you can reach your aim. "One step and he arrived."[372]

❁

Growing up with the Love and Light of God

If the faithful one holds an assumption about any person that he has grown up with the love and light of God since his ancestors, grandparents, and since the first days of his youth, let him keep that understanding about Blessed Muhammad. He said, "When Adam was just emerging from water and clay, I was already a prophet."

❁

A Companion for the Journey

When Bayazid was setting out on the pilgrimage, he was determined to go alone; he didn't want the companionship of some inappropriate person. Then one day, he encountered a traveler who had set out ahead of him. As he watched him and witnessed the brisk way in which he was walking, a certain taste came to him. He thought to himself, "Perhaps I might take this person as a companion. I might let go of this habit of walking alone on the journey, for he looks as though he would be an excellent companion. Then he reflected again, "'The highest companion (*hadith*)'; let God alone be my companion." Then again he saw that the taste for traveling with that man was prevailing over the taste for traveling alone.

---

372 This is a reference again to the *mir'aj* of the Prophet Muhammad and his stepping beyond the companionship of Gabriel into the very Presence of God.

He was in the middle of this debate about which choice to make when he noticed that the man had turned around and was facing him: "First, why don't you see whether I will accept your companionship or not," he said.

Bayazid bowed his head amazed at how this person had spoken his secret thoughts. The man quickened his pace.

The Strength of Muhammad

An attribute, a station is daunting to people, but according to Him, everything is easy. Even the heavens cannot pull the string of His bow. *We offered the trust to the heavens and the earth and the mountains; they turned away from the burden, but the human being took it up* [33:72]. According to this holy sign (*ayah*), even the earth and the heavens said, "It is not within our capacity to carry this trust," because their eyes are not fixed on God's granting of success. They might have said, "The bow is stiff, but there is someone behind us Who can pull it." Well, that vision and strength of relying on and trusting in the Truth belongs to Muhammad and those who follow him.

Now someone was speaking about the attributes of Muhammad or Jesus, mentioning the characteristics of one of the great ones and talking about their states and secrets.

One of those listening became excited and said, "I wish we had seen him!"

Another said, "O fool! Why don't you see this person who is talking about their qualities? Perhaps he is such a one, but he has veiled his face."

Focus on the Truth

Little by little become a stranger to people, for the Truth is not a friend with lots of people; He doesn't connect with them. I don't know what one could gain from them! What can they save a person from, or to what can they draw him or her closer? You've chosen the path of the prophets. You are following them. The prophets didn't mingle with people. They focused on the Truth, even though people were attracted to them and gathered around them.

The words of the prophets can be explained. They may say, "Go away!" but that "Go away!" actually means "Come near!"

Pass On, O Faithful One!

If someone calls a man of religion "little scholar," he is swearing; so what do you say about those who call someone "little dervish"? These are people who have not sensed any fragrance in "My poverty is my pride." Otherwise, how could they look down upon them as "little *fakir* (poor one)" or "little dervish"? What a blasphemy this is! And what a lesson we should learn from the voice of Hell saying, "Pass on, O faithful one! For without a doubt your light will extinguish my fire."

Perfect Philosopher

Ibn Sina (Avicenna) is a half-baked philosopher. The perfect philosopher is Plato—he claims love. But what a pity that in order to be well-regarded you try to talk of such conveyed things. It is absolutely necessary that you give up your command.[373]

Struggling with the Devil

When I was a child, I read a story about a shaikh who in the throes of death was suffering a great deal of pain. His disciples and those who had faith in him had surrounded him. They wanted him to make his declaration of faith: "There is no god but God (*La illaha illallah*)." But the shaikh kept turning his face away from them.

When they would go to the other side of the bed to the direction he was turning, he would again turn away. As those around him

---

373 Regard as a king someone unconcerned with kingship.
Only he who is an enemy to his own existence possesses real existence.
[*Mathnawi* II, 1469-70] See also I:3052-3101, "The friend who said I."

persisted and begged him to bear witness to his faith, he refused, "No! I won't say it."

The disciples began to wail and moan, "Oh! Especially in this moment, it is essential. What is going on? What is this darkness? What will become of us?" They wept and begged God for help.

The shaikh came to himself and asked, "What's happening? What's going on?"

The disciples explained what had been happening and the shaikh replied, "I wasn't aware of all that. Satan had come near me. With a glass of water in his hand, he was wandering around me and asking, 'Are you thirsty?' 'Yes,' I answered.

"'Then say that God has a partner and I'll give this water to you,' he said. I turned my face away from him. Then he came to the other side to which I had turned, and again he was repeating the same thing. And again, I turned my face away from him."

> During the day I look for Your pearls.
> All night until dawn, my eyes search the heavens.
> I'm not waiting for you to shed my blood,
> But if You do, I will be looking for You.

This is true, but when the moment of death comes for the pure servants of God, how could Satan dare come near them? Even an angel would walk around them carefully.

They say, "Umar (may God be pleased with him) struck his fist in one of the devil's eyes and blinded it." Most people don't understand it, but there is another meaning, a secret that is known—the devil is not a being with a body. "The devil circulates like blood within the veins of the children of Adam (*hadith*)."[374]

One day Satan came to Umar. "O Umar!" he said, "Come and let me show you something strange." He took him to the mosque. "O Umar! Look through the crack of that door," he said. Umar looked.

"What did you see?" he asked.

"Someone is making *salaat* and another person is sleeping in a corner of the mosque with his feet tucked in."

---

374 M. 295.

He said, "O Umar! By Almighty God who makes you dear by following Muhammad and Who saves you from me, if it weren't for the love in that one who is sleeping and fear of him, I could do to that man making *salaat* what a hungry dog would not even do to a bag of flour."

Nothing burns this devil—nothing but the fire of love of the man of God.[375]

Many people fast and follow disciplines, but cannot bind him—rather he becomes stronger, because he was created from the fire of desires. Fire doesn't accompany divine light—Hell cries out, "Pass on, your light extinguishes my fire (*hadith*)!"

❁

Gratitude Elicits Grace

I don't have the perfection of speaking. I wish there were someone who could listen. One has to speak with perfection, and one has to listen with perfection, too. "There is a seal on hearts, on tongues there is a seal, on ears there is a seal."

A little light is coming—it increases when one gives thanks for it. Expressing gratitude, with the tongue of one's state, one says, "My God! Show us things as they really are." The answer comes, "*If you are grateful, I increase My grace; if you are ungrateful, My wrath is stringent* [14:7]."

❁

Burning Candles

I came, because of my great love for you, to tell you that we should go again privately to the shaikh. And you recited that poem:

> Even if I go to gatherings and festivities,
> I won't put anyone's love within my heart.
> Someone who falls away from the sun,
> Instead of the sun, burns a candle in front of himself.

---

375 As Shams says elsewhere in the *Maqalat*, "Happy is the one whose eye sleeps but not his heart! Woe to the one whose eye is awake, but whose heart sleeps."

I said to myself, "He's saying,
'It's night, the sun has set,'
but I can see it hasn't set—the sun still stays
in its place."

✲

Moving Towards Completion

Someone asked another, "Is so and so mature?"

He answered, "His father was very virtuous and mature."

He said, "But I'm not asking about his father, but about him."

He answered, "His father was a very mature human being."

Then he said, "Don't you hear what I am saying?"

He answered, "You are the one who is not hearing. I've heard your words—if I hadn't, I wouldn't know what you were asking."

Come again, so that you may go further
than where you are now,
so that you may ripen, if you haven't yet matured.
In the time of war, you are the soul and the world,
Now, in the time of peace, see what you'll become!

It's not appropriate to give advice in front of a preacher or to sing in front of a singer unless you are a great master. If one says to him, "This veil is strange, but it hasn't been opened for you," he listens.

If you turn your face toward us, openness of heart is waiting for you! Lights appear through each veil opened. Whatever difficulty you see, you should know it is due to your own incompleteness and say, "This difficulty is due to myself!"

God shows interest in His servant in proportion to his or her worthiness. Whatever the servant does, God responds accordingly. Among such beautiful things, all that is pleasing is waiting.

✲

Preparing the Soil

A man was digging up the soil in a garden. Someone came by and complained, "Why are you ruining this beautiful soil?" That person didn't understand the meaning of building up or tearing down.

If you don't turn over the soil, if you don't tear off its surface, then it will be ruined. That tearing apart of the surface and digging up of the soil is really its building up. Without that, the crop won't flourish.

❁

Help from He Who Knows

If help didn't come from God who is the Owner of all wisdom and knowledge, from *One Wise, All-Knowing* [27:6], what would become of the work of the saints? Their work wouldn't be perfected in forty thousand years. If they were to live twenty times as long, still it wouldn't be enough.

Muhammad (peace and blessings be upon him) reached in a very short time what other prophets couldn't reach in a thousand years. The power was given to him from the rank of God, the Owner of wisdom and knowledge.

❁

Submission

Let's go out and shave these mustaches—we aren't going to war such that we would expect to frighten the deniers with our long mustaches.[376] But even if you were to throw as many spears as these hairs against the denier within, still it wouldn't be chastened. Mine is not like that. The work of my soul (*nafs*) was completed long ago. . . .

Somebody asked me, "What is the meaning of the secret in the saying: 'The worst of people is the one who eats by himself'?"

"It is very difficult to explain the meaning of this to people," I said.

I wonder which are "those who have prostrated" who are mentioned in the Qur'an. They are not the prophets who have come and gone. Nor are they the companions of our great Prophet and those who follow him; they aren't even the four hundred and forty saints.

---

376 Before men went to war, they grew long mustaches in order to frighten the enemy. I.e., since we are not going to war, let's shave our mustaches.

The Greatest Gift

There is good news within me. I am amazed by these people who are happy without having received such good news.

Even if they put golden crowns on their heads, they shouldn't be satisfied. "What are we going to do with this?" they should say. "We need that inner light, that joy of heart." Let them say, "We wish they would take whatever we have, but give us what really belongs to us."

When I was a child, they would ask me, "You are always sad—do you need clothes or money?"

I would say, "I wish they would take my clothes, and give me to me!"

Space for Love

A pious one said, "I have divided my stomach into three compartments. I have reserved two thirds of it for bread and one third for air." And I heard another pious one say, "I have divided my stomach into two, half of it is for bread and the other half is for water. Air is subtle and light." And a third one said, "Let me fill my stomach with bread first. Water is subtle, it will remain above it, and it doesn't matter whether the breath remains above that or not."

Now, they are talking about secrets! And we are saying, "Let's fill the whole of our inside with love, and nothing else. Revelation is a subtle thing. It makes its own place itself—if it needs a soul, it comes. If it wants to go, it goes.

I wonder what these people think this way of friendship with God is! He is God who created the heavens and the earth, and who made the universe come into existence. They think that His love is easy—as if they could just sit with Him, and they talk or listen. Do you think this is some kind of beef soup you can just take, drink up, and leave?

❊

Reflecting Light

The Prophet Job (may the greeting and peace of God be upon him) was patient with the worms that gnawed his body to such a point that he reached felicity in that way. They say that two hundred thousand worms and insects were gnawing at him. Since I haven't counted them, I can't tell you their number—as if they have counted them and can say that is how it was!

It is told that when one of the worms fell down onto the ground, he would pick it up and put it back onto his wound. When one would look at his body from one side in the sunlight, one could see through to the other side!

In order to be able to see God, one needs to be a real servant! Then let him see what is possible—how many kinds of games of love He plays—as though he were making love with the Lord of the heavens and the earth, he sees Him/Her. And so, what can we do? A light sprang forth from behind the veil of pure sincerity (*ihklas*), and it reflected onto a wall.

The light that reflects on the heart is one thing and the light that reflects on the wall is something else. The breath of the Truth appears, and so, of course, he prostrates.[377]

❊

Extremity

In Isfahan they sell bread along with nails. The clever salesmen say, "Eat the bread; hammer the nail into your shoe."

And the severely crazy ones say, "You should hammer the nail into your forehead, and sell the bread with coffins."

And to those who say, "What would I do with a coffin?"

They answer, "Aren't you going to die one day? You'll need it!"

---

377 See *Mathnawi* II, 708-9, *The Pocket Rumi Reader*, p.102:

> Sunlight fell upon the wall; the wall received a borrowed splendor.
> Why set your heart on a piece of earth, O simple one?
> Seek out the source which shines forever.

Because bread is expensive there, they talk in extreme terms.

Struggling in the Way of God

God Most High has said, "*Certainly we will show Our ways to those who struggle on Our way* [29:69]." Read this verse either from the beginning to the end, or if you like, from the end to the beginning—read it the way you want to read it. In other words, you can also read it as "to the faithful ones who struggle on Our Way, We have shown Our ways"—the result is the same. The purpose is to struggle on the way of God. Otherwise the ones who walk on this way should be able to walk without our guidance—then how would it be possible for us to guide them? They say that the purpose of those *who struggle on Our way* which is not said by the tongue of the Prophet, but directly by God, is the apparent struggle and service of our body. And what is meant by *We show Our ways to them* are the paths of our spirits or our faith. Someone fasts on extra days—he remains hungry on Sundays, Thursdays, and on random days. Ride on the back of the self (*nafs*) so that you may be able to say, "I am fasting." Be strict with your *nafs* so that one day it may be surrendered (*muslim*)!

Shaikh Muhammad

The Prophet said, "Speak with people according to the capacity of their understanding." He didn't say, "According to the degree of your understanding." . . . [378]

Shaikh Muhammad would often say that such and such a person has made a mistake, or such and such a person has erred. Then I saw that he was also making mistakes, and from time to time, I would tell him so.

He would bow his head and say, "My son, you are cracking the whip strongly." Over the mountain—he was a mountain.

---

378 M. 300.

Sometimes he would be in a state and speak about it, and then I would show him about how he was in that station.

For example, one day we were plunged in this topic—we were saying that if a *hadith* of the Prophet has its similar in the Qur'an, well, that tradition is regarded as a sound *hadith*. [Shaikh Muhammad][379] was speaking about a *hadith* and asked, "Where is the similarity of this in the Qur'an?"

Just then, I saw that a state had come upon him. I wanted to bring him to the universe of "Jem," the station of unity, from that universe of separation which he was in, with words appropriate for his question.

I said, "There is a controversy as to whether this *hadith* that you have spoken is a real one or not." I asked, "Where in the Qur'an is the verse equivalent to the *hadith*, 'The People of knowledge are like one soul'?"

Immediately he answered and gave examples, "*Indeed, the faithful are siblings* [49:10], and *The creation of you all and the resurrection of you all is but as a single soul* [31:28]," and then he plunged into himself. He recognized that my purpose was not the question. My purpose was something other than that.

He said to me, "Son, you are striking the whip strongly."

He used to always address us as "Son!" and then laugh—in other words, "How should I be calling you, 'son'?"

Bearing Witness

They used to ask the Prophet about faith. And he would answer according to the state of the questioner, so that it might be an answer that would be appropriate for him. Once he said, "A Muslim is one from whose hand and tongue Muslims are safe." At another time he answered, "He is one who offers *salaat* and gives alms." Let's also find a solution, we are not helpless.

---

379 It seems that this is Muhammad Ibn al-Arabi to whom Shams is referring. They spent time together while Shams was in Damascus.

Let's find the remedy of the universe. If you know what an *alif* is, this means that you know the whole Qur'an. Let's take the verse *He created the heavens* [6:73].[380] One does not say that this is in the ancient beginning; it has no beginning. Everything dissolves at His rank, and is created again, so that there may be a clear witness for His Divinity. When you see the sun, bear witness, for *We have sent you as a witness, as a good news giver and a warner* [33:45].

O the dead one in love with untying knots!
O the poor one who isn't born in union,
  who dies in separation!
O the ignorant one who sleeps beside the sea,
  thirsting for water;
O the wretched one who dies begging,
  right next to the treasure!

"I know that the situation is bad, but my power is not enough to stop it." What kind of thing is this to say? I know that this sea has the power to drown people, shall I dive further into it? Or, this fire burns; or this is a well as deep as a hundred arshins; or it is the nest of a snake; this is a fatal poison; or this is a dangerous desert! Although I know it, I still go? If you know, don't go. If you don't know, then how can it be knowledge? How can one call this reason or knowledge? I've spoken this advice and words all for you.

If I had said these things to people in the city, hundreds of thousands would be showing me great respect. Many of the people would become my disciples. Some would weep and cut off their hair. They would sacrifice their sweet souls and their possessions. But it has never left a trace in you—as though you are rock or harder, your heart has not softened. They speak of a soft temperedness that is not

---

380 *And He it is who has created the heavens and the earth in accordance with [an inner] truth—and whenever He says, "Be," His word comes true; and His will be the dominion on the Day when the trumpet [of resurrection] is blown. He knows all that is beyond the reach of a created being's perception, as well as all that can be witnessed by a creature's senses or mind: for He alone is truly wise, all-aware.*

soft in actuality. It is only asinine—otherwise, advice would leave some trace in a human being.[381]

The Greatness of God

I am occupied with Muhammad—I am not living with any other nature but yours. I am behaving as a brother and companion, because there's someone else above him—God Most High, who has no end.

Sometimes, when I mention His greatness, it is out of respect and exalting Him, not because of any obligation. The station of, "He is the Truth," is much higher than "I am the Truth."[382]

What can the servants who are a secret of the secrets of God say about God? Whatever they say, it becomes ugly. God doesn't speak, but through His power He makes all beings speak, even inanimate things. If someone were to say, "If it is time for Him to speak, He speaks with words and a voice," I would say, "Another God is needed to make him speak, because God Most High is the owner of that power that makes everything speak and He, Himself never speaks in words."

The Prophet said, "Qualify yourself with the qualities of God." The character of God is both gentleness and stringency. It isn't only one flavor. Just as it has been said about the characteristics of the faithful, *Stringent towards the deniers, but compassionate among themselves* [48:29].

Candy

In Baghdad, a shaikh had withdrawn into seclusion. The night of the festival had come and within his seclusion, he heard a voice. From another universe this voice that came to him said, "We have given you the breath of Jesus—go out and show yourself to the people."

---

381 Shams seems to be referring again to the situation with Alaeddin, Mevlana's younger son who was jealous of Shams, hard-hearted and resistant to his teaching, and other conservatives who were banding together in opposition.

382 Shams is referring again to Mansur al-Hallaj.

For a while the shaikh plunged into meditation. What was the purpose of this voice? A test? Is it to test what I want? A second time a more awesome voice came, "Give up these hidden fears and doubts! Go out; mix with the people. We have given you the breath of Jesus!"

The shaikh wanted to contemplate a while—he was meditating to understand what the purpose of this was, but a third time a stronger and sharper voice thundered: "Be quick and go out. Don't stay here—leap up from your place!"

The shaikh sprang outside. It was the day of the New Year's festival. He joined with the crowds in Baghdad and began to walk about. He came across a candy-merchant who was selling sugar halvah in the shape of little birds. He was calling out, "Bird candies!"

"Let me test it," he thought to himself.

He called to him. People who saw this were watching in astonishment to see what the shaikh would do, because the shaikh wasn't interested in halvah.

He took the halvah shaped like a bird from the tray, held it in his hand, and breathed upon it. *Let me create for you out of clay the shape of a bird* [3:49]. The bird began to stir, and suddenly flesh, skin, and wings appeared, and away it flew.

People gathered and watched a few of those birds fly away. The shaikh quickly tired of this crowd of people and the attention they showed him, prostrating in front of him in astonishment. He set out for the open country, but the people followed him. No matter how many times he said, "Don't come! We have work to do in solitude"—still they wouldn't leave him alone.

He walked for a long time in the countryside. "O Lord!" he was saying, "What kind of a miracle was it that has imprisoned me and left me helpless?"

At that moment an inspiration came to him: "Do something so that they might go away."

The shaikh passed a great wind from his belly, and the people all looked at each other. They all shook their heads in denial, and went away.

Only one single person remained. He wasn't leaving. The shaikh wanted to ask him why he didn't leave with the others, but because of the radiance of the man's longing and the brilliance of his faith the shaikh hesitated. Instead, awe filled the shaikh.

Then despite this state, he asked him why he was staying.

The man replied, "It was not because of that wind that I came in the first place, so why should I leave because of this wind. As I see it, this wind is better than that wind, because by this wind your blessed self has attained ease, while that wind only brought you pain and difficulty."

A Difference in Words

There are friends who with a single word save their friends from pain. They relate the reasons of the Friend to those who are entangled in false illusions, and they both help their friends reach comfort and also find ease themselves, while somebody else withholds a few words that might be needed, or wants to drown his friend with his words.

Aren't these words of yours worth something? Pay attention to which words are more mature—is this a more complete word or that one? If this word is more mature, more complete, the other isn't worth much. The only thing to do is to throw that outside oneself and fill oneself with this.

Good fortune is in this—don't keep speaking your own words all the time, so that they may not drive more mature words away! Remembering those incomplete words impedes the remembering of these mature words. Speak of this—that is, the good word; don't talk about that—that is the bad word! One should not speak words that tell of your secrets or the words that have been conveyed to you.[383]

---

383 As Mevlana says in his *Fihi ma Fihi* (*Signs of the Unseen*, p.73):

> Thus we advise our friends. When your "brides of intrinsic meaning" are manifested within you and the mysteries are revealed, beware! Again I say, beware lest you tell them to others. Expound them not, and do not relate the words you hear from us to just anybody. "Give not wisdom to the unworthy lest you wrong it; withhold it not from the worthy lest you wrong them." If you had a

❊

Though Love Is a Trouble, It Is a Joy

What is the meaning of *God has ascended upon the Throne* [20:5]?

A sultan had three sons.[384] They wanted to set out on a campaign. For several days, their father advised them, and maybe ten times repeatedly he cautioned them, "There is such and such a fortress on the way. It is a castle like this. . . . When you arrive there, say, 'Allah! Allah!' and pass by; never enter that castle!"

If the sultan hadn't given them this advice, maybe no curiosity or excitement to look in the direction of that castle would have been awakened in his sons, and they would have passed by and gone on. But because of his insistent counsels, a hidden curiosity and attraction awoke in them. They said, "We wonder what is in the fortress that our father so strictly forbids us to enter into it." As it is said, "A person becomes inclined toward what is forbidden."

When they came to the castle—it is a well-known story—they saw a wall upon which was the portrait of the sultan's daughter. As soon as they saw her portrait, they fell in love with her. They went and asked for the hand of the girl from her father. The sultan ordered, "Take them and show them the ditch filled with heads that have been chopped off."

The sultan's oldest son exclaimed, "Let me go to bring a sign, a token." But he was left helpless, and they killed him, too. The middle one was sacrificed the same way. It came to the turn of the youngest brother. He was bound by the same love.

The father of the girl said, "If you haven't taken a warning from the others, haven't you at least taken a lesson from the end of your own brothers?"

---

beloved concealed in your house and she had said to you, "Do not show me to anyone, for I am yours alone," would it ever be right to parade her around the marketplace and tell everybody, "Come and see this one"? Would your beloved like it? She would be furious with you and run off to another. God has forbidden these words to those "others."

384 M. 305.

The boy answered:

"In love, patience is not sufficient.
Patience isn't quick enough for yearning.
Patience might be nice,
But the heart won't listen to advice."

He felt compelled, and he persisted in asking for the hand of the girl. When the girl's nanny understood the sincere love of the boy, her heart softened. She counseled him to have a golden statue of an ox made, to enter into it, and to hide there. By a ruse, this ox was taken to the girl's pavilion.

At night, after others went to sleep, for these young lovers sleep would vanish under the tender light of love. The time of the tasting of love would begin. Under cover of the night, the prince would emerge from the ox statue. The candles were lit, wine was passed around, and the curly tresses of the girl became wet with the wine of love. When day broke, people would see signs, but nobody was in sight.

As a sign of this union, the boy received a bracelet from the girl. He would show it to her father saying that he had brought a sign from his daughter. Without even seeing any signs or miracles from him, the people also fell in love with his true, sincere love, and their hearts became bound to him. Because he was such a fine young man, they told each other, "If the sultan ever plots against his life, let's plot against the sultan's."

The prince found out about this and said, "There is no need for that. If I reveal this sign, as soon as he sees it, the sultan will die, and then you can take him by his feet and throw him out."

When he went into the presence of the sultan, he asked, "Where is the sign?"

The prince answered, "I've brought it, but let us—you, the vizier, and I—withdraw from the others, and I'll show you such a sign that reason will fly out of your head. Have no doubt about this—rest assured. They withdrew in solitude. The prince threw the scarf, ring and other presents that he had received from the girl in front of them, revealing them all.[385]

> With your grace, grief turns to joy;
> With your praise, life becomes infinite.
> Although love is a trouble, it is a joy.
> Though this wine is full of headaches, still it delights.
> Though being occupied with love is difficult,
> how sweet it is to trade hearts with you, O beloved.

❊

Developing the Inner Guardian

The Prophet Moses (may the greeting of God be upon him), even with his exalted station, begged for the help and companionship of Khidr, so that he might obtain an even greater subtlety as a prophet than he had. In order to perfect this attribute, he kept repenting.

A dervish must repent once and for all in his life, and regret what has happened and feel the pain of it, asking, "Why has this thing crossed my path?" The power of self-examination within us must become active:

How will I protect myself so that something that might be a veil for me might not come before me?—I get rid of one secret fear within me, and then a greater one comes and keeps me occupied defending myself, so that I lose the possibility of being occupied with my Self.

> When a cat snatches meat from me,
> I get busy with catching the cat.
> And lose the eating of the meat.

❊

What Is a Dervish?

At first, I didn't use to sit with the jurists, I would sit with dervishes. I used to say, "Those people are strangers to dervishhood." But when

---

385 Shams relates a short summary of the story that Mevlana later developed as the context for the conclusion of his *Mathnawi*. See "The Castle and The Three Princes," at the end of Book VI which emerged during his last days. Due to his illness, he was not able to fully express the tale of the third brother. The *Mathnawi* closes with the words, "Surely there is a window from heart to heart."

I understood what dervishhood is and where these people are, now I would rather sit in the company of jurists than with these dervishes, because the jurists have at least borne the burden of struggle. These people boast, "We are dervishes." But where is the dervish?

All the great prophets have burned within the love of dervishhood, to the extent that Moses cried out, "Make me one of the community of Muhammad." For those of the community of Muhammad are the ones to whom this has been given.

Every story has a kernel, an essential subtle point. The great ones have told stories for the sake of that kernel, not just to keep from being bored. They tell a story to reveal the purpose within it. Nevertheless, the one who remains silent will be saved in the service of the great ones, because:

> What a young person sees in a mirror,
> an experienced master can see in a brick.

When you converse with someone you keep watching to see—is there a veil in front of his eye and heart—how can it be removed? The point of speaking is to remove that veil.

The heart of a shaikh isn't informed only through the external senses, but through revelation and inspiration as well. Just as it is said in the Qur'an, "*I become his/her ear and eye. . . . He/she sees with the divine light of God. . . . His heart didn't contradict what he saw* [53:11-12]."

> They are aware of all the states of the heavens.
> They are the attained ones who search for the Truth
> and reveal the way.
> But because of their beautiful nature,
> they don't tear away anyone's veil.
> as though it is they who make time move.

❈

The Noblest Character

Adorn yourselves with the character of God. My dear Prophet! *Without a doubt you have been adorned with the noblest character* [68:4].

> When you are earning your livelihood,
> join together with others, and get along well with them.

> Strive for the gentle character of God,
> and discard ugly attributes.

Every child of a human being has an ego. If one could foresee where one would end up, would one ever support the claims of one's ego? Of course, everyone would avoid egoism. But those who came before could not see the end. Well, this is the superiority of Muhammad, who is the sultan and seal of the prophets. If a lover liberates himself from loving himself, the darling whom he loves and longs for also gives up love of her self.

> Whatever they say, this is its inner meaning:
> Death is dead and this is being alive.

❁

Enduring Blows

If a stranger strikes me a hundred times, I won't say a thing, but I'll take one I love to task for the touch of a tip of a hair. It's like the story they tell of Hallaj-i Mansur—ice rains from it. Only one of this state will catch the taste of this story.

They say that when they pulled Hallaj to the gallows, the decree of the Law was that the people of Baghdad should stone him. They all threw huge stones fit for a catapult.[386] His friends were also forced to do this—helpless, they joined in, but instead of stones they threw bouquets of roses. Hallaj moaned deeply and cried out. One of those who saw this asked him in amazement, "Why is it that you didn't make a sound because of those stones, yet you cried out when roses were thrown?"

"Don't you know," he said, "that harshness from a beloved is harder."

❁

The Wise One Can See in a Brick . . .

For years, a man had been searching for a spiritual guide. Whenever he heard of someone, he used to run to that person, but no door

386 M. 310.

opened. One day, he put his head on a brick and fell asleep. Then, in his dream, he saw what he had been searching for. When he awoke, immediately he began to kiss the brick, he embraced it. Then wherever he went, he tucked it under his arm. He didn't make prayers without it; he didn't go visiting people without it; when he went to express condolences to someone, or when he went to a wedding, or when he went to sleep, always, he and the brick were together. Even when he was sick and defecating he was never without the brick. If someone came and wanted to praise him, he would say, "First tell it to this brick of mine, this jewel of mine!" If a visitor approached him and wanted to shake his hand, he would say, "First acknowledge this brick with your hand." And to those who asked, "What is this?!" he would say, "What isn't it—whatever is good comes from it, and the bad goes. For thirty years I had lost something, but the night I put my head on this brick, I found it."

> O Darling! O Soul! How can my heart believe this?
> I never guessed I would reach you!
> I wasn't grieving, but heaven disliked this
> state of mine—
> yet the time when I was longing for you
> was to me even more pleasing.

❊

I Wish Infinite Life for all My Friends

I wish infinite life for all my friends. I am not praying for anything else, especially for you because you have nourished and matured both our outside and our inside; thousands of advantages have come to us from you. If you have been surprised at this news of mine, know that I am the attributes of the Truth and my attributes mean His attributes. My knowledge is His knowledge and His attribute. They say: God has a gentle nature and patience. Each instance of patience of His lasts a hundred or even a thousand years.

> O piece of moon! You were born and you shone,
> You wandered around your own heaven, swaying!
> You know you were together with the soul;
> Then suddenly, you waned and vanished.

Be Vigilant (Taqwa)

I complained about him that he did not protect me,
but he warned me to abandon my sins.

Everybody has his or her own sin. One person's sin is drunkenness and inappropriate behavior; it fits with his or her state. Another's sin is remaining far from God. There is an anger that from time to time rebels; at times it hides. Its business is to keep hidden. But how can any living creature protect itself from committing a crime? By knowing his or her own state.

In short, a cat doesn't leave the holes it's watching.[387]

The Gold of the Qur'an

A young man wanted to learn the Qur'an. Though he had already borne many difficulties in memorizing it, still a desire remained. "Where is one who recites beautifully?" he wondered. He was begging God to introduce him to someone who could recite from among the folk of the Qur'an who might also be one of God's folk.

Suddenly, he heard about such a reciter in Baghdad. Immediately, he went to find him. He repeated every verse he had memorized for the teacher, and the teacher corrected him, saying, "Recite like that . . . or recite like this. . . ."

This student of the Qur'an then saw that he had spent his whole life in vain and would have to begin his work all over again. "Whatever will be, let it be!" he said.

The teacher said, "It is my father's custom to ask one gold coin for the study of each page."

He answered, "Agreed."

He began to teach the secrets of the Qur'an to the young student. The student's heart was pleased with it, and happily he gave his teacher the gold coins. However, a day came when he had no more gold to give, and this made him sad.

---

387 I.e, Know yourself; watch to catch the compulsive self in its gyrations.

Not long thereafter, he encountered an old man who noticed his sadness and asked him the reason for his sorrow. When he told him about the situation, the old man laughed and took him home with him, welcoming him as his guest, but he couldn't eat anything because of his grief.

Then the old man said to him, "Your teacher is my son, and the gold coins you have given him are under this carpet. My son doesn't need gold. The blessed Prophet has said, 'Whoever is not rich with the Qur'an is not one of us.' Our gold is the Qur'an; our property, strength, and being is the Qur'an. We have not learned the Qur'an like this to be in need of anything else. This was only to test you. Look, all your money is here; take it and go," he said.

Test Your Donkey Now

If you hadn't forgotten remembrance, you wouldn't be in need of advice now, and we wouldn't have to appear to want from you a year old donkey foal that can't cross a bridge. You ride your young donkey; he shies and runs at a shadow; his legs tremble on a bridge; he binds the world to his soul. He has to carry some load; test him here. If he can pass over a bridge, all the better; if not, one must send him back immediately, because otherwise he will take you to the middle of the bridge, and even though his friends pass over, he won't be able to. Then it is impossible to return and impossible to move forward. So test him here, so that you may understand. Just as it says in the Qur'an, "*Allah who knows all, tests their faith* [60:10]."[388]

How will We Become Clean?

They say that one shouldn't mention the name of God when one is on the toilet, that it isn't appropriate to recite the Qur'an then

388 It seems Shams had given advice that wasn't followed, so Shams is offering advice again: dervish, train your donkey, your *nafs*, now, before the call to the other world comes.

even with a low voice. But then what will I do with the filth within myself, when I cannot get rid of it myself?[389]

❊

The Devil's Disguises

He said, "The king doesn't want to get off his horse—he's gathered his soldiers, and the devil is leading him, but the king keeps saying, 'Absolutely, this is God.' But so that they might accept him, the devil also appears in the form of God."

I said to that man, "How can the devil take the form of God?"

In his book, one can read the family tree of a hundred Bayazids. If he unfurls his sleeve, a hundred Abu Said's (Abul Khayr) pour out. He has both subtle energy and material powers.

Where does lust come from? It blurs the mind of those who cause veiling. Say, "Uncover your own self, and throw these thoughts away."[390]

Now, only those who have been properly brought up with courtesy by their parents can serve their parents.

> Mothers and fathers don't harm their children,
> but reason and spirit are within the hand
> of the saints.[391]

---

389 See *Mathnawi* II, 1366-1367, *The Pocket Rumi Reader*, p.108:

> Water says to the dirty, "Come here."
> The dirty one says, "I am so ashamed."
> Water says, "How will your shame be washed away
> without me?"

390 Such a person is causing others (women, the self) to be veiled because his own mind is blurred with lust. See discourse twenty of Mevlana's *Fihi Ma Fihi, Signs of the Unseen,* p.90-94.

391 I.e., spiritual parents, the parents of humanity—*wali* (*veli*) also has the meaning of "parent." The *veli* as guardian is also in charge of the child until the age of adulthood. Saints are our guardians throughout our lives. Taking their hand, with their help we learn true service/worship, and become perfected with God's grace. *The Hand of God is over their hands* [48:10].

❊

Rose Petals Are Falling

The wind blew—the rose petals fell
over the drunken lovers' heads.
The beloved arrived, and the wine was poured
into the goblets of the friends.
That hyacinth hair and those rose cheeks
have chased away the joy of the brave
attar-makers.
Those intoxicating narcissus eyes have shed the blood
of the sober.

According to our criterion, love is not in heads.
The strange thing is that our burden is heavier
than that of our saddle beast.
When the face, the beauty, of our beautiful one
is the subject of our talk,
we are not worthy of her, nor can we be her equal.[392]

If I look for a heart, I see it where you are.
If I want a soul, I find it in the curls of your hair.
If I am long without water and then drink,
In that bowl, I see the image of your face.

Can there be a more ruined state of heart than this?
Or is there an event more without beginning or end
than this?
In the whole universe, which poor one exists
Who has suffered and is more bewildered and in awe
than this?

O Soul of the universe, how pleasant it is to die,
when the sword is Yours, and the throat is mine.

❊

Catching the Fragrance

They have evaluated all the beauties of the universe, and for each one of them they have attributed a certain worth. O Dear Soul!

---

392 By speaking of her, we move into separation. Don't speak of the secrets of the beloved—keep that precious intimacy hidden.

What is the value of this ugly one whom no one appreciates?

You are saying, "Due to my wooziness after a drunken sleep, hundreds of jugs will break into pieces."

I wonder, if you haven't also caught that fragrance, since you, too, have become so drunk.

The True Heart

O heart! Go and be one of those who
contemplate the end![393]
In the universe of strangerhood, be one
of those of certainty!
If you want to ride on the morning wind,
Be the dust stirred by the saddlebeasts
of the dervishes!

The Trap of Self

One who interprets the verse, "*The All-Merciful is seated on His throne* [20:5]," needs to also speak about the subtle saying, "The one who knows himself knows his Lord." There is a hidden treasure here. Let it be explained and let there be no confusion, because someone who has dealings with his or her egoistic desires can correct neither himself nor others. "[*O My representative!*] *Whether or not you speak aloud; truly, He knows everything that is secret and that which is yet more hidden* [20:7]." The place of the *nafs* (ego-self) and its passions is only under one's feet. In Muhammad you can find *Ahad* (the One), but in *Ahad* you cannot find Muhammad.[394]

---

393 M. 315.

394 The dervish rides upon his *nafs* and is its master, rather than the other way around. See *Mathnawi* V:1089-1103. Let the Jesus of your spirit ride your ass; let it not be forced to carry it.

"Ahmad" is another name for Muhammad. "Ahmad," contains the letters for "*Ahad*," but the word "*Ahad*" is empty of the "m" consonant for the individual, "Ahmad." Within Muhammad there is Oneness, but within the One, any individual existence vanishes.

Witnessing

In court, the open confession of a crime by the defendant is better than hearing the testimony of eighty witnesses. Let's look at the wisdom in the words, *Say: which is the greatest testimony? Say: Allah is the All-Seeing* [6:19].

They say, "Does any Muslim say, 'This person is an unbeliever, a denier,' for someone whom he or she doesn't know?" They don't read their own letters, but they say, "So and so has become an unbeliever."

Yes, perhaps he was a denier, but now he is one of the faithful.

Discernment

Zeyneddin Sadaka said, "Let's bow our heads; let's be in the Presence and contemplate."

But because of the distance of a mere inch, you got stuck on the Way. Beyond this point are the desolate deserts. From Aksaray to Konya is a journey of only an inch, and yet you were left behind on that way of only an inch in breadth! The rest is the desert of non-being. But look for the Way and ask, "Is this the Way?" Investigate. Be wary; don't let those who mislead rob you! Be a person of clear vision and discern the right from the wrong! Because in the middle, the Way splits into branches. One comes from this direction, another goes in that direction. Keep going in the right direction. After you have arrived in Konya, there is no need to think of anything else. A just sultan lives there who causes no harm to anyone.

The Fortress of La illaha illallah

"*La illaha illallah* (there is no god but God) is My fortress. Whoever takes refuge in My fortress becomes secure (*hadith qudsi*)." Whoever goes into this fortress of oneness—He did not say, "whoever only says the name of the fortress." To say the name is easy; you say, "I have entered the fortress," or "I went to Damascus." But if it were just a matter of the tongue, in an instant you could ascend from earth to the heavens or to the Empyrean and the Throne.

The Prophet Muhammad said, "The faithful one who says "*La illaha illallah*" with purity and from the heart, enters Paradise." Now you sit and say, "He is One." But who are you? You are more than six thousand! Become One! Otherwise, is His Oneness your concern? You are a hundred thousand particles, and each particle of yours is being carried off by some desire; within each particle of yours, you are carrying an illusion. The one who demonstrates purity of intention, and sincerity of action, goes to Paradise. There is no need for a promise such as, "If he or she has been able to do this, he or she enters Paradise." If he or she has been able to do this, he or she is completely Paradise itself.

Running towards the Truth

Someone said to those who had gathered, "Now, let everyone put his head upon his knees and contemplate a while."

After a while, one of them raised his head and said, "I witnessed the greatness of the Empyrean and the Throne."

Another said, "My glance passed beyond both the Empyrean and the Throne—I dove through space into infinite emptiness."

Someone else said, "I am watching the back of the Ox of the earth and the Fish of the sea, and I can see even the angels that protect this Ox and Fish."

Another said, "No matter where I look, I can see nothing but my own helplessness. I am like a bird hung by its two feet. I have been hanged, but I am hanging in the trap of the Beloved. I say, "Welcome!"—I was asking for this. I don't want a spindle for winding thread, but two mines—a mine of gold and a mine of silver. Or rather, I am looking for the way of liberation from both mine and space—I want no one but Him. There are some who don't find poverty suitable, but wealth suits them.

It is poverty that leads the human being to the Truth—it makes one run away from everything other than the Truth. There is also another poverty that makes one run away from the Truth toward creation.

Those who prefer thorns to roses
Are fit for the gallows, not pulpits.

☼

Rosy Moments

O Darling! Just look—only a very little of this
soul is left.
Today, suffer my trouble just a little longer;
Only the time of a single dawn remains.
The color and shape of your beautiful cheek,
Have put roses into water,
And left the moon in difficulty.
I have no more gold or silver—
yet why would you turn away from us?
As a remembrance of my love,
only a golden bowl is left at your door.
You've claimed my heart,
but on Your way I've also sacrificed my soul.
Can one say any more than this?
Only a single right of Yours remains upon us.
At least for these few moments, suffer with us!
Because in the book of our lives only a single
page is left!

☼

Be Empty

Happiness belongs to the person who has been bound to a shaikh for a reason or a purpose, because a time comes when suddenly that connection occurs without expectation of anything in return. One relinquishes one's *nafs*, one stops being concerned about oneself and causality, and speaks like this:

We can't be contained by any measure[395]
We have lots to do, but like the ney,
on the inside we are empty.

---

395 Remember the *hadith qudsi*: The heavens and earth cannot contain Me, but I can be contained within the heart of My faithful servant. When the heart of the dervish is empty of self, God can enter.

If we look carefully at ourselves,
clearly and with awareness
and if we come to ourselves,
Then we understand that we are both
less than ourselves,
And yet we are also ourselves.

Why didn't God say to his Prophet, "Say: I am the one and only God," but instead He said, "*O My representative! Say: He* [*That is, God Who is unseen*] *is God who is uniquely one* [112:1]?"[396]

Samad means "empty in the inside" and "without a belly." Someone whose belly is empty is a witness to the existence of the One who has no belly, no need, in other words, *As-Samad*, God Most High.[397] He is like this. Similarly, *Ahad* is not one of the numbers itself but is the evidence of these numbers and their proof. In other words, numberlessness is also a proof for numbers. Now let's come again to the saying, "The one who knows himself knows his Lord." Then there is no doubt within the *nafs*; it is immersed in Him.

O You! Everything is You

Keep to the religion of old women—that is, "O You! Everything is You!"

Since the old woman says, "Everything," the old woman is also contained within this "everything." Therefore, to say these words is better than to say, "I am the Truth."

Even though he arrived at the Truth, he did not reach the reality of the Truth, the inner meaning of the Truth. If he had been aware of the Truth of the Truth, [Hallaj] wouldn't have said, "I am the Truth."

---

396 *Qul huwallahu ahad* [112:1].

397 *Allahu samad* [112:2]. *As-samad*, which occurs in the Qur'an only once, is applied to God alone. It encompasses the concepts of Primary Cause and eternal, independent Being, combined with the idea that everything existing or conceivable goes back to Him as its source and is, therefore, dependent on Him for its beginning as well as for its continued existence.

One whose "belly is empty," who is empty of self and ego desires, stands in unity as proof of that One, the Source of all that is.

And so, our spiritual guide, the one who holds our hand says, "Keep to the religion of old women." Learn from an old woman.

The proof they offer about the existence of God is that they say, "Nothing but God exists. God is."

❁

The Beloved's Trap

Your beauty is the grain
within the trap of troubles.
It is such a candle
That constantly it burns our moths.
O Darling! I love the chains of your hair,
Because they fit the feet of my crazy ruined heart.

When the dust settles down you will see
Whether it's a donkey you are riding or
an Arabian horse.[398]

❁

The Blessings of Poverty

A shaikh said, "I have a hundred distinguished disciples. Even if I am dying from hunger, none of them will give me a loaf of bread."

But ours aren't like this; they are completely the opposite. I said to the shaikh, "You are saying, 'I have a hundred disciples.'"

He said, "I wish I had one single *murid* (student)."

And I added, "And merge yourself with him, be with him!"

They came to Burhannuddin the Judge and told him, "Such and such a dervish insulted you after you left. He said, 'He is indigent.'"

The judge became angry. One of the assistant judges said, "Let me go see to that dervish."

He came straight to me and asked, "Why have you disparaged our master, the Judge? What are you thinking? 'He is indigent,' you have said! . . . Actually, he is occupied with the concerns of the indigent."

I replied, "With all his greatness, Muhammad (peace and blessings be upon him) used to beg God: 'O my God! Make me live as

398 M. 320.

one who is needy; kill me as one who is needy, and gather me after death within the companionship of the needy.'"

☼

The Real Madrasah

One day, some Companions of the Prophet came to see him. "There is a man here who is neither with the deniers, nor the Muslims. We see him pray, and we don't see him occupied in gaming or other such things. We don't see the attributes of the mad in him, nor the seeking for livelihood of the sensible.

Some others also spoke about him.

A feeling of compassion arose within the Master. He said, "Now go, and when you see him, convey my greeting to him, and say: 'Our Master wants very much to see you.' Don't command him to come here; do your best not to injure his feelings!"

They came near the man, and at first, they weren't able to greet him. After some time passed, the opportunity opened and they conveyed the greeting of the Prophet to him, and his love and strong wish to see him. All the while, he kept silent. They obeyed the command of the Prophet about not creating trouble for him and didn't speak further.

After a while, they saw that the man had come to visit Muhammad. For some time, he sat silently in the gathering. The Prophet sat silently and he was silent, too. At last, Muhammad stood up from his place. Both when the man arrived and when he was leaving, the Prophet behaved with great humility towards him. He said, "Abundant light has poured upon you"—great grace has poured down upon you. Our madrasah is this—these four walls made of flesh. The instructor is very great. I cannot say who He is. And His tutor is the heart; just as some people of God have said, "My heart has informed me about my Lord."

The House of God

Abu Yazid was going on hajj. It was his custom whenever he arrived in a city, to first visit the shaikhs, and then accomplish other work. He arrived in Basra and went to visit a dervish, who asked him, "O Abu Yazid, where are you going?"

He said, "To Mecca, to visit the house of God."

He asked, "What provision do you have for the journey?"

He responded, "Two hundred dirhams."

He said, "Get up and circumambulate me seven times,[399] and give that money to me."

Abu Yazid jumped up, took his money from his belt, kissed it and placed it in front of him.

He said, "O Abu Yazid, where are you going?! That is the house of God, and this heart of mine is also the house of God. But by the God who is the Lord of that house and the Lord of this house, ever since they built that house He has not gone into it, and ever since the day of building of this house He has never left it!"

Junayd Baghdadi

The children were pointing out to each other Junayd Baghdadi, may the Mercy of God be upon him, and saying, "He is the man who for God's sake stays awake all night."

When Junayd heard this, he said, "Let me not prove them wrong." Even though before that he hadn't been going to sleep until the middle of the night, from then on, he made a habit of staying awake all night until dawn. So it is possible that the faith and grace of the faithful may also have their effect upon the one in whom they have faith.

The people of God look for ways to hide themselves, but God wants to reveal Himself in a thousand ways.

---

399 When on *hajj* (pilgrimage), one of the rites is to circumambulate the *Kaaba* (the Holy House of God in Mecca) seven times.

To begin with, wakefulness was the soul of Junayd. Then later, they said, "You are too weak, you must rest at night, you must sleep!"

But in the beginning, one must strive continuously.

☼

The Awakened Heart

Happy is the one who gives his eye and his heart.
What a shame that they give their eyes,
but not their hearts.

Happy is the one whose eyes sleep,
but whose heart doesn't sleep!
Woe to the one whose eyes do not sleep
but whose heart does!

When stress increases, then the window of the heart opens. Unintentionally, someone knocks aginst the door and it opens. Now pay attention so that it doesn't shut.

Since the window is open, whether you want to or not, you see everyone who passes by. When it is closed, you hear the sounds of those who pass by and you sense a taste, but how can that be compared to this?

You will see, when the dust clears,
whether you are riding a horse or an ass.

Many times the dust has cleared, and we have seen that what we are riding is an Arabian stallion.

☼

Who Has the Remedy?

A bald person once said to another bald one, "Give me a remedy!"

And the other bald one answered, "Well, if I had a remedy, I would have used it on my own head."

☼

You Will See

"O My God," they say, "Do this," or "Don't do that." However, one needs to say, "O Great Sultan! Take this jug and put it there [near to you]."

How can the Sultan say, "No! That's impossible." He is the one who commands, "Do this," and "Don't do that!"

The Prophet (peace and blessings upon him) said, "What power do I have within my hand? I am only the Messenger of God."

God said to him, "*You cannot guide those whom you love to the right path. Only God can guide the one whom He wishes, to the right path* [28:56]."[400] Is He making us err? You will see.[401]

"You will see," is not usually said to everyone. How could it be correct to say it to everyone? It is not right to say to one blind from birth, "you will see." It is said to one of whose self and existence only a little remains—the rest has all become spirit. In other words, "Shake off the dust of existence!"

Muhammad and the Great Struggle

The Messenger of God develops and improves the fermentation of everyone who has yeast; but if there is no yeast, what will he improve?

I have seen that all the people of the house and the city were wandering and turning around him. Among his miracles, I have seen

---

400 *Surah al-Qasas*, The Story, 28:56:

Truly, you cannot guide aright everyone whom you love: but it is God who guides him that wills [to be guided]; and He is fully aware of all who would let themselves be guided.

401 God tells us "You will see!" in a number of places in the Qur'an, for instance, see *Surah az-Zumar*, The Throngs 39:53-70:

Say: "[Thus speaks God:] 'O you servants of Mine who have transgressed against your own selves! Despair not of God's mercy: behold, God forgives all sins—for, truly, He alone is much-forgiving, a dispenser of grace!'"

Hence, turn towards your Sustainer [alone] and surrender yourselves unto Him before the suffering [of death and resurrection] comes upon you, for then you will not be succoured . . .

And [so,] on the Day of Resurrection you will see . . . and lo! standing, they will begin to see [the truth]!

And the earth will shine bright with her Sustainer's light. And the record [of everyone's deeds] will be laid bare, and all the prophets will be brought forward, and all [other] witnesses; and judgment will be passed on them all in justice. And they will not be wronged, for every human being will be repaid in full for whatever [good or evil] he has done: and He is fully aware of all that they do.

such a divine light that it cannot be defined or described. I looked up and couldn't see the roof of the house.

Just then, my father said to me, "O my son!" And like two rivers, bloody tears gushed from his eyes. Within that state, he wanted to say something else, but his mouth was closed, and he could not speak. His illness increased, and suddenly he went.

In his kitchen, sacks of salt were consumed. Imagine the rest! But despite this wealth, he used to sell baskets (woven of rushes or palm leaves) and sit on the bare ground. He used to bring the poor and eat with them. "O Lord!" he used to say, "I am poor, I live with the poor."

The essence of the matter is that—I wish everyone were like that! Those who try to make claims about themselves—"I am like that," or 'I am like this"—are brainless people. My purpose in these insults and hard words is this—that harshness and roughnesss may come out from the inside and emerge to their outside, so that it might not fester and cause harm. . . .

As they say, "Someone who hurts others, without having been hurt, is an ass." But endurance and tolerance are at their maximum degree—I have nothing to do with hurt, because no existence remains in me. Suffering is due to existence. My body is full of pleasant feelings. Why would I gather outside troubles to myself. I cast them away with answers, and cursing. Just as after the return from battle the Prophet said, "Now, we have come back from the lesser struggle and begun the greater struggle!" What is the greater struggle? It is not fasting, it is not the *salaat.* The greater struggle of this community is to get along well with one another.

✲

If You Are a Duck, Act Like One

Someone came and said, "Alas! The Tatar raiders have arrived; how horrible a happening!"[402]

"Aren't you ashamed?" I said, "For such a long time you have been claiming to be a duck—so why are you trembling because of a flood?"

---

402 M. 325.

❁

Reading God's Book

The book of Muhammad, the Messenger of God, would not be useful for me unless first I have my own book—otherwise, without a heart, even if I read a thousand books, still I'll be left in darkness. Those who don't know the secrets of the saints of God read their books, but everybody adds their own imaginings, and then accuses the owner of the words, rather than finding fault with themselves. They never say, "The mistake is not in those words, but rather it is in our own ignorance and imaginings."

❁

Honey Preserves

I wish people knew that happiness is in the gathering of friends—that they might mingle with each other, and show their beautiful faces, so that love might appear among them. When one by one, desires come between them, their brightness vanishes.

If you keep something within honey, it remains fresh and sweet—the air cannot find a way into it to spoil it.

❁

A Master of Words

A master of calligraphy used to write in three different styles. One, only he himself could read, no one else could read it. The second, both he and others could read, and the third kind, he couldn't read nor could anyone else.

I speak, but I don't know these words, nor does anyone else!

Some talk about interpreting verses, but these are not that—what is really needed is for you to liberate yourself.

❁

One Witness

Somebody was suing someone. They wanted witnesses. He brought ten Sufis. The judge said, "Bring one more witness."

The plaintiff said, "Your honor, it has been said, *And call upon two of your men to act as witnesses* [2:282]. I have brought ten."

The judge answered: "These ten are all one single witness—even if you bring a hundred thousand Sufis, still they'll be as one."

❁

Bowing before Creation

Things that are very pleasing to people—desires and the beauties of the world—seem ugly to us. However, if it is for the wish or happiness of someone, I bow my head and endure everything. Because they are the *qiblah* of the Beloved and of everyone.[403] This is how it is evaluated. How could I argue with such a Beloved?

❁

Becoming a Full Moon

God advises His Prophet, "Say, 'My God! Increase me in knowledge [20:114].'" He is saying, "For the sake of my heart, don't acquire this knowledge! How can intellect fit into this?" Here, the clever are deniers—the intellect is a denier. Philosophers are under the judgment of the intellect. Those dogs were openly calling Shahabuddin a denier. How could Shahabuddin be a denier?[404] With such light! Yes, before the Sun, he is a denier, but when he sincerely enters service to the Sun, he becomes the full moon.

❁

Uways al-Qarani

Uways al-Qarani, may God be pleased with him, could not come to be in the presence of Muhammad while the Prophet was alive. Uways did not leave his homeland, but the veils in between them had disap-

---

403 Shams is indicating that creation is God's *qiblah* as in the *hadith qudsi*, "I was a Hidden Treasure, and I loved to be known, so I created the two worlds in order that My treasure of loving-kindness and generosity might be known."

404 Shams is referring here to Shihabuddin Suhrawardi (Maqtul).

peared.[405] His reason was that his mother needed his help, and he was helping her in obedience to God and His Prophet. The Prophet, peace be upon him, informed Umar and some of his Companions about him. He said, "If he comes after I'm gone, his mark is this. . . . Convey my greetings to him, but don't say much more."

After the Prophet emigrated from the world, Uways mother passed away. He visited the grave of Muhammad at a time when the Great Companions were away. Some of the other Companions asked many questions about his state. He answered them and told them of his reason for not coming. They said, "What is a mother or a father that a person could make such a mistake as not to come to serve the Prophet of God?"

No matter how much Uways explained his reasons to them, and how it was at the instruction of the Blessed Prophet and not due to his own desires or nature, he couldn't make them understand. They kept accusing him, and kept on talking.

At last, Uways turned to them and said, "How long did you live in the company of Blessed Mustafa?"

"For such and such years," each one of them separately answered. They said, "Each one of those days is worth more than a thousand years. How could we calculate it?"

> For a moment if you find yourself with the beloved,
> within that one moment of your life,
> you receive your portion of grace!
> Be careful not to waste that moment!
> Because only rarely is such a moment found again.

Uways said, "So, I ask you, what was the mark of Muhammad?" A few of them began to speak: "He was this tall."

---

405 M. 330.

Uways al-Qarani is an example of one who received his teaching directly through the Unseen. Since that time, other Sufis who do not belong to a particular *tariqah* (sufi brother/sisterhood), nor follow a particular teacher in the outer world, and yet reach enlightenment through the hand of the Unseen, have been known as Uwaysi Sufis, unless they themselves are confirmed as a Pir of a new lineage. Uways was among those who preferred to remain hidden.

"The complexion of his face was. . . ."

Uways said, "I am not asking about those."

They said, "He was so humble, so generous. Day and night he would worship . . . *awake [in prayer] nearly two-thirds of the night, or one-half of it, or a third of it* [73:20]."

"I am not asking about these things, either," Uways said.

Some of them said, "His knowledge was like this, his miracles were like that."

And he responded, "I am not asking about that, either."

If the great ones of the Companions had been there, he wouldn't have asked this question, because he would have seen Muhammad's mark in them, too. Hearing about something is not like seeing it with one's own eye.

> See how my face is yellow like gold, and don't ask!
> See these tears like pomegranate berries,
> and don't ask!
> Don't ask me what is inside the house—
> see the blood at the threshold, and don't ask.

When the companions couldn't answer the question, they said, "We don't know any signs other than these. Now you tell us."

When Uways opened his mouth to answer, seventeen people fell prostrate on the ground—they fainted and lost consciousness. And a soft-heartedness and weeping began in the others. No possibility remained for him to say anything—nobody had the strength to listen.

❊

Erzincan Moments

A few Sufis had become friends of mine on the way to Erzincan. They chose me as their leader. "Without your order we will neither halt at a caravanserai, nor set a table without your permission," they said. "Without your order we will not mention any trouble, even if one of us is hurt by another."

A few days passed, and they hadn't come across anything to eat. It was melon season. In the distance, a man in a vegetable field was gesturing with his hand and calling, "Dervishes, for God's sake, come here."

I said to them, "Don't hurry."

"But we are hungry," they said. "If you are hungry, don't be late—generosity shouldn't be denied."

I said to them, "After all, it's not going anywhere—that is in our hands—just as when the Sufi turned his face to that loaf of bread and said, 'If I find something better than you, you'll be saved from my hand. If I cannot, for the moment, you are at hand.'"

We pretended not to hear and waved our hands as if asking, "What are you saying?" He came closer and insisted.

I said to the man, "We will come on one condition—whatever you eat you'll also give the same to the dervishes."

He prostrated at my feet, because he had seen this all in his dream, and he was waiting for its time to come. He had gathered watermelons for the dervishes. I said to the man: "For God's sake, beware not to eat the good ones yourself and give the worst ones to the dervishes."

He cried out and fell to the ground.

Then for three days he hosted the dervishes. He butchered lambs for them. I said, "This is his lot. I have delayed the saints for three days, but you have also received your portion," and left.

When we arrived in Erzincan, I parted from those friends. During that time people didn't recognize me, and our days had passed in a pleasant way. We were playing games and joking with them. After they recognized me, they all gathered around me and would have given feasts and made celebrations.

For three days I went looking for work. Nobody would hire me, because I had become very thin. They took everybody else, but left me standing. Then as he was passing by, a great man's glance fell upon me. He sent his servant to ask me why I was waiting there.

I said, "Are you the chief of the road? If you've bought the city and the road, let me know."

Then the man came to me humbly and took me to his house. He invited me into a beautiful pavilion and had food brought. He sat on his knees with great courtesy. After I ate, he said to me, "As long as you are in this city, you must come here every day and eat your fill." Well, these words of his stopped me from going there.

One day, he saw me and said, "At last! Save me from this difficulty! Friendship is never one-sided. They say, 'There is a window from heart to heart.' I know that my own heart is burning. Why are you leaving me like this behind a veil? Won't you tell me why this is?"

"Yes," I said, "I have the habit that when I love someone, at first I behave with stringency towards him so that I may be wholly his—so that I may be bound to him with my flesh and skin—with my all, gentleness or stringency."

Because gentleness is such that if you show it to a five year old child, he becomes your own. But a man is one who sees how patient his leader is, and endures whatever trouble comes to him, and sees that behind it good fortune will show its face—he waits and considers where the secret will reach him and turns his face in that direction. He becomes a hero—he doesn't fear death, and in the end, he doesn't die. Instead he reaches immortality within immortality, or a thousand immortalities.

What Capacity Is in You?

I saw someone there who raised his finger.[406]

I said, "Even if you become a Muslim a thousand times, still, something of unbelief remains in you. Otherwise, why do you keep looking at me with those dark glances?"

There was a shaikh there. He attempted to give me some advice: "Speak with people according to the capacity of their understand-

406 During the *salaat*, while sitting, when one is reciting the profession of faith, "I witness that there is no god but God, and I witness that Muhammad is a servant and messenger of God," one raises the first finger of the right hand as testimonial witness.

ing! Then, relate to them according to their capacity for tasting[407] and friendship!"

"You are right," I said, "but I can't respond to you, because you have given me advice, and I cannot see in you the capacity to receive the answer."

❊

No Room for Words

The Spirit hadn't completely shown its face to Mansur al-Hallaj, otherwise how could he have said, "I am the Truth"? Where is "I" in relation to "the Truth"? What is this "I"? What is this word? If he had plunged into the world of the Spirit, how could words find a place there? Where could "I" fit? Where would "am" be contained?

❊

The Ease of Burning

The one who said, "Poverty is my pride," is a great human being—he cannot be contained within this world. What kind of poverty is it that he is proud of? Yes—he is poor and helpless before the Light of the Truth. His chest is burning with that Light of Truth, and all the while, he says, "I wish I had a hundred more chests, that everyday they might burn within this Divine Light. They would disintegrate, and scatter, and then be renewed again. Only one who knows the ease of that burning—only he can know its taste."

Had We bestowed this Qur'an from on high upon a mountain, you would indeed see it humbling itself, breaking apart out of awe of God [59:21]. If He had put it upon a mountain, it wouldn't have the strength to bear it—that Divine Light shines upon him.

The provision of the dervish is poverty, and poverty is dervishhood on the Way of God. What does dervishhood have to do with these cloaks—every year nine hundred thousand silver coins are spent for those who live within dervish cells, and every day ten sheep

---

407 I.e., Relate to people according to their purity and ability to experience spiritual states.

are butchered! Such income from nothing, and without rendering any service!

Muhammad said,[408] "I have such a moment with God. . . ." I have asked the shaikhs, "Is this moment with God continuous?" These foolish shaikhs say, "No, it is not continuous."

Come to Me as I Come to You

Did you, then, think that We created you in mere idle play [23:115]? They say that this is stringency—no it is gentleness.

In other words, "I have surged like a hundred armies and turned My face towards you, and you are busy somewhere else! You withhold yourself, I don't withhold Myself. My face is always turned towards you. 'My all is busy with Your all' is the appropriate response to 'My all is given to your all abundantly.'"

Someone weeps and moans in front of the door, "Let me come in for a moment."

They say, "You don't have permission to enter."

He moans, "No! How can that be?"

Sir! Everybody keeps talking about his own state, while saying that they are explaining the meaning of God's word.

With the Highest Companion

Why did the Prophet say, "God created the spirits before the bodies"? Suppose hundreds of thousands of years passed before bodies—still it is a veil, because they are newly arrived. That which is "newly arrived," of course requires ablution. One should be purified of "new arrivals" (*hadath*),[409] so that you might find the way to prayer and closeness with God.

---

408 M. 335.

409 Shams is playing with the words *hadith* ("newly arrived, newly created") and *hadath* (accidental bodily emissions) that require the renewal of ablutions for ritual purity.

I don't know how that which is newly arrived can grasp the words of God Most High. Only if he walks in a hidden way upon the path of the Truth. Until his spirit is annihilated and until his newly arrived being no longer remains, let him follow along this way. Just as that person of wisdom said, even though with cold and incomplete expression:

> Even though Muhammad was there,
> in what manner of existence was he there?
> Anything besides the Truth that was there,
> had entered nothingness and annihilation.

Yes, when he is annihilated, then He says, "I've come, peace be with you. I found only you alone."

Everyone was occupied with something. Each was pleased and happy with his work. Some were interested in spirit—they were pleased and occupied with their own spirits. And others were busy with their intellects, and some with their souls. But We found only you alone without companions. All the friends had gone after that which they sought, and they left you alone—I am the companion of those without companions.

What happened then has become famous: *What God has revealed to His servant, He has revealed* [53:10]. From the beginning of *Surah an-Najm* (The Star) until here, it has been revealed, although it hasn't been manifested openly.

Someone asked, "What did He reveal?"

He said, "What He said, He said."

His spirit comes and asks, "What did they tell you?"

The Prophet answers, "Whatever we spoke, we spoke." In the same way, intellect also comes and asks, and it also receives the same answer, "Now, a single line has been written on his forehead."[410]

---

410 See *Surah al-Fath*, 48:28-29. See also *Mathnawi* V:3593-3616 (translated by Nicholson, adapted by C. A. H.):

> Whoever has rose gardens to feast and dwell within,
> why should he or she linger drinking wine in a fiery furnace?
> The pure spirit's home is the seventh heaven;

Don't Dig Pits

Somebody was complaining, "They have plundered my property!"

I said, "That's like the story of the slave from India who was apprenticed to the grocer. The grocer used to steal a finger-full of honey or butter from the bowl of every customer after he weighed it, and then tuck it away. The slave would burn inside, but he couldn't say a thing.

---

it's the worm that finds its home in dung.
The purifying cup is for the God-intoxicated;
briny water is the drink for birds that are blind. . . .
Those who lack real faith are satisfied with painted pictures
of the prophets;
but having known the brilliance of those moons,
we aren't interested in shadows.
The person of the prophet sits here,
while his other body is in heaven, like the moon.
This mouth of his discourses with those beside him,
while that mouth intimately whispers with the Beloved.
His outward ear apprehends these words,
while his spiritual ear draws close the mysteries of Being.
His outward eye apprehends human forms and features,
while his inward eye is dazzled by the Face of that Friend.
Here his feet stand evenly in the row of worshippers within the mosque,
there he circumambulates the heavens.
Every part of him is reckoned in this way:
here within Time, there Eternity's companion.
One of his names is "owner of the two realms";
another is "Imam of the two places of prostration."
Religious seclusion and fasting no longer are his obligation.
His infidelity has become faith and disbelief has disappeared.
Like the letter *alif*, he stands foremost by his rectitude;
nothing of his qualities remains.
Putting aside the garment of his own weaving,
his spirit has gone, naked, to the One who gives it increase.
Since naked he arrived in the presence of that incomparable King,
He has woven him a holy raiment.
Putting on that robe of noble qualities,
spirit flew from the pit to the palace of majesty.
That's the way it is: when dregs become pure, lightening, they rise.

One day a big skin bag broke open, and all the honey inside spilled out. The Indian slave saw his oppportunity, "Yes! Bit by bit you've gathered it, and now bag by bag, it goes! Someone who digs a pit for his brother falls into it himself."

Don't do harm, because you yourself will live that way! Don't dig pits, because you yourself will fall in!

❊

Be a Person of Heart

One should not be a person of bodily instincts, but a person of heart. Seek the heart, not instincts! Where is the place of the heart? The heart is hidden.

He is a companion of God, but out of jealousy, they call him "a man of heart." The moment the bright light of the Truth reflects upon the heart, the heart becomes joyful. Then in a moment, that light disappears, but many times it happens like this so that the heart might become a heart. It burns, and many times the heart gets broken, until it melts and only God remains.

He indicated this to the Prophet David. David asked God, "Where will I look for you?" He said, "My heavens and my earth cannot encompass me, only the heart of My faithful servant can encompass Me." He also said, "I am with those whose hearts have been broken on My way." When you say, "a person of heart," say "those whose hearts have been broken," because brokenness of heart is necessary. When you reach the Truth, you will see the divine light of His Exaltedness from within the divine light of the Truth Itself, because "No one knows them but I."[411]

❊

Surely You Will Be Tested

Even if the mountain is full of snakes, don't fear;
the mountain also holds the antidote within it.

When he looked at the shaikh with loving looks, bright thoughts

411 My saints are under My dome—no one knows them but I (*hadith qudsi*).

would appear within him. Then when he dove into the shadow again, dark lurking fears would come: "Suppose that is his station—misleading people, dragging them into suspicions and doubts. Is that a manly way to act?"

When the shaikh saw this, he said, "Peace be upon you! How is it that you are thinking about us? Are you forgetting again? Do you suppose that you are free to accept or deny as you wish? *God alternates the night and the day* [24:44]. Again and again the light of day is drowned in the sea of darkness, and over and over again the sea of darkness is burned away within the rays of light. *Do people think that they will be saved by saying, 'We have faith,' and be left to themselves without being tested* [29:2]? What is there in the world that is accepted without passing through a test, or rejected without being tested? But if God wills, the work is corrected in the end, and you go along the right way, and then you understand who you are!"

A saint (*wali*) doesn't know that he or she is a saint when he or she hasn't matured yet, but is still on the way of completion. When a person arrives at Aksaray, how could it be that after he has arrived there he wouldn't know that he has arrived?

May Death Bring You to Ease

Khujandi says, "I am witnessing the tragedy of the Household,"[412] but he has forgotten his own calamity!

In Damascus, Shihab Hariwa, who was descended from that great family said, "Do you know how I see death? It is as though they have placed a heavy burden upon someone's back, and they drag him through the mud, or force him to walk up a high mountain, and in the midst of a thousand and one difficulties, while he is trying to climb that mountain, someone comes and cuts the rope of that sack on his back, so that it falls to the ground. Well, when he suddenly becomes light and is freed from that burden, his soul is refreshed. In

412 The "Household" is the family of the Prophet Muhammad, especially his daughter Fatima, her husband Ali, and their two sons, Hasan and Huseyn, who were martyred.

the same way, death also brings one to ease." Now, his state is like this—he who was the servant of that Household. So what might be the state of the Household?

If he had faith, he would see death like this. He would also be the servant of that Household. Instead, he mourns for the Household, and yet, with jealousy, he looks upon the lights of that family who are the servants of God, and he belittles them.

Give Light to This Eye!

Why aren't you pleading with God?[413] In the middle of the night, get up, prostrate your face on the floor and pour down tears—pass beyond this world of two-ness—saying, "O my God! If you don't want the prophets and saints to remain outside, like the knocker of a door, now that You have shown me such and such great one, enlighten my eye through him. Didn't the Prophet (peace and blessings be upon him) say, 'How happy is the one who has seen me, and happy is the one who sees him who has seen me'?"

Abundance Is Seeking the Beggar

In the early days, the Prophet (may peace and blessings be upon him) would strongly avoid people, because of his intimate friendship with the Truth. He would avoid both the good and the bad. He was careful, because he didn't want the people's love for him to become a veil for either a moment or an hour.

When he reached completion, it made no difference—the respect and love of eighteen thousand worlds or the love of two people. He said, "Sell me to the people!" In other words, "O Companions! Sell me to the people, because it is not of my own will that I come to the sale, so how can there be loss?"

If Muhammad has said this, look at what the Truth is saying—doesn't He cry, "Sell Me!" hundreds of times: "Make Me beloved

---

413 M. 340.

within the hearts of My servants. Remind them of My gifts and blessings, because hearts are filled with love for those who are good to them, and they bear a grudge against those who treat them badly."

The commanding self (*nafs al-ammarah*) says, "Sell yourself!" It is after gold or silver.

I am not after money, I am after that by which the donkey is able to pass over the bridge. They have become great men, they have become shaikhs, but what can I do for them? I am looking for someone who is still hungry. I am looking for someone who is thirsty! Clear and clean water, out of its natural gentleness and generosity, seeks someone who is thirsty.[414]

☼

In This World, Is There Really Any Difference?

Just say, "Hajjaj bin Yusuf! May the compassion of God be upon you!"[415] Yes, we do the opposite of what the people do—we reject everything they accept, and we accept what they reject.

One day, Hajjaj was secretly informed that someone coveted his position: "I wish I could sit upon his seat." And someone else was whispering to himself, "I wish I could spend the whole night on the divan of his harem."

Hajjaj called his men and ordered the cook of his palace to make pilafs of seven different colors. They brought the pilafs and placed them before them. He ordered them to eat, then he asked, "Is there any difference in their taste?"

---

414 See *Mathnawi* I: 2745, 2750, (*Rumi Daylight*, p.65):

> Abundance is seeking the beggars and the poor,
> just as beauty seeks a mirror.
> Beggars, then, are the mirrors of God's bounty,
> and they that are with God are united with Absolute Abundance.

415 Hajjaj bin Yusuf was the stern governor of Damascus during the Umayyad caliphate.

☼

How about a Little Humility, a Little Respect!

If it is blasphemy to call a scholar's shoes "little booties," what would you say of a poor one (a dervish)? Even if you were to spend a hundred thousand dirhems on me, it would never have the value of showing respect for my words. If you are respectful, come! If you are disrespectful, go! From now on, take your disrespect elsewhere. If you have respect for us, why do you reveal the things you've heard from us without receiving our permission?

He said, "A new vat may leak, but it keeps the water clean."

He said, "I have walked a long distance on this path."

I said, "If they make a person wander around within an area of twenty miles, if they take him all around the outskirts of the city, but never arrive at the city, what kind of journey is that?"

He said, "On the way of seeking for the Truth, I have sat closely with many great ones and lesser ones."

I said, "Either you were after comfort and ease, or you were just interested in gathering words!"

☼

Visions

I saw myself in a garden—I was in a state of having lost myself. A fever came to me, and I heard a loud voice. I cried out and came to myself. I wanted to put on my boots, but something else appeared in front of my eyes, and again I lost myself. I saw some of His servants, then I saw Mevlana at a pulpit. Through the air, two beings came near him with curling hair and large eyes radiating light. They brought plates one upon another filled with jewels, and they placed them in front of Mevlana.

☼

Testing

Let's say that a hawk came and perched on the wall of a castle. If someone takes a stone from the ground to throw at him, the bird flies up and leaves. But if there were a donkey on the wall, and I were to also take a stone and throw it to make him run away from there, either his neck would get broken, or he would fall into the mud and sink lower and lower like Croesus.

Also, look at that human being from whose face the light of faith is radiating. Hypocrisy has never touched him. It is such a light that no test has darkened or extinguished it. The difference between the other lights and this divine light is this—other lights darken and go out after a little test, but this one doesn't.

God hides some of His servants behind a veil, and He speaks of secrets with them.

Shaikh Awhaduddin Kirmani took me to a *sema*. He showed me great respect, and then he invited me to his private cell. "Please, why don't you stay with us?" He said.

I said, "This is possible only on one condition—openly, we must sit together and you must drink wine in front of your disciples, but I won't drink; I won't join you."

"Why won't you drink with me?" he said.

"Because you would become a happy sinner, and I would become an unhappy sinner."

"I can't do it," he said.

After this, I said but a single word, and three times he struck his forehead, exclaiming, "Allah!"

Merge with the Meaning

The scholars of the scriptures are still mumbling, just scratching the surface of "*alif*." They are not grasping its meaning at all, because they have no manhood. It's as if you put a beautiful woman in bed with an impotent man. What can he do? What can he do besides this tasteless fondling? He can do nothing but rub his face upon her face, that's all.

He is deprived of the means and real reason for it.

A Grace from the Truth

That Shahabuddin's knowledge overwhelmed his intellect. Intellect should overwhelm knowledge. It should dominate it.[416]

If you see God, convey my greetings. The Friend is very beneficent—you annihilate yourself in Him and you walk in His Being. If He no longer remains, neither do you. Everything, by coming into the realm of manifestation, is good news, a grace from the Truth.

With Whom Are You Busy?

A traveler was walking along the way, when he saw a horseman carrying light weapons galloping swiftly towards him. "Before this man tries to kill me, let me kill him," he thought to himself.

When the horseman approached, he called to the traveler, "Don't look at me with such an evil glance, because I am extremely unskilled in fighting."

The traveler responded: "You speak well; out of fear for my life I was going to fight with you, but now, come, let's shake hands."[417]

Now, things are also like this in the world of religion. If you want to wear this turban, you must wear it on your head in such a way that you may be able to take your head bravely out of this field of men, otherwise, you'll be left behind on the way. . . .

O judges, professors, and shaikhs! Those who show no humbleness of heart to the poor friend of God will themselves be wounded.

Perhaps they'll say, "We didn't know," but how can one walk on this path without knowledge?

"Allah has not taken the ignorant as His friend."

Perhaps you are busy; but I wonder—with us?

---

416 Shams mentions several Shahabuddins. One of whom he speaks positively, as on the previous pages, is probably Shahabuddin Suhrawardi. There was also Shihab (Shihabuddin) Hariwa with whom he spent time in Damascus of whom Shams was sometimes critical. This Shihab was a student of Fahkruddin Razi.

417 M. 350.

"No," he said, "with a neighbor."

"Who is that neighbor? I am your neighbor. Here, any claims are just empty words."

I like unbelievers because they don't claim to be friends. Openly, they say, "We are blasphemers; we are enemies."

Now, let me teach you about friendship: a friend is one who radiates the fire of compassion from his eyes. "O Educator! Save them from sin—forgive me, and all the Muslims!" he begs.

❊

The Turner of the Wheel

What is with these fatalists? How could a strong man not know that this whole existence is from God? You ask a child, "Who has created us?"

He says, "The Real."

If you say, "Does this wheel turn without a turner?"

"What are you saying? Are you crazy?" he asks.

"Allright, is the one who created us and who annihilates us stronger and more powerful, or are we?"

He answers, "Of course, He is. If He weren't stronger, how could He bring us into being and take us into non-being?"

The real man is the one who sees this victorious and exalted Giver of Being. He opens his eye, and sees the Creator without a veil or any limitation; he sees God.

❊

When the Help of God Comes

I saw you in that state and that station—I have tried so hard to help you give up that state. My heart was always with you. "I wonder why he is sitting down in that station of separation? Why is he so constricted and bitter?" I was reflecting; I wanted you to know what degree of compassion I have for you.

Now, touch me once with your hand like that. It has been a long time since you did. Even if you are busy with other things, just touch my hand a little.[418]

May peace be with you! May your holiday be blessed! Our greeting is a fortress. When you enter into it, you will be secure from all difficulty.

> When someone enters the fortress of God's help,
> Even a spider becomes his doorkeeper.[419]

❁

Recognizing a Pure Feast

He said, "Some lovers are magnificently glowing with energy, but the beloved ones are serene and still."

I said, "This magnificence and celebration, these feasts and entertainments are like when someone invites you to an orchard to eat walnuts. He climbs up the tree and begins to shake it and says, 'Help yourself! Eat them with your own hand.' The hands and sleeves of the guest become black.

"Someone else takes the guest to an orchard, seats him in a pleasant place, and orders his servants, 'Go and pick walnuts from the tree, clean them, take off the shell, and bring them after breaking off the skin.' And the servants bring the cleaned walnuts and put them in front of the guest, saying, 'Please, help yourself.'

---

418 I.e., Just connect a little. Even a little connection can be a powerful help and healing. Energy flows through a healing hand.

419 After years of persecution, divine permission was finally received for the Muslims to emigrate to Medina. Waiting until most of the community had safely departed, Abu Bakr and the Prophet Muhammad finally set out. The first night of their journey, they hid themselves in a cave on the outskirts of Mecca. Not long after their entry into the cave, suddenly a spider wove a large web across the opening, and a dove nested in the ledge of rock beside the cave door. When the Meccans who were pursuing them approached the cave and witnessed the spider web and the nesting dove, they assumed that such settled creatures could not have been disturbed by human beings in flight, and so they went to search elsewhere, leaving Muhammad and Abu Bakr in safety, trusting in the protection of God.

"The guest asks, 'What kind of a walnut is this? My hands have not blackened, neither have my sleeves. I cannot eat this—God knows what it is! They don't look like walnuts. I have never seen anything like this.'"

Real Lovers Are Not Confused

> Nobody could reach the secret of love,
> And the one who did arrive is bewildered.

Shaikh Ibrahim opposed these words of Khayyam. "Why would one who reaches the secret of love still be bewildered, and if he hasn't reached it, then why would he not be bewildered?"

"Yes," I said, "Khayyam is talking about the characteristics of his own state." He was confused and overwhelmed, so sometimes he complains of the heavens, another day he complains about the passing of time, another day about his lot, and another day he is accusing God Himself. In one moment he says, "There is no God," he denies Him, and the next moment he affirms. He speaks cloudy words mixed with fears and imaginings. A faithful person is not so confused.

The faithful one is one for whom the Presence has thrown away His/Her veil. He has lifted the veil, and he knows that for which he has been seeking. He serves, face to face, openly, and he knows that pleasure from east to west.

But an unbeliever always thinks negatively; he or she says, "No." If he says that to me, I still have no doubts about that Presence, because I can see clearly. I eat, I taste. What doubt could I have? I would say, "You can say what you wish," and I would just laugh.

It is the same as when, one day just before noon, a man with his stick in one hand and holding the wall with the other, comes to you with trembling legs, and sighing and moaning he groans and weeps, "O tell me, what is happening to us? Why this difficulty—the sun didn't rise today!"

And another says, "Yes, I, too, am bewildered just like you—why doesn't day come?"

Meanwhile you see that it is bright morning—bright light shines everywhere. Even if they were to say such things to you a hundred thousand times, you would only laugh at them.

Now, one who is of the faithful is not left in need, but where is there such a faithful one?

Wanderings through God's World

For a moment, let's stop by the tavern and see the helpless ones there. God created those poor women—whether they are good or bad—let's have a look at their state. Let's stop by the church, too—let's see how they are there.

Nobody is strong enough to do what I do. It is my work—others shouldn't try to do the same. They are right when they say that someone who is carefree like this shouldn't be followed.

Sweet Grapes

He kept complaining about his son. It was on the tip of my tongue to say, "He'll be fine in the end."

I said, "He is a child. These things he is doing are because of his youth; they are not intentional or deliberate. It is like unripe grapes and plums which are bitter and sour—these characteristics are due to the immaturity of the grapes and the rawness of the plums, not to their essence. However, there are also unripe grapes that have a sour scent, and remain hard as stones, and never sweeten.

> Unripe grapes should always be kept
> in front of the sun.

God has such servants—nobody could stand the troubles they suffer. The ones who drink from the pitcher that is continually refilled cannot return to themselves. Others get drunk and leave, but they stay near the barrel of wine.

Eating Wisely

Someone comes and says, "Teach me about how to eat, because this thing is very difficult for me, and it's giving me discomfort."

I answered, "Food should be eaten in such a way that you burden it—it shouldn't burden you. Eat in such a way that it carries you, but you don't have to carry it!"

He said: "Now, let us eat with you."

I don't say, "Eat!" I don't have that sanctity. That sanctity is only from God who can say, "I have given these pains to you to suffer, I myself will repair it again."

God has given me knowledge. If I don't behave bravely, that poor stomach will be disturbed for a day and a night, and I will have caused its pain.[420]

Passing Up Grief

What Mevlana says to people is not for my sake. I know his state within myself. If he frowns, I know that it isn't for me, because I clearly see and know Mevlana's state within me. I know that sour face is a sign for others.

Even if the whole universe is grieving, if I am joyful, it doesn't affect me. And when I am grieving, I don't let someone else's grief affect me, either.

Only God Is God

A person who is created by God can't be God, no matter whether he is Muhammad or anybody else.[421]

---

420 Shams said, "True knowledge comes of three things—a tongue which repeats the name of God, a heart which is grateful, and a patient body. A body which is not abstinent is like a tree which bears no fruit (*Menaqib al-Arifin*)."

421 M. 355.

Someone came, "Excuse us, we couldn't cook anything today," he said.

I answered, "What would I do with what you cook? You yourself must get cooked!"

"How will I get cooked?" he asked.

"What kind of a disciple are you that you don't understand any signs?" I asked.

He answered, "If the thing called 'understanding' were not of various kinds, the scholars of Islam wouldn't disagree about signs and phrases. They would derive the same meaning, especially from the verses of the Qur'an."

I said, "How can there be a disagreement among the wise ones of Islam? Seeing double and division is your work. If Abu Hanifah had seen Ash-Shafi'i,[422] he would hold his head and kiss his eyes. How can the servants of God disagree with their Lord? How could such a separation be possible? If you see a separation, sacrifice your self so that you might eliminate the distance."

He said, "How can I be liberated from this story of sacrifice?"

I said, "Sacrifice yourself so that you may be liberated."

To say, "God is greater" (*Allahu Akbar*) during the *salaat* is for sacrificing the self—to come near to God. "God is greater!"—the servant who worships with these words sacrifices himself. If you still have feelings of superiority and pride, you must say, "*Allahu Akbar*." In order to come near to Him, intend the sacrifice!

Now, how long are you going to come to *salaat* carrying an idol under your arm? "*Allahu Akbar*, God is greater," you are saying, but like the hypocrites, your idol still stands in your heart.

---

422 Abu Hanifah and Ash-Shafi'i were two of the wise ones of Islam upon whose example and principles schools of law were founded. Sometimes the followers of the different schools of law, (*madhhab*) argue with one another, but Shams is saying that their founders would have acknowledged the oneness between them within the Light of their Lord.

❊

A Pebble and a Pearl

Shaikh Muhammad[423] would often prostrate and bow down, saying, "I am the servant of the people of the Law." But he had no "following." I benefitted a lot from him, but not like I have benefitted from you. This is not like that. How different they are—a pebble and a pearl!

However, your children don't understand you. It is strange; they don't grasp who you are, but you are not here to show your children or others.

One person tries very hard to show something from himself, and another, with a hundred kinds of tricks, tries to hide himself. The more I make myself evident, the more troubles increase. Strangers gather around me, and I cannot live the life I need.

❊

Listen to the Pot Calling the Kettle Black!

He said, "Such and such person will never be close to you."

I said, "How do you know that he won't be close to me? You must be more mature than you are to know that!"

He said, "Because he is criticizing: 'It must be like this,' or 'It should be like that.' How can one find a place in the station of surrender if one says such things?"

I answered him, "You are criticizing him, saying it is not appropriate for him to say, 'It has to be like that; it must not be like this.' But aren't you also doing that? You are saying the same thing: 'It must not be like that.'"

It's like when during the prayer an Indian started talking. Another Indian doing the *salaat* next to him heard him and said, "Be quiet! You aren't supposed to talk while praying."

Then there was the man who went to the judge to lodge a complaint. They said, "There is no witness; you have to swear."

---

423 According to the tradition, Shams is referring here to Muhammad Ibn al-Arabi, while speaking to Mevlana (the pearl).

He answered, "By God, I swear that I won't swear. By God, I swear that I won't!"

The people of Ahlat said, "O disreputable one! Then go away, so that we may not swear at you!"

The Poor One

I said, "For you to speak in front of me seems as though you are saying, 'You don't know, and I am teaching you.' This is not pleasing between a shaikh and a disciple—this is not the way for a *murid*."

If there is rejection, there is no freedom. The ease of choosing freely what to do no longer remains. However, I need to behave freely; let me go if needed, or sit down or lay down if needed—in short let me behave with my own free will. But if you stay with me, no 'free will' remains—when I need to go, you go, or when you ought to go, I have to go. Either I become the servant, or I remain as a master who is served. In both cases freedom is lost.

He becomes neither the servant,
nor the master of anybody.
With mercy—a dervish has a pleasant world.

A truly poor one is one who neither has possessions, nor is he possessed by anyone.

Enter His Glance

One should get used to the state of poverty at a young age—it is easy to straighten a fresh branch, before it goes through the fire. But when it becomes stiff, things are difficult. You should fit your foot into the shoe while the leather is newly damp. Then the foot finds its place within the shoe, so that when it dries, your foot won't hurt.

He said, "Whether intentionally or not, to hurt anyone or behave coldly to anyone is not something a dervish does."

I said, "But if I don't submit him to the test, he won't understand who he is."

You see a person who has some faith, who displays self-sacrifice—when you begin to test him a little, just see what is left of his faith! He is left naked in front of you. Just once, ask for some money from one who claims to love! His intellect leaves, his soul departs, and he starts shaking his head and feet.

I have tested many of them so that they might see themselves. They begin to blame me, saying, "This man keeps making people who have faith in you cold."

I said, "He didn't do that. It is because of the love that God has for him—God Most High doesn't want people to know me. 'My saints are under my domes.' 'No one knows them but I' is on their foreheads. Who can see them? He is within the Glance of God. Those who want to see him must come into the Glance of God. Come into the Glance of God so that you may see him! How can His creatures comprehend the Truth? How can they see Him?

✲

There Are Those Who See

So, welcome this person who is within His Glance. . . . Everybody has a particular state—the preacher at the pulpit, the reciter of Qur'an on his seat, the listeners, and the disciple, and the shaikh—each has a state. The guide also has a state, a lover has a state, and the beloved has a state. *There is no god but God.*

What a perversity and blindness it is when one doesn't know that one is blind. I am not one of those, but I know of them. There is another group whose eyes see and who know what they see, and they, themselves, know who they are.

✲

Come See

The legs of intellect are weak. Nothing comes from it, yet it is not without a share. It is newly arrived, and as that which is newly-arrived it comes to the door of the house, but it doesn't have the power to enter.

An *alif* has been written on the Tablet. Whether we say it was written on the Tablet, or on the earth, or on the heart, everything has received light from it. Where is the speaker? Where is an eye? Where is vision that you might see?

Nasuh's Repentance

O you who have attained to faith! Turn to God with the repentence of Nasuh [66:8].[424] Some have interpreted this word "*nasuh*" as "that which has become pure and sincere." This is a pleasant expression. Some also say that Nasuh was a man whose face resembled a woman's, but he was fully a man, and he was lacking nothing as a man. He used to work as a masseuse in the women's bath. For thirty years he had worked at this job. One day, the daughter of the sultan came to the bath and the big ruby earring in her ear was lost. When they became aware of it, they realized that it was lost in the bath, and they commanded the guards, "Immediately, go and search every corner and crevice of the bath!" The guards immediately surrounded the domed area of the bath, inside and all around it.

> Unless the right moment arrives,
> the friendship of the friend is useless.

Nasuh retired to a private room and began to tremble with fear. "It will soon be my turn to be searched," he moaned and prostrated time after time, promising God, "O my God! If I am saved this time, for the rest of my life I will never again do such a thing as this—I will never again work as a women's bath attendant! I take refuge in Your Divinity and give my word. If you remove this burden from me, from now on, your servant Nasuh will never again commit this sin."

---

424 *Surah at-Tahrim*, Prohibition 66:8: *O you who have attained to faith! Turn unto God in sincere repentance: it may well be that your Sustainer will efface from you your bad deeds, and will admit you into gardens through which running waters flow, on a Day on which God will not shame the Prophet and those who share his faith: their light will spread rapidly before them, and on their right; [and] they will pray: "O our Sustainer! Cause this our light to shine for us forever, and forgive us our sins: for, truly, You have the power to will anything!"*

While Nasuh was within this state of pleading, he heard someone saying, "We have searched everybody. Only Nasuh is left, search her, too!" His mind flew from his head—he commended his secret to God.

Just at this moment, another voice was heard, "The earring has been found!" Those who had been searching said, "My God! We had begun to think ill of Nasuh! Now let her come and massage the sultan's daughter; she wants her to massage her."

They called Nasuh, and he replied, "Today my hand has stopped working; on the way here I had a pain in it."[425]

The companions of the Prophet would repent and then spoil their repentance. He said, "Repent with the repentance of Nasuh—that repentance endures for thirty years and is never relinguished."[426]

What Do You Worship?

The waves of the Ocean of Beneficence continually surge—it gives you whatever you want from it. Everybody worships something. One is fond of the beautiful ones, another is fond of money, and someone else is fond of status. In front of each, they say, "*This is my Lord* [6:76]." They don't say, "*I love not those that set* [6:76]," like the Prophet Abraham.

Abraham said, "I love not those that set." Where is the human being with the nature of Abraham capable of saying these words with the language of love?

The secret of this belongs to a different heaven. Because there are heavens in the universe of spirits. In the universe of inner secrets there are also heavens, suns, and moons. The one who passes through these images knows that these also have a Creator, and are also disappearing.

Once the image of the Friend opens from the inner universe, the divine light of manifestation appears. He says, "*I have turned my face to Him who has created the heavens and the earth* [6:79]."

---

425 M. 360.

426 See *Mathnawi* V:2218-2325.

When I fall ill, He heals me [26:80]. He attributes the sickness to himself in order to teach us. The Prophet Adam said, "*O Lord! We have wronged ourselves* [7:23]." In other words, "I am ill and my healing is only from Him." He is negating himself, putting aside the self. And when you remove your self, you have affirmed Him.

❁

Watch Out for the Thief

Satan says, "The thief himself shouts, 'There is a thief in the district'; and the people of the district shout with him, 'There is a thief! There is a thief!'"

On this Way, there are a hundred thousand satans with the face of Adam. Be careful not to think that everyone who has a human face, is a human being. These are the human devils. Their state isn't like your state, and their path is different than yours.

❁

Renewal

Even if this Christian speaks for a hundred days, one after the other I never feel bored. Someone who is boring and offensive I burn, because improvement is possible through burning; I crush him, because rebuilding is possible only after the demolishing. Such a person speaks about many branches of knowledge, but he doesn't know how to correct his own work. He does something and then thinks that the way of improving it is his own business. He has the wrong hole. He is praying, "O My God! Refresh me with the fragrance of Paradise!"[427] This prayer is right, but the hole is wrong—this prayer is done not when one is cleaning one's rear end—one should be washing one's face.

---

427 See *Mathnawi* IV 2213-2229. "In the ritual ablution, a separate prayer for each member of the body has been handed down. . . ."

※

You Alone Know

He said, "The one who knows himself knows his Lord (*hadith*)." Why didn't he say, "The one who knows his intellect" or "who knows his spirit?"

I said, "The self contains everything. The self is the being of a thing. One should train it when one is young. *You know all that is within myself, but I know not what is in Your Self* [5:116]."[428]

※

What Do You Really Want

I was embarrassed by these Muslims; they were about to kill me because of their hunger—they were swallowing everything and eating for their own pleasure. But God has revealed who the real human beings are.

"I spend a hundred dirhems for my own pleasure and attend musical celebrations, but I don't give the least money on the way of God!"—then where is servanthood or love of God? Let's say someone goes out and if he doesn't come across the silk he wants or the scarf from Yemen, he falls into terrible despair and dies. Even if one wants to do good for such people, they won't ever accept it.

But you are such a person that you are weeping for yourself! You have fallen into despair because of that fearful dream! And I am such a man that I have held your hand and saved you from those fears.

They said, "Today the Speaker is very ill."

"Yes," I said, "He called all the people to the path of health, and they didn't accept it, so he became ill—because happiness hadn't yet become dear to him.

---

428 *You know all that is within myself, whereas I know not what is in Your Self. Truly, it is You alone who fully know all the things that are beyond the reach of a created being's perception.* [*Surah al-Maida*, The Feast 5:116]

Who Is Influencing Who?

A sultan had two sons. One was well-behaved and beneficent, but the other one was ill-mannered, stupid, bad-tempered, and effeminate. In order to raise him to be a real man, the sultan looked for a wrestler like Rustam, who was of manly build, brave, and swift, to be a friend and comrade for his son.

Day and night, this friend of his would tell him stories of bravery, give him examples of heroism, and teach him about how to use weapons, and about the traditions of manhood. For a full two months, day and night, this brother and new friend of his spoke to him about stories of war and tales of heroism, but it was of no use. He kept making toys and dolls and playing like a little girl.

"Today, the sultan is coming," they told the man, "He wants to see what his son has learned."

And what does he see? The boy had plunged into a game with his friend—scarves were on their heads and toys were in front of them. The teacher had taken off his turban, and thrown it onto the floor; he was hiding himself next to him.

The sultan looked around to see where the teacher was: "Where's the teacher?"

The teacher uncovered his head, and with a woman's voice he said, "Salaam, I am the teacher."

The sultan said, "What's going on here?"

The teacher responded, "O Sultan of the world! No matter how much I have tried during these two months, I couldn't make him adopt my temperament—I wasn't successful. So in the end, I adapted myself to him."

When Happiness Becomes Dear

When happiness becomes dear to one, things become like in the story of the sultan and the vizier.

One day, the sultan called the vizier to himself and said, "I want my son to be a great scholar. Let him give advice to the people and awaken them; and let me sit at the foot of his pulpit, and listen to his talks. Now, which master should I send him to, so that he may educate him as a scholar? To such and such person, or to so and so? The vizier responded, "This thing is not the work of the scholars of religion. You are old; they won't be able to succeed in educating him quickly enough so that within such a short time you might sit in front of his pulpit and listen to his lectures and advice. Instead, you should send him to such and such a weaver."[429]

"Since you know of such a person, take care of it right away," the sultan replied.

The vizier left and went to see the weaver. From a distance, he greeted him with respect and sat down quietly.

The weaver asked, "How are you? What mischief are you contemplating?"

"What am I to do?" the vizier asked. "I have trusted in your greatness and come to you. For God's sake, grant my request!"

"The difficult part of this thing is that it is for God's sake," he said. He promised, "*You will see.*"

The vizier recounted everything to the sultan. The sultan became very happy. He immediately jumped off his throne and went to visit the weaver. He commended his son into his care. For two years, the boy worked beside the weaver.

After two years had passed, he said, "My son! Tomorrow, stand up at the pulpit and start preaching!"

The news was sent to his father, and he approached his son to see how things would go. He wanted to test him, so he said, "So, I offer my respects—please, make a speech!"

An outcry arose in the city—people came running in astonishment, and six thousand scholars with turbans gathered around the pulpit of the boy. The boy related about seven hundred sayings. He asked the experts about each of the traditions that he spoke: "Are these not the sayings of the Prophet?"

"Yes, that is so! It is true," they said.

---

429 Shams' first shaikh was a weaver: Abu Bakr Sellabaf.

"O My God!" the boy said, "You have learned so many branches of knowledge, but you have lived like the blind. Everything that I have spoken, was of my own speech!"

"O my God, O my God!" they exclaimed.

> Those who receive a share from the favors of God
> seem to be strangers,
> But their souls are the tablets of Divine secrets.

❊

Taming the Dragon

Someone was complaining about people of this world. To the eye of the people of God, this world is a toy—it is an imitation of the real. But according to children, rather than being a toy, it seems real.

Life is a loan. If today, you can't cope with playing and joking, don't play around with the world! If you can, then eat, drink, and amuse yourself, because its savor is not in weeping, but in laughter.

This world is both a treasure and a snake. Some play with the treasure, and others play with the snake. But those who play with the snake should be able to endure its bite. It strikes either with its tail or its head. If it strikes with its tail, one shouldn't go to sleep, because it may strike again with its head.

However those who turn away from this snake, and aren't caught by its wiles, are walking behind the guide of the intellect, because the guide of the intellect is the emerald that blinds the snake's eye.[430]

When the dragon-like snake sees that the guide of intellect leads the caravan, it loses its power, weakens, and slows. Once like a crocodile in that water, under the foot of the intellect, it becomes a bridge. Its poison turns to sugar, its thorns become roses. It was the waylayer of travelers; it becomes the guide. It used to be the ferment of fears, now it becomes the source of security.

---

430 It used to be thought that emeralds were protective against snakes, because a snake's eyes would become blind due to the rays it emits. The emerald is a symbol for the spiritual teacher whose radiance of divine light protects and aids the seeker in transformation of the *nafs*.

❊

Intellect Is a Skillful Archer

Intellect is a skillful archer; it can pull the bowstring to the ear. But the intellect of this world is weak in regard to being. It pulls the arrow, but it cannot pull it tight to the ear.[431] Even with a thousand tricks, it can only pull it to the mouth. What is the use of that—if you pull the string only to the mouth! You can hit the mark only if you shoot from the ear.[432]

Words that belong to the intellect of this world come from the mouth, but the words of the intellect related to the other world are the arrows that come from within the soul. *Yet even if a divine discourse by which mountains could be moved, or the earth cleft asunder, or the dead made to speak* . . .[13:31].

> A word that doesn't spring from real thought
> Isn't worth being spoken or written.

What are thoughts? First of all, one has to consider whether they bring benefit and gratefulness, or do they bring the opposite? Then, one has to look to see what the outcome of it will be. One must look in front of and behind oneself so that there might not be a wall or an obstacle in any direction. One shouldn't let love of the world create a barrier, for "Your love for something makes you blind and deaf."

When love for the world becomes greater than your love of religion, "it makes you blind and deaf." Then *We have put barriers in front of them and barriers behind them* [36:9] is revealed so that such people might repent and awaken. Then one's love for the world lessens, and the barrier thins. Most of the time, this happens through companionship with good companions. One's good companions should be sweet-tempered and far removed from ill thoughts.

---

431 M. 365.

432 In archery, the arrow is placed against the bowstring, and then the hand that holds the arrow on the string pulls it, stretching the string back towards the head of the archer. If the hand stretching the bowstring reaches only to the mouth, it is not a complete stretch; if it is stretched back to the ear, then it is a full stretch, and the archer will be able to convey the arrow with full force.

❁

Verses within Verses

One day a scholar awoke from sleep. His goods, his boots, whatever he had, he threw away. He moaned and wept, saying, "We have spent our lives distracted by the law of divorce; we haven't paid attention to the Book of God. How are we going to answer when God Most High asks us how we have consumed our lives, when we will be asked what we have seen with our eyes, what we have heard with our ears, and what thoughts have passed through our hearts?!"

Here, what he means by "The Book of God" is not the bound Qur'an; it is the one who shows the way, that is, the guide—he is the Book of God. He is the verse (*ayah*); he is the *surah*, and there are many verses within that verse.

❁

The Night of Power

Even as the "Night of Power" is kept hidden among the other nights, the people of God have also been hidden among the imitators. That they are hidden isn't due to their poverty or weakness, but perhaps because they are so openly bright, just as the sun is hidden for a bat. Even though it is right in front of him, he can't perceive anything of it. The veil of love of the world has made him "blind and deaf." When it is strong and powerful, love of the world is a magnet that pulls the world towards one. If one is weak, it can only pull the image of the darling [not the beloved herself], and in the end, the image of the darling also becomes an unpleasant veil unless the compassion of God rains. Just as, God, the Most Great, has said, "*For truly, We sent it down in the Night of Power* [97:1]."[433] In *We sent it down* there are several signs.

---

433 The "night of power" is the night in which the Qur'an was first revealed to Muhammad, during the month of Ramadan. One continues to watch for that night of power, hidden among the nights . . . See *Surah al Qadr* 97:1-5:

In the Name of God, the Infinitely Compassionate and Most Merciful
We have indeed revealed this during the Night of Power.
And what will explain to you what the Night of Power is?
The Night of Power is better than a thousand months.

It is *Better than a thousand months* [97:3]: it is brighter than a thousand full moons, but it has been hidden among the months—hidden because of its clarity. One day, he will see and cry out in repentance, "*Alas for me, that I did not turn towards Allah* [39:56]!" What an incomparable direction, and what a dimensionless dimension He is!

A Friend among Friends

I am happy, how could I not be happy? Whenever someone has denied me, a hundred thousand angels close to God always confirm me. Whenever someone has caused me pain or spoken ill of me, immediately, with a hundred thousand kinds of closeness and caresses God has compensated those griefs. No one has rejected me or become estranged from me without God Most High showing me a thousand kinds of nearness, and a hundred thousand sincere souls and angels of God appearing before me and bowing their heads in front of me.

Keep Shaking

The saying of the Prophet, "The world is the prison of the faithful," seems strange to me, because I have never seen a prison. All I have seen is happiness, majesty, and good fortune. Even if an unbeliever pours water over my hands, God forgives him and honors him.

Why then would I see myself as lowly? For some time I did not recognize my self—what greatness and exaltedness. It is as if I am a pearl, a jewel that has fallen into filth. Now, I thought I had been liberated from that, but no.

Now I speak happily, so that you may also be happy. Give me your hand so that we may take hands! Take the hand of your Muslim brother. While one is shaking hands, sins fall away. So one must keep shaking. O Muslims! Keep shaking, so that we may also shake.

Within it the angels descend bearing divine inspiration
by God's permission upon every mission:
Peace! . . . This until the rise of dawn!

☼

Don't Be Distracted by Blustering Snow

You should understand that what I say to others, I am also saying to you. And without getting irritated by it, don't think that what I am saying to you is just for yourself! Well, this understanding results from strong faith.

Let him know that the friend has said something about you—don't you understand? If you understand, then repeat it, but which one is it?

If you are afraid of him, thinking that it is not necessary to say it, know that within you dark thoughts and the power of understanding have become mixed—this is the harmful action of the devil who wants to separate you from the friend. A demon is calling you—he separates you from the friend, and pulls you from the right path into the wilderness.

The voice of that devil seems to be the voice of someone you know, or he tries to deceive you and block the way like a wolf who stirs up the snow.

☼

The Beneficent One Is Established on the Throne

What is the meaning of the verse "*The All-compassionate one is seated upon the Throne*" [20:5]?[434] About its outward meaning, they have said that to be "seated" upon the throne means to be dominant over it, just as in the verse:

> Bishr [the Persian King] sat upon Iraq
> without wielding a sword or shedding any blood.

From examples like these, they understand that the word is used in this sense. And Abu'l Hasan Ash'ari said, "We have faith in His words, *He sat upon the Throne*, without questioning how or why; we have faith that God's commands hold sway over the Empyrean."

What is understood by these words?

---

434 M. 370.

What have they said about this verse of *Surah Taha* in the commentaries? What have those who only know about the outside of things understood from this?

Have they not seen that we have appointed a sanctuary secure, while mankind are ravaged all around them? Do they then believe in falsehood and disbelieve in the bounty of Allah [29:67]?" Outside of the sanctuary of the heart, there are devils who cause hidden fears, terror, and dangers. *He whispers in the breasts of men* [114:5].

Just as Abraham who was thrown into the fire was then educated by the Truth to the completion of power,[435] even so, the Prophet Moses was also nurtured at the hand of the enemy.

✲

Balancing Gentleness and Stringency

There are certain things which I cannot say—I have said a third of it. They declare that, "Such and such a person is all gentleness, nothing but pure gentleness." They think that perfection is to be in a state of continual gentleness. However, it's not like that. One who is all gentleness is incomplete. It would never be appropriate to say about God "He is all gentleness," because then you will have abolished the attribute of stringency in Him. Both gentleness and stringency are needed, but these attributes must be in their appropriate places. The ignorant have both stringency and gentleness but manifested in an inappropriate or improper way.

Someone said, "Everybody has stringency towards enemies and gentleness for friends." But not everyone recognizes who is a friend and who is an enemy. If everyone could recognize his friend, God

---

435 See (*Mathnawi* III, 1388-1391):

When the kernel swells the walnut shell,
or the pistachio, or the almond, the husk diminishes.
As the kernel of knowledge grows, the husk thins and disappears,
because the lover is consumed by the beloved.
Since the quality of being sought is the opposite of seeking,
Revelation and Divine Lightning consume the prophet with fire.
When the attributes of the Eternal shine forth,
the cloak of time is burned away.

wouldn't have said, "*Do not take My enemies and your enemies as friends, showing them affection* [60:1]," or "*Behold, some of your spouses*[436] *and your children are enemies for you: so beware of them* [64:14]"[437] or "*Lo! It is you who love them, but they will not love you* [3:119]."

It is just as with the words of the Commander of the Faithful, Ali, "Love your friend but not excessively. Bear in mind that one day you may bear a grudge against him! Don't behave with hatred towards your enemy either, because perhaps one day you may become friends!" And *It may be that Allah will ordain love between you and those of them with whom you are at enmity* [60:7].

> To distinguish between an enemy and a friend
> you will need to live your life again.
> There is many an enemy who looks like a friend.
> What you need is that friend who is true.

To "live life again" is for the person who has not been able to be liberated from his or her first self and hasn't been able to find a new self. But the one who has found a second life has the promise—*Truly We shall quicken with good life* [16:97][438]—he or she sees with the light of God. Such a person recognizes his friend and knows his enemy. His or

---

436 I.e., "*sometimes, your spouses . . .* ," etc. Since, in the teachings of the Qur'an, all moral duties are binding on women as well as on men, it is obvious that the term *azwajikum* must not be rendered as "your wives," but is to be understood—according to classical Arabic usage—as applying equally to both the male and the female partners in a marriage.~M. Asad

437 Love of his or her family may sometimes tempt a believer to act contrary to the demands of conscience and faith; and, occasionally, one or another of the loved ones—whether wife or husband or child—may consciously try to induce the person concerned to abandon some of his or her moral commitments in order to satisfy some real or imaginary "family interest," and thus becomes the other's spiritual "enemy." ~ M. Asad

438 See *Surah an-Nahl*, The Bee 16:95-97:

And so, do not barter away your bond with God for a trifling gain!

Truly, that which is with God is by far the best for you, if you but knew it: all that is with you is bound to come to an end, whereas that which is with God is everlasting.

And most certainly shall We grant unto those who are patient in adversity their reward in accordance with the best that they ever did.

As for anyone—be it man or woman—who does righteous deeds, and is of the

her stringency goes where it should, and his or her gentleness also goes where it should. In reality, though, both return to one thing.[439]

The Faithful Are as One Body

That great man of knowledge, despite his great knowledge and authority, held the reigns of the shaikh's horse over his shoulder and walked along in front of him. Along the way, from moment to moment doubts would wander through his mind, and his faith in the shaikh would waiver. He was reflecting to himself, "A certain shaikh came near him and greeted him, but he didn't pay any attention to him. But after him, a young man came and greeted him, and he returned his greeting and showed great respect to him. How can I have faith in this man!"

---

faithful—him shall We most certainly cause to live a good life; and most certainly shall We grant unto such as these their reward in accordance with the best that they ever did.

439 One cold night, December 5, 1247, a few months after Shams' return from Damascus, while he and Mevlana were sitting together, a knock came at the door and Shams got up to answer it and went out into the garden. He was never seen again. Mystery still surrounds that moment.

According to many in the tradition, seven men, including Mevlana's son Alaeddin, attacked him in the garden and killed him. It is said that his body was thrown into a well (located under what is now the mosque of Shams-i Tabriz in Konya). No one spoke of this to Mevlana, who was half-crazed by his second disappearance, but he became estranged from Alaeddin, knowing his animosity towards Shams. Alaeddin himself became ill and died not long after. Mevlana immersed himself again in sema and would give the robe off his back to anyone who brought a hint of news of Shams, even though he doubted its validity. Poetry poured from his heart with Shams' name spilling everywhere. After some years of being cooked to ash within this fire, he found the Source of Love within himself; his soul was reborn and he became an even more profound witness to the Presence of the Beloved everywhere.

Some years later one of the friends saw Mevlana immersed in prayer at the tomb of his father, Bahaeddin. When he arose he asked for a reed pen and ink. He took these to the tomb of Alaeddin and wrote upon the plaster of his tomb, "If only the good were allowed to place their hopes in You, to whom could the sinner turn in refuge?" He then said, "I saw that in the world of the beyond, my Master Shamsuddin Tabrizi had made peace with and forgiven him. He interceded for him so that he was shown God's mercy." *Menaqib al-arifin* #404.
See also *Mathnawi* II:1030-1190.

Then he would repent again, come back to himself, and hold the reigns tighter. He was afraid that the shaikh might turn his face away from him. In this way, as a Muslim for one hour and as a blasphemer the next, he finally arrived at the door of the shaikh's house with the reins upon his shoulder.

He visited the shaikh again the next day, but saying, "I take refuge in God!" to himself, he was able to blind the eye of the devil.[440]

Then when he arrived at the door of the shaikh's house, he saw that he was playing chess with the young son of the chief. Again, his faith shook.

That night, he saw the Prophet Muhammad in his dream. He ran to be with him, but the Prophet turned his face away.

He cried out, "O Messenger of God! Don't turn your face away from me!"

The Blessed Prophet said, "Until when are you going to deny us? How much longer are you not going to accept us?"

"O Messenger of God" he said, "When did I deny you?"

"But, you have denied our friend," he said.[441] "'A person is with the one whom he or she loves (*hadith*),' is truly for the sake of such a friend. 'The faithful are as a single soul (*hadith*)' is for the sake of such a one."

He fell down upon his face, wept, and repented. Muhammad put a handful of raisins and nuts on his lap, and he awoke in this state.

When he ran to the presence of the shaikh, he saw that he was still playing chess with the boy. He had the dried raisins in his pocket, but again his faith shook, and right away he wanted to turn back.

The shaikh shouted from behind him: "Until when?" He said, "At least, be ashamed before the Prophet of God!"

---

440 *I.e., Rather than listening to the whisperings of the devil who was instigating doubt, he blinded him with auzhu billahi min ash-shaytan ir-rajeem . . . "I take refuge in God from Satan the accursed."*

Now whenever you read this Qur'an, seek refuge with God from Satan, the accursed. Behold, he has no power over those who have attained to faith and in their Sustainer place their trust . . . [*Surah an-Nahl,* The Bee 16:98-99].

441 M. 375.

Immediately he turned around and prostrated himself at the shaikh's feet. "Pass that plate," the shaikh said. He saw that from the plate filled with raisins and nuts only the place of a handful of raisins was missing. "Put that handful of raisins back on this plate," he told him. "Muhammad (peace and blessings upon him) took it from here."[442] In this moment he became one who has surrendered.

☼

Open-Mouthed

Now, when I am together with the Friend, with the Beloved, how can I be patient—how could I bear being with strangers? From the beginning, I felt a great deal of love for you, but I saw then as we began to speak that you weren't mature enough to understand the

---

442 When Shams left Konya the first time, Mevlana was distraught at the loss of his friend and sent his son, Weled, in search of him when word came that he might be in Damascus. Sultan Weled found him there and journeyed back with him, walking in front, carrying his reins over his shoulder. It is said that he had found him playing chess with a young Frank (whom some say was to become St. Francis of Assisi; even though the dates of Francis's time in the holy land don't quite coincide, the indication of a strong affinity is there). The event recounted here is similar to that event which may have occurred just before the return journey to Konya in the spring of 1247 C.E. (645 A.H.). On the route home, Shams conveyed many mysteries to Weled who became the inheritor of the Way that was opened by Shams and Mevlana. It was Sultan Weled who formed the ceremony of sema which encapsulates many of the teachings of Shams, and it was he who established the Mevlevi order after the passing of his father.

As Sultan Weled relates (*Menaqib* #251): My father said, "O Bahaeddin, when the seed of my teaching has taken root in your heart, you will understand; reflect deeply on my teaching and really try to absorb it and if you do, felicity will be yours. Know that the body of the prophets, the saints and their friends will never perish. A seed thrown on the earth may appear to die and disappear, however, at the end of a few days, it comes to life and flowers. In a similar way the body of the prophets and the saints will also come to life again."

He was absorbed in the mystery described in the Qur'an (51:21): *Have you not looked within?* There is nothing in the world that exists outside yourself; look into the depths of your being for that for which you are longing.

Cooked within the fire of love, Mevlana became love. The ocean of love that poured forth from Shams and Mevlana's friendship in Truth continues to surge and open a Way. We offer our gratitude. May great blessing and peace be with them both. *Hu/Hu.*

subtle indications. If I had spoken more then, you wouldn't have had the ability to understand! So, we closed our mouth, because in those days, you didn't have the state that would allow me to speak.

We Are Now One

Ghazal 1761 of Mevlana's *Divan-i Shams*
Translated by Helminski and Rezwani
Excerpted from *Love's Ripening*, Shambhala

We stood together hand in hand in primordial time;
Now at last, we are one again.
We are all of one soul struggling along one path,
And all drunk with the same wine.
From among the two worlds we chose Love alone;
Except for that Love there's nothing we adore.
What bitternesss did our souls suffer from separation!
At long last, we are free from separation.
A Ray from the Sun came in through an opening,
And raised us up in dignity, however low we were.
O Sunlight! Don't withhold Your
loving radiance from us!
Aren't we sitting in robes of Your radiance?
By Your radiance we are transformed into rubies,
It is because of You that we exist.
Dancing like particles before You;
In our yearning for You, we abandon our chains.

Rose Prayer

Traditional prayer of completion for Mevlevi Dervishes

May this moment be blessed.
May goodness be opened and may evil be dispelled.
May our humble plea be
accepted in the Court of Honor;
May the Most Glorious God purify and fill our hearts
with the Light of His Greatest Name.
May the hearts of the lovers be opened.
May our moments and joys be resplendent.
By the breath of our master Mevlana,
by the secret of Shams and Weled,
by the holy light of Muhammad,
by the generosity of Imam Ali,
and the intercession of Muhammad,
the unlettered prophet, mercy to all the worlds.
May we say Hu.

Index of Surahs

8. *Surah al-Anfal*, Spoils of War: [8:53] *(Allah never changes the grace He has bestowed)* p.36; [8:2-4] *(The faithful are those whose hearts tremble)* p.147
9. *Surah at-Tawbah*, Repentance: [9:11] *(forgetting all gratitude)* p.142; [9:21] *(They struggled by means of their possessions)* p.54; [9:40] *(Surely God is together with us)* p.166; [9:60] *(Alms are for the poor)* p.41; [9:111] *(God has purchased of the faithful)* p.42
10. *Surah Yunus*, Jonah: (see reference p.319)
11. *Surah Hud*, Hud: [11:107] *(Doer of whatever He wills)* p.296; [11:112] *(Be honest as you have been commanded to be)* p.5, p.222
12. *Surah Yusuf*, Joseph: [12:101] *(You have … taught me the interpretation of dreams)* p.121, p.180
13. *Surah ar-Rad*, Thunder: [13:11] *(God does not change people's condition unless they change their inner selves)* p.60; [13:31] *(a divine discourse by which mountains could be moved)* p.425
14. *Surah Ibrahim*, Abraham: (see references in Index)
15. *Surah al-Hijr*, Hijr: 15:19 *(I breathed into him of My Spirit)* p.79
16. *Surah an-Nahl*, The Bee: [16:50] *(They fear their Sustainer)* p. 110; [16:97] *(We shall quicken with good life)* p.430; [16:128] *(God is together with those who are conscious of Him)* p.166
17. *Surah al-Isra'*, The Night Journey: [17:27] *(The squanderers are the siblings of the devil)* p.288; [17:34] *(your promise)* p.55; [17:44] *(There is nothing that does not celebrate His immeasurable glory)* p.184; [17:70] *(We have honored the children of Adam)* p.333; [17:72] *(Whoever is blind)* 197; [17: 105] *(We have sent you as a herald of glad tidings)* p.278
18. *Surah al-Kahf*, The Cave: [18:18] *(the dog of the friends of the cave)* p.213; [18:39] *(There is no power save with God)* p.177-178; [18:44] *(power belongs to God)* p.178; [18:60] *(I shall not give up until I reach the meeting place of the two seas)* p.207-208; [18:65] *(One of our servants on whom We bestowed knowledge from Ourself)* p.13, p.208; [18:75] *(you will never be able to have patience with me)* p.205; [18:78] *(This is separation)* p.348; [18:94] *(Behold Gog and Magog)* p.79, 181; [18:109] *(Though the sea became ink)* p.54-55, p.194; [18:110] *(I am but a mortal man like all of you)* p.256-257 and *(Whoever hopes to meet his Sustainer)* p.299
19. *Surah Maryam*, Mary: [19:18] *(I take refuge in God)* p.188; [19:30] *(Witness, I am the servant of God)* p.38; [19:47] *(I will ask for forgiveness from God for you)* p.83; [19:56] *(Idris)* p.232

20. *Surah Ta Ha*, O Man: [20:1] *(Ta Ha)* p.236; [20:2] *(Don't suffer, We have not revealed this Qur'an to cause you difficulty)* p.294; [20:5] *(The Most Gracious is seated on the Throne of His Almightiness)* p.110, p.293, p.428; [20:6] *(Unto Him belongs all that is in the heavens and all that is on earth)* p.294; [20:7] *(He knows everything that is secret)* p.381; [20:17] *("What is it that you have in your hand?")* p.32; [20:18] *("This is my staff")* p.32; [20:114] *(O God, increase me in knowledge)* p.349, p.393
21. *Surah al-Anbiya*, The Prophets: (see references in Index)
22. *Surah al-Hajj*, The Pilgrimage: [22:23] *(silk will be their clothing)* p.319
23. *Surah Mu'minun*, The Faithful: [23:115] *(Did you, then, think that We created you in mere idle play)* p.292; p.399
24. *Surah an-Nur*, The Light: [24:21-22] *(forgive)* p.24; [24:35] *(Allah is the light of the heavens and the earth)* p.267, *(light upon light)* p.83, *(God guides to His Light whom He will)* p.299; [24:44] *(God alternates the night and the day)* p. 403
25. *Surah al-Furqan*, The Criterion for Discernment: 25:45 *(Your Lord has extended the shadow)* p.267; [25:58] *(the Living One who does not die)* p.26; [25:70] *(God exchanges their bad deeds with good deeds)* p.83; [25:23] *(All scattered dust)* p.195
26. *Surah ash-Shu'ara*, The Poets: [26:80] *(When I fall ill, He heals me)* p.420; [26:89] *(Bring to God a sound heart)* p.14; [26:79] *(He gives me to eat and to drink)* p.256
27. *Surah an-Naml*, The Ants: [27:6] *(One Wise, All-Knowing)* p.362
28. *Surah al-Qasas*, The Story: [28:12] *(We caused him to refuse other nurses)* p.327; [28:15] *(This is from the act of Satan)* p.343; [28:56] *(You cannot guide aright everyone whom you love)* p.60, p.222, p.275, p.390; [28:88] *(Everything is perishing except His Face)* p.218
29. *Surah al-Ankabut*, The Spider: [29:2] *(without being tested)* p.403; [29: 67] *(We have set up a secure sanctuary)* p.251, p.429; [29:69] *(Those who strive hard in Our Cause ... We will show Our ways)* p.137, p.365
31. *Surah Luqman*, Luqman: [31:28] *(as a single soul)* p.95, p.366
32. *Surah as-Sajdah*, Prostration: [32:11] *(the angel of death)* p.66
33. *Surah al-Azhab*, The Confederates: [33:4] *(God has not put two hearts)* p.316; [33:72] *(We offered the trust)* p.61, p.182, p.357; [33:45] *(We*

Index